Please remember that this is a library book,
and that it belongs only temporarily to each
person who uses it. Be considerate. Do
not write in this, or any, library book.

Ailing, Aging, Addicted

Ailing, Aging, Addicted

STUDIES OF COMPROMISED LEADERSHIP

Bert E. Park, M.D.

With a Foreword by
Arthur S. Link

THE UNIVERSITY PRESS OF KENTUCKY

Copyright © 1993 by The University Press of Kentucky

Scholarly publisher for the Commonwealth,
serving Bellarmine College, Berea College, Centre
College of Kentucky, Eastern Kentucky University,
The Filson Club, Georgetown College, Kentucky
Historical Society, Kentucky State University,
Morehead State University, Murray State University,
Northern Kentucky University, Transylvania University,
University of Kentucky, University of Louisville,
and Western Kentucky University.

Editorial and Sales Offices: Lexington, Kentucky 40508-4008

Library of Congress Cataloging-in-Publication Data
Park, Bert Edward.
   Ailing, aging, addicted : studies of compromised leadership / Bert
E. Park.
      p.   cm.
   Includes bibliographical references and index.
   ISBN 0-8131-1853-0 (alk. paper)
   1. Heads of state—Health and hygiene.   2. Diseases and history.
3. Nervous system—Diseases.   4. Biohistory.   I. Title.
D226.7.P37   1993
909—dc20   93-19550

This book is printed on recycled acid-free paper meeting
the requirements of the American National Standard
for Permanence of Paper for Printed Library Materials. ∞

For ARTHUR S. LINK
Mentor, friend, and scholar without peer

Contents

Foreword

Bert Park's new book is of singular interest and importance because it deals with the age-old problem of the impact of disease upon history, particularly upon some of the people who played a large part in making it.

Nothing startles so much as the obvious. One obvious fact is that history is biography writ large. Another obvious fact is that history has been changed, for better or worse, by a handful of people. The unknown billions have passed through the stream of history known only to God. They have been the sinews of the human race. Leaderless, they have been an inert mass. It is not fashionable to say such things these days; we historians are supposed to be interested in writing "from the bottom up," about the so-called common people. The difficulty is that we know virtually nothing about most of them except as aggregates. And, to repeat, history has been changed by a few individuals about whom we know a great deal.

Another obvious fact is that the lives of all people have been, in a determinative way, affected by good health or illness and disease. Most historians would say that this is a truism, and yet most of them are either startled or incredulous when confronted with the corollary of this trusim: disease often changes the course of history when it affects detrimentally history's shakers and movers.

From one angle I am not being altogether fair to historians, who have long been aware of the gross effect of disease upon macrohistory—for example, the depopulation of the Italian peninsula during the latter days of the Roman Empire, the Black Death of the 1340s, or the influenza pandemic of 1918. More recently, historians have discovered the devastating effects of diseases new to the peoples of the Americas after their contact with the Europeans in the sixteenth century. This resulted in the greatest demographic disaster in recorded history. It is biographers who have the most trouble in dealing with notable subjects whose behavior has been profoundly affected by disease. Often biographers simply pass the matter by. For example, one can read Ray Stannard Baker's multivolume biography of Woodrow Wilson without knowing that Wilson suffered during most of his adult life from hypertension and cerebrovascular disease. Actually, Baker knew this fact and may have thought it bad taste to discuss this aspect of Wilson's biography. But for most biographers, the medical histories of their subjects simply seem bodies of knowledge too esoteric and unknown for them to deal with; they are historians and biographers, not medical specialists. Dr. Park has some very wise things to say to them on this subject.

I first came to know Dr. Park in 1985, when he sent me a copy of the page proofs of his first book, *The Impact of Illness on World Leaders* (University of Pennsylvania Press, 1986), which contained a chapter on Woodrow Wilson. This was a time when, as editor of *The Papers of Woodrow Wilson*, I was approaching that period in Wilson's life when cerebrovascular disease, which culminated in a massive stroke on October 2, 1919, was beginning to have an unambiguous impact on Wilson's behavior. I invited Dr. Park to become a member of the Editorial Advisory Committee of *The Papers of Woodrow Wilson*. He accepted and was a wise counselor and guide through the labyrinths of Wilson's illnesses from 1918 to 1920. In addition, he contributed editorial notes to *The Papers* on Wilson during the Paris Peace Conference and the controversy in the United States over ratification of the Treaty of Versailles, the first article of which was the Covenant of the League of Nations.

Dr. Park has all the training and skills that every biographer would like to possess. To begin with, he is well-trained in history and historical methodology and, with his incredible energy, finds time to teach courses in that subject. Trained medically first in pathology, he has an astounding knowledge of disease in general. He then shifted to neurology, neuropsychiatry, and neurosurgery. I have never known anyone who is more avid or more honest in searching for the truth of the matter at hand. He is the first to say that he has made a mistake and to try to correct it. He knows the limits of medical historical knowledge and is skeptical when skepticism is in order, as it usually is. And his *bête noir* is medical reductionism, that is, saying that illness accounts for all deviant or uncharacteristic behavior. All these talents and devotion to the search for truth shine forth in the book for which these words are a foreword.

The three chapters in Part I on Napoleon, Henry VIII, and temporal lobe epilepsy as it affected (or did not affect) Hitler, Joan of Arc, St. Paul, and John Brown (of Harper's Ferry) show what a pathologist and neurologist can do in the absence of medical records (except for the report of Napoleon's autopsy). Medical records aside, we do have an enormous body of evidence (the observations of contemporaries, the writings and sayings of these subjects, and above all their behavior) on the subjects of this chapter. Dr. Park's conclusions are cautious, sometimes tentative, but I find most of them convincing. He is now not so sure as he was in

The Impact of Illness that Hitler was afflicted with TLE. It seems to me that he has discovered the disease, schistosomiasis, contracted in Egypt, that did Napoleon in over the long run, although arsenic poisoning may have hastened his death; that he has proved that Henry was not a syphilitic; and that John Brown had a classic case of TLE. As for St. Paul, it is hard for Dr. Park to believe that he suffered from the seizures and hallucinations of TLE: "As intriguing as the evidence for TLE is from my perspective as a neurosurgeon, it is difficult for me as a Christian to believe that so many theologians who have studied Paul could be wrong. Yet nothing clouds rational thinking as much as deeply held convictions born of faith. The question remains whether in regard to Paul we have allowed that to happen."

The three chapters in Part II on Stalin, Wilson, and Churchill attack the central questions of the biographies of these twentieth-century leaders: whether their careers were affected by disease or psychological deficits. About these individuals we have enough medical evidence to enable Dr. Park to write with a sure hand, when he argues that each suffered from an identical underlying disease that accentuated their psychological deficits. The evidence on Stalin is now voluminous and is becoming more so every day of *glasnost*; he was, as Park says, a "premier paranoic," the victim of one of the worst diseases that can affect a functioning person. In Stalin's case, it turned him into the incarnation of evil. The chapter on Wilson ought, it seems to me, to settle the question of whether neurological disease and stroke *or* psychological defects caused the collapse of Wilson's leadership during the treaty fight. (Dr. Park has covered Wilson's earlier cerebrovascular disease in *The Impact of Illness*, and, on the basis of new medical evidence, has been able to validate his earlier clinical judgment). Dr. Park does not go much into Churchill's medical history before 1945, because Churchill's hypertension strokes did not begin until 1949. For the pathetic story of the great prime minister's decline, he relies mainly on the detailed evidence in the diary of Lord Moran, Churchill's physician.

In Part III, Chapter 7, Dr. Park greatly expands his discussion in *The Impact of Illness* of the abuse of amphetamines that certainly played the major role in Anthony Eden's bizarre behavior and downfall during the Suez Crisis of 1956. Chapter 8 on John F. Kennedy will probably interest American readers most, particularly its account of how the Kennedy family and entourage effected a complete cover-up of the young president's Addison's disease and dependence upon steroids. Then, along came the semiquack, Dr. Max Jacobson, who frequently gave Kennedy injections of amphetamines as well as steroids. They probably enhanced the president's sexual appetite, but Dr. Park doubts that they had any effect on Kennedy's political behavior, for example, during the Cuban missile crisis—the Vienna summit setback with Krushchev perhaps excepted. However, as Park says, "Given the huge dosages of amphetamines and steroids to which Kennedy was subjected, it is a wonder that his performance as president was as exemplary as history recalls."

Dr. Park has long been concerned about ways to deal with the problem of presidential disability. He is, I think, quite right in saying that the Twenty-Fifth Amendment fails to provide a reliable method to assure the succession of the vice president in the event the president becomes incompetent to perform the duties of his office. In *The Impact of Illness*, Dr. Park proposed the establishment of a Presidential Disability Commission composed of physicians, neurologists among them, to examine sick presidents and make "an objective recommendation based on the data it gathers." That suggestion did not evoke much support, even much discussion by politicians, political scientists, and the media.

In the last two chapters of the present book, Dr. Park comes back to the same problem and proposal while reviewing the crippled presidencies of Garfield, Wilson, Franklin Roosevelt, Eisenhower, and Reagan. But Park would now expand the duties of the commission to include examining presidential *candidates* and monitoring the health of presidents during their incumbency. Whether the merits and possibilities of this plan outweigh its demerits and are politically possible, I must leave to the reader to decide. However, thoughtful Americans will surely demand a second opinion on a subject of such enormous importance.

But to get back to *Ailing, Aging, Addicted* in general, let me conclude by saying that it is a *tour de force*. It will be indispensable for historians and biographers and fascinating for general readers.

ARTHUR S. LINK

Preface

This study is a sequel to my first book, *The Impact of Illness on World Leaders*. At least one motive for undertaking the original work was admittedly self-serving: to make some small contribution that might afford me an opportunity to rub elbows with members of the fraternity of historical scholars. On a less narcissistic note, I hoped to show that an interdisciplinary approach to history can provide valuable insight into a few of the more obscure and neglected aspects of our past, among them the blinders we have worn while chronicling the health of leaders in general and American presidents in particular.

So what came of that effort? At least with respect to my fragile ego, I got my wish. The book caught the attention of Arthur S. Link of Princeton University. Among other scholarly credits spanning five decades, he has edited a truly monumental work entitled *The Papers of Woodrow Wilson*. That led to a fruitful association as a member of the project's Editorial Advisory Committee with this esteemed scholar, who became my mentor, collaborator, and (what I cherish most) dear friend. His willingness to explore the medical dimensions of the president's changing personality prompted Link to ask me to write several editorial essays for the *Papers* on Wilson's long-suffered cerebrovascular disease, its impact on him personally, and its influence on some of the most important events of the twentieth century.

Equally encouraging, a plethora of works dealing with leadership health and presidential disability have appeared since the publication of my book some seven years ago. If such studies have enhanced the scholar's awareness, it is fair to say that the general reader—not to mention those in a position to effect changes for the better—remains somewhat in the dark. Until the hue and cry from the public at risk becomes so deafening that the politician can no longer ignore it, the potential for calamity will remain. Hence the impetus for a sequel. Yet to capture the attention of both requires speaking their language, drawing upon familiar historical figures, and critically reassessing what has been written about their infirmities, both perceived and real.

In the preface to my first work, I lavished praise on Arno Karlen's incisive critique entitled *Napoleon's Glands and Other Ventures in*

Biohistory. Having once partaken of this inviting smorgasbord of pathology, I thought it only fitting to introduce my second bill of fare by ruminating on the virtues of Karlen's perspective with respect to Napoleon himself. Well enough. But why then regurgitate, in part, the medical histories of Woodrow Wilson, Adolf Hitler, Winston Churchill, and Anthony Eden for a second tasting? For one thing, the thesis of my first book was framed around the political collapse of Europe between the world wars. That alone precluded a detailed recounting of the latter two case histories. For another, Hitler warrants resurrecting if for no other reason than to cast doubt on my former belief that he was a victim of epilepsy. And as for Wilson, previously unpublished primary source materials now attest to the fact that his medical history remained incomplete at the time my first manuscript went to press. That said, I am grateful that its original thesis has since been validated.

So much for particulars. If taking the message to the general reader is the intent of the present work, why market it through a university press, which has fewer inroads into the large bookselling-chains that dictate what we read today? Simply because this issue of physiologically compromised leadership is a delicate and exacting pursuit that deserves the imprimatur of peer review both before and after publication—and is not a matter to be left to whimsical interpretations with the proverbial Bottom Line of sales in mind. Not that any university press editor who publishes such material need worry. Properly presented, there is enough of the bizarre and macabre to be found in these pages and similar works to compete with the most felicitous wordsmiths of popular history. Whether that is enough for the reader to sit up and take notice, and our legislators to take action, only the future will judge.

Introduction: On Prudence and Skepticism

Can one man's sickness make millions suffer? Have diseases of the brain in particular adversely affected the behavior of certain leaders? If so, how did that change history—and when did it signify nothing more than a footnote to the past?

To answer such questions, historians and physicians bedded down in the unkempt lair of "pathography," where studies of disease as it has affected famous people are conceived. Following what their critics would dismiss as unseemly one-night stands in biographical research, these odd bedfellows often face the morning-after of peer review with self-reproach—as if they have awakened in some sort of cheap flophouse on Scholars' Row, chastened by the prospect of having their reputations impugned.

On occasion, to be sure, stimulating works with redeeming value come out of such academic trysts. Yet to flaunt them as serious scholarship without first making certain one's backside is covered entails some hazards.

For historians who have made their marks in more traditional pursuits, established reputations are at stake; physicians who ignore their history risk being labeled medical reductionists. All too often such self-appointed diagnosticians have forsaken the virtues of prudence and skepticism in their haste to conceive a viable thesis. Even if the diseases these writers ascribe to their subjects seem plausible enough, they usually fail to convince their colleagues that poor health had any bearing on individual behavior, much less on history.

Some of this criticism is justified. More than its fair share, however, stems from a Tolstoyan prejudice that discounts the role of any one person—sick or healthy—in shaping the past. Thomas Carlyle's Great Man theory of historical causation has fallen on hard times. So has the credibility of pathography. Biohistorians deem it less relevant to conjure up the effects of hemorrhoids on Napoleon's conduct at Waterloo, for example, than to highlight the typhus epidemic and its depletion of his troops in Russia.[1]

Many psychohistorians too are critical of their sibling rival. They would have us believe that virtually all behavior can be traced to childhood, that we need to know less of diseases that come later and more of how character is formed. Mapping out those delicate connections in the brain known as "synapses," they say, tells us nothing about motives.[2] Reduced to the lowest common denominator, what they are naively proposing is that physiology has little bearing on behavior. Perhaps suppressing unpleasant memories of their own struggle for respectability, the psychoanalysts have dismissed pathography as little more than an obscure subject in search of an audience.

Before we allow such skeptics to hurl this fledgling discipline out of academe, maybe we should ask ourselves whether there are not elements of truth in these retrospective postmortems. Must psychoanalysts be allowed to claim that only they have the tools necessary to reconstruct the comportment of kings, the genius of artists, or the behavior of madmen? Can pathographers, who concentrate on physical disease, carve any niche for themselves in the writing of history and biography?

I believe they can. Although environment, economic forces, and the like play a large if often mysterious role in the historical process, the lone individual may play an equally crucial role independent of those factors. To exemplify the point, perhaps no man had a greater impact on twentieth-century history than Mikhail Gorbachev. Not that the port-wine stain on his forehead accounted for Gorbachev's genius (or something more sinister). To argue either would be to view history through pathographical 3-D: deceiving, derisory, and dumb. Rather, drawing attention to a harmless birthmark on the scalp serves to remind us that unrecognized disorders of the underlying brain may have a determinative influence on behavior. In a leader, that can have disturbing implications.[3]

To confine behavioral analysis to childhood influences, as some psychoanalysts would have us do, limits the biographer's perspective. There is both an alpha and an omega to the evolution of character, as any physician familiar with the aging process knows. And those mysterious brain-cell connections to which we have referred have something to do with that: how they transmit environmental stimuli has as much bearing on a grown man's behavior as do undescended testicles, thumb sucking, or psychological abuse in childhood. Not only do high blood pressure, hardening of the arteries, and just plain old age affect the way these synapses function; drugs, epilepsy, or hormonal imbalances may cause them to misfire altogether. Perplexing behavior results, and character changes.

Those who counter that these physiologic derangements remain indecipherable without a barrage of confirmatory tests risk exposing their lack of familiarity with how physicians diagnose disease. Should the doctor lack a strong suspicion of what it is that ails the patient after taking a careful medical history, he or she is unlikely to uncover the cause with a physical examination or laboratory tests. Similarly, the pathographer has the observations of the historical figure's associates and his or her own clinical intuition to rely upon in the absence or unavailability of complete medical records.

Sources are sources—whether they are grounded in medicine, psychology, or history. All the data, both physiological and psychological, must be weighed before a full understanding of individual behavior can be had. To eliminate either, just as to ignore the political circumstances in which decisions are made, is to select out the evidence beforehand; the result is medical or psychoanalytical reductionism. Little wonder that neither alone has convinced the historian trained in more traditional methodology.

On the one hand, there is much to be said for being skeptical of retrospective medical diagnoses; on the other, we should be just as wary of knee-jerk criticisms of the pathographer's methods. Yet to demonstrate that this relatively new discipline can make significant contributions to biography demands some housecleaning. We must discard the junk that clutters pathography's hallways, which the unwary biographer stumbles over on his way to the door separating fantasy from reality. To open it requires what the historian calls "the verdict of peer review." The clinician would see it as "asking for a second opinion"—or a third or fourth.

Perhaps the best way to reach common ground is to review pathography's literature in an attempt to uncover what worthwhile questions it has raised, and then to offer second opinions on its diagnoses on behalf of a number of historical personages. This book attempts to do that by organizing a critique around the most mortifying of diseases identified as crucial determinants of behavior—say, syphilis and epilepsy—and then by clarifying the possible influence of more common ailments: premature or age-related senility, depression accompanying a stroke, drug abuse, chronic disease and pain—any one of which weighs on the psyche and affects the way a person thinks as much as do more dramatic blows to the brain.

Yet what repulses in the literature at the same time it intrigues also manages to sell. That is why pathographers who cater more to marketing than to scholars have tended to ignore the mundane for the morbid. Similarly, some biographers, in an effort to make the historical personality come alive, have assumed the role of armchair psychologists, though lacking the necessary training. As a result, both psychohistory and pathography have been viewed as little more than shams.

Perhaps the fault stems as much as anything from a lack of expertise in *both* medicine and history. Arno Karlen succinctly describes the problem. Historians, bound by what he terms the "Law of Repetition," are guilty through lack of medical knowledge of recounting worn and hackneyed views posited by alleged medical scientists.[4] For example, until Dr. I. MacAlpine and others made a very credible case that George III had been victimized by porphyria, historians had accepted as gospel a manic-depressive state leading to alleged insanity.[5] (MacAlpine's methodology should serve as a model for future pathographers; whether or not her conclusions are embraced by everyone, the depth and breadth of commitment to detail set this investigation apart from its predecessors.)

Another rule of clinical prudence—that the truly important disease must *not* be missed, whereas the less serious ones may well be ignored—is equally important for the biographer. Many health problems, though interesting in themselves, offer little insight into behavior. Mary, Queen of Scots, was allegedly a victim of a veritable smorgasbord of diseases—Marfan's syndrome, rheumatoid arthritis, anorexia nervosa, amenorrhea, peptic ulcer disease, and yes, porphyria—but none that can be linked to her role in the succession crises in England of the sixteenth century. From the historian's perspective, there is little to recommend what remains of obscure significance.

Nor, as the old saying goes, should one who hears hoofbeats think first of zebras—unless, of course, zebras happen to be in the vicinity. That is, the wary physician disdains the unusual cause when a more common disease suffices to explain a set of symptoms. Yet it behooves us to remember that diseases decidedly rare in one location may be quite common in another. Take, for example, a parasitic disease like schistosomiasis: at first glance that would appear to the European or American scholar an unlikely affliction for Napoleon—until one recalls that schistosomiasis was endemic in the Middle East precisely where (Egypt) and at which point (1800) his health began to fail. This is merely to suggest that, on the African plain at least, hoofbeats may quite validly suggest zebras.

Still another prudent rule of thumb is a willingness to continue to debate the evidence even after the data are ostensibly established. Few maladies deserve as much skepticism as does syphilis. It is unlikely that much more primary source material will be uncovered on such historical figures as Ivan the Terrible and Henry VIII, for whom that diagnosis has been accepted by most biographers all too ready to embrace what previous pathographers assumed. Like a resourceful blind man selling pencils out of a tin cup on the street corner, the clever writer pushes his wares upon the gullible biographer while recounting a story he once overheard about an infamous despot who suffered from syphilis. The buyer, in his haste to dash off and record the story he has just heard, overlooks the fact that his new pencil has no eraser. Presumably such pencils were used to brand still another tyrant with syphilis—until new data on Adolf Hitler came to light to debunk that myth.

Just as the honest diagnostician acknowledges the prejudices that characterize his or her own clinical style, the biographer must guard against the tendency to address only those data with which he or she feels comfortable, to the exclusion of the less familiar. Historians who are uncomfortable with medical jargon must either undertake the necessary training to deal with it or seek the advice of medical specialists. Likewise, medical writers must immerse themselves in the social, economic, military, and political evidence that is the historian's stock-in-trade; otherwise, they run the risk of blowing a medical diagnosis totally out of proportion to its impact on the past.

Finally, the skeptical pathographer must be wary of hunches. He may well choose to gamble with his own reputation, but not at the expense of his defenseless historical subject. If a Swedish toxicologist once made a valuable contribution to the study of Napoleon with his landmark discovery of the emperor's arsenic intoxication, he nevertheless lapsed badly by playing a hunch that the presence of arsenic was grounds for the charge of premeditated murder.[6]

What both biography and biohistory require is not medical reductionism that ascribes to disease the sole or even primary force behind a leader's conduct, but pathography soundly based upon medical factors weighed carefully in the totality of causation. For their findings to be taken seriously by other scholars, then, pathographers must be skeptical enough to refuse to fall victim to the Law of Repetition; be willing to master the nuances of both medical diagnosis and historical method; be prudent enough to obtain second opinions; and above all, be honest enough to accept that some of history's most intriguing cases will still defy their best efforts at resolution. The chapters that follow deal with cases in which divergent opinions as to biohistorical diagnoses exist and with whether the medical condition itself may have made an impact on history. Moreover, they examine only those instances in which disease appears to have affected either the behavior or the thought processes of the individual in question and, consequently, his or her decisions. I can only hope that I have followed my own advice in the second opinions I have proposed.

The first section of the book rehashes the medical case studies of a number of historical figures whose meteoric rise and fall have often been linked to disease. The case of Napoleon Bonaparte introduces the term "differential diagnosis"—establishing that plausible range of alternatives which might account for the symptoms described—whereas Henry VIII's medical history illustrates the opposing tendency to hone in on a single disease, with all the pitfalls such as an approach implies. If only to propose that a second look is of value in exploding some popular myths that continue to color our understanding of both men's behavior, these chapters concentrate on certain shortcomings of the methodology used by earlier pathographers. By emphasizing the excessive passions (sexual and otherwise) of two select monarchs to explain either their slow burnout at the top or more spectacular crashes in the fast lane, previous investigators may have led both themselves and their readers astray.

Similarly, epilepsy has been suggested as a plausible influence on some of history's most colorful characters—among them, Adolf Hitler, Saul of Tarsus (the Apostle Paul), Joan of Arc, and John Brown of Harpers Ferry fame. Seizures were the first phenomenon that neurologists identified as an alternative explanation for the bizarre behavior[7] that many persons have seen as divinely (or demonically) inspired. And indeed, psychologists who followed in the neurologists' wake may have overlooked physical disease as an underlying cause for the pathologic behavior they described. The intent here is to offer at least an opinion that mysticism and clairvoyant behavior may have deeper roots than those uncovered by the psychoanalysts.

The second section deals with three leaders of the twentieth century who labored under pressures as much physiologic as political. Josef Stalin, Woodrow Wilson, and Winston Churchill shared a common disease that predictably accentuated certain underlying character traits. Long burdened with high blood pressure, Stalin became more paranoid, Wilson more self-righteous, and Churchill more egocentric as they aged; their leadership suffered as a result. The purpose of the second section, then, is twofold: to refocus upon previous psychoanalytical accounts of their character through the retrospectoscope of neurological disease, and to highlight the impact of accelerated brain aging on human behavior and history.

The third section dramatizes the role that drugs have played in the health and conduct of world leaders in the twentieth century by comparing two men who used them to excess. Both Anthony Eden and John F. Kennedy embroiled themselves in covert military operations and duplicitous diplomacy that compromised their credibility and the nations they governed. The question remains to what extent, if any, the amphetamines they abused governed their actions. Merely indulging in the same drug does not assure that different individuals will react in the same way, as these two chapters make clear. Even so, the price paid (both potential and real) is disturbing.

The last section chronicles the effects of poor health on the behavior of selected presidents of the United States and examines the impact not only on the workings of the office itself but on the succession crises that frequently resulted. Yet it is not enough simply to identify the problem; if there is any value in such exercises, they must, as their parting gesture, offer some suggestions for dealing with the specter of compromised leadership in the future. As these two chapters demonstrate, the public would do well to seek a second opinion from someone other than the presidential physician when judging medical disability in its chief executive. How that can perhaps best be done is the intended legacy of the final chapter.

Using a case-study approach, then, I have tried to offer first a critical look at pathography as a legitimate discipline; second, exploration of those areas in which it can make and has made meaningful contributions to the study of biography and history; and last, some suggestions it might offer us for the future.

That much of the material is not new explains, in part, the need to cite a larger number of secondary sources than is typically found in more "scholarly" accounts. For the ultimate intent of this project is to reexamine existing medical and biohistorical interpretations in search of those defensible observations that may enhance our understanding of the individuals in question.

Not that I presume to have had the proverbial last word on these important subjects. Pathographers' pencils still need erasers. In the continuum of historical and biographical analysis, this work represents but one pathographer's attempt to offer his own second opinions. Undoubtedly, and for the good of the discipline, there will be more in the future.

PART I

Sick Heads and Tall Tales

Few things threaten biographers more than finding themselves on grounds as unfamiliar as disease and its impact on behavior. Emboldened by a fistful of what were considered irrefutable scientific data in the first half of the twentieth century (when biohistory came into vogue on the heels of psychoanalysis and the now disgraced musings of phrenology), they found it expedient to assault their subjects with such diagnoses as defective glands, syphilis, and epilepsy. After all, contemporary medical thought assured them that any one of these conditions, untreated, could dramatically alter personality.

Appreciative reviewers and unwary readers, encountering something both novel and intriguing, passed on what they had read without much reflection and even less understanding. Were one to believe those writers who have ignored more prudent seconds in their own corner, virtually every tyrant has at one time or another let his guard down, only to be rendered punch-drunk by the slings and arrows of pathophysiology. Yet with time and the evolution of medical knowledge, a few discerning critics began to suspect that some "classic" matches between disease and behavior were little more than charades.

Napoleon Bonaparte is a case in point. To explain his mid-life transformation, the voyeur with books to sell began by pummeling below the emperor's belt at his infested genitals and an unruly case of piles—or changed tactics and jabbed at Napoleon's seizure-riddled brain. Yet assuming that the defenseless subject could not have been totally irrational and still rule an empire or win a battle, some writers pulled an ill-defined "hormonal imbalance" from the grab bag of diagnoses for the knockout punch. By such sleight-of-hand has the corpse of the Little Corporal grown larger than life.

The same applies to a despot of an earlier time whose girth grew as if to accommodate his self-indulgence; few men in history were said to have matched sex, sport, and suds with Henry VIII. In time, however, the king's formidable reputation was eclipsed by the very excesses that marked his reign. No one disputes that the years were unkind to Bluff Hal. What is less certain is whether the regal head or tail took a greater beating at the hand of the syphilitic sphirochete while he lived or from the imaginative pathographer long after he died.

Once more sophisticated explorers of the mind came to disdain the medieval belief that disease and peculiar behavior were attributable to moral transgression or divine retribution, they were left to ponder the secular and often competing contributions of neurology and psychology. If the former was initially limited to identifying infestations growing within the brain, the identification of epilepsy some fifty years before the emergence of Freudian psychoanalysis catapulted the concept of a seizure-induced personality into the mainstream of pathography. Few theses have been so liberally exploited, though it is one that all too often smacks of medical reductionism in the hands of imprudent sleuths frantic to uncover pathography's next Rosetta Stone. I know that from experience: as an older, other person, I now recognize the limitations of having once applied the temporal-lobe-epilepsy thesis to Adolf Hitler. Mark it well: no second opinion is more painful than that which brings one's own first into question. Whether the same might pertain to the other case studies presented in the final essay remains to be seen. Despite what the skeptic would surely term a hackneyed concept, this thesis deserves a second look with regard to Hitler and other zealots, if only to reexamine one admittedly rare physiologic phenomenon that subsequent psychoanalysts have managed to ignore.

CHAPTER 1

Napoleon Bonaparte: Heads or Tails?

Can the pathographer make head or tail of Napoleon's perplexing medical history? Despite the attempts of a myriad of imaginative specialists to reduce this Corsican upstart to little more than a walking textbook of disease, even the most skeptical investigators are willing to consider that Napoleon might have won the battle of Waterloo had he not been indisposed; for thrombosed hemorrhoids were said to have diverted the general's attention during his final curtain call on the stage of European history.[1] In that sense, a painful tail wagged what remained of the dog days of Napoleonic France. The more cerebrally inclined believe the causes for his downfall lie elsewhere: whether as a result of an imperial pituitary gland that failed, a brain that occasionally misfired in sporadic bursts of epilepsy, or a psyche warped with Freudian complexes, Napoleon was a psychophysiologic wreck waiting to happen. Yet perhaps the real answer to biohistory's most popularized enigma may be found in neither the emperor's head nor his tail but somewhere in the middle—in what physicians of the Victorian era discretely termed the "equatorial zone" of the abdominal cavity.

About Waterloo itself, at least one thing seems certain: Napoleon lost the battle on June 18, 1815, by closing his window of opportunity the day before. Although on June 16 the struggle against the British and Prussians had proved indecisive, a rout of Napoleon's adversaries on June 17 looked propitious, given the strength of French reserves. Yet as historian Frederick Cartwright has concluded: "It was in those twelve hours from 9:00 P.M. on the 16th to 9:00 A.M. on the 17th that the campaign was lost."[2] What is now known is that Napoleon was uncharacteristically indecisive during that twelve-hour period and lost contact with the Prussians during the morning of the seventeenth. We also know that he was in a great deal of pain. Quite unlike the disciplined warrior of earlier years, Napoleon slept late and confined himself to his tent on that fateful day, losing the advantage in the early morning hours. Why such perplexing behavior?

Dr. William Ober offered an intriguing clue in his essay "Seats of the

Mighty." Napoleon, he says, was suffering yet again from painful hemorrhoids occasioned by long hours in the saddle. He had earlier ridden in a bouncing carriage across the Alps to Paris after his daring escape from Elba, only to endure further the subsequent journey to Waterloo. On June 13, portents of disaster gripped the imperial loins. As the biohistorical critic Arno Karlen so aptly described its implications: "Riding horseback with piles is a fate to be wished on one's worst enemy." [3] That is precisely the painful position in which pathology placed Napoleon before the decisive conflict with Blücher and Wellington. History tells us that when a leader crosses the Rubicon of his career, what goes on in his head is usually the decisive factor. Yet for French history, what came out of the tail in a very literal sense may have weighed as heavily—and as painfully. From the pathographer's perspective at least, the future of Napoleon's empire rested less on his shoulders than on his sensitive and fragile bottom. [4]

If the emperor's bulging hemorrhoids obscured a more penetrating look at his behavior through the historical proctoscope, the persevering medical investigator might do well to hang Napoleon in the stirrups of the urologist's examining table to study his diseased bladder. After his return from Egypt in 1799, he began to suffer from painful and hesitant urination that plagued him until the end of his military career. Victor Hugo recorded that not only did Napoleon ride through the day at Waterloo with "ghastly bladder pain" but that similar symptoms had begun as early as 1800 during the Battle of Marengo, only to recur at Borodino and Dresden during the 1812-13 campaign. Nor did the painful malady ever unleash its grip. In captivity at St. Helena during his last years, Napoleon was often observed leaning his head against a tree, trying in vain to urinate. [5]

No one knows for sure whether the front or back of Napoleon's imperiled loins was more of a burden for him at Waterloo. What washes this discussion out of gossip's gutter and into the mainstream of historical analysis is that his military conduct arguably suffered as a result. Yet were bleeding piles or a shriveled bladder enough to account for a dethroned emperor's ultimate failure on the battlefield? Hardly so. To argue that Napoleon lost his tactical advantage to the fickle dictates of disease is to ignore those military historians who have already given us good and sufficient reasons for his defeat. Though he may have been in some distress at the time, the weight of the evidence suggests that Wellington's superior resourcefulness and patience in battlefield command were the decisive factors.

It is one thing for the diagnostician to reduce a set of symptoms to their lowest common denominator; it is quite another to lead the gullible historian down the primrose path of medical reductionism by

attributing historical effect to pathologic cause. Still, subsequent revelations will at least risk suggesting that underlying illness did account
in large measure for Napoleon's dramatic change in appearance and
behavior—and perhaps even a change in history itself—but not before
other myths concerning his health are dispelled and the limits of the
medical argument defined.

If civility and common sense are reasons enough to dispense with
further speculation about an unruly case of hemorrhoids, greater liberties continue to be taken with Napoleon's chronically inflamed bladder.
His heavily sedimented and painful urinary stream brought to mind two
distressing—if undeserved—implications linked to the emperor's recalcitrant genital hardware. The first was his failure to produce heirs
during his marriage to Josephine, leading to the spurious assumption
that chronic infection of the urinary tract accounted for his suspected
impotency. This theory was dispelled by imperial ejaculates that produced Napoleon II and at least two illegitimate children.[6] Reversing
their steps to the entrance of that blind alley, a few intrepid gumshoes
entered another by suggesting that Napoleon had returned to Josephine
from a lengthy military campaign in Egypt with venereal disease. There
was much of medical significance in that campaign (revealed below),
but syphilis was not a part of it. No credible evidence links Napoleon to
that source, despite what some biographers have said.

The tail end of the medical legends that surround Napoleon and
other historical figures cannot be told without paying homage to the
testicles of the elite, which always seem to weigh so heavily for the
Freudian investigator. The heaviest on record, at least by the criterion of
literary license, were the testes of Harry S Truman, of whom someone
quipped that after his victorious showdown with John L. Lewis in the
coal strike of 1946, one could "hear his balls clank" as he walked down
the halls of the White House.[7] Though fumbling with the genitalia of
deceased generals and presidents recalls the naiveté of the phrenologist,
who once assumed that greatness could be mapped out by the contour of
the skull or the convolutions of the cerebral cortex, Napoleon was not
immune to such ribald scrutiny. He was said to have suffered from
underdeveloped genitalia (once attributed also to Adolf Hitler) by tem-
erarious genital fixators, smug in their assurance that a small penis is
injurious enough to the afflicted's psyche that he overextends himself to
bolster his compromised masculinity. This charge can be dismissed in
Napoleon's case, given the discovery of normal, albeit retracted, genitalia at his autopsy.[8]

Nor did Napoleon's drive and ambition wither away in time like his
private parts ensconced in an increasingly corpulent groin, as boldly
asserted by those who refused to look above the Corsican beltline for

explanations of Napoleon's inactivity and lethargy in his later years.[9] Some have even gone so far as to cite Napoleon's deprived manhood as evidence linking his deterioration to a hormonal deficiency[10]—which brings matters to a head in a very literal sense.

We are not referring in this instance to Napoleon's brain; rather, a few pathographers have drawn attention to a small organ at its base (the pituitary gland), which is the control center for hormonal and endocrine balance in the body. A British neurologist was the first to suggest that Napoleon suffered from a deficiency of this master gland, a disease known as Froehlich's syndrome.[11] That surmise was pounced upon by other physicians, one of whom referred to the emperor's "infantile genitals,"[12] while another pronounced him a "pituitary eunuch" on the basis of his corpulence, lethargy, thinning hair, and pudgy hands.[13]

True, these changes in Napoleon's physical appearance were universally acknowledged at the relatively young age of thirty-six. Truer still, the renowned Napoleonic self-discipline disappeared as rapidly as did his theretofore insatiable vitality and capacity for work. For one who had always prided himself on burning his candle at both ends, the wax of Napoleon's genius had clearly begun to melt down. Could his physical and mental decline, at least descriptively consistent with a burned-out pituitary gland, have been responsible? Hence the opening of the door of the bony vault at the base of Napoleon's skull encasing this tiny organ to the pathographer's examination—a door that has been forced open despite the absence of a key to fit the Froehlich lock.[14]

Though Napoleon may have suffered from a relative degree of thyroid deficiency,[15] it would represent a quantum leap of imagination to blame the pituitary gland as the cause. An underactive thyroid is certainly a more common condition in the aged than has been previously recognized, but to postulate this in a man of thirty-six defies the law of averages, unless some underlying pathology in the pituitary could account for a hypothyroid state in concert with other hormonal deficiencies. At first glance, the observations of one British physician who had attended Napoleon's autopsy cannot be dismissed out of hand as incriminating primary data implicating a lack of testosterone. "The pubis much resembled the mons veneris in women," he recalled. "The muscles of the chest were small, the shoulders narrow, and the hips wide. The penis and testicles were small."[16] In his most imaginative (if not politically motivated) prose, Dr. Walter Henry was depicting an effeminate male with a glandular deficiency. In reality, he was describing a pear-shaped habitus that probably reflected the physical inactivity of Napoleon's later years. As for the alleged "defective genitals" found at autopsy, allowance must be made for the well-known fact that the penis and scrotum normally contract against the body after death.

Moreover, Napoleon had hardly been impotent or infertile, a distinction at variance with persons victimized by Froehlich's syndrome. Nor is an underactive pituitary gland an evanescent condition. Without drug replacement it remains a pervasive, day-to-day physiologic burden, one hardly consistent with the brief displays of energy, brilliance, and vivacity that characterized the ailing emperor until very near the end.

And what of Napoleon's alleged short structure? Could this have been due to a lack of growth hormone from the same "failing" pituitary gland? Once again, the imaginative investigator has harnessed a recalcitrant Froehlich steed to a wagonload of unsupportive data. In truth, Napoleon was not as short as popular mythology recalls. At five feet, six inches, he was of average height for a Frenchman of that age. That he was not taller perhaps speaks as much to the misguided anticipations of those who, upon meeting a giant by reputation, were disappointed to find a middle-aged man of average size who had let his body balloon over a slender frame.[17]

The charge of homosexuality[18] has proved equally indefensible. Sensationalists are peculiarly prone to conjure up defective or overactive genitals, venereal disease, or homosexuality to explain a despot's character. In the most intriguing scenario of all, an unrestrained libido inevitably lands one in the lap of syphilis. And if that tenuous relationship cannot be sustained, then it is posited that the genitalia in question must have been embraced by members of the same sex. Like the Freudian psychoanalyst always searching for the "complex" to explain defective character, or the neurologist who sees an epilepsy sufferer behind every tyrannical leader, the sex researcher implicates "homosexual tendenices" to emasculate the powerful.

For that matter, no group of researchers has spilled more ink over the greats and not-so-greats of history than have the psychoanalysts and psychologists. Depending on how the ink blots their pages—and more important, which investigator examines the image conveyed—Napoleon has become the Rorschach of the psychohistorical world. Some attribute his behavior to his small stature, which allegedly led to overbearing and tyrannical compensation (the so-called "little man syndrome"). To Freud himself, Napoleon embodied the essentials of the Joseph complex, more familiar to today's reader as the "big brother syndrome."[19] Defense of these theses makes interesting reading but hardly provides the necessary push to roll the stone away and resurrect the essence of the man in his later years. Rather, it is the combination of physical changes coinciding with Napoleon's altered behavior that continues to spur the search for a single underlying disease process to unify the biohistorical verdict.

A few physicians, presumably putting their training in comparative anatomy to good use, sought answers in comparative pathography. The medical biographer Boris Sokoloff was among the first to perceive a continuity of behavior between Alexander the Great, Julius Caesar, and Napoleon Bonaparte, characterized by certain tragic if self-defeating flaws in the ambitious tyrant consumed by delusions of grandeur. No one would dispute that Napoleon epitomized that description during the ten-year period preceding Waterloo. Not only had he declared himself emperor; he personally designed his own coronation robes, adopted the sword and insignia of Charlemagne, and placed himself in service at the right hand of God (if not to reverse the relationship in his own mind on occasion). In Sokoloff's view, Napoleon eventually became a victim of the same psychological complex—hubris—that had accounted for his success in earlier years as it did his ultimate failure.[20]

So much for the complex; could there have been an underlying neurophysiological cause for it? For example, one specific type of epilepsy sufferer occasionally exhibits peculiar personality traits, among them erratic and intemperate behavior, alterations in sexual activity, and grandiose delusions of his rightful place in history. These are enduring qualities that persist between episodes suggestive of seizure activity, and even the most cynical would be hard pressed to dismiss out of hand their plausible application to Napoleon after 1805. It behooves the proponents of this theory,[21] however, to identify suggestive behavioral disturbances that might be interpreted as manifestations of epilepsy. True, Napoleon was said to have suffered several seizures between 1803 and 1805, which must have made him fear for his sanity on occasion.[22] As he once lamented: "One cannot lie in the bed of kings without catching from them the madness of destruction."[23] One of his mistresses, awakened by the rigors of a full-blown seizure gripping her lover, ran screaming from the room—only to meet the displaced (and presumably distraught) empress in the hall.[24] That Napoleon suffered from some form of seizure disorder, then, is not at issue. Whether this alone could have accounted for his personality change is another matter.

Though at least two investigators proposed precisely that by equating what they termed "*formes frustes* of epilepsy" with psychomotor seizure activity emanating from the temporal lobe,[25] on closer review the incidents in question bear little resemblance to the brief periods of unawareness ("fugue states"), behavioral automatisms, or repetitive motor or speech activity devoid of meaning that would be identified with this category of seizures per se. Moreover, acquiring the personality features that result from this specific type of epilepsy usually requires a lifelong experience of hundreds of such episodes left untreated.[26] The fact that none of the handful of seizurelike episodes found in Napoleon's extant record is said to have occurred after 1805 diffuses their plausible impact on his enigmatic behavior beyond that point. If their occurrence is undisputed (Talleyrand himself witnessed one such episode) and their description convincing enough to be compatible with epilepsy ("face distorted," "appeared to lose consciousness," "fell to the ground"),[27] it would still be imprudent for the retrospective diagnostician to call them anything but grand mal seizures—which, insofar as neurologists have been able to determine, are not accompanied by a well-defined personality disorder.

Persistent seizure activity of any sort is both uncommon and debilitating enough that it would have been unlikely for Napoleon to rise to such a high position under its onus—or, once he had arrived, for such abnormal behavior to pass unnoticed in one so frequently before the public eye. More damning still, those who argue that epilepsy was a pervasive influence on Napoleon's behavior have made inaccurate associations to substantiate their claims: for example, citing the emperor's slow pulse and paroxysmal behavioral disturbances as evidence of a conduction defect of the heart, incongruously attributed to "some disturbance of the . . . pituitary gland."[28] Nor is there evidence to support the audacious assertion of one writer that the epilepsy thesis represents the "key" to his military triumphs, that "Napoleon's triumphs were triumphs of epilepsy."[29] If still another concluded that "the endocrine origin of Napoleon's nervous paroxysms is more than reasonably certain,"[30] the skeptic would at least agree that it is indeed *more* than reasonable; it is pure fantasy.

We can do little else with Napoleon's brain, then, but to offer speculative explanations for why the man behaved as he did: Examination of neither that organ nor the pituitary gland was permitted at autopsy. Yet diseases outside the brain can have an impact on its function and indirectly, therefore, on behavior. Consider the biochemical induction of abnormal constriction and painful dilatation of blood vessels under the scalp known as migraine. Napoleon's behavior throughout his career, but more notably after 1805, was punctuated by frenetic periods of constructive activity and creative thinking, alternating with interludes of lethargy and inactivity that characterize some artists, executives, and leaders today who are victimized by these painful vascular systems. Yet those who have defended the migraine hypothesis have overshot the mark, not only ascribing the alleged "fits" to "vascular spasms" of his brain (a distinctly unusual occurrence in migraine), but proposing consequent permanent damage to that organ.[31] Some have gone so far as to lay the mysterious lethargy and physical changes postdating his midlife crisis at migraine's doorstep. Better such notions be laid to rest. The vast majority of migraine sufferers lead useful and productive lives; very few are victimized by the permanent complications some investigators have suggested. Nor was Napoleon. That he suffered from migraine is, at best, problematic; the allegation that it accounted for his changed behavior at the turn of the century underscores the limitations of fitting ill-defined data into a preconceived thesis.

The inroads of normal aging left the same scars on Napoleon as they do today on the rich and powerful—not to mention the commoners among us. Those who have lived a lifetime burdened with ambition, realized or not, often have difficulty tolerating the stress that accompanies it as they wrestle in older age with more mundane matters of clouded memory or recalcitrant genitalia. At least in their younger years, three primal motivations have been said to goad the movers and shakers of the world: sex, money, and power (and usually in that order). Yet like the roles of their wives in the dynamics of such men's lives— mistresses in their youth, companions in middle age, and ultimately nursemaids—these formative motivations not only change but become relatively unimportant as the overachievers are undermined by aging. The question that remains to be answered in Napoleon's case is why he aged so rapidly.

Chronic illnesses of the least intriguing sort prematurely age the national leader no less than the ordinary mortal. Any combination of long-standing afflictions might be anticipated to accelerate that process, not to mention a destructive lifestyle that ages the body even in the absence of overt disease. Living on three hour's sleep a night, bolting his food (as he did his sex) while plunging from one project into another, traveling on military campaigns almost incessantly during his last active years before final captivity on St. Helena, Napoleon had arguably signed his own death warrant long before Waterloo.

His military travels in particular may have exposed him to a chronic debilitating infection that could account for the myriad of symptoms from which he suffered. During the Egyptian campaign of 1798-99 Napoleon may have been infested with the schistosome, a ubiquitous parasite endemic to ponds and rivers of the Middle East.[32] The resulting disease, schistosomiasis, has been found in autopsies of several mummified Egyptian pharaohs[33] and has reached epidemic proportions during frequent periods of that region's later history. As was his custom, Napoleon bathed frequently while in Egypt as elsewhere. Perhaps, then, the unheralded schistosome gained entrance into his bloodstream by burrowing through the skin, thereafter traveling to other organs of the body.[34]

To argue the point, one needs to know something about this relatively unknown parasite. Depending on the species responsible, schistosomiasis presents itself as two distinctly different diseases in humans. One causes dysentery; the other (*Schistosoma hematobium*) affects the pelvic region and is the type of schistosomiasis that is endemic in the Middle East. After invading the skin of its host, the parasite first implants eggs in the bladder wall and veins of the rectum. The latter infestation causes painful dilatation and thrombosis of venous structures, which the victim ruefully recognizes as hemorrhoids. As for the bladder, the eggs chronically inflame its walls and lead to the excretion of mucous, pus, and blood. Concretions develop around the implanted eggs, eventually obstructing the urinary tract altogether. Once the veins lining the pelvis are infested, the schistosome rapidly spreads in the bloodstream to the lungs and may be deposited there. In severe cases, the lungs prove ineffective filters, and the larvae proceed to infect the liver, stomach, and even the brain.[35]

Schistosomiasis remains the second most common parasitic disease (next to malaria) in humans. Involvement of the bladder, rectum, and stomach is found 80 percent, 75 percent, and 30 percent of the time, respectively, in patients who die of the disease.[36] Though frequently a silent invader in its early stages, rigor and fever eventually occur and are indistinguishable from symptoms of malaria, its partner in crime. These facts are perhaps of more than passing interest in relation to a French general who was a compulsive bather, who was documented to have suffered from at least one episode of "the ague" while in Egypt,[37] and who was later victimized by diseases of each of the three organs most prevalently involved by the schistosome.

It may, then, be more than coincidental that Napoleon began to show all the usual symptoms of schistosomiasis (not to mention an exacerbation of hemorrhoids) only after his return from Egypt.[38] These included an increasingly prominent ache in his right side, perhaps reflecting kidney, liver, or even stomach involvement with the parasite; painful urination with subsequent stone formation as a possible result of bladder infestation; and a hacking cough that may have been related to the calcified granulomata or "tubercles" found in his left lung at autopsy.[39]

Proceeding from the defensible to the more speculative, any disseminated disease in the bloodstream (whether of tumor or parasitic origin) involves the pituitary gland with greater incidence than its small size and location would suggest, ostensibly on the basis of this gland's rich blood supply.[40] Though the supposition that Napoleon suffered pituitary failure is fraught with contradictions, those who cling to this hypothesis have yet to posit a cause for its alleged occurrence. Perhaps the schistosome thread offers a rope with which the Froehlich-syndrome advocates might one day hang their critics. That intriguing surmise will be left for others to argue.

For the purpose of this review, schistosomiasis may prove to have important ties to still another maligned theory concerning Napoleon's demise that deserves a second look: the popular belief that Napoleon had been poisoned, based on the arsenic that detailed photospectrometric analyses of samples of his hair revealed.[41] Yet modern toxicologists are now aware that antimony may be confused with arsenic in the type of analysis used.[42] And that is of singular importance, as antimony was a mainstay of treatment for parasitic diseases of all kinds in the eighteenth and nineteenth century.[43] This leaves the skeptic with food for thought: Was Napoleon being treated with antimony for a parasitic disease that was believed at the time to be malaria but was really a case of schisotosomiasis heretofore undocumented in the medical record? Even if the schistosome was not the culprit, the record indicates that he suffered a bout of "malaria" at Auxonne in 1789.[44] Setting the arsenic question aside for the moment, what this ubiquitous parasite affords the pathographer is a single unifying disease that could account for a host of seemingly unrelated symptoms, and which had a chronicity that links long-standing illness to the phenomenon of premature aging.

Many investigators have accepted out of hand that Napoleon's recurring abdominal pain, nausea, and vomiting were manifestations of a peptic ulcer that eventually transformed itself into a cancerous growth in the stomach.[45] No doubt his dietary habits, perpetual stress, and destructive lifestyle might have predisposed the emperor to the former condition in any case. The real question is whether the "cancer" was the cause of his death, as his physicians certified following the autopsy.[46] Given the various accounts of the autopsy findings, however, it is by no means certain that the growth found to be penetrating the back wall of his stomach was in fact a cancer. For one thing, a chronic yet benign peptic ulcer (not to mention an indolent schistosomiatic infestation known to induce ulcerations) can produce such scarring that it resembles a tumorous growth. For another, it may also penetrate the outer layer of the stomach, as every general surgeon knows.

Nor does stomach cancer, in and of itself, kill its host merely by being present. An overwhelming number of its victims die for one of four reasons: the cancer obstructs the gastrointestinal tract, leading to starvation; it spreads to other vital organs, most notably the liver and lungs; it induces an infection in the abdominal cavity known as "peritonitis" once a perforation of the stomach occurs; or the patient slowly (on occasion, precipitately) bleeds to death as the ulcer enlarges. Not only is the evidence for obstruction (until the very end) unpersuasive in Napoleon's case; his autopsy affirms that there was no dissemination of cancer to other organs. Moreover, the location of the perforation precluded a fulminant infection (despite some investigators' assertions to the contrary),[47] as the rent was in effect sealed by the juxtaposition to it of the liver.[48]

While recognizing that the Corsican pathologist who performed Napoleon's autopsy was a borderline clinician (not to mention that some thought he was a confirmed liar as well),[49] it would be imprudent to dismiss Francesco Antommarchi's findings altogether. After all, he had been trained by an eminent anatomist and at least recognized his limitations as a clinician, having had only corpses to deal with in the past.[50] Though Antommarchi found no evidence of peritonitis, the intermittent episodes of acute abdominal distress that his patient experienced while on St. Helena at least suggest that earlier infections might still have occurred. To be more precise, descriptions of these illnesses implicate some form of inflammatory process, possibly on the basis of a transient perforation of the ulcer into the abdominal cavity. Beginning in 1816 Napoleon suffered from spasmodic abdominal cramping and vomiting that were accompanied by a rapid pulse, fever, profuse sweating, and pain referred to the right shoulder. Not only does the shoulder discomfort suggest diaphragmatic irritation from an inflammatory source in the abdomen with referred pain to that area, but the notation of jaundice thereafter raises the possibility of liver involvement—precisely as might be expected by the close approximation of the ulcer to the liver's edge, found at his autopsy.

Simply stated, there are unresolved problems with the cancer thesis to account for Napoleon's death, unless the amount of gastrointestinal bleeding that did occur over time was enough to induce a life-threatening anemia and subsequent shock. On the surface, there is much to suggest that his frequent episodes of loss of consciousness were due to blood loss rather than to the mysterious "seizures" that some have proposed. Count Monthalon recorded in his diary that Napoleon's lips and fingernails were "entirely colorless" in the end, only to embellish his observation with an equally colorless metaphor: "There was no more oil in the lamp."[51] This was enough for some pathographers to conclude that chronic anemia was slowly snuffing the flame of Napoleon's vitality. True, there was evidence of active bleeding in the stomach just prior to his death; true, too, chronic infection is known to induce a gradual fall in the blood count, even in the absence of overt hemorrhage. Nevertheless, descriptions of Napoleon's last hours do not convincingly match those of patients dying of hypovolemic shock. One therefore could hardly be faulted for looking elsewhere for the cause of his death, as a Swedish dentist with a lifelong interest in toxicology has done. We return, then, to the arsenic theory.

Readers familiar with pathography's literature will readily surmise that this account of Napoleon's health thus far is quite in keeping with Arno Karlen's incisive critique. This is only to emphasize that Karlen's examination, as far as it goes, represents the most balanced and thought-provoking study of its kind that has been written to date. It is not to say, however, that second opinions are out of order, for Karlen largely ignores the arsenic question. Yet it can now be argued that arsenic ties in closely to the phenomenon of chronic infection in particular (and premature aging in general) that the record has already highlighted in bold relief. To fit the puzzle together requires reexamining the arsenic thesis in some detail.

In 1961, Dr. Sten Forshufvud published a landmark study documenting the presence of large quantities of arsenic in hairs taken from Napoleon's shorn head at the time of his autopsy.[52] Using a sensitive activation-analysis technique, Forshufvud pursued a hunch (and the hair) after reading previously unpublished diary entries of a member of the emperor's entourage. Two literary phenomena followed, the first of which was based on Forshufvud's jump from an assimilation of hard data substantiating the presence of arsenic to a far softer assumption that one of Napoleon's associates had systematically poisoned him at the behest of French royalists who feared his return to power.[53] The second body of literature to emerge was a series of vituperative disclaimers concerning that assumption, published in the distinguished British medical journal *The Lancet*.[54]

As a result of this debate and subsquent studies, Forshufvud's theory has been largely discounted[55]—albeit not for all of the right reasons. Forshufvud dismissed his critics in kind with a cynical riposte: "History belongs to the historians, not the scientists."[56] Still, if historians could not ignore the fact that many of his fellow scientists disputed the Swedish dentist-toxicologist's claims,[57] neither could investigators dispel the data indicating that arsenic was present in higher concentrations than is normally the case. Though later independent analyses of different locks of Napoleon's hair revealed even higher concentrations of antimony, the weight of the evidence still suggests a place for arsenic in his medical history. Even so, Forshufvud may have overlooked the real reason why it was there. That toxic levels of a heavy metal were found in fragments of hair (and that they belonged to Napoleon) is not at issue. What is really in dispute is, first, did arsenic contribute to the emperor's decline and death, and second, was it administered as a poison?

With regard to arsenic's contribution to Napoleon's deteriorating health, Forshufvud drew an important distinction between acute and chronic poisoning. He surmised that Napoleon's own doctors missed the telltale symptoms of chronic arsenic intoxication because these were not precisely known until a hundred years later.[58] Forshufvud emphasized loss of body hair, swollen feet and legs, an enlarged liver, somnolence and paradoxical insomnia, and obesity as typical symptoms of the condition (the last two features are open to question) but failed to mention one of the most prevalent signs of this particular type of prolonged heavy metal exposure: a blotchy pigmentation of the skin in general and thickening of the skin of the palms and soles in particular.[59] Napoleon's hands were described in detail at his death (mention is made of their "puffiness" but not thickness per se), and though his torso was examined closely enough that the absence of body hair was observed, no pigmented lesions were noted.[60]

Further, one does not advance to chronic arsenic intoxication without first going through its subacute stage. Patients with subacute poisoning suffer from puffiness of the skin and eyelids, which Napoleon had, but where are the bouts of diarrhea so characteristic of this stage of the disease?[61] On only two occasions during Napoleon's stay on St. Helena is diarrhea even mentioned,[62] hardly in keeping with the universal observation of frequent bouts of "the runs" each time the heavy metal is ingested. In short, not all of Napoleon's clinical signs and symptoms fit today's textbook descriptions of this particular type of exposure.

To add to the confusion, not all who have studied the problem are consistent in their findings. One investigator acknowledged that most of the signs and symptoms descriptively fit arsenic poisoning, underscoring the presence of leg swelling and loss of hair, yet concluded that Napoleon's symptoms did not fit that condition after all.[63] This is not to dismiss his and others'[64] contributions to the debate altogether. They are on more solid ground in debunking Forshufvud's theory that the remarkable preservation of Napoleon's body at the time of his exhumation two decades later was due to the preservative effect of high levels of arsenic in the body.[65] One suspects that Forshufvud was hearing zebras where horses' hoofbeats signaled their far more familiar cadence: Napoleon's entombment in four airtight coffins was a more than adequate explanation for his well-preserved remains.[66]

These caveats to Forshufvud's thesis notwithstanding, even the most cynical observer would be hard pressed to dismiss his subsequent studies masterfully correlating Napoleon's hair growth with sequential clinical stages of the disease.[67] True, some scientists have reminded us that antimony can be confused with arsenic, despite the alleged specificity of the activation analysis test; still others have pointed out that the tartar emetic that Napoleon took on his deathbed contained antimony, even though it may not have been used to disguise the real poison as Forshufvud suggested.[68] On balance, however, the impartial pathographer would view with skepticism the claim that arsenic wasn't there or that the amounts weren't clinically significant.[69] It was, and they were.[70] The question that really needs to be addressed is how it got there. What the record suggests is the possibility that Napoleon had been treated all along, for a number of recurring symptoms, with either antimony or arsenic—or, more likely still, both.

To illustrate the difficulty in following a trail that has long since grown cold, we would do well to remember that a little knowledge can go a dangerously long way toward turning the casual scholar in the wrong direction. By way of example, I recall one French professor who smugly reminded me of a "fact" that accounted for the presence of arsenic in Napoleon's hair: "As every good pharmacist knows, arsenic was used as an aphrodisiac in France in the eighteenth and nineteenth centuries." He got the genital part right, but made the wrong association: drugs containing arsenic were used to treat syphilis—and all manner of other illnesses, including parasitic diseases.[71]

One such preparation was Fowler's solution. Although this tonic did not reach widespread use until the mid-1800's, it was available in Napoleon's day.[72] Strange indeed that the emperor's health seemed to improve during those periods in which he was medically unattended.[73] Was there more than meets the eye in the numerous references to purgatives, tonics, and paregorics that Napoleon received from his doctors, of which some had side effects at least suggestive of subacute arsenical effect?[74] Taking an optimist's view of my predecessors rather than searching for the diabolical motive behind every action, one might conclude instead that Napoleon had unwittingly become a victim of polypharmacy—including certain drugs containing arsenic that were used for medical purposes.

Not that the chronic consumption of arsenic necessarily leads to physiologic incapacitation or death. During the nineteenth century, Austrian peasants of the Styrian Alps habitually consumed huge quantities of arsenic as a means of promoting physical stamina—testimony to the fact that one may become acclimated to quantities known to produce immediate death in the individual without prior exposure.[75] Apothecaries and physicians had long used that fact to advantage. Not only had the Chinese been treating syphilis with arsenic since the seventeenth century; it was also administered as a cheap antidote for malaria, which Napoleon was believed to have had.[76] Moreover, one of its most prevalent uses in Napoleonic France was to treat recurring skin eruptions, and history records that the emperor was no stranger to that affliction either.[77]

Perhaps Napoleon even believed that he had syphilis and requested arsenic surreptitiously—a reasonable enough suspicion until his fears of impotence resolved after his divorce from Josephine. Though some have argued that he characteristically refused all manner of medication until very near the end, when failing health softened his resolve, on balance the extant data suggest that he was not averse to taking medicines on occasion, even as a young man.[78] The syphilis connection seems rather far-fetched to account for the presence of arsenic, but its use as treatment for a parasitic infection has a ring of plausibility about it. Coupled with at least two other diseases that Napoleon was perceived to have had, and for which arsenic was the treatment of choice of that day, the chances are good that it found its way into his body as a medicine rather than a poison.

Further, there is still the possibility of environmental exposure. Both the wallpaper and heavily brocaded curtains in the emperor's room contained arsenic,[79] which was frequently found in interior decor of the eighteenth century, and inhalation of arsenic from such sources is one means of acquiring toxic levels of the heavy metal in the body. It can also be ingested in substances other than medicine. Could the unwary prisoner on St. Helena have eaten vegetables or drunk spring water contaminated with it? Arsenic *was* used as a pesticide during the eighteenth century.[80] What has yet to be clarified is whether such pesticides were used on the island before or during Napoleon's captivity, and whether the volcanic soil or water of St. Helena was laden with arsenic.

Such important questions may defy the retrospective tools of investigation that today's science affords. Proponents of the poison hypothesis dismiss these possibilities out of hand, arguing that inadvertent environmental exposure would have affected others on St. Helena. Yet much in the way of defensible inference can still be made. For one thing, hepatitis (or at least a variation of that liver ailment) was almost endemic on the island. To date, its origins there remain unclear. What is now known is that heavy metals of various types, including arsenic, adversely affect liver function.[81] Moreover, rats were prevalent on St. Helena—virtually every diary mentions their presence—and we know that arsenic was used as a rat poison on the Continent in the eighteenth and nineteenth centuries.[82] Perhaps the British had exported it to St. Helena in an attempt to eliminate the feared rodent—for Europeans had much in their past history to be skittish about when it came to rats.

None of these potential sources of arsenic can be established with certainty. They do, however, seem more plausible—if admittedly less intriguing—than the poison theory. Forshufvud believed he had discovered both how the poisoning was perpetrated (chronically) and how it was covered up (with calomel and tartar emetic). He was postulating the perfect crime; all he needed was a motive—suggestive elements of which were found in obscure diary entries.[83] These were enough to convince this modern-day Hercule Poirot that one of Napoleon's trusted entourage had been sent to St. Helena at the behest of French royalty to assure that the audacious Corsican would not be around to haunt any future succession crisis.[84]

In one sense, Forshufvud appeared to be his own worst enemy. After reading Louis Marchand's diary, and before documenting the presence of arsenic in Napoleon's body, the fertile imagination of the toxicologist had all but closed his mind to any alternatives to premeditated murder. Slamming shut the diary, he had exclaimed to his wife: "That's how they did it. They poisoned him with arsenic!"[85] Yet constructing an engrossing spy thriller on subjective premises, complete with motive, method, and murderer, would leave such purists as Sherlock Holmes exasperated, to say the least. If poisoning was the name of the game once Napoleon reached St. Helena, then how explain the earlier documentation of arsenic in his hair when he was neither incarcerated on St. Helena nor in the company of his alleged assassin? As Forshuvfud himself admitted, "Napoleon was exposed to substantial amounts of arsenic . . . before being exiled to St. Helena."[86]

Although arsenic alone did not kill Napoleon, it may have contributed to his death, for it is now known to decrease the immune response to all kinds of diseases.[87] If the emperor in fact suffered from chronic schistosomiasis, then his immune response to the spread of the parasite to other organs may have been compromised by the arsenic present. That surmise at least deserves more consideration than the conclusions of one cynic, who not only asserted that thirteen times the usual amount of arsenic in the body was "within the range of normal" but lamely argued in the end that "corrosion of the soul" and "asphyxiation of the spirit" accounted for Napoleon's death.[88] People don't die of depression and loss of self-esteem alone. These factors do, however, affect an individual's willingness to push on in the face of chronic disease— and may arguably have affected Napoleon's long-standing battle with schistosomiasis every bit as much as did the arsenic that lowered his immune response.

It seems hardly necessary, then, to postulate an exhaustion of the pituitary gland, a brain full of spirochetes, or a lifetime of seizures to explain Napoleon's changed appearance and behavior. Probably victimized by a chronic parasitic infection with frequently painful manifestations, depressed and tired of life, perceptive enough to realize in the stifling confines of his barren captivity that he had met his match in the British, and weakened further by progressive anemia from a bleeding ulcer and chronic heavy metal exposure, Napoleon lost his last battle in 1821 to overwhelming psychological and physiological forces. Yet history had already passed him by. And that, in the judgment of more sober scholars, may be reason enough to account for his terminal decline.

CHAPTER 2

Henry VIII:
Syphilitic Sovereign?

What more need be said of King Henry VIII? His popularly recounted life story reads like a soap opera: eventually falling victim to syphilis after years of debauchery, Bluff Hal spent the rest of his life captive to murderous passions that earned him the dubious distinction of being among the most violent monarchs who ever ruled England. At mid-life, we are told, both his health and his character changed for the worse, such that the royal flagon was by then more half empty than half full. Yet in retrospect one wonders whether the pathographer, with his yard of "ail" in hand, has proved too intoxicated to assimilate the meager pool of medical facts left to ferment in the dregs. To render its contents more potent, he has filled the remainder with more than a splash of inference, thereby masking the real physical ailments that may (or may not) have accounted for Henry's perplexing behavior.

Those who subscribe to the syphilis theory to explain the king's transformation peddle their wares out of four shopworn containers. First, syphilis burst upon the English scene in pandemic proportions during a period when Henry both sat on the royal throne and presumably slept in some less-than-regal beds.[1] Second, the obstetrical histories of his wives, most notably Catherine of Aragon, bear a striking resemblance to those of syphilitic women who bear children, and the medical histories of some of Henry's surviving offspring to those of the children of such women.[2] Third, Henry later manifested certain features suggestive of an individual afflicted with syphilis of the nervous system: difficulty in walking, behavioral changes, loss of judgment, poor memory, fits of rage—all said to be typical of "paresis of the insane."[3] Finally, an "ulcer" of Henry's leg (and an obscure scar on his nose) appeared during the time he was deteriorating physically and mentally, raising the possibility that both lesions were syphilitic gummas known to affect the bones in late stages of the disease.[4] From such evidence comes the "presumptive diagnosis" of syphilis.

What gave birth, as it were, to the syphilis theory in the first place? It all began with the obstetrical histories of Henry's wives. On the basis of their multiple premature births and stillbirths, the earliest pathographers embraced the theory that syphilis lay behind these failures of propagation. After all, no effects of disease are said to be quite so predictable as what happens to syphilitic women who attempt to have children. Catherine of Aragon's track record set the stage for the medical reductionists. During her first two years of marriage alone, she produced a stillborn daughter and a son who lived only fifty-two days. A year later the queen suffered both a second miscarriage and another stillbirth. After four unsuccessful pregnancies, Catherine finally delivered her only viable child, a daughter who one day would rule England and earn for herself the tasteless epithet "Bloody Mary."

With no male heir forthcoming and the royal succession in doubt (for no queen had ever been crowned sole ruler of England), the king's patience was sorely tried by Catherine's labors. The same could be said for his later detractors, who labored in vain to uncover that elusive venereal "sore" responsible for bringing the scourge of syphilis to the Tudor line.[5] Both Henry and Catherine have been repeatedly "tried" in the court of pathographical review through the years, yet neither has been found guilty of harboring such a sore beyond a reasonable doubt.

Quite frankly, the indictment of Henry smacks of the ex post facto. Because his later history suggests an avid interest in sowing the royal seed, some have assumed that the prince must have had a lot of practice prior to meeting Catherine. But did he really? One historian who was hardly an apologist for Henry admitted that, for all the rumors of his sexual excesses as a young man, "he was careful to contain his passions within bounds."[6] Moreover, the tight reins held by his father, the austere Henry VII, were restrictive enough to dampen the excesses of a son who, by all accounts, was kept well under thumb.[7] If, as one "syphilophile" surmised, Bluff Hal had "probably forgotten the trifling incident" that exposed him to syphilis in his ribald youth,[8] no scholar has yet uncovered it. Though the elusive sore was first ascribed to Henry, such inferential scabs have left no scar.

Of necessity we turn to Catherine. Here the extant data are as titillating as they are subjective. A solicitious Spanish ambassador once took it upon himself to alert the royal court to Catherine's "scandalous involvement" with one Diego Fernandez, a confessor to this recently widowed matron whose first husband happened to have been Henry's brother. Whether their relationship was purely platonic and aboveboard (or at least out-of-bed), as the queen asserted to her dying day, Fernandez certainly lived up to his racy reputation. He was later convicted of fornication and driven from court.[9] Though no evidence exists to support the notion that he ever had syphilis, perhaps there was more than meets the eye in the comment of Catherine's doctor: "The only pains from which she now suffers are moral afflictions beyond the reach of her physician."[10]

A third and often discussed possibility as to who got sores from whom ignores the fact that simple chronology belies the hypothesis. In 1514 (some four years *after* his marriage to Catherine), Henry returned from a military campaign in France. A few weeks later he contracted a rash that one observer cavalierly labeled the "French disease," a parochial term of the day for syphilis. Henry, no mean healer and producer of nostrums himself, proclaimed that he had smallpox, as did his physician Thomas Linacre. Still others who were charged with monitoring the king's health saw nothing more in the affliction than a case of measles.[11] It was left to future speculators who never saw the rash themselves to attribute it to syphilis.[12] If so, had Henry acquired it during an uncircumspect tryst in France? Or did the queen infect her husband on his return? Either way, the verdict is moot, because Catherine had already experienced three miscarriages and stillbirths. For the syphilis thesis to fit her obstetrical history, Henry would have to have contracted the disease long before the French campaign.

Few would dispute that Catherine's predicament was unfair, trapped as she was between the demands of royal prerogative and a recalcitrant womb. Aside from her suspicious obstetrical history, is there anything objective with which to substantiate the claim that she was given to sexual excess, regardless of who was the alleged guilty party linking lues to the loins of Tudor? In all too few instances can the pathographer's retrospective postmortems be tested against the real thing: an autopsy of the deceased. Lest one mistakenly suppose that the sixteenth-century autopsy provided unassailable scientific evidence upon which to base retrospective suppositions, we must be prudent enough to recognize that what is found at autopsies, then and today, lies largely in the eye of the beholder.

In Catherine's case, a candlemaker turned embalmer found no abnormal pathology except in her heart, which was described as "black and hideous, with a black excrescence that clung closely to the outside."[13] It is less than informative to see what some have made of this description, ranging from a distinctly unusual cancer of the heart, on the one hand, to "syphilitic aortitis" on the other[14] (ignoring the rudimentary fact that the aorta is quite distinct from the heart itself). Yet far removed from any manifestation of syphilis, perhaps a more mundane explanation fits the clinical context of the queen's death: a myocardial infarction that extended itself over a period of days might have rendered a portion of the heart necrotic (and possibly "black") with a postmortem clot lodged under the thinned-out wall of heart muscle that has died.[15]

Suffering from pangs of false labor himself over a thesis that is scarcely more viable than the corpses and stillbirths he ponders, the syphilophile is forced to throw out some babies with the bathwater that don't mesh with his preconceived scenario. Failing that, he remakes the survivors in his own image. As for Henry's next wife, Anne Boleyn, her firstborn was a normal girl, Elizabeth I, who sat on the English throne for nearly a half century and never showed any stigmata of the dread disease. This birthing record contradicts that usually found among syphilitic mothers.[16]

Faced with healthy progeny to explain away, at least one writer seized on the contemporary rumor that Elizabeth may not have been Henry's daughter after all. Citing Anne's known proclivity for flirting, why not brand her a nymphomaniac and proclaim her daughter to have been born out of wedlock?[17] But as one who held the king at arm's length for six years, steadfastly refusing to be Henry's mistress until his divorce from Catherine assured the throne for herself, Anne would hardly have risked it all in the eleventh hour by involving herself with another man.[18] There were other ways to provoke Henry's jealousy, which she had exercised already. To jeopardize both the royal prize and her head as well squares with neither her motives nor the dictates of prudence.

Nor is Anne's the only obstetrical history that doesn't fit the syphilology party line. Henry's third wife, Jane Seymour, successfully gave birth to a viable if admittedly frail male heir, the luckless Edward VI. What at first glance, then, suggests an engaging thesis born of the failed birthing process suffers from illegitimacy, as two of the king's first three wives simply do not fit the mold of syphilitic maternity history.[19]

That is, of course, unless the undaunted researcher can prove that his surviving children themselves bore the stigmata of syphilis. Not surprisingly, just such an argument has been advanced with regard to three of Henry's offspring. If the cases of Henry Fitzroy (Henry's bastard son born to Anne's sister Mary) and Edward VI are similar insofar as both died at a young age,[20] no one has convincingly portrayed either as a syphilitic child.[21] Apart from their fragile health, the extant records fail to describe any incontrovertible signs of congenitally acquired venereal disease.

What we do know of congenital syphilitics who survive into childhood is the following: the child's growth is usually stunted, and the perceptual senses of hearing and seeing are impaired. The teeth resemble foreshortened pegs, the nose may be flat, and the skull prominent. Mental development is slowed, and many victims are institutionalized on that account.[22] To be sure, some of these features have been attributed to Henry's daughter Mary: one investigation asserts that her portrait by the Spanish artist Moro depicts a "classic hereditary syphilitic" with its frontal bossing, flat nose, and wrinkled face.[23] Yet the restrictions that apply to the interpretation of autopsy reports also apply to art; others who have studied the same painting have failed to see in it any damning physical stigmata.[24]

Proponents of the syphilis argument have also catered to the less than scientific practice of selecting the evidence. More discerning critics, drawing upon other portraits and unbiased descriptions by Mary's contemporaries, have refused to allow the oil depicting her as a syphilitic to dry on the canvas of historical reappraisal. Though some might take exception to the Venetian ambassador Michiel's description of Mary as a "seemly woman" (enough to posit the hope that he was a better diplomat than a judge of beauty), perhaps Michiel was taking into account her other redeeming features. For one, she had become an accomplished musician by the age of four; for another, she was fluent in four languages by the age of ten—achievements that hardly reflect the intellectual attributes of the congenital syphilitic.[25]

Those researchers who embrace more objective data than aging portraits still must consider Mary's poor eyesight, which some have argued to be representative of interstitial keratitis so prevalent among hereditary syphilitics.[26] Sad to relate, the skeptics' cause was hardly strengthened by one otherwise incisive critic of the syphilis thesis who lamely attributed Mary's failing vision to "severe eye strain" induced by long hours of study as a youth or, worse yet, to "the incessant weeping" provoked by Henry's treatment of her mother Catherine![27] The less romantically inclined would point out instead a multitude of other causes for compromised vision, not to mention the lack of documentation for Mary's having had poor hearing or pegged teeth. And the latter is of singular importance, as the presence of interstitial keratitis supports the diagnosis of syphilis only when linked with these other two defects in what is collectively known as Hutchinson's triad.[28]

Given the history of childbirths during that era, the frequent birthing failures in Henry's family probably matched what the times allowed, even for pregnancies among the well-to-do. His older sister Margaret had an obstetrical history little better than that of the unfortunate Catherine: two of her children died at birth, and three others expired in their infancy.[29] Not all failures of propagation can be laid at syphilis's doorstep, even during the worst of times when the scourge had reached pandemic proportions.

That brings us to the best of times to consider whether the quasi-incestuous relationships in which Henry and his kin were involved might have contributed to a larger share of congenital defects, miscarriages, and stillbirths than a more diversified genetic pool would have afforded. In truth, consanguinity was no more prevalent among the Tudors than within other royal families of the sixteenth century. That bit of circumstantial evidence probably warrants more consideration than the suggestion that something known as "Rh incompatibility" accounted for Catherine's frequent fertility failures.[30] Whereas the obstetrical histories of Anne Boleyn and Jane Seymour contradict the syphilis thesis in that their firstborn survived, Catherine's history is at odds with Rh incompatibility precisely because her first did not. For a woman to acquire the Rh factor leading to abortions and miscarriages in later pregnancies, her firstborn by definition is unaffected, as circulating antibodies in the mother's blood militating against subsequent normal pregnancies are not present until Rh positive and Rh negative serum combine.[31] Moreover, Mary's survival so late in the picture further serves to negate the hypothesis.

If, as the record could be interpreted to suggest and the natural history of syphilis transmission allows, Henry became less infectious with time,[32] he still had ample opportunity during the course of his subsequent marriages to reload and fire at will, as the saying goes, in an attempt to father a son. Viewed from this perspective, the syphilis thesis remains at best a blip on the screen of Tudor history—unless, of course, it can be proved that Henry's later behavior itself bore the stigmata of neurologic involvement. And here again subsequent argument will suggest that the imaginative pathographer has gone too far.

That said, are we justified in labeling Henry an unwary syphilitic simply because much of the population undeniably *was* victimized by this new and frightening venereal disease? After all, syphilis had burst upon the scene with such alacrity and virulence that during the first thirty years of the sixteenth century alone, one-half to two-thirds of patients admitted to asylums and sanatoriums were said to be afflicted by the scourge.[33] To some scholars, this statistic alone solidified the case: "Syphilis was a common disease at the beginning of the sixteenth century, and the simple explanation is that Henry suffered from it."[34] Yet the skeptic might suggest substituting the word "simplistic" for "simple" to underscore the shallow appeal of circumstantial evidence in the face of more unassailable data.

Though its origins were at best poorly understood, the manifestations of syphilis were so descriptively specific by 1520 that few victims of what was then called the "Great Pox" passed undiagnosed. Therein lies one very telling argument against Henry's having been so afflicted: despite the best medical care of the day (not to mention the scrutiny of ambassadors dutifully charged—and handsomely rewarded—with keeping abreast of the king's health), no account of his ever having the disease, much less having been treated for it, exists.[35] Certainly it would have been difficult to disguise, in a victim with Henry's imposing physical credentials and social standings, the slobbering that would have occurred under the influence of mercury ingestion, the accepted treatment of the day.[36]

That syphilis was the latest in a long list of plagues to ravage the English countryside does not imply that everyone in Tudor society got it. For those who did succumb, its skin eruptions alone were so striking and loathsome that the spirochete's presence could hardly be missed. Obviously, there are inherent dangers in applying what we know of syphilis today to its manifestations at the turn of the sixteenth century; still, a few facts are generally accepted as timeless. Statistically, only one-third of those who contract the disease and pass without treatment go on to central nervous system involvement; and of that subgroup, only one-third are infected in such a way as to affect their behavior.[37] Not only would Henry have been unlikely to develop neurosyphilis on percentages alone, then, but his later conduct hardly suggests the need to raise the issue in the first place.

Most investigators now refute the popular myth generated by a handful of earlier biographers that Henry's behavior dramatically changed as he aged.[38] On balance, they regard as more apparent than real the much touted midlife crisis that allegedly transformed him at about the time he obtained his divorce from Catherine. The underpinnings of Henry's character, including an unbridled egotism and an insistence on having his own way, were already well entrenched in what today's physicians would identify as his "premorbid personality": that is, before the onset of any disease that might have afflicted him during this period. One prudent scholar has spoken for most of his colleagues in asserting that "something of the King's cruelty and inherent assumption that clean breaks with the past could solve deep-rooted problems was already in evidence" at an early age.[39] Much of this has been ascribed to an inferiority complex suffered at the hand of his father, though it seems excessive to embellish that with an Oedipus complex, as one psychologist has done.[40]

What we do discover very early on in Henry's reign is a dearth of illness per se but a plethora of frustrations. Take an individual intent upon legitimizing a line that had very tenuous foundations, add his lifelong pretensions against the French, then throw at him a succession of diplomatic affronts, a wife who could not bear him a male heir, and a mistress who refused his entreaties for six years. Is it any wonder that this consummate egotist would become more paranoid and vindictive seemingly overnight? Henry's ego had always been his Achilles heel. Crafty enough to fend off potentially lethal arrows shot from the bows of opponents and subordinates alike, the king's pride nevertheless suffered grievous wounds. He was as victimized by his own passions as he was by self-perceived offenses, either personal or diplomatic. Not only had his erstwhile allies turned archrivals—Ferdinand, Maximilian, and Charles V—renounced a treaty that had earlier made them common enemies of Henry's much coveted France;[41] his sexual passions neither produced redeeming progeny nor found an outlet in Anne, who steadfastly refused his amorous advances.

As a self-styled Renaissance man, Henry's intellectual passions were equally boundless. Into the ferment of anticlericalism rocking the foundation of the English church dropped his divorce of Catherine. During the proceedings, the king became, as one historian well put it, a "mendacious theologian."[42] Using his perverted theological constructs just long enough to effect a legitimate divorce (at least in his own eyes), he just as quickly dropped his obsession with formulating doctrine and began to exercise it. Perhaps that was just as well, insofar as his reputation as a serious theologian was concerned. Shakespeare, for one, implied that the king's religious views extended no higher than the bodice of his mistress's gowns. In the second act of *Henry VIII* the Lord Chamberlain remarks: "It seems the marriage with his brother's wife has crept too near his conscience." To which the Duke of Suffolk retorts: "No, his conscience has crept too near another lady."[43]

Straining under the yoke of Rome as much as the barrenness of Catherine's womb, Henry vigorously enforced his self-serving tenets for the purpose of removing both problems altogether. The measure of his resourcefulness is that he succeeded—but not without immersing himself deeper in self-indulgence. That only opened his eyes to the limitless bounds of what his will alone could accomplish, some of which was admittedly unwarranted. The later beheadings of Anne Boleyn and Sir Thomas More were cases in point.

Yet falling victim to one's passions (even sexual ones on occasion) hardly equates, a priori, with succumbing to a social disease. It was not the dread spirochete but Henry's overweening will that embroiled him in crises of both a personal and political nature—to the effect that he was corrupted in the end by his own sense of power.[44] The influence he wielded in temporal and spiritual matters was so formidable that, his perennial designs on the French excepted, Henry's reign was marked by one success after another. In the sober analysis of one authority: "On the twin issues of monarchic theory and lust for conquest, there is everything to be said for the view that Henry VIII's policy was consistent throughout his reign."[45] Indeed, at this point in the story he had succeeded in gaining control of both church and state—a supreme compliment for an alleged victim of syphilis who had accomplished what virtually all other kinds had sought in vain since the lay-investiture crisis of the Middle Ages.

If any change in Henry's character occurred at all, it arguably came only after a literal blow to the head and a later figurative blow to his fragile ego. While participating in a jousting tournament in 1536, Henry had been knocked from his horse and rendered unconscious for two hours. That was a landmark incident whose possible physiologic significance is discussed in further detail below. From the standpoint of appearance and behavior, the king became a changed man—and not the least of the changes can be attributed to the fact that he never rode in the jousts again, forfeiting the one physical activity that had not only afforded him self-esteem but had kept him thin and robust. A man who has found pleasure in physical contests that are now denied him may well become depressed. Moreover, obesity is a cardinal sequela of both depression and a sedentary lifestyle, as depressed and inactive individuals both eat more and expend fewer calories. Hence the king's transformation within a three-year period into the gargantuan blob with which history identifies him. For those who have used Henry's expanding waistline as a measure of progression of whatever intriguing diseases they have attributed to it—whether syphilis,[46] gout,[47] or amyloidosis[48]—such a bland equation as balancing caloric expenditure with dietary intake is bound to disappoint.

Equally disappointing for the retrospective voyeur, Henry's gluttony no longer extended to his erstwhile prodigious sexual appetite. Shortly after his fortieth birthday, word spread that England's most renowned womanizer had become impotent. There is no documentation to support the allegation, though the rumor alone was enough for some later writers to suggest that his alleged impotence was yet another sign of advancing syphilis.[49] Prudent physicians who deal with depressed patients on a daily basis would recognize instead that Henry's depression may have had more to do with his diminished sexual drive than did organic disease per se, for depressed patients often complain of their loss of interest in sex.[50]

Their mates may turn by default to other sexual outlets, as seems to have been the case with Henry's fifth wife: the scandalous Catherine Howard was described by one chronicler as a "nymphomaniac from the age of twelve" and by another as little more than "an animated flapper with the glitter of a jewel and the morals of a female guttersnipe."[51] Morals aside, Henry loved Catherine dearly. When she was ultimately convicted of adultery in 1541 at the behest of Henry's councilors, rival ambassadors could hardly fail to remark to their superiors how terribly affected he was by the queen's treason, which he was powerless to pardon. The Venetian ambassador, Chapuys, reported that Henry had "greatly fallen away" into melancholy since learning of Catherine's misconduct; Marillac, the French liaison to Henry's court, found him still a year later to be "very old and gray since the *malheur* of his last queen."[52] Now rapidly aging, he would soon turn to a sixth wife, who would afford him the solace of a nursemaid.

Not all his scars were emotional. Even before Catherine Howard's indiscretion, physical ailments other than obesity and depression were nipping at the increasingly vulnerable heels of poor Henry. In 1537 Lord Montague confided that the king had developed an "ulcerous leg," the serious nature of which was underscored by Henry's belief that it might someday kill him.[53] A later scholar ascribed undue significance to the lesion's occurrence at precisely the time Henry's physical incapacities accelerated, going so far as to interpret this and other physical manifestations as late sequelae of a syphilitic gumma that had ulcerated and become infected.[54]

To begin with, the lesion's date of onset is as unclear as most of the other physical stigmata with which popular history has castigated hapless Hal. According to one source, as early as 1515 (at age twenty-five) Henry had developed a "leg ulcer," presumably of traumatic origin; another set the date at 1528—noting in passing that the ulcer eventually affected both legs.[55] That both extremities were involved is supported by primary sources such as the deposition of the Duke of Norfolk and any number of ambassadors' recollections.[56] To account for this, the prudent diagnostician might be inclined to invoke a generalized condition, the most common of which, given Henry's increasing corpulence, would be varicose veins.[57] If compresses could not heal the bulging and unsightly veins in Henry's thighs, it would be natural for his surgeon, Sir Thomas Vicary, to incise them and, in so doing, perhaps induce a superimposed abscess in the process. Each time the draining ulcer sealed, Henry would be wracked with fever.[58]

To be as precise as possible, descriptions of Henry's leg malady closely parallel our present-day understanding of something called a "post-thrombotic syndrome" that occasionally occurs in varicosities of long standing. This is a perversely chronic affliction that defies even the best treatment available today. Acute blockage in one vein may lead to dilatation of interconnected tributaries in the leg, predisposing in time to chronic occlusion of the entire system. Blood is forced into less resilient pathways in the venous system, increasing pressure against thin-walled channels whose eventual rupture leads to subcutaneous hemorrhage, scarring, and ulceration. The condition then becomes a self-perpetuating process.[59]

Not only is the thigh an unusual location for a syphilitic gumma (and most authorities are of the opinion that his ulcers emerged there, as they were visible to neither contemporaries nor portraitists),[60] but Henry had both the physical attributes and lifestyle that would have predisposed him to such a common disorder as varicose veins. To a king who demanded prompt resolution of problems—whether in marriages that soured, wombs that did not work, or popes that defied him—the skills of an aggressive surgeon would seem tailor made—even if, by applying them, Vicary may have induced recurrent infections that would plague Henry to the end.

One of the most feared complications of sluggish blood flow in the legs is a potentially fatal condition known as pulmonary embolism. Evidence suggests Henry suffered precisely that on one occasion when he lay at death's door for several days, "black in the face without speaking." [61] Though this has been considered by some a manifestation of epilepsy or neurosis,[62] ascribing it to a blood clot that had traveled from chronically thrombosed veins to his lungs is far more believable. Even if one were to postulate a petit-mal variant of epilepsy, a blackened face has less to do with that condition than with a lack of oxygen as a result of blood clots lodged in the lungs.

Even less tenable is the supposition that Henry's leg affliction was due to a build-up of uric acid crystals in the subcutaneous tissue, which occurs in individuals afflicted with long-standing gout. This pervasive malady has allegedly afflicted, at one time or another, virtually every gluttonous monarch of biohistorical interest. Even Henry's father was said to have suffered from it, though that surmise is far from convincing. All that is known is that Henry VII was a victim of an ill-defined arthritic condition (among other maladies), hardly a firm basis upon which to build an open-and-shut case for gout. What Henry's father died of was "a disease that wasted his lungs." Not that there is any known association between excessive uric acid in the bloodstream and lung disease; nor is there any direct relationship to the high blood pressure and depression that one researcher mistakenly ascribed to gout in Henry VIII.[63]

Inference must also serve those scholars who have asserted that "indirectly, through its derangement of his renal functions, gout was responsible for Henry's headaches and, eventually, his death" as a result of uremia.[64] In point of fact, there is no evidence that he ever had kidney failure; it was merely supposed by some observers (more likely, suggested by one and repeated as fact by a few that followed) that he died in a uremic coma. Individuals suffering from uremia typically manifest stupor, either intermittently or continuously, for long periods of time before dropping into coma. Nothing of Henry's demise suggests that this occurred. Nor does corpulence (to cite another bit of specious circumstantial evidence) equate with having gout. Henry's sedentary lifestyle and depression alone were enough to account for this, the most obvious of the physical changes that befell him.

To bury the argument completely, consider a few well-known facts about gout. There is both a high incidence of kidney stones in its victims and painful swelling of the big toe, the latter so common as to be almost synonymous with the disease—yet Henry never contracted either condition. Moreover, only a small percentage of individuals with high uric acid levels ultimately develop gout.[65] The limitations of subjective opinion are nowhere more apparent than in one investigator's attempt to prop up what was already a wobbly case by dragging out yet another musty portrait—this one of Henry's father, allegedly depicting "physical suffering long endured" from the pain of gouty arthritis.[66] Perhaps we should take the portrait at face value for what it really depicts: a prude with sour features.

This "art" of viewing portraits with the intent of making retrospective diagnoses catapulted the gumma thesis back into the limelight long after it had already been dismissed. A Danish physician suggested that the vaguest hint of a "lesion" on the right side of the nose in some portraits and sketches of Henry done after 1536 was yet another gumma of the type that allegedly afflicted the king's legs. The qualifier "some" is of more significance to the critics of such a supposition than it apparently was to its lone supporter, who took the liberty of dismissing three other portraits of the same period, which failed to show any lesion on Henry's nose, on the grounds that the king's vanity compelled him to order the portraitists "to leave the deformity out."[67] This is culling the evidence that supports one's claim from any contradictory data that do not. What the retrospective investigator chooses to see in portraits—as in autopsy reports and obstetrical histories—is largely what so speculative a diagnostician wishes to emphasize.

If a selection of aged portraits has failed to convince the skeptic of the merits of the syphilis thesis, and an examination of Henry's physical infirmities and the obstetrical histories of his wives only further refutes the assumptions undergirding it, can the spirochete's trail still be uncovered in poor Henry's cerebral cortex? Should objective data fail such diehard proponents, vituperation must suffice: having been accused of our own improvisations when "the obvious medical truth [of syphilis] is staring us in the face," what could we "mindless fools . . . who love to hug [our] little delusions" have missed? With all due respect, certainly nothing as foolish as linking Henry's "terrible mental and moral degeneration" to the scourge of venereal disease.[68] Reducing Henry VIII's phobias and obsessions to symptoms that are uniquely linked to syphilis simply doesn't wash. Yet galloping naked to the field of scholarly combat, the syphilologist proclaims that Bluff Hal's central nervous system was running amok with burrowing spirochetes. For their part, most laypersons would equate the term "syphilis" with the cerebral form of the disease; hence the "terrible degeneration" responsible for the excesses of Henry's reign.

If syphilis alone cannot account for all the symptoms described, there is always the shotgun approach: "Valvular diease, atheroma, and arteriosclerosis were causing 'dropsy' of [Henry's] legs. . . . Due to his rising blood pressure, he began to suffer from very severe headaches . . . [while] his corpulence was aggravated by the development of cirrhosis [of the liver]."[69] There you have four distinctly different diseases postulated a priori—without a shred of evidence presented to support any one of them—to cover all the physical ailments the spirochete has missed.

The most explosive indictment of all, however, Henry's "syphilitic" behavior, assumes a change of character so dramatic that only an underlying disease affecting the brain could account for the delusions of grandeur, megalomania, paranoia, and cruelty that emerged.[70] More prescient biographers have concluded instead that his behavior (with some minor augmentation of earlier character traits) was consistent from beginning to end—his moral persuasions and *modi operandi* hardly out of step with other monarchs of his time. In one historian's summary: "The pattern of his life did not change; it simply sharpened."[71] Admittedly, this entailed a ripening of his fears and suspicions (many of which were well founded), his lust for power, and an increasing compulsion to control. Yet in thought and deed, Bluff Hal remained as much a realist in adulthood and old age as he had been as an adolescent seeking to carve out a niche for himself in the Tudor hierarchy.[72]

Despite a plethora of physical changes quite compatible with aging, Henry remained in remarkable control of the diverse social, political, and diplomatic forces bearing down upon him. In the face of rival factions vying for power within his own kingdom (not to mention the machinations of the Holy Roman Emperor, the Pope, and the King of France), he managed to balance the scales weighing against him by the sheer force of his personality.[73] Beyond a doubt, Henry endured the last eighteen months of his life gravely ill, wracked by recurring fevers from his ulcerated leg. Even then he "thrust and parried like a master," never losing his grip; in the assessment of those around him, he now appeared more confident and more formidable than he had ever been.[74]

Again, this is hardly the portrait of a neurosyphilitic madman. Henry's remarkable last speech to Parliament but one year before his death was considered a masterful, if histrionic, stroke of royal prerogative. And the detail of his will, intent as it was in assuring the Tudor lineage, reflected the same capacity to weigh the consequences of his actions: he committed neither to the Catholic nor to the Protestant splinter groups in the end, entrusting some powers to both within his own council during his son's regency.[75] For those who would decry Henry's executions and terrorist methods, it bears remembering that such treacherous acts were superseded in their zeal not only by the French and Spanish Inquisitions but by his father as well, who executed large numbers of opponents through acts of attainder and forfeiture.[76] Henry's reign, compared with those of sixteenth-century rulers (Ivan the Terrible and Henry's own daughter among them), seems almost benign. He never killed anyone with his own hand, or used poison, or burned victims at the stake.[77]

What the king required was not so much blind obedience from his subjects as an absolute freedom from restraint for himself, whether in the realm of religion, war, or wives.[78] In matters of religion, Henry fervently believed that spiritual deviation might open the door to social revolution. His wars, on the other hand, resulted from a combination of factors, not the least of which were pretensions born of his youth to secure French conquests for himself, added to in time by more pragmatic concerns for securing Tudor legitimacy (if not hegemony) in European affairs.[79] As for Henry's vindictiveness, that resulted in part from being paradoxically ruled by the wombs and whims of Catherine of Aragon and Anne Boleyn. Nor should we forget that the king treated his last four wives (Catherine Howard excepted, who arguably deserved her fate) far better than he did his first two. Such behavior is hardly consistent with neurosyphilis, which by its very nature is a progressive disorder.

For that matter, Henry actually learned from experience, a quality that a diseased brain would have precluded. He had learned a bitter lesson in public relations with Anne Boleyn's execution. Thereafter he assiduously prepared public opinion before acting and skillfully drew Parliament into assuming responsibility for some distasteful actions— the execution of Catherine Howard among them. As one biographer concluded: "He had reflected and mastered his lesson."[80] And in personal relations, one would expect a syphilis sufferer's latter years to be marked by more treachery than existed earlier. Certainly Sir Thomas More, Cardinal Wolsey, and Ann Boleyn—all either executed or dismissed relatively early in Henry's reign—would have had difficulty in seeing that claim. So have countless scholars who have examined his conduct with more than a stethoscope or tongue blade applied retrospectively to the primary sources.

Though Henry's reign had profound historical significance, it was hardly of the sort that the medical reductionist would have us believe. For one thing, the absence of a male heir was said to have signified the "beginning of the end of the Tudor dynasty."[81] Surely feminist readers today would be offended to have fifty years of Queen Elizabeth's beneficent reign overlooked—though the preceding bloody interlude of her half-sister is an era they would like to forget. Even if the brief reigns of Bloody Mary and the immature Edward VI bespoke a rapacity that prevented a Catholic restoration, the syphilophiles have ignored a sizeable anticlerical sector of English society that would have made such a reconciliation difficult at best.[82] With or without their allegedly disease-influenced leadership, a period of strife and turmoil was already in the cards. Though Henry's break with the Roman Catholic Church eventually led to civil war, there was little the spirochete did to make way for the ensuing "attempted absolutism of the weaker Stuarts."[83]

Where else do the allegations of Henry VIII's central-nervous-system involvement with syphilis not fit the mold? If some physicians have unwittingly ignored much of the social and political data while rewriting history, a few have unaccountably taken liberties with the medical facts as well. For some things about neurosyphilis ("paresis of the insane") have been agreed to by all, both at the turn of the century when the syphilologists were constructing their arguments and in the context of our present understanding of this disease. Perhaps the most esteemed medical authority during the period syphilis was intensively studied was Sir William Osler. His textbook *Modern Medicine* highlights the most common symptoms and physical findings found in neurosyphilis.

In its earliest stages, the victim of cerebral syphilis experiences disturbances in speech and becomes indifferent to his surroundings. Henry had no such symptoms, at least none recorded by his doctors or the ambassadors who monitored his behavior with a critical eye. Thereafter a marked change in temperament and behavior occurs, arguably of the sort that might account for the king's "fits of rage," so frequently alluded to. In conjunction with this, however, memory becomes progressively defective, a trait hardly in keeping with Henry's ability to stay abreast of the myriad of diplomatic, theological, and state concerns that consumed his working day.

As the disease progresses, delusions of grandeur emerge, and some reductionists would argue that just such disease-induced obsessions characterized Henry's dealings with the church and his claims to primacy in state affairs as well. Yet here Osler adds an important caveat: these delusions are "wholly unsystematized extravagant utterances that do *not* constitute the basis for purposeful actions," such as might occur in the paranoid state alone.[84] By all accounts, Henry's "delusions" most assuredly led to decisive actions that were as consistent as they were distorted to some degree by paranoia. Yet they had a purpose: the need to assure the Tudor line and to control the apparatus of state and church affairs to promote stability.

As untreated syphilis evolves, speech becomes more affected still, acquiring a tremendous quality. Words are difficult to find, and articulation becomes indistinct. Osler himself underscored that point: "The suspicion of general paresis rests *more often* upon this one symptom than any other" (emphasis added); indeed, the "paretic speech" of the tertiary syphilitic can hardly be mistaken for any other speech disturbance.[85] Again, there is no documentation that Henry had difficulty in speaking.

In the disease's late stages a tremor of the facial muscles and hands develops, and writing is difficult. The victim becomes progressively demented, unaware of his or her surroundings and incapable of meaningful personal interaction.[86] None of these descriptions fit Henry VIII. Nowhere is there mention of a tremor of any sort, nor have cursory analyses of his handwriting uncovered consistent deterioration in his script. And certainly overt dementia did not ensue even during the last sad year of his life.

True, most authorities agree that the disease either in Osler's time or in its rare occurrence today seems to run a much slower course than it did in the sixteenth century, when victims succumbed to the scourge within two to three years. But if Henry's death at the age of fifty-three seems a relatively youthful demise, recall that even the fifth decade in Tudor times was considered old age. He outlived both his father and elder sister, neither of whom was ever accused of having the Great Pox.

Despite the effectiveness of penicillin in reducing the incidence of neurosyphilis, there is little reason to suspect that its neurological manifestations have significantly changed with the passage of years. Textbooks published seventy years after Osler presented his findings and still in use today list garbled speech, facial and extremity tremors, and impaired handwriting as the most common features[87] of tertiary syphilis. Yet in the one hundred years since the disease was first ascribed to Henry VIII, no authority has been able to document any of these findings to substantiate that case. Some have skirted the edge of incredulity instead by asserting that such nondescript behaviorial changes as violence, cowardice, and obscenity are "diagnostic" of syphilis.[88]

To muddy the waters further, a leading advocate of the syphilis thesis is willing to admit that Henry may not have had full-blown neurosyphilis.[89] But syphilis does not stop at the edge of the brain and still give rise to fits of rage, personal indiscretions, and self-glorification without infesting the cerebral cortex. Either one has neurosyphilis or one does not. There is no halfway house of diagnosis to protect the medical reductionist from his own inferences. Such arguments only drown in their self-contradictions.

Neurosyphilis can, of course, affect the spinal cord, with or without concomitant brain involvement. This is a condition known as "tabes dorsalis," which some have imputed to Henry in an attempt to explain his difficulty in walking during his last year.[90] Yet they fail to mention two other characteristic symptoms recognized to be almost diagnostic of tabes dorsalis. First, well over 90 percent of its victims have sharp, "electric" pains shooting into the legs, appropriately termed "lancinating pains." No description of Henry's "sore legs" is consistent with these. Second, many sufferers experience "gastric crises" of neurologic origin that mimic acute abdominal catastrophes. None appear in the king's medical history. In concert with both types of pain, tabes dorsalis patients also experience hyperesthesia, contact with clothes, for example, is exceedingly painful. Again, no mention is made of this on Henry's behalf.

Bladder disturbances also occur with tabes, principally in the form of incontinence. It is instructive to see how often a failing bladder is equated in the mind of the less than circumspect investigator (not to mention an unwary lay public) with impotence—which, as noted above is another unsubstantiated charge laid on Henry's later years. More incriminating yet less defensible still is the allegation that syphilitics are impotent. One imprudent writer called attention to what he admitted to be an "inference" by asserting that Henry's "impotence" represented the most damning evidence available substantiating the syphilis thesis.[91] In reality, only a small percentage of syphilitics suffer from impotence.[92] Nor are there any hard data to substantiate that Henry was indeed impotent; rather, inference is again substituted for evidence.

How, then, did this whole fabrication of Henry's syphilis gain such widespread acceptance? To begin with, neurosyphilis was one of the first mental disorders for which a definite cause could be established. That led to its getting more than a fair share of ex post facto credit in history. Popular literature and the cinema have embellished the image of Henry as a mad and gluttonous despot, as excessive in his rule as he was in the royal bedchamber. The discovery of syphilis as a cause for insanity, coupled with its mode of transmission, made the spirochete at least an intriguing and explicable culprit to explain away Henry's behavior. If the study of syphilis was in the mainstream of medicine during the first quarter of the twentieth century, as seems to have been the case, perhaps the pathographers of that period took Osler's warning too much to heart: "Know syphilis in all its manifestations and relations, and all other things clinical shall be added unto you."[93] Precisely at the time the study of pathography was coming into vogue, the pervasive spirochete ruled the roost of diagnostic alternatives.

As animals evolve over time, however, so do diseases—and biohistorical appraisals of them. In making a retrospective diagnosis, analysts must be aware first of the disease as it presented itself at the time it afflicted the subject; second, of the disease as described by their predecessors; and third, of the disease as it is currently understood. Witness what used to be known and feared as the Great Pox versus the mild skin manifestations of the second stage of the disease today. Our knowledge of any given disease is in a continual state of flux. Failing to recognize how strongly the times influence one's perceptions locks an already much maligned discipline into simplistic diagnoses peculiarly attractive only for that period. Hence they run the risk of becoming as dated as their methodology is flawed. Perhaps the eminent physician John Hunter said it best: "Never ask me what I have said or written, but ask me what my present opinions are and I will tell you."[94] Few have been so honest as this prudent skeptic, who appreciated that medical knowledge changes with time, compelling us to accept changes in our thinking.

Nor should we forget that the perspectives we bring to a given historical case, based on our experiences as clinicians, color our outlook—if they do not blind us entirely to other alternatives. To take but one example which I can legitimately address: as a neurosurgeon, I found myself reading the data in such a fashion as to incriminate Henry's head injuries as a suitable explanation for his behavior.[95] While discounting a previous scholar's view that a rather trivial blow to the faceguard of Henry's helmet in 1524 had much to do with his headaches or later behavior,[96] I would submit that the more serious injury in 1536 was of singular importance.[97] This had not been simply a concussion; by definition, a two-hour loss of consciousness signifies, at the very least, a contusion of the brain with possible permanent injury resulting from bruising of the cerebral cortex.

Nor does the evidence exclude the possibility that a small blood clot on the surface of the brain might have resulted. That it was not a large hematoma in any case is suggested by the absence of paralysis or sensory loss thereafter—unless the bleeding occurred in the frontal lobes, in which case only behavioral disturbances, changes in affect, or a deficient memory might have evolved. Either way, these blood clots break down and occasionally form membranes over the brain, which are prone to recurrent hemorrhages in the future with trivial blows to the head.[98]

If untreated, such hemorrhagic fluid collections begin to cause physical signs of brain compression. One of the most frequently observed results of this evolving process is an unsteady gait[99]—precisely the most noticeable symptom from which Henry suffered during the last two years of his life. The fact that he could not move his legs at all during the week prior to his death only adds further fuel to the suspicion that his head injury in 1536 was perhaps more significant than most investigators have acknowledged.

Lest we place all our alternative diagnostic eggs in one basket for future pathographers to shatter, still other neurosurgeons might be inclined to ascribe the ultimate impact of his head injuries and falls to a traumatic myelopathy in the cervical spine. Myelopathy implies injury to or chronic compression of the spinal cord in the neck, with resultant spasticity and difficulty in walking. Hyperextension of the spine, such as occurs with blows to the face or forehead, is a common mechanism of injury. Viewed from this perspective, either of Henry's head injuries may have accounted for his subsequent gait disturbance.

But cervical spine injuries do not cause behavioral changes or coma. Therefore, a panel of neurosurgeons might well favor an intracranial cause for the multiplicity of symptoms from which Henry VIII suffered—perhaps his coma and death as well, should the postulated fluid collections have re-bled one final time. Yet even this is not as straightforward as it may seem. It is offered only to make a point: as convincing as such an explanation is to a neurologist or neurosurgeon weighing the evidence today, the prudent skeptic would point out that because chronic subdural hematomas and spinal cord myelopathy are frequently seen by these specialists in their medical practices, there is an inherent prejudice in the way they would interpret the evidence—just as an expert in venereal disease or an obstetrician might be inclined to support a diagnosis of syphilis, or a rheumatologist to suggest gout or amyloidosis as the underlying disease process that best explains virtually all of Henry's medical history.

So what is the answer to this most perplexing enigma? Quite simply stated with respect to the impact of disease, I believe there is *no* answer that the extant data can support with full conviction. Perhaps one of the king's biographers had the last word: "Enough sins have been laid at Henry's doorstep without adding a social disease to the list."[100] To paraphrase what was abundantly clear to at least this one observer: the results of a man's life are easy enough to chronicle, but his innermost thoughts and motivations may defy our best analytical efforts. Leonardo da Vinci discovered the same in his art: "A good painter has two objects, to paint man and to unveil the intention of his soul; the former is easy, the latter hard."[101] In like manner, it is easy enough to recognize disease and old age, but measuring their impact on the minds and motivations of people in general, and rulers in particular, is more difficult. Unless the data with which one molds his opinions are unassailable, the difficult becomes indefensible in the court of scholarly review.

From a neurosurgeon's perspective, the cerebral contusion–chronic subdural hypothesis has a natural—however biased—ring of truth. But like all other retrospective diagnosis, it remains a hypothesis at best. Such one-dimensional thinking is precisely what has obscured the merits of some otherwise telling criticisms of the syphilis thesis—the best examples of which are Ellery's Rh incompatibility theory, Barrett's amyloid hypothesis, and Shrewsbury's arguments for gout.

Perhaps—as is occasionally the case among our own patients—we should be prudent enough to recognize that suggesting any one disease to explain what ailed poor Henry will continue to frustrate our best efforts. Have we lingered too long over sparse medical data that defy retrospective analysis? Ponder an opened bottle of wine for too long, and it turns sour; subject Henry VIII to too much medical scrutiny, and the essence of the man evaporates. Perhaps Mark Twain, no sufferer of either fools or pretentious scholars, understood poor Henry and his ilk best of all. As his Huckleberry Finn declares: "All I say is, kings is kings, and you got to make allowances. Take them all around, they're a mighty ornery lot. It's the way they're raised."

CHAPTER 3

Fanatics and Saints: The Case for Epilepsy

If personality can be defined as "an enduring style of relating to one's environment" as the mind perceives it,[1] then it follows that physiologic changes within the brain may profoundly affect how a person behaves. Perhaps the most enigmatic of all personalities to have had an impact on history are those mystical leaders who embraced the burning issues of the day with an eye toward molding them in their image, if not to their own benefit. Whether divinely inspired or physiologically unbalanced, such persons have run the gamut from altruistic self-sacrifice to heinous crimes carried out in God's name.

As one measure of how broadly this spectrum of "inspired" leadership extends, the lives of Adolf Hitler, Joan of Arc, John Brown, and even the Apostle Paul have seductive parallels that have been ignored. All were alleged to have spoken and acted at the behest of mysterious forces outside themselves. All left a prodigious legacy of written and oral testimony to justify their actions. And all, most assuredly, continue to perplex the historian no less than the psychoanalyst who dissects their characters with Freudian scalpels. Yet those who treat organic diseases of the brain for a living might wonder whether these four movers and shakers among mystics of the past can be reduced to a single, shared disease that explains their behavior in pathophysiologic terms.

In an earlier publication I built a much too detailed case for Adolf Hitler's having been a victim of temporal lobe epilepsy (TLE).[2] At the time I offered that diagnosis as hypothetical at best. Still, the facts in the matter were suggestive enough to warrant ongoing study. Rehashing the available data from the perspective of devil's advocate some years later has failed to dispel that lingering suspicion altogether, yet it remains nothing more than that. Of one thing, however, I am certain: any deleterious impact such a condition may have had on the Fuehrer's behavior during the last four years of his life pales in comparison with the effects of an astounding combination of drugs and central-nervous-system stimulants prescribed by his unprincipled physician. More germane to this study, I soon discovered other subjects to consider with respect to the impact of seizure disorders on history.

While reviewing the medical literature on temporal lobe epilepsy, I was first struck by the relatively high incidence of that condition in the general population. Fully three persons per thousand suffer from seizures arising from the temporal lobe,[3] a figure not far below that of insulin-dependent diabetes and of inguinal hernias, to mention but two of the more familiar conditions that afflict humankind. Acknowledging that some seizure-riddled personalities manage to become charismatic enough in their own right to attract attention, I turned to the historical literature in search of other possible victims. To my surprise, I found the genre of popular history replete with largely speculative accounts of all manner of seizure disorders among the greats and not so greats of the past.[4] Just when I thought I had stumbled upon a diagnostic coup or two, I was made to feel like the interloper in Robert Louis Stevenson's *Treasure Island*, who threw open the shutters of an empty room and shouted in exasperation: "Pew, they've been before us!" My disappointment was tempered by the discovery that virtually every founder of the world's great religions, from Buddha to Mohammed, was also said to have been afflicted by the scourge. If Confucius's neurologist has yet to be heard from, that seems to be the exception and not the rule. Countless saints and prophets alike have also been linked to temporal lobe epilepsy.[5]

To have uncovered such a potpourri of alleged epileptics bearing witness to faiths that mankind has lived and died for raises some disturbing questions. Wouldn't the law of averages alone speak against there being so many prophets victimized by a single disease? That said, could there still exist an underlying thread of illness linking at least a few of what past generations reared on the Good Book assumed to be divinely inspired actions? As for those agnostics among the psychoanalysts who claim to know better, have they too missed a seizure suspect or two along the way?

What of the darker side of messianic leadership, whether divinely or demonically driven? God knows, what with television evangelists running amok nowadays, there is no lack of suitable candidates. If some would have us believe they are picking up where their predecessors left off by feigning apocalyptic visions of Jesus and prophecies of their own death, the one thing they seem to be picking for sure is our collective pocket. And if speaking in tongues (even forked ones on occasion) seems faintly reminiscent of temporal lobe seizure activity, we would be giving some of the world's truly great actors far too much succor by attributing their behavior to diseased brains. It may well be more appropriate to remove such Guardians of the Faith from the medical examining table and consign them to the Temple with those money changers to whom we sell not only our souls, but occasionally our senses.

As prevalent as TLE is alleged to be, my search for its victims in history took me back some 130 years before I stumbled upon a case so suggestive of that malady that its story simply begged to be told. Enter John Brown of Harpers Ferry fame, self-presumably descending to the stage from God's right hand. Brown's lengthy diaries and texts, laced as they are with religious and moral themes, epitomize one singular preoccupation of the long-standing TLE victim known as "hypergraphia." Those documents alone offer the pathographer a wealth of primary source material from which to reconstruct a prototype of this seizure-induced personality disorder.

That leads one to wonder where still another enigmatic warrior such as Joan of Arc might fit in this bevy of divinely inspiring (or sporadically misfiring) brains. On the strength of her apocalyptic visions she managed to rally the French populace behind the pathetic figure of one Charles VII, whose royal legitimacy was dictated by those same visions as interpreted by a French teenager. Though Joan's execution at the youthful age of eighteen perhaps precluded the development of the entire spectrum of personality change one associates with TLE, any neurologist familiar with her story, replete with celestial voices from above commanding her to secular combat below, might rush to slap brain-wave electrodes on her head in search of a seizure focus. As with John Brown, readers will have to decide for themselves.

On the other hand, a few intrepid authorities seem to have decided for us already when it comes to categorizing the conversion and subsequent behavior of Saul of Tarsus. Some have seen in his vision of Christ on the road to Damascus and resultant conversion little more than a seizure disorder, complete with hallucinations and a religiosity that simply reeks of the theological preoccupations of the TLE victim. And like both Hitler and Brown, Paul's writings arguably reflect the hypergraphia of a psychomotor-seizure-induced personality. Most physicians who have examined this case study remain as captivated by the TLE thesis as theologians are perplexed and horrified by it. Who, then, possesses a monopoly on truth?

If some readers have difficulty believing that Adolf Hitler's diabolical nature can be explained, in part, by misfiring neurons in the temporal lobe, surely it would test their credence to suggest that at least three other figures of the past may have been afflicted in kind. To be sure, that consideration will remain the strongest argument *against* what follows. Yet to dismiss out of hand a recognizable personality disorder stemming from a specific anatomic structure in the brain is no longer a tenable position. Confusion in the past arose when earlier

researchers mistakenly applied an all-encompassing "epileptic personality" to seizures of whatever origin.[6] Recent investigators have confined such a profile to those suffering from TLE, and even the data
generated by their critics support the notion that some identifiable
personality characteristics do in fact exist.[7]

No one disputes that type-specific personality changes arising from
epilepsy are uncommon. This may explain why the diagnosis is missed
in a few of our patients today, as it may have been overlooked in a
handful of tyrants and saints of the past. Before truly bizarre behavior
becomes so obvious that it can no longer be ignored, even a zealot may
be taken at face value. In too readily identifying the mystic with a
religion or sacred cause, perhaps we have overlooked the disease for the
sake of the divine.

To understand the argument, one needs to know something about
the salient features of the personality profile that develop in approx-
imately one-fourth of those suffering from the "complex partial" or
"psychomotor" seizures of TLE. This personality disorder must not be
confused with the seizures themselves; rather, it emerges years after
they begin and occurs between them in the form of enduring behavioral
traits. The intensity of these changes appears to parallel the duration of
the underlying epileptic condition rather than the frequency of seizures
per se. Of paramount importance, it is the occurrence of several recognizable but seemingly unrelated traits *in combination* that raises the
wary clinician's suspicions, whether in the clinic or on the pages of
history.[8]

What, then, are these collective features that separate seizure-
induced behavior from the merely peculiar or eccentric? To begin with,
there is an intense preoccupation with religious, cosmic, or even de-
monic themes. The victim may undergo multiple religious conversions,
often precipitated by hallucinations during a typical seizure episode.
Second, the sufferer feels compelled to write copious volumes pertaining to these themes in general and as they might apply to the writer in
particular. Such texts are filled with underlined words, sentences in
capital letters, and repetitious phrases. These autobiographical accounts characteristically unmask a third attribute of the TLE personality, referred to as "hypermorality," which is reflected in their speech
as well as their writing. Victims embrace a rigid sense of right and
wrong, brood incessantly over issues that seem less pressing to others,
and fail to see humor in anything. Long-winded monologues imbue
them with what the clinician has picturesquely termed "viscosity" in
relations: they miss obvious social cues to terminate a conversation.
Finally, what few friends they manage to keep describe them as being
indifferent to sex. They may experience a gender crisis or deny normal

sexual drives altogether—although in a few instances TLE sufferers paradoxically evince hypersexuality, fetishism, or transvestism. Either way, the sex lives of these seizure victims are far from normal.[9]

A less frequent but very characteristic phenomenon that occurs in TLE subjects of long standing is something called an "organic delusional syndrome": the victim is so overwhelmed by delusions that he or she assumes a new identity.[10] More often, only a dramatic change in life view occurs. Given the proclivity for hypermoralism and religiosity, a conversion experience may result. Interestingly enough, organic delusional syndromes associated with religiosity and hypermoralism are said to occur more frequently in those with a left-sided seizure focus, whereas emotional lability and overt aggression are more common in those with right-sided lesions of the brain.

The association of left-sided seizures with mood disorders and right-sided with mood disturbances is consistent with split brain function as neuropsychologists understand the concept. Though this distinction is not as clear-cut as it is sometimes made to seem, the left (or dominant) side of the brain generally processes intellectual information, whereas the right side tends to control emotional response to the environment. That may also explain why those with a right-sided seizure focus tend to minimize or deny the negative attributes of their behavior, whereas victims of more "ideative" left-sided seizures express an intense reaction to their shortcomings, as would be expected in ruminative individuals who intellectualize everything to the extreme.[11]

To be sure, the most ostensibly normal individual may manifest any one of these qualities. What sets the TLE sufferer apart is their occurrence *in concert*.[12] To ignore that fact is to neglect any consideration of what clinicians would term the "differential diagnosis" in a given case: that plausible range of alternatives which may explain unusual behavior in either a patient or a historical figure.

Reduced to its lowest common denominator of anatomy and physiology, temporal lobe disorder involves both an underlying substrate and an identifiable mechanism that triggers the evolution of such a personality. The mechanism involves an inability to assign appropriate emotional significance to external stimuli; its anatomic substrate resides in an area of the brain known as the "limbic system," comprising delicate, multiconnected pathways linking the temporal and frontal lobes with deeper structures that propagate emotional impulses in the human brain. In a word, this system is "overcharged" in the TLE sufferer. Whereas destruction of any one of these pathways results in precisely the opposite behavior (that is, the patient becomes placid, tame, and indifferent), temporal lobe epilepsy brings about a functional "hyperconnection" that suffuses experience with charged emotion.[13]

What one sees in the TLE personality, then, is an exaggerated response to previously neutral stimuli or events. Taken to the extreme, that only enhances the self-righteousness and even paranoia that victims experience should no one take them seriously. They refuse to allow themselves (or others) to become passive pawns in the hands of more powerful forces. Whereas the pathologic religious zealot may use this as a divinely inspired calling card to sway an apathetic flock, afflicted political mavericks may feel so fervently about rules and laws, right and wrong, that they take the law into their own hands.[14]

It is an axiom of clinical and laboratory experience that permanent changes in the brain's physiologic function may occur as a result of repeated stimulation. What we are less certain of is the degree to which such changes depend on, or are determined by, external events. Yet to those who have studied this distinctive subset of fascinating patients it does seem that episodic changes in limbic activity of the brain temporally related to coincidental happenings in the environment can lead to altered modes of "processing" the significance of external events: hence the telltale alteration of personality in times of crisis, both perceived and real.[15] A precise medical understanding of these personality changes can not only lend plausibility to the four cases under consideration, but even, on the basis of available sources, substantiate beyond a reasonable degree of medical doubt which side of the brain was affected.

This assumes, however, that yet another diagnostic criterion, apart from the personality itself, has been fulfilled: the occurrence of distinct episodes retrospectively identifiable as seizure activity. And here the screws of certainty loosen considerably, as temporal lobe seizures by their very nature are notoriously difficult for even the most astute clinician to detect. More perplexing still, a few authorities contend that overt seizures do not have to occur at all, that underlying pathology in the temporal lobe—perversely silent—may effect enough physiologic change to induce the personality disorder described.[16] This conclusion may not be as unfounded as its critics claim, because the change in personality appears to be more dependent on the *duration* of the disease than on the epileptic manifestations themselves.

To diagnose a seizure, the investigator first applies certain general criteria to individuals not previously known to have experienced overt epilepsy. These may be summarized as (1) an abrupt onset of psychosis in a previously healthy individual; (2) a sudden occurrence of an unaccountable delirium; (3) episodes characterized by unusual behavior; or (4) a history of unexplained "falling out" spells. Yet identifying any of these in our historical patients is far from conclusive; to confirm a

diagnosis of TLE, evidence of much more specific behavioral disturbances is required.

Transient periods of unawareness known as "absence attacks" are
among the most frequent manifestations of temporal lobe epilepsy.
Though the victim may appear to be interacting with the environment,
he or she has no recall of the period in question. Unawareness is suggested by certain activities such as smacking of lips, repeating stock
phrases, or other symptoms that the unwary observer ascribes to nervous tension or habit spasms.[17] The sufferer of such a spell then picks up
where he or she left off as if nothing had happened, without appreciating
the consequences of what has occurred.

One of the most intriguing examples of psychomotor seizure activity is that elicited by a specific sensory stimulus. Flashing lights,
certain strains of music, or even such mundane activities as reading or
walking can precipitate an attack of TLE. These fall in the category of
"reflex epilepsies."[18] Sleep deprivation, fatigue, or anxiety states may
also precipitate psychomotor seizures. They may begin and end with an
absence attack or, as a prodrome to a more elaborate psychomotor
seizure, go on to full-blown epilepsy.

To make the diagnosis more difficult still, the pattern of behavior
associated with a psychomotor disturbance may differ from seizure to
seizure in the same patient. Even so, an unexplained feeling of fear
accompanies well over half of all TLE episodes, whether they take the
form of absence attacks or more elaborate stereotyped motor activity.[19]
The victim perseverates on fears unexperienced by anyone else and
becomes enslaved to their dictates, for these ideas force themselves into
the patient's mind to the exclusion of all others.[20]

Overt delusions and hallucinations are other forms of temporal lobe
epilepsy which can be more readily recognized. These may manifest
themselves as imaginery voices, horrifying nightmares, or flights into
fantasy. The patient's ability to regain composure after the seizure has
passed separates such sporadic delusions and hallucinations from those
of the schizophrenic.[21] Either way, the fear, anxiety, and even dream
states that usually accompany such disorders of perception are more
characteristic of TLE than of other delusional syndromes.

That both the personality disorder and the seizure manifestations
are characteristic enough of TLE for the wary clinician to send today's
patient packing to the electroencephalograph (EEG) lab for confirmatory testing is of little solace to the biographer left to wrestle with
bizarre and unexplained behavior. Armed only with records of descriptions given by associates and subordinates or family and friends of the
subject, where does one draw the line between the merely peculiar or

egocentric and the pathophysiologic? Some "authoritative" accounts to the contrary, not every mystic, martyr, or man of war can be reduced to a clinical case study, whether in the neurologist's imagination or the psychoanalyst's dreams. To confine our efforts to either branch of analysis is not only to risk falling prey to reductionism but to run counter to the laws of nature that make for the great diversity of personalities characterizing the human condition. As one wag so aptly described us all: "There is much of human nature in mankind."[22]

As a corollary, there is also much of human nature in the scholar longing to make a reputation. Perhaps the most ingenuous method used by the pathographer is to describe an obscure disease process, selectively apply available data to it, and then sanctify the diagnosis with medical jargon and case studies from literature quite foreign to the average reader. To underscore the point, few diseases have been invoked so often as epilepsy to disarm the pathographer's archrival, the psychohistorian. As convincing as the epilepsy thesis may be made to seem, it behooves the investigator first to rule out more common causes of abnormal behavior.

No individual has been skewered on the horns of this pathographic-psychoanalytic dilemma with more relish than Adolf Hitler. To be sure, some contributions to the debate have proved less than edifying. For one, it is simply no longer adequate to ascribe his behavior to an Oedipus complex or an undescended testicle. To do so is to fly in the face of so much incriminating data concerning his poor health that one of the few remaining questions to be answered is how Hitler managed to carry on under such duress for so long—and to carry Nazi Germany with him. In my own recent account, I not only proposed that the Fuehrer suffered from gallbladder disease and Parkinson's syndrome but also suggested that his personality disorder might have been explained on the basis of temporal lobe epilepsy, accentuated by at least seven central-nervous-system stimulants he took to excess during the last four years of World War II.[23]

Yet the question remains: just how convincing is the epilepsy thesis, particularly when other scholars have heretofore failed to support it? Moreover, the amphetamines Hitler abused can elicit some of the same behavior often associated with temporal lobe epilepsy. Taken to excess, they not only unleash the aggression, volatility, irrational fear, and paranoia typical of TLE paroxysms but may transform the indivdual's personality into a striking likeness of one afflicted with this seizure disorder.[24]

Though imaginary fears and bizarre behavior are part and parcel of TLE, the neurologist must also distinguish between what might be seizure-induced and something known as "parasomnia" (of which sleepwalking is the most obvious manifestation). This is of particular relevance to Hitler, who was frequently victimized during later stages of the war by terrifying hallucinations that woke him from sleep. Parasomnia is a far more common disorder than TLE, is frequently associated with "night terrors," and is *not* a seizure as such. Nor are night terrors the same as nightmares; they last much longer, and the sufferer cannot be convinced that the terrifying images are imaginary. The parasomniac may also exhibit violent, purposeless behavior and have no recollection of it. Yet insofar as parasomnia is not seizure activity, it carries no implications for personality development.

Critics of the TLE hypothesis would further point out that the amphetamines and cocaine Hitler took to excess can interrupt the sleep cycle, thereby predisposing the abuser to this rather common disorder— not to mention the deleterious effects of sleep deprivation alone. We would do well to remember, after all, that the overwhelming majority of the behavioral disturbances in question occurred *after* Hitler became an unwitting victim of Dr. Theo Morell's potpourri of some seventy-odd medications. By that late date, perhaps there were simply too many ingredients in the differential diagnostic pot to extract a single diagnosis accounting for the Fuehrer's increasingly bizarre behavior.

Moreover, the psychohistorians at least deserve credit for underscoring other factors that may have made him behave as he did. No one who has read Robert G.L. Waite's incisive psychoanalytical treatment, *The Psychopathic God*, has put down the book without having gained some insight into those inner demons that drove Adolf Hitler.[25] Nor would skeptics of the TLE hypothesis accept out of hand that those various and sundry irrational outbursts attributed to misfiring neurons in the brain necessarily signified seizure activity per se. Take such a man, who is suspicious to begin with, place him in an isolated setting where his world is both literally and figuratively tumbling down over his ears, add a host of central-nervous-system stimulants that enhance his suspicions, and he may well become overtly paranoid—enough to provoke unbridled anger at best and totally irrational acts at worst.

While few individuals appear at first glance to fit the cardinal features of a seizure-induced personality more than this fanatical Jew-baiter and mastermind of the Master Race, undeniable caveats remain. On balance, a few reviewers of the epilepsy thesis as it was applied to Adolf Hitler found the idea intriguing; fewer still, I suspect, were convinced.

The same probably applies to the conversion experience of the apostle Paul. Though French scholars of the mid-nineteenth century were among the earliest writers to profile the religiosity of the epileptic, it was not until 1873 that a physician first ascribed a specific conversion to the effects of a seizure.[26] This academic revelation of sorts opened a Pandora's box from which a number of suspect mystics emerged, culminating in the 1960s when several landmark studies on temporal lobe epilepsy appeared in the medical literature. Not only were mystical delusions quite common among the patients described, but those that embraced them were convinced of their validity as bona fide religious experiences. One clinical investigator drew attention to states of ecstasy in which the victims saw the heavens open, heard God speaking, and felt themselves transfigured.[27] Another described TLE patients who had visions of Christ "coming down from the sky" as part of their hallucinations.[28] Still others treated individuals who had a series of visions, during which they were made to feel that their lives were being judged.[29]

It was only a matter of time until someone emboldened by these clinical observations examined the most famous convert of all from the perspective of TLE. Saul of Tarsus was a man who, until the time of his fateful encounter on the road to Damascus, had made it his vocation to persecute Christians. Yet his life's view was completely changed by what happened on that day, when, by his own account, a vision of Christ cast him to the ground and rendered him blind and out of sorts for fully three days. As a result of that experience Saul of Tarsus, orthodox Jew, became the Apostle Paul, convert to and major spokesman for Christianity. Yet he lived his remaining years in fear and dread of a mysterious "thorn in the flesh" that some believe was a seizure disorder, the price paid for his conversion.[30]

Few words have caught the pathographer's eye more than Paul's own description of that seminal event: "I know a man . . . who fourteen years ago was caught up to the third heaven. In the body or out of the body? That I do not know . . . [yet] this man was caught up to paradise and heard sacred secrets which no human lips can repeat."[31] By portraying himself as being in a state of unreality in relation to his body, Paul was describing a dreamlike state that arguably predisposed him to auditory and visual hallucinations. Suffice it to say, it was a depersonalizing experience of the sort that one often associates with TLE, for by now he was referring to himself in the third person.

Had Paul been made to feel (as other psychomotor seizure victims are wont to recount) that at this moment in his life he was being judged? Undoubtedly. Did his subsequent impairment reflect the experience of another TLE victim who believed that he was in heaven, became depersonalized, and "took three days for his body to be reunited with his soul?"[32] Was not Paul's experience much like that of yet another seizure sufferer who believed that "God had sent the seizure as a means of converting him?"[33] Was epilepsy the "thorn in the flesh" to which Paul alluded? In short, did his experience mirror that of countless other victims of temporal lobe epilepsy? These are all hypothetical considerations, of course, but they seem so compelling when considered together that some would have us believe Paul to be the standard by which all other seizure suspects in history can be judged.

Yet I am not quite so certain. Suggesting that Paul's visions were nothing more than hallucinations is one thing; tracing his activities thereafter is quite another—and far removed from what usually follows figments of the imagination or sporadic discharges from the temporal lobe. In view of the total record, it is really defensible to ascribe to epilepsy not only his conversion but that of the five hundred or more who also claimed to have seen Christ after his resurrection?[34] If so, what should we make of countless prophets of the Old Testament, not to mention John, whose visions are spelled out in explicit detail in the Book of Revelation? To extend the argument to so many would imply that TLE had reached epidemic proportions and affected all sufferers in much the same way.

Can we even be sure that the "thorn" to which Paul referred was really epilepsy? At least one piece of evidence implicates instead the failing vision that plagued him throughout his life. As Paul himself exclaimed: "But even though my physical condition was a great trial to you . . . I myself can say that you would have taken out your own eyes, if you could, and given them to me."[35] Some would conclude from this that Paul's eyesight, not his brain, was the "thorn that wracked him."[36]

One final note of caution: since much of the New Testament consists of Paul's writings, it would be troubling indeed if subsequent Christian scholars have been misled by the delusions of a hypergraphic TLE victim. Perhaps we should give Paul the benefit of the doubt instead, which he himself referred to: "Even if I am unskilled in speaking, I am not in knowledge."[37] What Paul was implying is that he knew that he had trouble reaching his audience with the spoken word. From that perspective, his copious letter writing may not have been the product of epilepsy after all but simply a reflection of his awareness of what he did best. This is all to say that we must not allow our scientific training and biases as retrospective clinicians to cloud our thinking. As intriguing as the evidence for TLE is from my perspective as a neurosurgeon, it is difficult for me as a Christian to believe that so many theologians who have studied Paul could be wrong. Yet nothing clouds rational thinking as much as deeply held convictions born of faith. The question remains whether in regard to Paul we have allowed that to happen.

Few cases on record mimic Paul's conversion experience, complete with visual and auditory hallucinations, more explicitly than that of the Maid of Orléans, Joan of Arc. For her exploits in delivering an oppressed people and their depressed king from the yoke of England, as God had directed her to do, Joan ultimately joined the ranks of a long line of persecuted saints. Make no mistake about it: such folk are different from you and me. If the Catholic Church has underscored that distinction by immortalizing them, a few skeptical medical observers have pointed instead to a litany of seizures that may have made them so. To date, Joan has not been included beyond a reasonable degree of medical certainty on this list. That would only add to the embarrassment of a church loath to surrender the supposition that its pope, who is elected by a college of mortals, has a direct pipeline to Peter. Presumably fishermen plumbing for saints, like physicians diagnosing disease, are circumspect enough to obtain second opinions. One can only hope that somewhere along that pipeline, if not behind the Pearly Gates themselves, there is an EEG lab spitting out brain-wave tests on saints-to-be.

After all, the list of seizure-suffering saints is legion. As an adolescent, St. Teresa of Avila (1515-82) experienced a series of apparitions of such intensity that she likened the chronic noises in her head to "a number of waterfalls" interrupted on occasion by "voices of birds singing and whistling."[38] She also suffered from chronic headaches, but not before having been given up for dead at the tender age of twenty-four. For four days she was wracked by one seizure after another that left her with a bitten tongue, dislocated joints, and bruises and abrasions all over her body. After she emerged from her coma, Teresa's visions became laden with religious overtones—enough to lead her to sainthood rather than to the sanatorium where she arguably belonged.

Three centuries later a saint of the same name but different locale, Lisieux, fell victim to a series of mystical states strongly suggestive of TLE. As a young girl she was seized by "strange and violent tremblings all over her body," later to be transformed into terrifying hallucinations that merged on occasion with celestial visions. Like Joan of Arc some four hundred years before, this Teresa too had undergone a quasi-religious experience in adolescence that brought about a "complete conversion."[39]

Still other saints are alleged to have suffered from abnormal mental states. Some bordered on hysteria; more than a few were attributed to psychomotor seizures. Included in the epilepsy category were St. Catherine of Genoa (1447-1510), St. Marguerite Maria (1647-90), and the Florentine saint, Catherine dei Ricci (1552-90).[40] To be sure, the last had a series of visions peculiarly governed by the clock, enough to suggest that such bizarre behavior was not seizure-induced; for irritable neurons would be unlikely to misfire precisely at noon on Thursday and revert to normal at 4:00 P.M. the next day, as invariably occurred in Catherine's case.[41]

Lest one detect an unseemly Catholic addiction to epilepsy, let me add that both Buddha and Mohammed were said to be afflicted by the same disease. There is also the case of the Mormon founder, Joseph Smith, to consider. In the spring of 1820, Smith experienced such an overpowering apparition that it left him speechless. After encountering two celestial beings whose brightness and glory "defied all description" as they spoke to him, Smith found himself "delivered." He also found himself lying on his back "looking up to heaven,"[42] as would be the position of one who had just experienced a grand mal seizure.

Those who would dismiss the epilepsy link out of hand have left at least one troubling question unanswered. How could God, or Allah, or whatever deity one acknowledges as *the* Creator, select out so many leaders of different faiths to be the Chosen Few? As for Joan of Arc, why should God have seen fit to choose a province or two of oppressed French peasantry and a pathetic imitation of a king over the fortunes of England—or of Burgundians? Could it be that these suddenly enlightened subjects were duped by a seizure victim?

The details of Joan's short-lived existence are a matter of record. At about the age of thirteen this ostensibly normal, albeit pious, farmer's daughter experienced a celestial vision that altered the course of French history. Amid a flash of light, Joan was visited by angels whose intent was unclear to the frightened girl. When the visions recurred with increasing frequency, she came to believe that two apparitions in particular, St. Michael and St. Catherine, were commanding her to take up the banner of an Armagnac regent (soon to become Charles VII) in order to deliver her people from the yoke of English and Burgundian tyranny. Somehow, Joan managed to convince Charles that together they could rid France of its predators. Their fortunes soared with one victory after another. Yet she ultimately fell into the hands of the enemy and was tried in an ecclesiastical court as a heretic. Joan was found guilty, temporarily recanted, and then reverted to her visionary claims. That assured her death at the stake. Some twenty years later her reputation in the Church was rescued, leading to her canonization in 1920.

Joan's conversion experiences and subsequent behavior bear a striking resemblance to those of persons victimized by a seizure-induced personality disorder. Her own description of what occurred in the garden one day, detailed in testimony during her later trial, recapitulates the essential features of a temporal lobe seizure: "I heard the voice on my right hand, towards the church," she recalled. "There was a great light all about." Two angels then appeared, reminding her of the "pitiful state of the kingdom of France" and beseeching her to "depart and go to France . . . to succor the king." For days thereafter she heard the voice precisely at the time the church bell chimed, and the message was always the same. Yet Joan was perplexed by what she had heard: "I answered . . . that I was but a poor girl who knew nothing of riding and warfare." Nevertheless, she eventually steeled her resolve and vowed to keep her virginity "for as long as it should please God," until the issue was resolved in His and her compatriots' favor.[43]

Joan was visited by her celestial guardians for three years before she eventually left home against her parents' wishes and made a pilgrimage to Chalon to convince Charles of her legitimacy. In the meantime, her visions had become as elaborate as her revelations proved prophetic. Not only were her guardian angels adorned with rich crowns; they were often accompanied by hundreds of knights bearing torches. Her revelations from heaven included a number of events that came to pass: the English siege of Orléans would be lifted; the citizens of Rheims would come out unsolicited to meet Charles and anoint him on the spot; and before many years were out the English would be defeated and driven from France. All this Joan learned firsthand from those she called her three counselors: "There is one who remains with me always, another . . . visits me often, and the third is He from whom the other two take command."[44]

Strange indeed that God would see fit to take sides in a squabble over a few French provinces. Stranger still that her celestial visitors spoke fluent French and would require her to wear men's clothing. If Joan, in her perpetually rapturous state, failed to see something odd in all of this, her trial inquisitors begged to differ. So have future historians and psychoanalysts who have wrestled with Joan's personality, but still failed to solve the enigma of the French Maid. As one investigator has said: "In all other respects she was quite healthy. . . . Further than this, history cannot go, and the choice between insanity and inspiration must be made by another science."[45]

Welcome, then, to the science of neurology—and to questions begging for answers. Are insanity and inspiration the poles between which lies the entire list of differential diagnoses? Was there something overlooked in Joan's youth, not to mention her underlying health? In a word, was temporal lobe epilepsy the missing link tying her to other saints and mystics who may have suffered from the same disease? No doubt the environment in general and certain happenings in childhood in particular profoundly influence the evolution of one's personality, seizure victim or not. From that perspective, the Maid's early years may offer more clues to this enigma than preceding investigators have realized.

Consider what was happening in the village of Domrémy, where Joan grew up, just prior to her conversion. At a time when marauding bands of Englishmen and Burgundians were ravaging the countryside, the townspeople remained loyal to their Armagnac leader, Charles. When Joan was thirteen, Domrémy was overrun.[46] It was shortly thereafter that she began to hear voices in the garden beseeching her to go to the aid of her people and their beleaguered leader.

Each of these factors undoubtedly influenced Joan's subsequent mind-set. Like many TLE victims who undergo a religious conversion in such charged circumstances, what arguably began with hallucinations was transformed in her mind into a covenant with God. As she wrestled with unconscious conflicts that were superimposed on her religious background and the mayhem of her environment, Joan's visions provided a suitable impetus for her conversion. The question that remains is whether the visions were seizure-induced.

If one of the hallmarks of TLE is unexplained fear, it should not pass unnoticed that Joan had been "much frightened" when she first heard the voices in the garden. Yet what she already knew added a peculiar twist to her fears. For one thing, Charles had taken St. Michael as his patron saint only six years before and had recently erected a statue of St. Catherine in the town square. For another, Joan was aware of the popularly held prophecy that France was to be "ruined by a woman and restored by a virgin."[47] Hence, perhaps, the identity of the angels and the perceived need to remain chaste until her work was done. She even insisted on wearing men's clothing, a practice that paradoxically pushed her closer to the martyrdom she may have sought all along.

Any impact that TLE may have had on Joan's suppressed sexuality could have related to its age of onset. Experts in the field have discerned that "if seizures begin before puberty, normal sexual interests may fail to develop."[48] That the seizure victim evinces little interest in sex is of no particular concern to the afflicted; if anything, that seems entirely in keeping with his or her new life's view. Joan of Arc was no exception. Such thinking extended to her insistence upon disengaging herself from the hedonistic lifestyle of the rabble.[49] She forbade profanity in her presence, detested camp followers, and sought to isolate herself from any situation smacking of sexual connotations. That went a long way toward convincing Joan's contemporaries that she was somehow different. As one authority on TLE makes clear: "These victims seem different because they feel different; [accordingly] they tend to withdraw from ordinary social interactions."[50] From a sexual perspective at least, Joan's vibrations were ambivalent at best; no man who rode with her ever admitted to any carnal feelings toward the Maid, believing as they did that "she was from God."[51]

Comparable behavior can be found in many TLE suspects today who have yet to reach puberty before their first seizure occurs. Joan's perceived mission and virginity pledge mirror the account of one of the first described seizure victims on record: "After a seizure, the youth declared he had been given a mission by God to reform the world!" He had heard the voices of God and the Virgin Mary, who commanded him "not to eat until the project was finished." Still another patient, who had experienced her first seizure at the age of ten, became so devoutly religious four years later that a conversion experience occurred, sealed with the same vow of chastity that the French Maid had embraced.[52]

That Joan felt compelled to act in the face of her parents' disapproval was evidenced by her later testimony: "Since God had commanded me to go, I must do it. . . . Had I had a hundred fathers . . . and mothers, I would have gone."[53] What Joan was alluding to, as many later TLE victims have done, were unbridled obsessions that drove her, even against her will. One such patient experienced "a sudden dream-like feeling, saw a flash of light, and proclaimed 'I have seen the light.' He suddenly knew that God was behind this, and that he could have power from God if he only asked for it." Another had always perceived herself as a religious person, but her feelings intensified during periods of inner conflict. Despite the assurances of voices telling her that the strong and upright like herself had "the hand of God," she later attempted suicide—just as Joan did in a fit of despair when she leaped seventy feet from a tower in which she was incarcerated. A third patient described having "heard a voice, soft and tender." Later the same day a church bell chimed in her right ear and a vision appeared of a woman wearing a black dress, extending an arm with lights. At such times the Almighty would then speak to her.[54]

There is much, then, to suggest that Joan of Arc's celestial visions and voices, as well as her subsequent behavior, may have had their roots in temporal lobe epilepsy. Yet a few loopholes remain. Where, one wonders, are the cardinal manifestations of hypergraphia in Joan's record? Without that, her behavior falls short of the typical profile of the seizure-induced personality. Yet there is a simple explanation: Joan was illiterate.[55] Nevertheless, she did from time to time dictate the equivalent of letters, pronouncements that bore the indelible stamp of self-righteousness and hypermoralism so typical of the TLE victim's writings. For example, her communiqué to the English before the siege of Orléans commanded them to lay down their weapons lest the scourge of God visit itself upon them. Even the banner she carried into battle betrayed her holier-than-thou attitudes; she bore it with the same self-righteousness as did a later seizure victim who walked the street carrying a sign with the inscription "Be prepared to meet thy God."[56] For all intents and purposes, Joan was warning the English to do the same. Moreover, her trial testimony betrays an excessive compulsion with choosing her words and weighing her arguments carefully. True, Joan was very much aware that the prosecution was trying to coax her into contradicting herself, and that she assiduously avoided. Yet her measured responses may have also been a reflection of the hypergraphic TLE personality, for these individuals are obsessed with the clarity of their thinking in a subconscious effort to control their emotions.[57]

In an indirect sense, Joan's warrior mentality mirrored the aggression that later investigators have identified as yet another cardinal feature of the TLE personality. Time and again her dogged persistence in countermanding orders by her more experienced subordinates turned the tide of battle when all was believed lost. On one occasion her commanders wanted to skirmish before reaching Paris. Joan ignored them and crossed the moats to engage the more heavily fortified enemy there. In like manner, she had ordered her soldiers and the townspeople to rush out and assault the bastille at Orléans. That eventual success was literally in the wind was intimated by a sudden shift in its direction which allowed the boats to cross the river. To Joan's ways of thinking, that was a sure sign of divine intervention.[58]

These events bring to mind the strongest argument *against* Joan's meteoric rise having been the result of temporal lobe seizures: how does one explain the military successes of a farmer's daughter described as having formidable aptitudes as a horsewoman and military tactician without prior training in either? For all the stigmata suggestive of a psychomotor seizure victim, the retrospective diagnostician must acknowledge the possibility of supernatural forces at work, particularly when it comes to chronicling results rather than merely describing behavior.

This scarcely negates the hypothesis that Joan of Arc might still have been a seizure sufferer. One of the attributes of such victims is their ability to interact effectively with others, despite their disability.[59] Viewed from that perspective, and acknowledging that her people had every reason to support any self-proclaimed savior who might reverse their shared misfortune, Joan's pivotal role in what transpired deserves a second look from neurologist and historian alike—if only to suggest that future scholars should give some consideration to a diseased brain that may have driven her.

If being driven by a sense of hypermoralism, self-righteousness, and religiosity characterized Joan of Arc's behavior, those same qualities apply to few persons more than to John Brown before, during, and after the Harpers Ferry debacle. Whereas the life of the French Maid was so short as perhaps to preclude the full development of every aspect of the TLE personality, Brown epitomized those characteristics to a degree that would be anticipated in a man who lived six decades. For all his eccentric mannerisms, history records that something transformed Brown during the last years of his life. As fate would have it, that happened to be a time of gathering storm clouds before the thunderclap of civil war divided the country.

Though obviously concerned with the slavery issue throughout his life, it was not until the 1850s that Brown became totally consumed by it.[60] At virtually the same time, this now very militant abolitionist became inordinately self-righteous, embellishing his behavior with such evangelical fervor that his associates found him insufferable.[61] Perhaps an undue sensitivity, pathophysiologically induced, accounted in part for Brown's conversion once a truly worthy cause became ripe for the picking. Not only do the last years of his life recapitulate many attributes of TLE to the letter, but both psychological and and physical evidence coincides with what the pathographer might expect to find.

Recall that victims of a left-sided seizure focus can be distinguished by their ideative, contemplative, or religious conceptualizations, while those with a right-sided focus demonstrate more emotive and impulsive actions.[62] Whereas Adolf Hitler's behavior was suggestive of the latter, given his proclivity to act through instinct and emotion, Brown typified the obverse by being profoundly introspective and contemplative. Selected photographers taken as early as 1856 suggest why this might have been so. A noticeable flattening of the right side of Brown's face in conjunction with a sagging lower eyelid raises at least the suspicion of a subtle paralysis—perhaps on the basis of a structural lesion in the left side of his brain.[63] Though the long beard and mustache he grew after that date were put to good use by disguising the features of the fugitive from justice that Brown had become, they may have inadvertently disguised something more deeply seated in a literal sense: a tumor of the left temporal lobe. Despite the limitations of relying on musty reproductions (acknowledged in the preceding chapter), the implications are at least intriguing: was there more than messianism brewing in the brain of one of history's more infamous zealots?

That unproved surmise notwithstanding, one critical link is missing to tie this wizened warrior to the scourge of epilepsy. In contrast to both Paul the Apostle and Joan of Arc (and arguably Adolf Hitler), there is little in the record to suggest that John Brown suffered from recognizable seizures. But such an omission is not as damaging as it may seem, since we now know that the subsequent behavior of these victims correlates more with the duration of the epilepsy than with the number of seizures per se. Indeed, overt seizures (at least those apparent enough to be recognized) do not have to occur at all. The behavioral syndrome may develop instead as a result of subtle damage to the temporal lobe in the absence of obvious epilepsy.[64]

Yet perhaps we are getting ahead of the story. To understand John Brown requires knowing something of his early years and influences long before the changes that became obvious after 1848. Much of his childhood was spent in the Western Reserve of Ohio, a hotbed of abolitionism to which his father had become an early convert through his work with the underground railroad.[65] It would also be safe to say that the son's views on the subject were colored at an early age by religion.[66] Such influences exacerbated his imperious nature. Above all, John Brown longed to lead. Even as a young man he took himself and his causes very seriously. Witness his audacity in interrupting a sermon on one occasion to debate certain scriptural points with a startled minister and his perplexed parishioners.[67] That said, Brown's subsequent record in one failed business after another reveals a tragic flaw in his character. As one contemporary later recalled: "He failed not for lack of ingenuity and perseverance, but because his basic judgment was wrong."[68]

Although Brown's education was paltry, he was an avid enough reader to immerse himself in the works of other fanatics and revolutionaries such as Toussaint l'Ouverture and Oliver Cromwell—the latter of whom, prophetically enough, believed himself to be an instrument of God. Eventually, such weighty influences would sink home; Brown's "god-idea" begat in him a feeling that he was "the Moses that was to lead the Exodus of the colored people."[69] All the same, such plans would have to wait for a man still struggling to make his way in an increasingly wayward world. George Delamater, who perhaps knew Brown as well as anyone during the early years, described his high-strung neighbor as one whose mind "was rather intent upon his business pursuits, the education and improvement of his family and . . . other projects of public interest or utility."[70] Only after he had failed repeatedly at the first did the last consume him—and with such intensity that it terrorized his contemporaries as much as it has perplexed historians.

For all his highbrow pretensions, John Brown was a self-righteous boor. Yet "however unlovely his personal characteristics," one editor noted, "he was lifted above the herd because he was inspired."[71] If so, then by what? How could one observer revere Brown as "an exalted hero" while another saw nothing more in him than a "horse thief and a murderer?"[72] Did this "volcano beneath a covering of snow,"[73] simmering with frustrated intentions superimposed on fundamentalist pretensions, require merely a spark from misfiring temporal lobe neurons to activate it?

Or was Brown simply insane, as attested by nineteen separate affidavits provided by family members during his trial? After all, a long line of insanity was said to have run on his mother's side and believed to have been inherited by a few of Brown's sons.[74] To argue the case on these terms, however, misses the point on at least two counts: first, insanity is not necessarily hereditary; and second, the affidavits supplied by family members to validate his insanity have proved to be transparent in the extreme. His second wife, who probably knew him best, vehemently denied the charge.[75] Nor did Brown's closest associates testify to his madness, including those members of the highly educated Secret Six in Boston, who underwrote the entire Harpers Ferry scheme. One of the six, himself a doctor who treated the mentally disturbed, categorically denied that Brown was insane.[76]

Certainly the Old Man was no psychotic like Nat Turner, who had unleashed his own slave insurrection some thirty years before at the behest of celestial visions and voices. In that sense, the eminent historian Samuel E. Morison's assessment of John Brown rings true: "He was a madman with a method."[77] If the method was so firmly rooted in Brown's mind that he overcame formidable obstacles to bring it to fruition, Morison has less to say about the behavior of madmen, who are erratic in connecting means and ends. And on that count Brown was obviously guilty. Yet that in itself does not make him insane. Zealots and fanatics may behave the same way. So do some temporal lobe seizure victims.

Sensing failure as a provider for his family, Brown's "cast of mind began to alter" during the late 1840s.[78] Until his exploits in "Bleeding Kansas," however, it might be argued that Brown's actions "flowed from normal human drives." True, he had an insatiable appetite for command. Truer still, his involvement in the antislavery cause reflected in part an "overcompensation for all his failures."[79] But there was something more: a true metamorphosis of personality from mere advocate to ardent fanatic. A little reflection from the neurophysiologic perspective might shed some light on why this was so.

As early as 1848, antislavery themes began to dominate what now seemed Brown's compulsion to write. From letters devoted to family matters or a plethora of personal travails, there emerged a distinct turn toward hypergraphia, sermons composed with heavily underlined script based upon a single theme. As such, "Sambo's Mistakes," a series written for the Negro paper *The Ram's Horn*, marked a watershed. Written as if Brown were a black man reciting his own errors,[80] the work heralded his preoccupation with the antislavery issue. Further intimations of things to come appeared in a letter to Joshua R. Giddings, in which Brown began to display imbalance and strange ideas about abolitionism.[81] Even so, these essays did not yet reflect the patent religiosity and aggression that would come to typify his later efforts.

In his letter to the League of Gileadites, an organization for the protection of fugitive slaves in Massachusetts, Brown took on the air of a self-appointed counselor, embellishing the title *WORDS OF ADVICE* in capital letters with the byline "as written and recommended by John Brown." The letter is filled with prophetic warnings (for example, "All traitors must die") and heavily underlined words: *"Do not delay one moment after you are ready."* While religious overtones lent some respectability to the message, Brown's aggressiveness only hardened the tone of his rhetoric: *"Let the first blow be the signal for all to engage,"* he wrote. "Make clean work of your enemies. . . . *Stand by one another . . .* while a drop of blood remains; and be hanged if you must."[82]

Still other letters reflect the cosmic bias of the psychomotor seizure personality. To cite an early example written in 1852: "My attachments to this world have been very strong, [but] Divine Providence has been cutting me loose one Cord after another. . . . All ties must soon be *severed."* By 1853 he was rebuking his son in a sermonlike epistle, again filled with underlining, capital letters, and bits of scripture. About the same time he drafted an essay, titled "Law and Order," to the black leader Frederick Douglass.[83] Here was but one of many hints that, as TLE victims are prone to do, John Brown was prepared to take the law into his own hands in order to right the wrongs that others passively accepted.

It was not until the mid-1850s in Kansas that Brown irrevocably committed himself to militant abolitionism, come what may. By his own hand, he dragged out five proslavery advocates in the middle of the night at Pottawatomie Creek and massacred them. As was now typical of virtually everything he did, Brown justified the heinous crime as part of a religious crusade. "May God still gird our loins and hold our right hands," he wrote, "and to him may we give the glory." Presumably the unbalanced warrior wished to include among his gifts the heads of murdered victims served up to the Lord on a bloody platter. Yet as one measure of the derangement of his mind at the time, Brown denied that he had ever taken part in any slaughter—all other witnesses' accounts to the contrary.[84]

From the neurophysiologic perspective, two possible explanations for Brown's denial emerge. The first, and one emphasized by all investigators to be distinctly rare, is episodic aggression that occurs *during* a psychomotor seizure. Consumed by impulses beyond his control, the TLE sufferer may commit a violent act[85] (much like those later attributed to the infamous Boston Strangler) as part of a seizure and not remember what he has done. Yet it would be stretching the argument to suggest that Brown was in the throes of epilepsy at Pottawatomie, for he had planned all along to perpetrate just such a crime.

The second possibility involves what the neuropsychologist terms a "dissociative state." In its extreme form, the victim becomes a bona fide split personality; failing that, he blames his behavior on benevolent or malevolent powers[86]—just as Brown attributed his actions to God's will. Recalling for the moment that no issue is minor for TLE sufferers, slavery could scarcely be seen from either Brown's background or his now distorted perspective as anything but "the greatest sin against God."[87] Yet there are problems with attributing what happened at Pottawatomie to the dictates of a dissociated personality. In the absence of ongoing seizures, it is distinctly rare for perpetrators of such to claim amnesia for what they do; indeed, they usually recall these actions with considerable regret—particularly when the underlying pathology involves the left temporal lobe, which has already been attributed to Brown.

This is simply to say that not every activity of even the most pathologic individuals can be explained in physiologic terms. Even so, virtually the whole of John Brown's subsequent behavior appears to fit the mold of a TLE personality. One aspect of his meteoric rise and fall that has perplexed historians to the present day is how this failed sheepskinner and erstwhile businessman turned renegade managed to gain the support of a few highly educated members of Boston society, who underwrote not only his activities in Kansas but the sad debacle at Harpers Ferry. Yet once one learns that the temporal lobe epileptic may prove to be an engaging conversationalist, Brown's hold on the Secret Six may be more readily understood. As one measure of the "viscosity" that characterizes the TLE victim, he startles the unwary object of his conversation with instant intimacy and extraordinary candor.[88] Moreover, he takes both himself and his world quite seriously—and what could be more appealing to this band of abolitionists than just such a man with a plan, one willing to assume the martyr's role? The partnership proved mutually beneficial: Brown needed a cause as much as abolitionism needed a martyr.

True, the winsome warrior gave the Secret Six a misleading account of his future plans. They were made to believe that he would embark on a limited military engagement in an unspecified setting.[89] That too might come as no surprise to the neuropsychologist because many long-standing TLE sufferers have difficulty giving straight answers to direct questions. Yet Brown's circuitous recitations seem to have held him in good stead when it came to soliciting support from ardent conspirators who failed to do their own homework.

The tragedy, of course, was the extension of Brown's powers of persuasion to the naive young men who were to accompany him to Kansas and Harpers Ferry. He corrupted these youths by turning them from nonentities into Real Men like himself once they embraced the antislavery issue. He granted them high offices in a phantom government and handed out commissions in a nonexistent army in exchange for the blind obedience that cost many of them their lives. And that is why Edwin Coppoc's later deposition at Brown's trial weighed so heavily on the outcome. "You don't know John Brown," he told the jury. "When he wants a man to do a thing, the man does it."[90]

Brown's predilection for cosmic and social issues only intensified during those frenetic months before Harpers Ferry, paralleled by his equally frenetic turn from mere advocate to messiah. As he later proclaimed: "You know that Christ once armed Peter. So also in my case I think he put a sword into my hands."[91] Here was a telling reflection of the epileptic's intensely emotional response to his environment. Brown's Bible-thumping fanaticism had become his raison d'être. He was as consumed by what God had in store for him as he was by efforts to define the cosmos in his own terms. While bivouacking on a cold, snowy night with his clan on the way to Virginia, he conducted what his son Owen described as a "hot discussion upon the Bible and war, . . . commerce and manufacture, also upon the . . . civilized world." A few of Brown's contemporaries excused his fanaticism as a reflection of the times. Many more dismissed it as the ravings of a madman.[92]

Either way, by 1858 the Old Man was clearly more irascible and nervous than he had ever been before. He remained completely absorbed in an idea that most believed transcended "ordinary thought and reason," scarcely acknowledging his critics as he spoke.[93] That was but one measure of what the psychiatrist would term a "viscous affect," for Brown remained as insensitive to social cues as he was to unwelcome advice. Perhaps that is why the hypergraphic syndrome served him so well, allowing him to lecture through the written word to silent and unseen audiences that might otherwise have turned him a deaf ear.

Brown's letters also depict the depersonalization that evolves over time in some TLE sufferers, referring to himself as he sometimes did in the third person. He even considered writing a book about his life, only to abandon it as his mercurial mind set roamed the gamut of delusional thought. As he wrote at about the same time in typically abstruse prose: "I believe, when you come to look at the *ample field* I labored in and the rich harvest . . . the Whole World . . . *may reap* from its cultivation; you will feel that you are out of your element unless you are in it."[94]

As the pace of his writing picked up, Brown's "element" became captive to the limitations of his hypergraphic pen. Incapable of erudite prose, TLE victims rely instead on heavily stylized script laden with underlining and capital letters. In just eight lines of a letter to the Reverend Thomas Wentworth Higginson, Brown italicized nine words. A letter to his daughter about the importance of her husband to his scheme declared: "I have a PARTICULAR and VERY IMPORTANT (but not dangerous) place for HIM to *fill*. . . . I know of NO MAN living so well adapted to fill it." A seven-line letter to his wife in the same year bore the indelible stamp of hypergraphia with its twenty-four under-lined words.[95]

On the eve of Harpers Ferry, John Brown was treading a fine line between the militant abolitionist he had become and the pathological personality that had already defined him for upward of ten years. Preparing himself on the morning of the conflict that would catapult him into infamy, Brown rose and "prayed as in a trance, eyes closed, his hands swaying, [enforcing] conformity to his ideas of what must or must not be done." He was acting now as but "an instrument of God," ready to die "for God's eternal truth on the scaffold" if that were required.[96]

For all his fanaticism and self-righteousness, Brown's judgment remained as impaired as it had ever been. In choosing Harpers Ferry, he turned the original plan as understood by the Secret Six on its head. Here was no mountain redoubt but a pit. The raid itself was not to be an avoidance of bloody confrontation, as Brown had intimated, but just the opposite. And if twenty-one diehards seemed a pathetically small number to rescue thousands of oppressed slaves, Brown had already convinced himself that they would be deluged with black reinforcements the moment hostilities began—though in fact, not one slave voluntarily joined the insurrection. Misreading his history and his religion as much as he had misinterpreted the advice of those foolish enough to counsel him, Brown mistakenly assured his flock that Nat Turner had "held Virginia captive for five weeks"; now he assured them in kind that "God [has] appointed us as the men to do his bidding."[97]

In the absence of divine intervention, the enterprise was doomed from the beginning. Trapped in the armory's wagonhouse with shells splintering through wooden peepholes that his terrified man ducked under rather than fired through, Brown became confused and indecisive. Failing to negotiate an escape in exchange for an end to hostilities, he rashly surrendered his pretensions and his arms, but not before ten of his men had died—among them, his son Oliver, whom he admonished in the strictest terms: "Be quiet, son. If you must die, die like a man."[98] Captured and hastily tried in the county court of Charles Town, the forsaken prophet was hanged six weeks later. Even in defeat he had refused to accept that God had never been at Harpers Ferry at all—much less, perhaps, aligned against him. He expressed no remorse during his incarceration and refused to implicate anyone else. "No man sent me here," he testified. "It was my own prompting and that of my Maker." Asked whether he believed himself to be an instrument in the hand of God, he responded simply: "I do." [99]

No doubt Brown's Calvinist ideas about predestination and salvation had always been an overriding influence in his life. Yet today's neuropsychologist might identify his religiosity as one element of a seizure-riddled mind. Surely something more than religious upbringing compelled this zealot to quest for martyrdom with such little regard for human life. If, as he fervently believed, "God had often covered [his] head in battle" so that he would be left to do good works, Brown evinced little concern that those he loved were not protected in like manner. His response in either case was fatalistic. As for Oliver: "I guess he's dead." As for himself, on his way to the scaffold: "Now, when He intends to use me in a different way, shall I not most cheerfully go?" [100]

Like other fanatics, John Brown carried his pretensions with him to the grave. On the morning of his execution he handed a note to a guard that, perhaps more than any other single sentence, epitomizes the self-righteousness and aggression of the TLE personality: "I John Brown am now quite *certain* that the crimes of this *guilty land* will never be purged away; but with Blood." [101] John Brown lived and died a fanatic, and the impact of fanatics on history has been immense, as every historian knows. To cite but one: "Without such men there would be no organized religion and few, if any, 'causes.'" [102] Without temporal lobe epilepsy, perhaps those numbers might be fewer still.

So what is one to conclude from all of this? First, the vantage point from which we have examined this handful of zealots suffers from a very narrow perspective; and second, the intent was not so much to fill in the blanks of perhaps unanswerable questions as it was to raise them with an eye toward enlarging our retrospective focus beyond the psychoanalytic. That said, most readers will still want answers. Within the limits inherent in studies of this sort, here are mine. Whether Adolf Hitler really suffered from an overactive temporal lobe probably deserves less notice than the drugs he took, which changed the course of German history after 1941. Likewise, the data supporting the TLE thesis for Paul and Joan seem less than conclusive, particularly when it comes to weighing concrete results. For all my scientific and medical training, I concede that there may indeed be an element of the supernatural here. Only with John Brown do the data appear to fit to the exclusion of virtually every other consideration. This may seem paradoxical, as

Brown was the only one of the four in which overt seizure activity lacks documentation. That in itself speaks to the need to have raised the issue of TLE in the first place. After all, this diagnosis is probably missed more often than any other in the psychiatrist's clinic. The question remains whether it has been overlooked elsewhere.

PART II

Brain Failure at the Top: Psychology or Pathology?

Second opinions are as valuable in rehashing history as in diagnosing disease. Accepted schools of historical thought are forever being challenged by what that profession has termed "revisionist views," often influenced as much by the scholars' own biases and the times in which they write as by new data. Digging up a treasure trove of documents may occur but once in a lifetime for the historian; as for the pathographer, a public figure's medical record may remain buried under mounds of doctor-patient confidentiality. Still, as every good researcher knows, the same data may, in receptive soil, sprout different conclusions. Yet far from stumbling upon undiscovered diamonds in the rough, many revisionist gumshoes have soiled the soles of their reputations with discarded excrement long after foraging familiar fields has lost its appeal for the rest of the herd. Some are left to wallow in obscure journals; others are butchered on the spot or put out to pasture without a publication.

No doubt knowledgeable physicians offering their own second opinions on the musings of the preceding chapter would hesitate to push its thesis too far. Relatively few men and women suffer from seizures; fewer still, the personality disorder that accompanies them. On the other hand, everyone has a mother and father. Sigmund Freud put that elementary fact to good use in deciphering human nature. Viewing peculiar behavior not as some short circuit of the neuronal network but as the subliminal outgrowth of one's childhood, Freud went to great lengths to imprint that notion on society's collective conscious in the 1920s. It was only a matter of time before his converts began to apply such thinking to history.

Today the limitations of psychoanalytical theory are common knowledge to practicing physicians. Not that this discipline should be dismissed out of hand by either the historian or the biographer; rather, the prudent scholar would merely ask that its disciples strike a proper balance. Reenter the neurologist, now armed with more substantial data than seizure-riddled psyches, to highlight more prevalent diseases that have been all but ignored.

One of the most disabling is poorly controlled high blood pressure. As if to underscore its impact on history, four world leaders in the twentieth century alone suffered from particularly virulent cases of hypertension that adversely affected their brain function. Yet to date, Josef Stalin, Woodrow Wilson, and, to a lesser degree, Winston Churchill have been indicted on the pages of history by the psychoanalyst more than by the neurologist. (The exception among the four is Franklin D. Roosevelt, for whom the psychohistorians—excluding the effect of polio on his subsequent quest for office—have managed to leave well enough alone.) Whereas both agree that all three men were but shadows of their former selves in the end, neither discipline has been willing to revise its thinking enough to admit what they have in common: that each of these leaders manifested signs of accelerated brain aging, which magnified those personality attributes the psychologists have so capably identified. In short, Stalin became more paranoid, Wilson more rigid, and Churchill more egocentric as a result of hypertension-induced cerebrovascular disease.

It follows that a complete historical appraisal of the first half of the twentieth century must include the largely overlooked issue of physiologically compromised leadership, if for no other reason than that few men in modern history (sick or healthy) exercised so much power over so many for so long. It therefore falls to the pathographer, as something of a revisionist in his or her own "write", to offer second opinions on that issue's implications, both psychological and political. As such, the chapters that follow attempt to shed some light on what has been to date an obscure contribution by pathography to psychohistory.

CHAPTER 4
Josef Stalin:
A Premier Paranoic

Before condemning the proponents of revisionism (or impugning their motives), we would do well to acknowledge that some revisionists have contributed immeasurably to our understanding of the past. To cite but a few examples: Did the Age of Jackson truly signify the emergence of the "common man" in American politics, or was it a time in which mere deference was paid to the common man by the "uncommon men" who really ran things?[1] Was the Spanish-American War the logical culmination of our Manifest Destiny or a byproduct of imperialistic pretension?[2]

Nor have the revisionists ignored the origins of the Cold War and America's responsibility for it. Did a headstrong president really push Josef Stalin into a defensive posture at the end of World War II, thereby initiating the Cold War?[3] Can a single individual have such an impact on history? Surely there is something to be said for the suspicions of contemporaries and later scholars alike that Stalin's paranoia also had something to do with dropping East-West relations into the deep freeze. Taking that argument one step further than the psychoanalysts have done to date, we now have medical support for the view that his lifelong paranoia may have been augmented in the end by hypertension-induced brain aging. On this subject, the pathographer is singularly blessed with an increasing quantity of medical data trickling out from the former Soviet Union that adds a new dimension to Stalin's psychological profile.

Of course, historians have already given the origins of the Cold War a detailed second look. Whereas the consensus view suggests that Soviet designs on Eastern Europe were largely responsible for the split that emerged, some revisionists believe it was the United States that abandoned the wartime partnership and subconsciously backed the Soviets against the wall long before they chose to build a real one for themselves.[4] At best, America's twentieth-century infatuation with international peace-keeping organizations ran counter to age-old Russian preoccupations with spheres of influence; at worst, some suspect that

Harry Truman was guilty of deliberate provocation.[5] Emboldened by the gloved fist of Marshall Plan aid slammed into the open palm of Europe on the one hand and the strong-armed threat of nuclear hegemony on the other, the United States, it has been argued, shouldered legitimate Soviet considerations aside.

How else to explain Truman's aggressive rhetoric when, on the eve of the Potsdam Conference in the summer of 1945, he gave the Soviet ambassador a "straight one-two to the jaw"?[6] That was more than a verbal tongue-lashing, for Truman's bite was as penetrating as his bark was shrill. At least for the moment, America's diplomatic clout was sustained by a self-conscious awareness of its economic and military might. In contrast, Russia, with its twenty million dead and an economy in dire need of resuscitation, not only had to rebuild but also feared capitalist encirclement and future expansion. Whether or not the Soviet Union was truly the object of an international conspiracy led by the United States, the Soviets perceived itself as such. And it is the mind of Josef Stalin in particular that offers the most sensitive barometer of pressures coming to bear on postwar Soviet behavior.

Here the argments of both traditionalist and revisionist dovetail in an ironic fashion, hinged as much to the cornerstone of individual disease as mutual distrust. Whereas the revisionists have argued that the United States was guilty of several actions that only augumented, if not justified, much of the Soviet Union's somewhat paranoid machinations, proponents of the traditionalist school such as Arthur Schlesinger, Jr., highlighted that paranoia in peculiarly personal terms: "Stalin . . . was plainly a man of deep and morbid obsessions and compulsions. . . . His paranoia . . . led to the terrible purges of the mid-thirties and the wanton murder of thousands of his Bolshevik comrades." In time, it would lead to much more, including the execution of a best friend, a lover, and members of his own family. As Schlesinger bluntly concluded: "In the end nothing could satisfy Stalin's paranoia. His own associates failed. Why does anyone suppose that any conceivable American policy [designed to keep the Soviet Union as an ally] would have succeeded?"[7]

This distinguished scholar was implying that the Cold War was in all likelihood unavoidable. Much of that thesis rests on Russian history in general and Stalin's morbid obsession in particular, which made any diplomatic rapprochement between the superpowers an exercise in self-deceit. Through the centuries, Czarist paranoia had been spawned by invasions and conquests that compelled its leaders to protect the motherland's borders from Huns, Mongols, and Germans alike.[8] Lenin's later perversion of Marxist ideology to a death struggle between capitalism and socialism, rather than a predetermined progression from one to the other, accentuated this peculiar aspect of the Russian psyche. So long as capitalism existed anywhere in the world, the Soviet Union and its newly acclaimed ideology were at risk. By the end of World War II, what had seemed a theoretical risk now became an overt threat: bourgeois capitalists were knocking on Russia's western door. To complicate matters further, what had been a movement led by a strongly centralized party of revolutionary elite had devolved during the Stalin era to a personality cult—a personality that alone spoke and acted for Soviet interests.

Historians on both sides of the fence have for some time now been willing to recognize these underpinnings of Soviet Russia's postwar paranoia. Perhaps one of its most astute contemporary observers was the United States attaché in Moscow, George F. Kennan, who emphasized what he felt to be a permanent and enduring feature of Russian psychology that resulted in a "neurotic view" of world affairs. What Kennan appreciated more than most was an "age-old sense of insecurity of a sedentary people reared on an exposed plain in the neighborhood of fierce nomadic peoples."[9] Schlesinger took this geopolitical factor one step further and tied it to two others: any analysis of the origins of the Cold War must include not only what he termed these "sinister dynamics" of Russian society but also the intransigence of Leninist ideology and Stalin's "madness."[10]

Neither ideologies nor pathologic personalities develop in a vacuum. No understanding of postwar Soviet mentality can be had without acknowledging past grievances that contributed in large measure to the profound paranoia of the Stalin era. On two occasions during a twenty-five year period of Russia's recent history alone, its borders had been overrun by jackbooted Germans swarming across the Polish corridor. It was perhaps understandable, then, that Stalin would perceive the post-war reorganization of Poland not as a question of honor but as a "life and death" struggle.[11] To make matters worse, after both world wars overt German hostility was supplanted by Western interference in Russian and Soviet affairs. From the beginning, Bolsheviks reacted with dismay to Western support of the Whites (which occurred despite Woodrow Wilson's objections to Allied interference in Russia) during the six years of civil war before the Reds established control within their own borders.[12] Now, a quarter of a century later, Russia's erstwhile allies were denying the Soviets their spheres of influence in Eastern Europe as well. Nor had Stalin forgiven the Allies' delay in opening the western front until June 1944, at the expense of millions of Russians lost before Germany was required to divert its forces to its defenses in the West. And if Soviet interference in Polish affairs and elsewhere offended Western liberal thought, Stalin could point to the unilateral surrender and dismemberment of Italy without Russian input as justification for later Soviet incursions in Eastern Europe.

What Stalin really feared was contact with a more powerful and economically healthy West—unless, of course, the Soviet economy might benefit from that without any strings attached. Hence his early refusal to allow potential satellite states in the eastern *cordon sanitaire* to participate in the Marshall Plan.[13] Not that their suffering population would have cared where the aid came from; what had become a pervasive neurosis framed in insecurity afflicted Soviet rulers far more than it did the ruled.[14] In one sense, the tribulations of war had moved the Russian people away from the internationalist pretensions of the Communist Party toward a more protective, if pragmatic, embrace of the motherland. Stalin recognized that himself. As he ruefully admitted to Averell Harriman during the war: "We are under no illusions that the people are fighting for us. They are fighting for Mother Russia."[15]

While tying its people by the necessity of hard times to a totalitarian dictatorship, Communist ideology itself no longer tugged at the heartstrings of popular emotions at war's end. Yet sustenance and survival did—and Stalin believed that he alone knew how to assuage those elemental concerns. Such hubris hinged on a submissive Russian mentality as much as it stemmed from what Dostoevski termed the "mental degeneration" of Russian revolutionaries, who believed that human beings, "vicious and depraved as they are," have to be coerced into accepting ends and means for which they are not ready but which will ultimately serve them well.[16] That the Soviet people perceived freedom of choice as a luxury they could scarcely afford was to their immediate benefit but long-term distress, because subjugation and murder thereafter became part and parcel of the state's means to achieve desired ends. As Freud assessed Soviet leaders through the confessions of Dostoevski: "Truly they were like the barbarians of the great invasions who murder and do penance, whereafter pentience becomes a technique to enable murder to be done."[17]

This was all, of course, a magnified reflection of Russia's history as personified by past tyrannical rulers, Peter the Great and Ivan the Terrible among them. A preeminent Russian scholar of the Stalin era, Gustav Bychowski, perceived what evolved under Stalin's rule as "unconscious identification" with the methods and ideals of his forebears.[18] In addition, the anxiety and frustration of the postwar world created in the shell-shocked Russian mind set a deeply seated need for ideals backed by material power. Providing these was a mandate Stalin intended to preempt for himself by whatever means proved necessary.

If despotic oppression had long blighted Russian history, that same instrument now buried its blade to the hilt in a malleable populace to effect a cure for ills that its rulers had, in large measure, created. Ivan the Terrible was among the first to initiate a system based on *opriezniki*, faithful servants of the czar who carried out the functions of a modern-day secret police.[19] In Lenin's time, by extension, the "haves" were no longer masters over the "have-nots." Hence the suppression of the wealthy, quasi-capitalist kulaks, farmers whose rural districts were completely depopulated by forced mass exportations. By such stringent measures were the oppressed compelled to take their medicine as retribution for the wrongs done by a few to the subjugated many. The prescription for Russia's ills was deceptively simple: scalpels wielded by its leaders must penetrate deeply to cut out this bourgeois cancer.

It was left to Lenin to administer the anesthetic that ultimately allowed his successor to operate. As one admirer recalled: "Lenin appeared to be burdened, oppressed with all the pain and . . . suffering of the Russian people."[20] Like all good revolutionaries, he needed a scapegoat, which capitalism and the bourgeoisie supplied: they were the alleged persecutors of Russia's oppressed classes. As such, Soviet ideology found its psychological catharsis in the persecution of the bourgeoisie within and the defense against capitalists without.

This only intensified the inveterate Russian suspicion of a hostile West—but not before opponents from inside Soviet borders fell victim to its excesses. Once Stalin came to power, the purge trials from 1928 to 1938 transformed one individual's neurosis into collective paranoia. Terrorism became palatable in the defense against traitors, allowing Stalin to use any means necessary to exact social obedience, including mass murders without parallel in human history (his former enemies, the Nazis, perhaps excepted).[21] In addition, Stalin's own past only fueled the flames of his paranoia. As a Georgian, he ruminated over the domination that Russian officials had exercised over his homeland.[22] Vengeance would be had, as he consciously or subconsciously identified past oppressors with allies-turned-internationalists.

Stalin was hardly the first Bolshevik to perceive the utility of violence and terror in gaining his ends. That *modus operandi* had been sanctified long before by Leon Trotsky in his "Defense of Terrorism," which justified the use of violence to "break the class will of the enemy."[23] Lenin subsequently put that theory into practice with the systematic use of terror by one class against another.[24] In the process, a notable contradiction in Marxist theory evolved: Though the state was supposed to "wither away," the revolution evolved in precisely the opposite direction—toward increasing its power. In such a fashion were the redeeming features of socialism ultimately subverted by terrorism.

Lenin's successor would elevate that practice to such a level that Stalinism became "the enduring legacy of Leninism," as one perceptive

student of Soviet culture, Zbigniew Brzezinski, defined it.[25] Whereas
Lenin had rationalized the development of totalitarianism by the mere
presence of capitalist enemies at home and abroad, Stalin extended its
application to all opponents, perceived and real. In his mentor's collected works, one sentence most assuredly caught his eye: "The scientific concept of dictatorship means nothing other than unlimited
government unrestrained by any law . . . [and] supporting itself directly
by force." [26] One might imagine Stalin closing the book, rubbing his
hands together, and exclaiming through tobacco-stained teeth in his
Georgian-accented Rusian: "*Harasho* [good]!"

Into the maelstrom of collective Soviet insecurity, then, dropped
one who was already paranoid in his own right. Habitually mistreated as
a youth by his drunken father, blighted with a withered left arm that
paradoxically compelled him to strong-arm his opponents, having
chafed under the yoke of inquisitors and monks at the seminary he once
attended (not to mention the oppression of his Georgian people by
previous Czarist regimes), Josef Stalin was a physically and emotionally
deprived captive of his past. If Soviet leadership in general has been aptly
characterized as having "unconsciously identified" with past Russian
tyrants, Stalin in particular had just as unconsciously "identified with
aggressors" (or so one psychohistorian has argued), among them, past
czars who had thrown off institutional restraints and behaved as out-
laws and autocrats in their own right.[27] When employed against pu-
nitive authority figures, identifying with aggressors is not in itself
pathologic. Yet when projected against innocent persons, the practice
becomes pathologic in a very real sense. Both before and after the war,
Stalin was guilty on all counts. (It did not pass unnoticed by his infre-
quent visitors in later years that a portrait of Ivan the Terrible graced the
wall over his desk. Yet the paranoid premier had exercised the worst
excesses of his identified benefactor long before consulting his interior
decorator).

As the first writer to explore Stalin's "heart of darkness" systematically, Gustav Bychowski compared the rise of Stalin to what occurs in
primitive societies, in which the other sons of a past venerated leader
are eliminated one by one by the most cunning and powerful among
them.[28] The motivation is simple: the would-be new father figure fears
retaliation. Once all pretenders are eliminated, subordinates ingratiate
themselves with ostensible loyalty to the survivor, who then becomes
the idealized leader in his own right. Yet the anger of suppressed hostility always remains. To protect himself, the idealized leader creates
powerful safeguards. In primitive societies, restrictive taboos suffice;
in a modern totalitarian stage, they include terrorism and subterfuge
through the secret police.

Stalin subconsciously followed this hypothetical construct to the letter. He had to—for even Lenin mistrusted the Georgian Bear from the beginning, as well he should have. A loyal cadre of spies infiltrated Lenin's administration, Stalin's wife among them: while serving as Lenin's secretary, she acted as a double agent on her husband's behalf.[29] After Lenin's death Stalin proceeded to eliminate his potential opposition in a timely fashion through numerous purges. And some of those directly involved in drawing up lists of their comrades to be executed continued to sit on the Politburo even after their wives had already been carted off, on Stalin's orders, to forced labor camps.[30]

Lenin's death from cerebrovascular disease in 1924 rekindled a Stalin-Trotsky feud that had been smoldering since 1918. Lenin's biographer Louis Fischer asserts that the Moscow purge trials of the 1930s, which cost the country its top leaders, were in reality "trials" of Trotsky, reflecting Stalin's paranoid vendetta against his exiled archrival. Nor can one ignore the impact of that on state policy, leading to the premature implementation of industrialization and collectivization that resulted in famine for millions.[31]

This is all to underscore what one modern psychiatrist was driving at when he observed that "paranoia is the most political of all mental illnesses." Should the victim happen to rule in a totalitarian state, and hence not be constrained by the political system he dominates, then the consequences not only for his enemies (perceived or real) but for the state can be enormous.[32] Ironically, the system itself may both contribute to the evolution of paranoia and obscure its presence, particularly in closed societies such as existed in Russia long before Josef Stalin ever came to power.

Having left the seminary to follow Lenin along the road toward a future Bolshevik revolution, Stalin reentered a society rife with conspiracy, intrigue, and paranoia that had epitomized the czarist state since the turn of the century. The eminent psychiatrist and founder of Russian neurology, Mikhailovich Bekhtenev, dared to diagnose this unhealthy state of affairs as early as 1897 with a stinging social critique. He likened the Russian people to a "distinct personality" that was being "systematically repressed, . . . gasping for air in the vise of arbitrary despotism as dark and suffocating as a dungeon."[33] Just such an oppressive environment not only reflected but magnified Stalin's life view and suspicions.

With the substitution of one authoritarian system for another, Soviet society under Stalin became more closed than ever. Hence, perhaps, the collective torpor that permitted its suffering millions to ignore these increasing manifestations of Stalin's suspicious nature. Dr. Jerrold Post has described their predicament succinctly enough: "In the

1930s, Stalin's suspiciousness mounted to a degree that would have warranted a diagnosis of 'paranoid personality disorder' in an open society. Yet the question of pathology was masked by the conspiratorial environment in which he lived and to which he contributed."[34]

In fact, that diagnosis had been made in Russia long before—though never divulged in Stalin's lifetime—by none other than Mikhailovich Bekhtenev. As early as 1927, this preeminent psychoneurological authority was called to the Kremlin by Stalin himself to treat the premier's depression. What Bekhtenev encountered was a man enslaved by irrepressible fears. That was enough for the improvident doctor to render, at once, both a diagnosis of "grave paranoia" for Stalin and a death warrant for himself. Bekhtenev never left the Kremlin. He died the same day, poisoned by the hand of his own patient.[35]

Even Stalin's wife fell victim to her husband's paranoia in the end. Rather than confront Stalin with reports of widespread famine in the South, Nadezhda Alliluyeva surreptitiously traveled there herself to investigate and presented her report without her husband's consent to the Central Committee of the Party. Stalin's fury over her meddling in Party affairs was further inflamed by Nedezhda's rebuke for his involvement in the shooting death of nine of her fellow students at the Commercial Institute outside the Kremlin. In a fit of rage, Stalin shot his wife on November 21, 1932, according to the nurse of one Dr. Pletnev, who had been Stalin's physician in attendance during the 1930s. That crime of impassioned paranoia was enough to trigger some later uncharacteristic remorse on Stalin's part, for Nedezhda was the only person he had ever loved. Yet remorse did not sit well with Josef Stalin, nor was it enough to divert this disturbed man from completing what had to be done in its aftermath. He later brought Pletnev to trial on trumped-up charges, along with other physicians who had knowledge of the crime, and executed them as well.[36]

Recalling the psychoanalyst's dictum that the projection of aggression onto one's opponents becomes truly pathologic only when it is directed at friends, siblings, spouses, and other undeserving persons, we can see how truly pathological Stalin became at a very early stage. He personally shot his one-time best friend, Avely Yenukidze, who was secretary of the Central Executive Committee at the time and a close friend of Stalin's wife. A son by his first marriage was discovered in 1941 to be a prisoner of the Germans; for reasons that still defy explanation, Stalin ordered his agents to find the boy and kill him. Then there was the fate of one Liza Kazanova, with whom Stalin had carried on a passionate love affair after the death of his wife. Ridding himself of her fiancé by having him deported to a gulag was not enough to satisfy Stalin's morbid obsessions; he later had Liza gang-raped by four OGPU thugs and thereafter arrested his former lover and sent her to prison, where she mysteriously disappeared.[37]

Naturally, Stalin reserved most of his unbridled aggression for his political opponents. The murder of Trotsky and countless others aside, the assassination of Maxim Gorky is perhaps the most celebrated example of his pathologic excess. Hero of the poor, the oppressed, and the forgotten in Soviet society of Stalin's day, Gorky was a thorn in the hypersensitive side of the Georgian Bear. Accordingly, Stalin had the writer strangled in his own apartment. To cover the tracks of blood running straight to the Kremlin's door, the assassin himself was eliminated, as was Gorky's doctor, who had been entrusted with his patient's papers and diaries before the assassination. Three other witnesses to the crime also disappeared, as did Gorky's manuscripts—but not before he had inscribed his own epitaph memorializing a self-fulfilling prophecy: "All you Russians are still savages," he had charged. "Evidently killing is easier than persuasion [for the Communist hierarchy]."[38]

Bychowski's linking of Soviet behavior to that found in primitive societies also explains much of the projection of aggression onto hostile outside forces—and brings us back full circle to the origins of the Cold War. In theory, the latent hostility of rebellious sons (read, Kremlin subordinates) frequently breaks through in a form of what the psychoanalyst calls "paranoid projection." Too unsure of their own strength to take on the substitute father who has become an idolized leader, they turn on one another or, more acceptable still, on their past oppressors, perceived and real. In practice, this led to a singular result in Soviet Russia. Not that the merging of international Bolshevism with Russian nationalism (that is, the fusion of a revolutionary ideology with nationalist sentiments) was unique; similar circumstances had arisen before in history. What imbued the Russo-Soviet blend with an insidious persecution complex in the 1920s and 1930s was that both were breaking out from perceived repression.[39] Hence the hatred and suspicion of all foreigners forged with the sickle and hammer of ideology on the anvil of past historical conflicts. That this fusion was solidified by one who was already paranoid in his own right assured a morbid intransigence in postwar diplomacy.

Psychoanalysts have pointed out that the war itself only contributed to Stalin's paranoia. Some have gone so far as to call him a prototypical "warfare personality," suggesting that he possessed paranoid characteristics unique to such individuals.[40] That simply was not the case; rather, Stalin's complete life history affirms that the exigencies of war merely augmented a personality disorder already well entrenched. That said, it would come as no surprise that imperialism after the war was justified in Stalin's eyes by a few paranoid projections of his own—

the fear of Western encirclement among them. Wrestling in the diplomatic arena with capitalism became a singular obsession. George Kennan, for one, underscored this and fingered the paranoid premier as its source: "Stalin sees the world only through the prism of his own ambitions and his own fears." Given the depth of his obsessions by 1948, the pathographer might justifiably transpose the word "prison" for "prism," for Stalin was enslaved by his compulsion for self-preservation, as Kennan had made clear: "His fundamental motive was the protection of his position. . . . This is the key to his diplomacy."[41]

Not that the United States was in any mood to salve Stalin's wounds or assuage his paranoia—Harry Truman least of all. "If the Russians [do] not wish to join us," he once warned his advisers in typical Trumanese, "they [can] go to hell."[42] It was precisely this mindset and some of the activities it engendered that made the United States an accessory to the division of Europe at war's end. In that respect, the revisionist argument may have more merit than the traditionalist has been willing to acknowledge.

Truman's secretary of war, Henry L. Stimson, himself a classical balance-of-power advocate, spoke to deaf presidential ears when he told his superior that "the Russians [are] perhaps being more realistic than we [are] in regard to their own security." To Stimson's way of thinking, accepting the spheres-of-influence doctrine represented a rational alternative to "a head-on collision." As for George F. Kennan, he was just as out of step with his president in supporting a "prompt and clear recognition of the divisions of Europe into spheres of influence," arguing that nothing could be done to alter the course of events in Eastern Europe.[43] Acknowledging Stalin's paranoia as he did, Kennan was being entirely consistent with what his observations of the man told him.

The often maligned Henry A. Wallace agreed, perceiving the situation as analogous to James Monroe's hallowed doctrine, which isolationist America had long before embraced: "We have no more business in the political affairs of Eastern Europe than Russia has in the political affairs of Latin America."[44] Nor should we forget (as Stalin most assuredly did not) that Churchill had for some time been more tolerant of spheres-of-influence preoccupations than his American allies. Long before war's end Churchill had proposed that, with the impending liberation of the Balkans, Russia should run things in Rumania and Bulgaria in exchange for British control in Greece.

It was only natural, then, for a person with Stalin's psychological profile to believe that America was his mortal enemy. The paranoid premier did not have long to wait to see his suspicions confirmed. In January 1945 the Russians asked the United States for a six-billion-dollar credit for postwar reconstruction. That request was reported to have been inadvertently mislaid in the State Department, a circumstance that even the least paranoid of the Soviet leadership had difficulty believing. This was followed in May 1945 by the abrupt termination of lend-lease shipments to Russia. Describing the manner in which they were terminated as "brutal," Stalin was equally mortified to learn that reparations from Western Germany would be delayed. When that issue had arisen at Yalta, Roosevelt deferred any definitive consideration of amounts to be paid to his ally. Schlesinger spoke for traditionalist and revisionist alike, then, in observing that the "Russian hope for major Western assistance . . . foundered on three events which the Kremlin could well have interpreted respectively as deliberate sabotage (the loan request), blackmail (lend-lease cancellation) and pro-Germanism (reparations)."[45] The Kremlin *could* have believed this—and a paranoid Josef Stalin obviously did.

All the more unbearable was his realization that by 1948 the United States was generating one half of the world's industrial output—not to mention its possession of the atom bomb, which was guaranteed to impress even the most psychologically stable Kremlin power brokers. At this juncture in history, Harry Truman was speaking none too softly and carrying big sticks loaded with bangs and bucks. As might be anticipated in such Machiavellian times, the realists accepted that the United States would use its formidable power to best advantage, whether as a diplomatic tool to forge agreements or as a weapon to compel compliance.[46] Stalin characteristically assumed the worst, as paranoics are wont to do. He reacted as if these Western-style cattle prods were being used to gore the hind parts of the Russian Bear where, as presumably existed behind the Iron Curtain, the sun never shone.

After all, Stalin had his own opinions of Western leaders, which Harry Truman's machinations hardly dispelled. "Churchill is the kind who, if you don't watch him, will slip a kopeck out of your pocket," the premier charged. "Roosevelt is not like that. He digs in his hand for bigger coins."[47] Presumably Truman had in mind robbing the bank with an eye to mortgaging Russia's future security—or so Stalin perceived the situation as his paranoia accelerated to alarming levels after the war.

Obviously, then, there is nothing new to be said about the Soviet premier's paranoia or the psychoanalytical theses that sustain it. If any contribution is to be made by subsequent writers, it remains to define the physiologic context within which this condition became pervasive. And here the medical record has much to tell us. One investigator who spent a lifetime studying this enigmatic personality struck to the heart of the matter: "In the period after the Second World War, Stalin's inappropriate accusations of treason and morbid suspiciousness . . .

suggested a pathology associated with the process of aging and his increasing sense of isolation."[48]

To begin with, Josef Stalin was a very sick man by 1945. For years he had suffered from recurrent heart trouble aggravated by high blood pressure. Rumor had it that he had suffered a mild heart attack just prior to the Potsdam Conference.[49] How high his blood pressure was at the time is uncertain, but the results of Stalin's later autopsy in 1953 attest to the severity of that underlying condition. Like Franklin D. Roosevelt eight years before, he died of a massive hemorrhage in the left side of his brain.[50] Far and away the most common cause of such hemorrhagic strokes in an individual seventy-three years old is poorly controlled hypertension.

Long-standing high blood pressure also leads to heart failure. As Stalin's autopsy report makes clear, hypertension had contributed to "arteriosclerotic modifications of particularly important vessels in the brain's arteries," as well as "considerable hypertonic disturbances of the left ventricle of the heart."[51] In lay terms, the Soviet premier suffered from hardening of the arteries to his brain and an enlarged heart, both the results of accelerated hypertension. Though no mention of a stroke appears in the medical record prior to his demise, Stalin had experienced at least one transient disturbance of blood flow to his brain's speech center as early as 1937. Again, far and away the most prevalent cause of such stroke warnings is either poorly controlled hypertension or atherosclerotic cerebrovascular disease. That would come as no surprise to Stalin's pathographers; we now know that both conditions had already reached life-threatening levels fully fifteen years before his death—more than adequate confirmation of the severity of his underlying hypertension.[52]

So much for the physical aspects of Stalin's health after 1945. How might hypertension and atherosclerosis have contributed to his psychological deterioration? In fact, both diseases adversely affect brain function; in particular, they can change the way the victim behaves. As one biographer assessed Stalin's increasingly bizarre conduct during this period: "Apart from its physical effects, illness seems to have caused some change in personality. . . . He was prone to bouts of irrational anger and . . . appeared increasingly suspicious of those about him. In this he exhibited some symptoms of paranoia."[53] That indictment was not unfounded. Stalin was once reported to have interrupted a meal with his Kremlin colleagues to stare icily at a senior official, only to ask: "Why are you looking at me like that?" On another occasion, Nikita Khrushchev recalled, his mentor reproached him in a Party meeting for failing to look him in the eye.[54] Such behavior is typical of paranoics, who are always searching for clues to substantiate their suspicions.

Any physician familiar with Stalin's underlying physical deterioration might have understood at least in a subjective sense what subsequent medical data have confirmed as an objective effect of long-standing hypertension and atherosclerosis on brain function: premature aging of the brain. That alone is often accompanied by unwarranted suspicion and paranoia as the victim struggles to remain in control. In someone who is already paranoid to begin with, these qualities may be magnified tenfold. What catches the pathographer's eye is the pervasiveness of this behavior on Stalin's part after the war and until his death in 1953.

Though Stalin's paranoia has recently been described by one Russian psychiatrist as having been "cyclical,"[55] it ultimately became a permanent fixture in his personality. Marshal Zhukov believed that Stalin himself was aware of this, but only as late as 1946, when he readily admitted to "living in fear" of his own shadow.[56] That was perhaps Stalin's last recorded bit of self-revelation. From that point forward, in fact, several associates would describe him in private as bordering on the senile—a circumstance that can now be directly attributed to his hypertensive cerebrovascular disease. Indeed, one psychiatrist who has managed to disengage himself from the bondage of psychoanalysis concluded that "age and cerebroarteriosclerosis moved [Stalin] along the continuum from paranoid suspiciousness to full-blown paranoia."[57]

Senile individuals often assault or harangue members of their own families or close associates, whether or not they harbored paranoid tendencies before the onset of their deterioration. In Stalin, this behavior accelerated after the war—as would be anticipated with the passage of years. His daughter Svetlana recalled one such event in 1947 during a dinner with the Politburo. Silence terrified Stalin, and on that occasion Andre Zhadanov was deemed responsible for contributing to it. "Look at him," Stalin angrily exclaimed to the others, "sitting there like Christ, as if nothing was of any concern to him." Zhadanov, himself quite ill and aware of his superior's penchant toward vengeance, grew pale, and beads of perspiration stood out on his forehead. Everyone fell silent out of fear of both Stalin's wrath and the possibility that Zhadanov might have a heart attack under the duress.[58] Such outbursts, which occurred time and again, were entirely consistent with the disease that drove him; the hypervigilant paranoic characteristically expresses disdain for the weak, sickly, or defective.[59]

Meals always seemed to bring out the worst of Stalin's paranoia. According to Khrushchev, he was forever looking for hemlock in every chalice. Stalin always had others taste the dishes first, though everything served at the table had already been tested by Kremlin analysts.

"Look, here are the giblets, Nikita," he would say. "Have you tried them?" If such rudimentary activities as eating disturbed the morbidly suspicious premier, going out in public absolutely terrified him. Traveling in a motorcade of five identical cars wherever he went, Stalin would invariably have the order of the cars changed to foil possible assassination attempts. He never felt safe even in his own home, where security was at a premium. Only carefully screened servants had access to his dacha, and none was allowed to become accustomed to his routine. Changes of the guard took on an air of interminably revolving doors— doors that were armored, bolted from the inside, and activated by remote control. No one ever knew until the last moment where Stalin would sleep. He had four identical rooms to choose from, their windows blocked by slabs of reinforced concrete, and would bed down unannounced in any one of the four with a loaded revolver under his pillow.[60] To the very end, Stalin lived in total isolation with his fears.

Physicians today would characterize such obsessions as being grounded in a disease-induced paranoic state: "Once such character defenses as rigid thinking and unwarranted discretion fail to protect the individual from his deepest anxieties, persecutory symptoms emerge as a means by which the personality defends against fears of death and impending loss of functions and satisfactions."[61] So why, one might ask, did Stalin's physicians fail to recognize what their empirical observations should have made clear all along? The fact is that no doctor was close enough to the premier to establish an effective patient-physician relationship, for Stalin's paranoia extended to those entrusted with his health. Any doctor who had been allowed the chance was inevitably dismissed on trumped-up charges, and the closest of all were executed, just as Pletnev, Bekhtenev, and others had been.[62] His daughter, for one, believed that Stalin's self-imposed isolation from the medical profession shortened his life.[63] It also increased his paranoia.

A few writers have suggested that there must have been something in his doctors' conduct for Stalin to have so distrusted traditional medicine; why else would he have banished them when he needed their skills the most? The answer lies in the premier's morbid preoccupation with controlling his environment. Any individual who potentially held sway over his physical well-being was a part of that. One doctor's "plot" after another was uncovered at Stalin's behest, yet there is no evidence to support that any were plotting to do away with their feared patient— who nevertheless continued to believe otherwise. As late as 1953, *Pravda* reported that Stalin had uncovered yet another sinister medical conspiracy. Nine physicians in all were blacklisted, and only Stalin's death saved them from the fate of their predecessors.[64]

In the final analysis, Stalin's paranoia on all matters—from security and eating to medicine and diplomacy—was only accentuated by his failing health. As his trusted adviser Milovan Djilas perceived as early as 1948: "He seemed to be failing fast. . . . When I last saw him in 1945, he was still lively, quick-witted, and had a pointed sense of humor. Now he laughs at inanities and shallow jokes." More distressing still, Stalin's abstract thinking suffered in kind, as Djilas testified: "On one occasion he not only failed to get the political point of an anecdote I had told him in which he outsmarted Churchill and Roosevelt, but I had the impression that he was offended, in the manner of old men."[65]

Despite his lack of medical training, Djilas was a more astute diagnostician than he realized. Aging frequently unmasks the underlying flaws in a person's character. Should he or she also be in poor health and relatively isolated, such traits are exhibited in bold relief as the temperamental fuse shortens and adaptability disappears. One medical authority adds that such individuals become "conspicuously more pedantic, self-righteous, petulant . . . irascible, suspicious and withdrawn."[66] The morbid accentuation of Stalin's lifelong paranoia and later self-imposed isolation related in the end as much to physiologic compromise as to political considerations.

Before examining further the impact of aging on Stalin's paranoid state of mind, I should make clear that I am not using the term "paranoid" in only a descriptive sense with reference to Stalin's personality. Obviously, every one of us has paranoid moments. For the most part, however, we manage to disavow our suspicions when presented with a reasonable explanation. The true paranoic, in contrast, will turn defensive and even hostile. When such behavior becomes pervasive (that is, pathological), it most often reflects one of three underlying conditions: schizophrenia, a manic-depressive disorder, or dementia. In Stalin's case, recent evidence suggests that the last of these conditions transformed what some have described as paranoid tendencies into a truly pathological state. To argue that point requires knowing something of both dementia and paranoia as contemporary investigators have defined them.

From the strictly medical standpoint, pure paranoia is characterized by persecutory delusions that cannot be explained by other psychiatric disorders. As opposed to those of schizophrenia or manic-depression, these delusions are generally well developed and systematized logically. Stated another way, the essential feature of paranoia is a permanent and unshakable delusional system accompanied by the preservation of clear and orderly thinking.[67] This also differentiates *de novo* paranoia from that which frequently accompanies an organic brain syndrome, in which loss of memory, disorientation, and impaired judgment and impulse control are also manifest.[68] This is not to say, however, that dementia cannot exacerbate an underlying paranoid state. And that, the record suggests, is precisely what happened to Josef Stalin some five years before he died.

Once having eliminated other psychiatric diseases, and in order to substantiate a diagnosis of pure paranoia, the suspect must fulfill several specific criteria, among them an unwarranted distrust of others, hypersensitivity, and stifled emotions.[69] Few of history's leaders better fit both the general character of the paranoid personality and its specific criteria than did Josef Stalin. As has already been suggested, his childhood had much to do with that. Many paranoics are victims of physical beatings or mental cruelty, as was Stalin, and their parents are described as distant, rigid, sadistic, or weak and ineffectual—all attributes shared by his father. If parental figures cannot be relied upon to help deal with humiliations and frustrations, the child tends to perceive the entire environment as hostile and become hypersensitive to imagined slights. Consumed with anger and hostility, and unable to face responsibility for their rage, paranoics both project their resentment and anger onto others and protect themselves from further rejection by turning their positive feelings into negative ones.[70]

Projection comes into play in other ways. Intolerant of criticism, they criticize others. Overaggressive themselves, paranoics see imagined aggressors in everyone around them. They sublimate feelings of inferiority with delusions of superiority, grandiosity, and omnipotence—part of an elaborate system of fantasies that they embrace to bolster their self-esteem. It is also of interest that paranoia is more prevalent among minority and immigrant groups.[71] After all, Josef Stalin was a Georgian among the Russian ruling class.

Yet a deprived childhood alone does not assure a priori that a paranoid personality disorder will emerge. Environmental influences outside the home may assist in its development. Psychiatrists have identified at least seven situations that may be contributory: (1) anticipation of receiving sadistic treatment; (2) situations that increase distrust and suspicion; (3) social isolation; (4) predicaments that increase envy and jealousy; (5) affronts that lower one's self-esteem; (6) circumstances that cause the individual to see his or her own sublimated defects in others; and (7) situations that lead to ruminating over hidden meanings and motivations.[72] From these perspectives it is readily apparent how Stalin's childhood predispositions toward the development of overt paranoia were only augmented by what he himself later acknowledged to be a distressing postwar situation—even before the physiologically induced hardening of such attitudes that his hypertensive brain disease would ultimately assure. Grievous Soviet losses during the war, the threat of capitalistic encirclement by the West, and the less than sympathetic U.S. attitude toward his spheres-of-influence preoccupations all contributed to an acceleration of Stalin's paranoia at war's end.

When frustration from any combination of perceived slights exceeds the limits that the paranoid personality can tolerate, the victim becomes anxious and withdrawn. So do leaders faced with predicaments that they have difficulty understanding, particularly if they have limited resources to effect a change: "They realize something is wrong, but cannot explain it."[73] The formation of a "delusional system" offers a solution to the problem. That is precisely the answer Stalin subconsciously embraced vis-à-vis Eastern Europe and the West.

Such sufferers begin by attributing malicious intent to others' actions. In the diplomatic environment the intentions of allied nations turned adversaries may be similarly misread, just as Stalin failed to acknowledge that the termination of lend-lease applied not uniquely to the Soviet Union but to other nations as well, such as Great Britain. Eventually, they see these perceived adversaries as organized into a community of plotters, much as Stalin came to view the West as a monolithic bloc engaging in an active conspiracy against the U.S.S.R. Finally, they react to these threats, both real and imaginary.[74] Hence Stalin's perception that U.S. interference in Polish affairs, the announcement of the Truman Doctrine, and the implementation of the Marshall Plan were nothing more than all-out attempts at quarantining the Soviet Union. One psychiatrist has labeled the evolution of this delusional system as a "pseudocommunity" with which paranoics bind together their projected fears and justify their own aggression toward some tangible target they have previously been unable to identify.[75] That was but one reason why the West became the feared Soviet bogeyman in the immediate postwar era.

A hypervigilant if not paranoid approach may also prove to be a highly adaptive style with which to relate to one's potential enemies—particularly during periods of social disruption such as war. Moreover, preoccupation with small details and incessant questioning lend credence to paranoics' reputation for being businesslike and astute. Their speech is both goal directed and logical, even if some of their premises are manifestly false.[76] They would like others to believe that they are convincing and in control, simply because control of their environment is essential to their well-being. That is why a delusional system becomes paradoxically therapeutic.

Whether one chooses to embrace Bychowski's hypothetical construct relating paranoia to primitive societies or feels more comfortable with theories of "delusional systems" or "pseudocommunities," few can deny that Stalin epitomized what would be identified today as a classic paranoid personality. Though that condition in its early stages is said to be distinct from such causes for paranoia as an evolving organic brain syndrome, the two in time may become interdependent. It was precisely the union of the two after 1945, with Stalin's rapidly accelerating hypertensive cerebrovascular disease, that contributed to his unpredictable and at times potentially explosive behavior.

In both a literal and a figurative sense, refractory high blood pressure lay at the heart of Josef Stalin's deterioration. Yet the impact of that disease process on his brain has failed to capture the attention of historians and psychoanalysts alike. Long-standing hypertension causes premature aging—and aging, in the end, magnifies character. Less resilient to change, the elderly become caricatures of themselves over time. It is within this context that such a one-time admirer as Djilas could have become so disillusioned with Stalin's increasing paranoia that he believed his leader was "bordering on the senile." As if to solidify the case, Khrushchev drew attention to Stalin's rapidly failing memory after the war. Now unable to recall the names even of some of his closest associates, Stalin invariably became "very much unnerved" when such slips of memory occurred. Above all, his increasing vulgarity of speech and manners, "the primitive rudeness of his behavior," marked him as a rapidly aging man.[77]

Prone to excess in everything he did, the rapidly aging premier's morbid obsessions were given such free reign that it was difficult for him to assign anything but the most vile and base motives to Western activity in postwar Europe. While his own doctor (before an untimely death at the hand of his feared patient) had already perceived Stalin as a "victim of mania of grandeur and persecution" long before the outbreak of World War II,[78] a few of his later physicians may have recognized that the premier's increasingly compromised health thereafter had much to do with this deterioration in his character. Yet few survived to offer an opinion. That is why Bychowski, as a layman, can be forgiven for failing to acknowledge that underlying disease accounted, in part, for this transformation. As he himself put it: "I am not aware of any new material that might significantly add to an understanding [of Stalin's personality]."[79] As for Cold War diplomacy itself, the genesis of that personality proved to be not nearly so relevant as its accentuation, the result of hypertension on the aging process as Josef Stalin's biologic clock began to run down.

In time, new information did surface, most notably in the diaries of N. Romano-Petrova and the revelations of Stalin's daughter.[80] Khrushchev bared the facts to the entire world in his celebrated "secret" speech of 1956, which, for all its self-serving motivations, only confirmed the suspicions of Bychowski and others. "Everywhere and in everything,"

Khrushchev recalled, "Stalin saw 'enemies,' 'double-dealers and spies.'
. . . The negative characteristics of his [personality] developed steadily
and during the last years acquired an absolutely insufferable character."
Above all, he had become "capricious, irritable and brutal." What
Khrushchev concluded to be a "persecution mania" reached "unbe-
lievable dimensions" before Stalin died.[81] For his part, Bychowski had
been perceptive enough to describe his premier as early as 1948 as "a
criminal paranoic of the type described by the French classic school
of psychiatry—the 'persecuted persecutor.'"[82] If both Bychowski and
Khrushchev were at least descriptively correct, they still lacked enough
medical information to implicate an underlying disease that magnified
the psychiatric condition they had identified so well.

This is all to say that until the release of Stalin's autopsy report the
medical record was unknown and that subsequently (with one notable
exception)[83] no physician has sought to link its findings to Stalin's
personality. Tying physical health to psychiatric disease is long overdue, not only when specifically applied to Stalin but as it applies to
leaders in general, for hypertension and aging share with virtually all
afflictions the dubious distinction of transcending national boundaries.
Just as certain tragic elements of Woodrow Wilson's character can be
shown to have sharpened under the duress of hypertension and cerebrovascular disease in the aftermath of the first world war,[84] a perceptible accentuation of the worst aspects of Josef Stalin's personality
became apparent, in part, as a result of the same at the close of the
second. Though both leaders were on the winning side of wars that were
truly international in scope, they were losing very personal battles at
home to an identical disease.

The irony is compounded by the realization that Stalin's ally-in-
arms, Franklin D. Roosevelt, lost his own individual struggle on the
same account; had he not, subsequent U.S. history might well have
been different. Schlesinger has highlighted the lasting significance of
FDR's death at such a pivotal time: "Roosevelt retained a certain capacity to influence Stalin to the end. . . . It is in this way that the death of
Roosevelt was crucial—not in the vulgar sense that his policy was then
reversed by his successor, which did not happen, but in the sense that no
other American could hope to have the restraining impact on Stalin
which Roosevelt might for a while have had."[85]

Little wonder that revisionist historians who have already taken
offense at the more traditional views of the emerging Cold War that
Schlesinger and others have presented may have difficulty accepting a
new thesis that seems to smack of medical reductionism. Yet some
extrapolation might help to reconcile the two disparate views. Whereas
some revisionists have argued that the United States used its superior

status as a "weapon" to compel compliance with American positions,[86] the medical record may add to our understanding as to why, at least in part, Josef Stalin responded to the challenge as he did. Beyond a doubt, more than a few American diplomatic maneuvers were responsible for triggering some reprehensible Soviet actions. If it is also true that Truman's foreign policy was often "haughty, expansionist, and uncompromising," the question remains as to just how "flexible" Soviet policy was in the immediate postwar years: whereas some revisionists assert that Truman "failed to orient eastern Europe toward the United States,"[87] it now seems obvious that Stalin forbade that region the chance to become so oriented.

If it might also be argued that American diplomacy was "self-consciously expansionist,"[88] none perceived this more than Josef Stalin. By 1945, that perception and others were distorted by more than their fair share of paranoia in all matters, however aggressive U.S. intentions proved to be. In that sense, the traditionalist perhaps had the final word, at least insofar as the neurologist or psychiatrist has come to understand the Georgian Bear. As Schlesinger points out: "A revisionist fallacy has been to treat Stalin as just another Realpolitik statesman, as Second World War revisionists see Hitler as just another Stresemann or Bismarck. But the record makes it clear that in the end nothing could satisfy Stalin's paranoia."[89]

Whether or not the Cold War was truly unpreventable hinges on much larger and weightier issues than a medically oriented thesis can hope to address. Yet there is more than an element of truth in the assertion that any analysis leaving out past Russian history, the intransigence of Leninist ideology, the sinister dynamics of a totalitarian society, and the madness of Stalin is obviously incomplete. It has been the intent of this study to define his "madness" in a less perjorative and more medically precise sense. For the neurotic premier was not altogether mad, nor—for all the manifest changes in his personality—was he overtly senile. Yet Josef Stalin was most assuredly paranoid. And that quality, arguably accentuated by hypertension and artherosclerosis, imbued the divisions that separated the two former allies with what one scholar termed the "apocalyptic potentiality" that we all lived with throughout the Cold War.[90]

CHAPTER 5

Woodrow Wilson: Paralyzed Prophet

Perhaps the lingering nightmare of the Cold War (and most assuredly the hot one that preceded it) had its origins in both irony and tragedy as early as 1920, once the United States Senate had failed to ratify the Versailles Treaty ending World War I. Ironic, because this was precisely the period when Bolshevism, intoxicated by a recent revolution that effectively removed Russia from the war, turned its back on Europe and its attention toward the motherland, intent upon consolidating its tenuous gains. And tragic, because America had just as effectively removed itself from the game of governance in world affairs by rejecting entry into the League of Nations. True, events in Russia were probably well beyond the reach of the victorious, if beleaguered and exhausted, Allies—with or without Woodrow Wilson's cherished League. Yet the tragedy remains that these two slumbering leviathans on the world stage left Europe to fend for itself during an era that would shortly usher in yet another unstable dictator.

What also marked that misguided turn of events with pathos was Wilson's self-defeating behavior during the Senate deliberations, which left his reputation in question and his New World Order in shambles. For Wilson had the most important political and diplomatic victory of his career at his fingertips, had he but chosen to accommodate those senators who favored ratification of the treaty with reservations. That much is unassailable history.

If some writers have already offered compelling psychological reasons for Wilson's refusal to yield, subsequent revelations in the medical record compel a second opinion as to why poor health dictated his behavior, at least in part.[1] That the same three words—irony, tragedy, and pathos—time and again characterized Wilson's last two years in office is agreed to by all. And each devolved from the stricken president himself, whose character has been rigorously dissected by psychoanalytically inclined scholars. The best among them, Alexander and Juliette George, published a landmark work in 1956 depicting Wilson as

a man forever struggling with inner conflicts that arose from his childhood, largely at the hand of a strict, if well-intentioned, father.[2]

To date, few have taken exception to their engaging thesis, defended
as it was with felicitous detail at a time when psychohistory was
maturing into an accepted discipline. One who did, however, happened
to be the recognized doyen of Wilson scholarship, Arthur S. Link of
Princeton University. And for good reason. As the Georges themselves
acknowledge in their revised edition of *Woodrow Wilson and Colonel
House,* a sizable portion of critical materials being edited for the Wilson
Papers had remained unexamined by them when their book had first
went to press.[3] Adhering instead to Edwin Weinstein's view that a series
of strokes had more to do with Wilson's perplexing behavior than his
psychosocial background, Link was on solid footing that befit the wisdom of a scholar who had already painstakingly reconstructed some
fifty-six volumes of primary Wilsonian sources.[4]

Subsequent publication of later sources has done nothing to weaken
Link's position. True, much of what the Georges and their allies have to
say provides a valuable framework upon which to reconstruct Wilson's
evolving character as he prematurely aged. Yet it is the pervasiveness
and depth of deterioration resulting from a diseased brain that marked
Wilson, in the end, as a tragically flawed leader. For this is precisely
what the primary sources from volumes 58 through 65 of the Wilson
Papers reveal in no uncertain terms. The complete record now affirms
that both his personal behavior and presidential conduct were adversely
affected by the inroads of a progressive illness that culminated with a
major stroke in 1919 at the height of the crisis.

To begin with, there is no longer any doubt that Wilson suffered
from severe hypertension long before he became president in 1913. That
this condition was hardly inconsequential is confirmed by the documentation of well-advanced vascular disease of his retina on that account as early as 1906. It would be overstating the case, however, to
accept one historian's assertion that "Wilson should never have been
nominated in 1912," given his "medical history of strokes and atherosclerosis."[5] That ignores the president's formidable achievements
during his two terms in office—not to mention no such medical history
was known to anyone prior to 1912, much less accepted by all later
scholars. Psychologists and neurologists today, however, at least agree
that subtle deterioration of brain function occurring in the hypertensive
patient of long standing (with or without obvious strokes) can highlight
some less desirable attributes of the personality. This accounts in large
measure for why Wilson and the League of Nations both fell victim to
the most self-defeating elements of his character during a crucial period
in American history.

To ignore the psychodynamics of the man as they were dictated, in part, by childhood influences and dysfunctional relationships would do a disservice to those who have so capably identified them. But those alone have not been enough to explain why a man of Wilson's acknowledged intellect and ability could himself later "destroy what he had invested his lifeblood to create" in 1919.[6] Recently published documents suggest that a catalyst added to his psychological ferment precipitated the destructive reaction. Hence the importance of reconstructing Wilson's medical history. For it was precisely the disease-induced blunting of his keen judgment and prodigious memory, on the one hand, and an accentuation of his self-righteousness, intellectual arrogance, and Calvinist life view, on the other, that ultimately unleashed the "demons" goading Wilson.

Long before a relatively complete medical record of the president's failing health was established retrospectively, a physician, Walter Freidlander, suggested that repetitive "small strokes" may have aggravated some of Wilson's more unfortunate character traits. Those often seen in such patients suffering from something called an "organic brain syndrome" included defective control of impulses and emotion. That led, paradoxically, to a perverse magnification of his underlying personality. If the barbs from his political opponents affected Wilson "as the proverbial red flag affects the proverbial bull,"[7] it bears emphasizing that the president's disease-induced egocentricity left him isolated in a treacherous political arena where he was ill suited to fend for either himself or his cause.

Still other equally consequential (and controversial) issues have clouded the last two years of Wilson's presidency. One involves the matter of presidential disability and Dr. Cary Grayson's role in orchestrating an alleged cover-up of his patient's final stroke. Some have assumed that limited medical knowledge of the day precluded a precise diagnosis. In light of recent revelations, that view is now untenable. Others assert that Grayson was on solid ground in withholding information for fear it might have been misinterpreted or prove politically damaging for the president. This brings to mind the larger issue of restricting the public's right to know and whether the nation's best interests were served by so doing. That Wilson was impaired in the medical sense and disabled in a constitutional sense—and that his physician and closest associates knew it—is now a matter of record. Both had singular implications for the Senate's rejection of the Versailles Treaty and, ultimately, the fate of the League of Nations.

To pick up the story in the middle of its most important chapter, Wilson had ventured to the Paris Peace Conference in January 1919, tragically unaware of both his mortgaged future and that of the nation-state system he sought to reconstruct. Yet in the final analysis, his tireless efforts there reflected little of the progressive neurologic deterioration that would become so apparent during the following spring and summer. That statement itself signifies a revision of previous accounts (including my own) depicting a seriously ill president making numerous concessions to the French premier, Georges Clemenceau, and thereby compromising the treaty's legitimacy in the eyes of American opponents.[8] To argue the point requires a proper understanding of Wilson's underlying medical condition.

Once untreated hypertension reaches an accelerated phase, untoward effects on the body's blood vessels occur, such that retinal hemorrhages and scarring appear, soon to be followed by intractable headaches, congestive heart failure, renal insufficiency, and strokes. The first manifestation of malignant hypertension was documented by Wilson's opthalmologist six years before his patient assumed the presidency. That thirteen further years of this untreated disorder would eventually lead to overt multiple organ-system failure in 1919 should come as no surprise.

To be sure, subtle alterations in brain function may occur long before such physical changes appear. Recognizing their limitations, victims revert to familiar themes and modes of behavior that served them well in healthier times. That is to say, they become caricatures of themselves, just as Wilson did during the latter half of his second term. Yet like many patients with high blood pressure, he also appears to have suffered a series of small strokes through the years on the basis of hypertension's effects on small penetrating blood vessels deep within the brain on both sides. That led to a perceptible degree of dementia as defined retrospectively by specific medical criteria. These changes were obvious to every medical observer following Wilson's severe, large-vessel, atherosclerotically induced stroke in October 1919 but were arguably manifest even before he ventured to Paris the preceding December.

Criteria for establishing a diagnosis of dementia, or organic brain syndrome, include (1) cognitive changes that interfere with occupational or social obligations; (2) memory impairment; and (3) impaired abstract thinking, faulty judgment, and behavioral aberrations.[9] Bear in mind that these changes do not occur overnight, nor are obvious strokes required to account for them. In that sense, perhaps too much emphasis has been placed on the postulated occurrence of the latter, their arguable identification as lacunar infarcts notwithstanding.[10]

Knowledgeable contemporary observers in fact believed that a significant turn for the worse in Wilson's behavior was already apparent a year and a half before the Paris Peace Conference. In August 1917 the president confided to Secretary of War Newton D. Baker that he was becoming absentminded and his memory "leaky." A year later, Supreme Court Justice Louis D. Brandeis bemoaned the fact that Wilson's judgment was no longer infallible. Before that time, he had been a "bold and imaginative leader"; now he was doing things that were "unnatural" for him.[11] That Wilson became increasingly reclusive, suspicious, and defensive perhaps accounts as much as anything for the "glacial disdain" he showed for the interpersonal aspects of his conduct in office from that point forward.[12]

For example, from the time the armistice was declared, Wilson sought to eliminate his opposition from any participation in the impending peace conference by appointing to the American Commission in Paris men he believed would support his position without question. He became less discreet in his personal criticism of opponents and supporters alike and dismissed unwelcome advice. Moreover, Wilson downplayed unpleasant political realities, including the repudiation of his appeal to the voters to send only Democrats to Congress in the off-year November elections of 1918, and the vindictive mandates that his negotiating allies brought with them to the bargaining table. Equally telling, his relative disdain for detail and limited preparation before going to Paris reflected a noteworthy change in one who had prided himself on being so precise and methodical.

If an obvious loss of the president's ability to abstract would not become manifest until after his return from Paris, other signs of cognitive compromise began to appear well before the conference. Issues for Wilson became black and white. Allies were transformed into adversaries. Abstract morality drew the sword against the self-interest and balance-of-power considerations he anticipated meeting there. For him, the League was now all that mattered. Yet he failed to appreciate that his perception of it cut both ways: either the League as Wilson perceived it would be too supranational for the Senate to accept, or else it would be rendered impotent by the pious idealism underpinning it.[13]

Certain changes that occur are recognized only in retrospect as nascent manifestations of a condition that later becomes obvious with time. Wilson's behavior during the period encompassing the Paris Peace Conference underscores that fact. Such sufferers become increasingly self-absorbed and exhibit a lowered threshold for frustration. This was particularly characteristic of Wilson during the last week of March and came to a head during a serious viral illness that he suffered in early April. They also show less respect for and insensitivity to the opinions and feelings of others—a quality that French Premier Clemenceau, British Prime Minister David Lloyd George, and the later German delegation were exposed to, not to mention Secretary of State Robert

Lansing throughout the conference and Wilson's personal adviser, Colonel Edward House, during its latter half.

Some dementia victims tend to harbor unwarranted suspicions; Wilson remained to the end as suspicious of alleged French spies as he later became of advice from his most trusted subordinates. Still others indulge in impulsive acts as a substitute for intuitive reflection; Wilson's compulsion to tie up loose ends at the conference within a ten-day time limit in April prompted his insistence that participants hurriedly sign a memorandum on the Kaiser's war guilt shortly after inexplicably reversing himself on the same isue.[14] The president's refusal to deal with specifics may also in retrospect betray an incipient dementia sufferer's inattention to detail. Those who are so afflicted cling to more familiar themes to disguise both this and the loss of memory that goads them. Hence Wilson's belief that the League Covenant and the League's existence would in themselves suffice to overcome obstacles he refused to confront on a point-by-point basis.

Not that these and other features of an evolving organic brain syndrome necessarily translate into compromised leadership or negotiating skills. Changes in cognition, abstraction, and memory occur relative to the individual's prior intellectual capacity—and few would deny that Wilson's capacities were formidable. Gifted persons may well function adequately enough in the early going to match wits with those of lesser caliber. Perhaps that accounts for the failure of Wilson's associates (and many later scholars) to recognize the subtle changes overcoming him during the Paris Peace Conference. Although he was prostrated by illness on at least two separate occasions while there, for the most part the president remained an effective leader and negotiator throughout the proceedings. This hardly negates the dementia thesis, as Wilson fulfilled virtually every criterion of its earliest manifestations while still in Paris. Yet to argue his effectiveness requires a brief reexamination of the issues that confronted the president.

Wilson returned to the United States in February after securing acceptance of his much-beloved Covenant in Paris. He had exercised enough flexibility to amend the Covenant in order to promote some measure of domestic jurisdiction in League disputes, assure recognition of the Monroe Doctrine, secure the right of the United States to withdraw from the League if necessary, and implicitly limit the council's power to issue a legally binding order of military intervention on its members.[15] Despite Wilson's critics, who found much of political value in arguing each of these points to the contrary, he was not so compromised at this juncture as to preclude his taking the opposition's concerns into account.

That attitude began to change once the president had returned to

Paris in March and the conference entered its "dark period." Intimations of things to come occurred on April 3, when Wilson was felled by a brief but debilitating viral illness during which he suffered a fever-induced delirium. Although a precise diagnosis of influenza is debatable, the illness undoubtedly accelerated his neurologic decline. For fever in and of itself frequently induces transient confusion in older people, particularly those already suffering from underlying cerebrovascular disease or organic brain syndromes. Moreover, the intensity of the delirium seems less dependent on the height of the fever than upon psychogenic factors related to the preexisting personality.[16] That is why Wilson's "temperamental defects," to which all scholars have alluded, may have had more to do with his literally feverish state of mind at the time than his critics have been willing to admit.

That Wilson failed to demonstrate overt disorders of perception, inappropriate behavior, or lapses in judgment during the Peace Conference itself is hardly proof that a delirium did not occur. Its manifestations are characteristically worse at night; indeed, the most common form of delirium in older patients is the so-called "nocturnal confusion" or "sundowning." Hence the significance of Dr. Grayson's discreet comment that Wilson suffered two "very restless nights" during his illness, and another close associate's observation that he had never known the president to be "in such a difficult frame of mind as he is now" or that "even while lying in bed he manifests peculiarities."[17]

The identification of a delusional state, like a diagnosis of dementia, rests on specific criteria—all of which Wilson met during his four-day febrile illness. That is important simply because delirium may accelerate the process of dementia in a predisposed individual—which Wilson was, on account of his far-advanced hypertensive cerebrovascular disease. Many such persons in fact fail to return to their prior level of function.[18] And that is precisely what Wilson's valet, Irwin Hoover, intimated when he recalled that "the President was never the same after this little spell of sickness."[19]

Given the wide range of compromises reached during a two-week period surrounding Wilson's illness, can the disease be said to have adversely affected the president's judgment? Much to the medical reductionist's surprise, the weight of the evidence on such key issues as reparations, occupation of the Rhineland, surrendering the Saar coal mines to the French and formulating a mutual security treaty with them suggests that few of Wilson's principles (or the interests of the United States) were compromised. In point of fact, Wilson appears to have wrested as much as he had a right to expect from Clemenceau in exchange for the "essentials" of the Covenant and the League. To argue otherwise not only ascribes too much to an isolated disease but ignores the primary sources as they reflect Wilson's previously espoused positions.

Despite some disturbing implications for his future health, Wilson had not suffered a stroke in early April, as at one time was alleged.[20] The same cannot be said for a second, less-publicized illness later that month: on April 28 he suffered a small stroke that affected his right arm. In his consulting physician's convoluted prose, this "made of him a changling with a very different personality and a markedly lessened ability."[21] As one measure of his (transient) disability, Wilson began to write with his unaffected left hand.[22] Regardless of the stroke's impact on the conference itself (which seems minor, except for the postulation that the president may have been "in a daze and did not know what was going on" when on May 1 he inexplicably allowed a change in the wording concerning the Kaiser's guilt),[23] the incident is significant insofar as it substantiates the impression that Wilson's hypertension was now out of control.

For one thing, a number of associates noted thereafter how tired and worn Wilson appeared; Dr. Grayson himself admitted a day after the stroke that these were "terrible days for the President physically and otherwise."[24] For another, his memory seems to have undergone a precipitate decline. Baker was perplexed to find a man of Wilson's formidable recall reading over his cherished Fourteen Points to refresh his memory! Indeed, on May 3 the president admitted to being too tired to remember the day's events.[25] A deficient memory may also have accounted for one of his worst speeches on record six days later. In midsentence he lost his train of thought and fell back on an oft repeated metaphor about the "light streaming upon the path ahead, and nowhere else."[26] That is typical of aging individuals, who characteristically resurrect familiar themes or well-rehearsed vignettes to disguise their inability to shift reflectively in their thinking.

That inability may also account, in part, for a perceptible hardening of Wilson's attitude against further compromise. It was as if, a month before, the president had crossed his last bridge of conciliation; he had gone as far as diplomatic realities could push him. If both illnesses accentuated the most tragic elements of Wilson's character, as seems apparent, that is because they were superimposed on his underlying neurologic condition. In a word, he had become increasingly egocentric. His lofty principles began to shade into prejudice, his strong will into intransigence.

Dr. Edwin Weinstein has synthesized the psychologic and neurologic aspects of Wilson's persona into perhaps the most succinct and proper balance possible: "The *content* of [his] behavioral alterations was closely related to personality and motivational factors . . . [yet] their *occurrence* was a sign of . . . Wilson's underlying brain damage."[27] Charles Seymour, historian and Peace Conference commissioner, now ruefully alluded to the president's "one-track mind." Colonel House was disturbed by his friend's "inflexibility." He was of the opinion that Wilson's "prejudice and self-will" were becoming liabilities, enough so to predispose him to "getting into inextricable situations" in the future.[28] House did not have long to wait to see his worst fears realized once Wilson returned home to meet the opposition in the United States Senate.

The fact of the matter was that between his June 28 departure from Paris and mid-July, Wilson was no longer operating at his normal capacity. The record speaks for itself. Not only did he have difficulty composing his forthcoming speech of July 10, in which he was to present the treaty to the Senate, but he was forever confusing the legal technicalities inherent in the terms "reservations" and "amendments" and the degree to which they would affect the treaty's ratification. No longer willing (or able?) to adapt to new circumstances, he failed to develop any realistic strategy for forming a pro-League, bipartisan coalition in order to assure that the Senate would consent to ratification.

Not that Wilson didn't have the chance. Public sentiment and a clear majority of senators from the beginning were strongly in favor of the concept of a League and its ratification. Fatefully enough, the chairman of the Senate Foreign Relations Committee, Henry Cabot Lodge, knew this. More fateful still, he had harbored an intense dislike of Wilson for years and had his own presidential ambitions to consider. Recognizing that he simply did not have the votes to defeat ratification initially, Lodge proceeded slowly and deliberately to influence public and senatorial opinion against the treaty. The strategy was nothing if not brilliant. Lodge had no inclination to beat down the treaty with a frontal assault; rather, he counted on Wilson to play into his hand through the "indirect method" of reservations.[29] Though Lodge had assumed the mantle of a master psychologist, he had no way of knowing just how compromised his adversary had now become.

As if to underscore his decline, Wilson suffered yet another physical setback on July 19. Inexplicably, Grayson hustled his patient aboard the presidental yacht *Mayflower* for a cruise, despite warnings of an impending storm and despite the doctor's official diagnosis of "dysentery"[30]— for which being whisked out of the capital onto stormy waters seems hardly a suitable treatment. Perhaps Grayson was only warming to the public relations task before him, given Wilson's prior medical history. At any rate, on his return the president was still too ill to tend to business and canceled all appointments. That, coupled with his subsequent collapse in October, only strengthens the suspicion that he may have suffered a second small stroke in mid-July.

Perhaps the most outwardly visible sign of Wilson's progressive neurologic compromise during July and August was his increasingly suspect memory. In response to Lodge's inquiry on July 22 as to whether arrangements for the distribution of reparations had been agreed upon at Paris, the president denied any knowledge of them—though it turned out that he had already drafted a letter to Lodge on the very subject.[31] In like manner, on August 4 he denied having received any protests from members of the American Commission against the controversial Shantung settlement, yet at the same time was planning to send Lodge a copy of a letter that registered one commissioner's displeasure in no uncertain terms.[32] In another letter to Lodge just two days later, Wilson again erred, both in denying having any formal drafts of the Covenant except "that presented by the American commissioners" (who in fact had never presented one) and in insisting that there were no exant records of the commission proceedings.[33]

To make matters worse, Wilson's increasingly irascible nature and petulance were now given free rein. On August 8 alone he characterized one of House's disclosures as "amazing and deeply disturbing," lambasted Rumania for acting in a "perfectly outrageous manner," and threatened to withdraw the French Security Treaty. Three days later he reacted vehemently against Lansing's advice to consider compromise with the mild reservationists, leading his secretary of state to lament Wilson's inflexibility and defiance.[34] Within the week he considered divorcing America from the League altogether, while vowing in the same breath to send his opponents to Berlin to negotiate a new treaty with Germany themselves should they succeed in emasculating his own.[35]

It was at this juncture that Wilson met with members of the Senate Foreign Relations Committee in an extensive give-and-take discussion. Not surprisingly, he stumbled through at least sixteen overt errors, misrepresentations, and self-contradictions during the three-hour interview on August 19. Whether in recalling dates of what happened in Paris, what documents he did or did not possess, or simply forgetting some of the treaty itself, Wilson's memory was consistently faulty.[36] More incriminating still, he failed to perceive either that his performance had been less than exemplary or that he had not changed any of the senator's minds.

By now Wilson was so set in his beliefs that he had become a caricature of his former self. Labeling his opposition "intriguers and robbers,"[37] he threatened to keep the United States out of the League altogether unless he got his way—which he could have had if only he had accommodated the mild reservationists. Yet failing to shift reflectively as changing circumstances dictated, the cornered president refused to bend—despite reminders from virtually everyone that he simply didn't have the votes for ratification without compromise.

To revive an earlier theme, there were touches of irony, pathos, and tragedy in Wilson's behavior during the latter half of 1919. Irony, because Wilson had written years before in his critically acclaimed *Constitutional Government in the United States* that it was the chief executive's "plain duty" to reach an accommodation with the Senate on matters that divided them, rather than to go over its head (as he did in September) with an appeal to the people.[38] Pathos, because his decision to turn his back on what he had once perceived to be a president's solemn obligation was less the result of rational calculation than of disordered thinking. And tragedy because Wilson had unwittingly written his own epitaph as early as 1890 when he singled out "uncompromising thought [as] the luxury of the closeted recluse."[39] If the slings and arrows of outrageous fortune would thrust Wilson into that very predicament some thirty years later following his final stroke in October 1919, his premorbid mind set had already betrayed such instincts long before—as Senator Lodge, at least, was well aware when he had set his tactically flawless trap.

Lodge's prescience was further vindicated once the failing president chose to go on a speaking tour in September to defend the treaty. That decision in itself was made in anger and bordered on the irrational.[40] Perversely egocentric by then, Wilson challenged the Senate not to reach an accommodation but to prepare for a fight. Impervious to all advice, he vowed to give his opponents "a belly-full," ignoring both his own tenuous health and the consequences of his absence from Washington for a month. Although it was obvious to everyone else that the battle for the treaty was to be waged in the Senate and not out on the hustings, they also recognized that Wilson had already mortgaged much of his influence in all quarters. That was enough for Lansing to concede that his president was no longer likely to be listened to as he had been in the past.[41]

As if to lend credence to Lansing's surmise that Wilson was compromising both himself and his office at that time, essays in the Wilson *Papers* and elsewhere have applied guidelines routinely employed by physicians today to quantitate the president's impairment in September 1919 on a percentage basis.[42] Such a determination entails making a clear distinction between the terms "impairment" and "disability." Whereas impairment is solely related to the health status of the individual, disability can be determined only within the context of occupational requirements that he or she is unable to meet as a result of that impairment.[43] Wilson was at the very least medically impaired during the summer and fall, even before his October stroke; recent evidence suggests that he may have been disabled in the constitutional sense as well.

To argue the point requires an understanding of those criteria that a neuropsychologist would apply to any person suffering enough brain dysfunction to affect his or her social or occupational conduct. One standard that has withstood the test of time relates to the failure of the individual to utilize what is known as the "abstract attitude," resulting in an inability to (1) shift reflectively as circumstances change; (2) account for personal acts or thoughts; (3) keep in mind various aspects of a task to its completion; (4) grasp the essential parts of a given whole; (5) learn from previous experience; (6) accept what is, and is not, possible; and (7) detach the ego from interpersonal conflict.[44] No doubt the psychologist would point out that Wilson brought a few of these liabilities with him to the White House. What catches the eye, however, is the pervasiveness of all of them once his physiologic compromise accelerated.

With regard to the first, Wilson's perception of the treaty and the League was set in stone from the moment he left Paris. He simply failed to acknowledge what others told him of the necessity to shift his focus toward gaining the best possible compromise once the opposition began to coalesce. Although the mild reservationists could hardly believe that Wilson would remain blind to the fact that they were offering their president a way out of Lodge's trap, he seemed perversely incapable of shifting reflectively to any point of view outside his own.

Virtually all of Wilson's associates were perplexed and dismayed by the president's inability to account for why he thought and acted as he did during the summer and fall. True, to a great extent he had always possessed the artist's temperament, preferring to work alone.[45] Yet he had never totally isolated himself to the extent that he did following his break with House in the spring of 1919. Wilson had always resented the intrusions of others into matters that he reserved for himself—and somewhere in the halls of Versailles, Colonel House had finally crossed the line. If it is also true, as others have surmised, that Wilson always acted as if he "must fight to have his way,"[46] he never satisfactorily explained why he felt it necessary. Nor could he render a convincing account of himself to others in a more literal sense when the time came to report what had happened in Paris, as his performance before the Senate Foreign Relations Committee in August sadly attests.

Wilson's faulty memory betrayed him on so many occasions that he was forever asking his associates to send him memoranda of their prior discussions so he could keep in mind details of the task before him. His amnesia, at first selective and later pervasive, occasionally led to some embarrassing and inexplicable gaffes. The most obvious was a nineteen-day delay in informing the Senate of the French Security Treaty, which he simply appeared to have forgotten to mention upon his return from Paris. That made the task before him even more difficult, as Senate opponents and supporters alike questioned his motives in not revealing it earlier.

Wilson's failure to grasp the essentials of a given whole was nowhere more apparent than in his inability to distinguish Lodge and the irreconcilables from the mild reservationists. His paranoia fostered the delusion that "the given whole" was none other than a monolithic Republican party, embodied in the person of Senator Lodge. Nor was it at all certain that the "whole" of the problem was an inevitable renegotiation of the entire treaty should even mildly distasteful reservations be accepted, a position from which Wilson never wavered despite its unsubstantiated premise.

Evoking prior experiences with an eye to learning from them likewise proved increasingly difficult for the beleaguered president. How else to explain his turning a deaf ear to the results of the off-year election "referendum" of 1918, not to mention his misdirected appeal to the Italian people in April 1919 concerning its government's controversial claims in the Adriatic? Wilson's decision five months later to take his case for the League to the American public over the head of the Senate seems equally irrational (if not tragically consistent) and proved just as futile in the end. Having set his course, he would accept nothing short of total victory on his terms, reflecting an inability to distinguish the possible from the impossible. If that also reflected Wilson's lifelong "refusal to yield to interference in that sphere of authority in which [he] sought compensatory gratification,"[47] his premature aging had something to do with magnifying this characteristic in the long run.

Finally, and most painfully obvious to his associates, Wilson was never able to divorce his ego from the issues at hand. At one point in the Senate conflict he was asked: "Do you never think yourself wrong?" To which Wilson responded with typical egocentricity: "Not in matters where I have qualified myself to speak."[48] That self-fulfilling prophecy betrayed his unwillingness to consult when matters became emotionally charged, for Wilson loathed exposing himself to potential criticism. It also bespoke a pathologic augmentation of his character. Under the duress of accelerated brain aging, the president's most undesirable traits were unmasked—and his ego, arguably, most of all.

When Wilson embarked on the western speaking tour in early September, only his physician and a handful of his closest associates were aware that their president was seriously ill. Yet even later scholars little inclined to gauge the impact of his illness acknowledge that Wilson had been suffering severe headaches as early as the month before. Grayson himself alluded to them during the tour on at least nine separate occasions, the last of which—just prior to the president's collapse in Pueblo, Colorado, on September 25—he described as being "so splitting" that Wilson "could hardly see."[49] That, coupled with his small stroke in Paris and his documented retinal disease, is more than enough to substantiate that Wilson's hypertension had reached a fulminant, or "malignant," stage. Added to this alarming medical history were eight separate references to "congestion" and nightly coughing spells that prevented Wilson from sleeping. On September 26 these telltale signs of congestive heart failure reached crisis proportions; indeed, Grayson's diary entry just the day before provides a classic description of that condition.[50]

Moreover, the president had experienced at least two separate stroke warnings during the trip before his overt breakdown occurred in early October. Grayson had been the first to notice "a curious drag or looseness of the left side" of Wilson's mouth, which he recognized to be "a sign of danger that could no longer be obscured."[51] Even the press correspondents sensed a problem, once the president's speeches became uncharacteristically repetitive and rambling. One later news release alluded to an ill-defined "fatigue neurosis" that was said to have "affected the nerves of one of his arms and to have been responsible for a twitching of the muscles of his face."[52]

While the latter had nothing to do with the massive stroke Wilson suffered a week later (he suffered from a chronic—and classic—case of hemifacial spasm),[53] it now seems clear that a transient ischemic attack occurred on September 26. Though Grayson found his patient to be suffering terribly and in "a highly nervous condition" early that morning, he made no mention of a temporary paralysis of Wilson's left arm, to which both Mrs. Wilson and Joseph P. Tumulty later alluded.[54] To make matters worse, the cumulative strain on Wilson's heart and an apparent acceleration of his hypertension were such that the president himself remorsefully volunteered that he "had gone to pieces." On balance, Wilson's collapse on September 26 was far more than "a nervous reaction in his digestive organs," as Grayson proclaimed.[55] The stroke five days later amply confirms in retrospect the occurrence of a transient ischemic attack induced by hypertensive cerebrovascular disease.

That raises two heretofore unanswered questions: what did Grayson really know, and how candid was he in his revelations to the public that he also served? Insofar as he at least recognized this convergence of symptoms as a portentous development, Grayson's ministrations to the president (and the appropiate restrictions he placed upon him) reflect well on the man as a treating physician. Yet it was left to Ray Stannard Baker and Irwin Hoover to record for posterity that on October 2, after returning to Washington, Wilson had in fact suffered a severe stroke that paralyzed his left side. Despite speculations to that effect in the press, the furthest that Grayson's medical bulletins ever went was to describe Wilson's collapse as "nervous exhaustion," a condition he later upgraded to a "functional," not organic, "fatigue neurosis."[56]

Any suggestion that medical knowledge at the time precluded his arriving at a definitive diagnosis, or that Grayson may have really believed that exhaustion alone was the culprit, is now hard to defend in view of the fact that he knew all along that Wilson had suffered a devastating paralysis.[57] In Grayson's defense, one might assume that as a general practitioner he was merely adhering to the diagnosis of "neurasthenia" rendered by his esteemed neurologic consultant, Dr. Francis X. Dercum. To concude otherwise, then, requires examining the data in some detail in relation to what was known of both neurasthenia and stroke at the time, and Grayson's refusal to affirm publicly any diagnosis other than the former. Once having done that, it remains comforting for the retrospective diagnostician to have at his disposal Grayson's unpublished records, which tell a story very different from anything he ever divulged in his own lifetime.

Textbooks of Grayson's day defined neurasthenia and stroke as two distinctly different entities.[58] The former was believed to be a psychosomatic condition; the latter was attributed to structural damage in the brain. Not only were strokes recognized to be caused by thrombosis or embolism, but those involving the carotid, middle cerebral, and perforating arteries were already so explicitly described in the medical literature that even the general practitioner was expected to know the difference between them and neurasthenia. Above all, the signs and symptoms of vascular disease elsewhere, especially in the heart and retina, were said to "readily clarify the diagnosis" of stroke.[59]

Neurasthenia, on the other hand, was described by textbooks of the day as a "functional neurosis" and was expected to yield readily to "very simple treatment of the nerves," including enforced bed rest and dietary modification. No other disorder was said to produce such multiplicity of symptoms of the *subjective* physical type, among them fatigue, indigestion, palpitations, headaches, and insomnia.[60] No wonder Grayson proposed just such a diagnosis to explain Wilson's collapse in late September; after all, his patient initially had most of those symptoms.

Yet ascribing to a functional neurosis a devastating paralysis six days later ignored the accepted medical precept that precluded a diagnosis of neurasthenia if an organic disease of the brain was present. When Dercum himself referred to neurasthenia after examining Wilson on October 3, he took great pains to emphasize that he had "merely confirmed Dr. Grayson's diagnosis," and not the other way around.[61] Dercum never publicly commented on Wilson's illness again. As perhaps the most eminent neurologist of his day, he could hardly have failed to recognize that Wilson was now paralyzed. And as an acknowledged authority on neurasthenia himself, Dercum obviously knew the difference between that entity and a stroke; indeed, he wrote out the latter diagnosis in very precise terms two weeks into Wilson's illness, a copy of which has recently been uncovered in Dr. Grayson's files. Yet the closed-lipped Grayson went to his grave without ever acknowledging that.

The dearth of revealing public statements notwithstanding, there is now no doubt that on October 2 Wilson suffered a major stroke that left him permanently paralyzed and cognitively impaired. Its underlying pathogensis entails three possibilities: (1) a thrombosis or rupture of a small, perforating vessel deep within the right side of his brain—of the sort that may have repeatedly taken place as early as 1896 and as late as April 1919; (2) a blood clot under the brain cover known as a "subdural hematoma," which could have resulted from Wilson's fall at the time of his collapse; or (3) an occlusion of the right carotid or middle cerebral arteries that supply the superficial cortex of the brain.

The last seems the most plausible, if for no other reason that that was the diagnosis Dercum himself arrived at from his painstakingly detailed and recorded examination. On October 20, 1919, and only after several further examinations, Dr. Dercum submitted to Dr. Grayson what he described as a "final and complete" revised statement regarding Wilson's medical condition:

> THE DIAGNOSIS made on October 2 and confirmed at the subsequent examinations was that of a severe organic hemiplegia, probably due to a thrombosis of the middle cerebral artery of the right hemisphere. . . . At the time of the first consultation, the diagnosis was communicated to Mrs. Wilson and Miss Margaret Wilson. The subsequent course of the case revealed the hemiplegia to be persistent. Notwithstanding, because of the improvement noted at various times, *Dr. Grayson* thought it wise to issue general statements only [emphasis added].[62]

Wilson's impairment, then, was profound, was for all intents and purposes permanent, and involved those portions of the brain most commonly affected by a large-vessel occlusion. Small-vessel strokes of the lacunar type are rarely so devastating or permanent; moreover, deficits accruing from a blood clot overlying the brain seldom evolve so rapidly after a blow to the head—and there is no doubt that Wilson's paralysis came on suddenly.

Regardless of the precise etiology of his stroke, the president's condition remained shrouded in mystery for the remainder of his term. Whether Grayson or Mrs. Wilson was responsible for that is unclear, though the preponderant evidence seems to implicate the president's wife in the decision to withhold any damaging medical information. What *is* clear is that for at least the first three months of his illness Wilson was disabled in both the medical and the constitutional senses of the word: he was unable to carry out the duties of his office effectively—if at all.

Bear in mind that, retrospectively, the president already warranted an impairment rating of from 15 to 45 percent of the whole person during the summer and early fall.[63] After his stroke, not only was Wilson unable to perform most activities of daily living at a level even approaching his previous norm, but he was forbidden to do so. That equates by today's standards with an additional 15 percent impairment. Disturbances in the use of language, a second criterion used to compute neurologic impairment, have been elaborately detailed in Weinstein's neuropsychological treatment of Wilson and warrant, at the very least, a 15 percent rating.[64] Third, Wilson's nervous anxiety and burgeoning paranoia so far exceeded the lowest level of "emotional disturbances under stress" as to equate with a further 15 percent impairment. Finally, his paralysis fits the criterion of focal neurologic disturbances to the letter, with their own specified percentages of impairment. Most important of all, percentages from separate categories are *additive* in arriving at a final figure, attesting to the sobering conclusion that the stricken president would be labeled today as well above a 50 percent level of impairment of the whole person![65]

The salient point to address from the historical perspective, of course, is the impact of Wilson's impairment on his conduct in office: that is, his disability. For the treaty fight in the Senate, that impact was immense. To solidify the case, and to demonstrate that the nation's best interests were poorly served while the president's true condition was concealed, requires a closer examination of events following his fateful stroke.

Prior to early February 1920 any role that Wilson's illness may have played in the ratification struggle and a host of other suspended isues relates primarily to his imposed isolation. As access to the president was severely restricted, little was then known of his personal behavior or official conduct. The recently published record now affirms that Wilson failed to act as chief executive in any meaningful sense. His isolation cut both ways: not only was he unable to assess issues in context, given the limited information he received, but his real thoughts on any issue were obscured by those who were writing his responses and memoranda for him—including even a few *to themselves* over the stamp of the president's name.[66]

Any executive matters not deemed urgent by Tumulty or Mrs. Wilson (and even some that were) were pigeonholed, among them the *Imperator* controversy with Great Britain, return of the railroads to private ownership, Italy's claims in the Adriatic, an impending treaty with Turkey, the unstable Mexican situation, and a host of diplomatic appointments. As if to highlight the impasse, when Tumulty himself submitted a list of suspended business to the president as late as December 18, most of the items passed unacknowledged.[67] Secretary of State Robert Lansing convened more than a score of cabinet meetings during the interlude in an attempt to keep the executive branch abreast of its obligations.

As for the treaty fight itself, Wilson's resistance to reservations only hardened in the sludgy amalgam of his imposed isolation. Despite his entourage's attempts to protect the president from disturbing news, Wilson simply had to be informed of Senate minority leader Gilbert Hitchcock's urgent plea on November 18 that he reach an accommodation with the mild reservationists.[68] Now gripped by paranoia, Wilson could not help but feel that even his supporters were abandoning him. That may have led to his refusal to see Hitchcock on November 29, despite Grayson's assertion that there was no medical reason why the president could not have kept the appointment.[69]

Wilson's December declaration of "no concessions and no compromise," then, represented but the tip of the iceberg of his growing intransigence. If Lansing now believed that his own "independence of opinion" and "frankness of expression" displeased the president, Baker and others had recognized all along that Wilson lacked the "compliment of consultation" and the ability to "play upon men's vanities," which were instrumental in gaining desired political ends.[70] That lack, coupled with his increasingly pugnacious temperament, would only multiply the administration's problems in the weeks ahead.

Despite official pronouncements in December that Wilson's "complete recovery was now assured,"[71] the feebleness of the stricken president's attempt to compose his thoughts matched what any neurologist would expect from a recent stroke victim, who has trouble completing tasks that demand sustained attention. All too often, others were obliged to think and act for him. On those few occasions when Wilson did take the initiative, confusion as to his true intent frequently resulted. Even from afar, Colonel House had learned enough from his many visitors to conclude that "the President is in no condition . . . to direct important business."[72] Lansing foresaw as early as mid-December that he would soon be forced to resign, given the "violent passions and exaggerated ego" resulting from Wilson's illness.[73]

How else to explain the president's abortive challenge to the Senate opposition on December 17 to resign their seats and seek reelection on the treaty's ratification? Rather than abandoning this unprecedented idea and seeking an accommodation, Wilson transformed it into a suicidal instrument of partisan politics in his Jackson Day letter.[74] That may have been a reflection of his thinly disguised desire to seek a third term; perhaps he even believed that the treaty's defeat would be in his own best interests, since it would give him an excuse to run again.[75] If so, such a self-serving if pathetic rationalization offers a possible glimpse into the convoluted recesses of Wilson's diseased brain and is quite in keeping with the thought patterns of other victims of dementia, whose ability to appreciate the consequences of their actions is typically diminished.

Whether or not such thinking was truly the product of an "illogical mind," as Lansing believed, few denied that Wilson had painted himself into a corner. Self-righteousness, always a hallmark of the Wilson persona, was only magnified by his illness, highlighting the medical axiom that strokes may induce "a marked and almost grotesque accentuation" of prior personality traits.[76] In any case, all that could be hoped for was a change for the better in the president's condition. As if on cue, Dr. Grayson obliged with a press release predicting that Wilson would be "as well as ever" by February.[77] Others were less sanguine. With Tumulty's list of duties for the president to act upon still unfulfilled by the new year, he gently prodded Wilson at least to change his position on the treaty. That suggestion fell on deaf ears, and Edith Wilson's reply to Tumulty a day later speaks for itself: "The President does not like being told a thing twice."[78]

Although Wilson's increasingly active role by February appeared to fit Grayson's timetable, he was a very different man from the one the people had reelected in 1916. To underscore the public's misperceptions of their leader, Wilson's preeminent editorial supporter, Frank I. Cobb, missed the mark entirely when he asserted that his president would never reject an honest compromise.[79] Those few who knew better (Lodge among them) still failed to understand *why* Wilson acted as he did. Yet once the president became more "visible" in early February, it did not take long for at least the medical experts to form their own opinions as to his inability to lead. Surmising that he had suffered a stroke (which only Wilson's urologist had been willing to admit),[80] a former president of the American Medical Association, Arthur D. Bevan, flatly stated that "under no circumstances" should Wilson be permitted to return to his former duties.[81]

If anything, subsequent events belied the White House party line that "in many ways the President [was] in better shape" than before his illness.[82] A mere three days later Wilson not only peremptorily dismissed Lansing but erred in allowing their private correspondence on the matter to be publicized. He then laid what was by then a typically "unalterable" proposal before a delegation of railroad leaders, and ended the week by issuing to the Allied Supreme Council a "virtual ultimatum" on Italy's "unjust claims."[83] Wilson's critics were less than kind, even if their observations were on the mark. In the captivating prose of one editor, the president's correspondence to Lansing bespoke "the wormwood and gall of the isolated, hermited [and] imperious mind."[84] Even the more supportive *New York Evening Post* asserted that "those always disconcerting qualities of the President's temperament" were now being exaggerated by his illness and consequent isolation.[85] Any neuropsychologist reviewing the evidence today would agree.

Having charged Lansing with insubordination for holding cabinet meetings without the president's knowledge or approval, Wilson failed to acknowledge (or remember) that his secretary of state had informed both Tumulty and Grayson directly, and Wilson indirectly through correspondence, that such meetings were taking place.[86] Not that Wilson's charge concerning Lansing's usurpation of power marked the president as a tyrant, as his displaced subordinate would have posterity believe. It did, however, signify an increasingly rigid and suspicious individual's obsession with controlling his environment. Whether Wilson's actions were "childish" or even "unbelievably stupid," there is little doubt that his behavior bordered on the pathological. He was now acting as much from the heart as the mind, and that, too, is in keeping with a stroke-induced psychosyndrome, of which impaired control of emotions and impulses is said to be the cardinal feature.[87] Perhaps Baker had the last word when he described the way in which Lansing was dismissed as "the petulant and irritable act of a sick man."[88]

Once Wilson resumed speaking and acting for himself in early February, his character defects affected everything he did. If Italy's claims in the Adriatic were indeed unjust, he "intended to resist them to the end, *no matter what the consequences*" for his allies (emphasis added).[89] On February 3, Baker was moved to describe Wilson's disease induced state of mind as "tragic" for a man who was now willing to skewer his brainchild on the horns of his temperamental difficulties. Ruing the "utter confusion" that had existed in the State Department before Lansing's dismissal, Baker blamed it on the president's stubbornness and closed-mindedness.[90]

Wilson's impairment led to some embarrassing displays of emotional lability as well. On February 14 he was reduced to tears upon hearing Homer S. Cummings's effusive peroration of him—only to recover long enough to castigate his opponents for having "disgraced America."[91] (Still later, Wilson broke down in the middle of a story being read to him, while his perplexed son-in-law, Stockton Axton, sought in vain to find something in the text to account for it).[92] Whereas Baker had learned enough of Wilson's peculiar behavior to appreciate how illness could unleash the "ungovernable element of [his] strong nature," Lansing, in his more self-serving style, now dismissed his president as a man who had become unable to control his "warped and distorted passions."[93]

Naturally, Wilson reserved his most flagrant outbursts for his sworn enemies. Despite accepting in principle William H. Taft's draft of a reservation to Article 10 that hardly differed from the opposition's, Wilson exclaimed that "he would see both the treaty and Lodge in Hades" before giving his nemesis the satisfaction of having the reservations labeled in his name.[94] At this stage in his illness, Wilson's distorted logic had convinced him that the political stage was simply too small to accommodate any views other than his own. The same sort of pathologic arrogance compelled him to dismiss even the advice of his few remaining close associates, once he had chosen to shelve the treaty by equating the acceptance of any reservations as a "nullification" of it.[95] In effect, Wilson heard only what he wanted to hear. That precluded granting individual interviews to those senators who were still on the fence, a practice he had dutifully cultivated (albeit with some distaste) the previous summer.

By late February the "splendid attention" that Wilson was allegedly giving affairs of state was as questionable as his ostensible recovery. The *New York Times* openly discussed the impasse in Washington and the responsibility for it of the president's health.[96] If, as he fancied himself, Wilson was the only legitimate peacemaker who placed international stability above the interests of nation and self, why would one commentator speak for the majority of his colleagues in categorizing the president's personally revised and vituperative letter to Hitchcock on March 9 as "another war message?" Even the usually supportive *New York World* was openly critical of Wilson and acknowledged that his rigid stance and bullying methods were "weak and untenable."[97] Whatever his motivations, everyone now recognized that Wilson was a changed man. That alone was enough to assure the treaty's subsequent defeat.

With respect to both his functional impairment and his disability, Woodrow Wilson's medical history can be divided into two periods. The first was roughly a twenty-year interval, up to and through the September speaking tour of 1919, which was characterized by slowly progressive multi-organ system failures on the basis of advanced hypertension. Following his atherosclerosis-induced large-vessel stroke in early October, Wilson's health underwent a more precipitate decline—after which few could deny that his mental faculties and comportment had changed permanently for the worse.

From the strictly neuropsychological perspective, it is not until 1918 that a reduction in what might be termed his "adaptive versatility" can be detected in the primary sources. Individuals suffering such a reduction typically manifest a lower threshold of frustration, are prone to make unwarranted criticisms and judgments, and complain of tiring easily. Unable to adapt to rapidly changing circumstances, they tend to concentrate on one issue at a time in order to reduce their mistakes, yet still pay less attention to detail as they become increasingly self-absorbed. As their memory grows more impaired and their emotions less restrained, they become impervious to advice and insensitive to others' reactions. The complete record now affirms that these qualities characterized Wilson to the letter during the spring and summer months antedating the western tour.

Only during the accelerated phase of cognitive decline are their associates' suspicions confirmed that something is definitely abnormal about the behavior of such persons. That certainly applies to Wilson's conduct in the aftermath of his stroke on October 2, 1919. Yet it is of paramount importance that a major determinant of impairment is one's preexisting ability to adapt, as defined by the underlying personality. And that is why some elements of Wilson's character and lifelong inner conflicts, which others have described, bear reemphasizing. Those who, like Wilson, have more rigidly defined adaptive patterns to begin with usually manifest greater impairment in the long run.[98] This last observation, of course, has singular implications for Wilson's conduct during the final year of his presidency, and perhaps squares the circle of debate into a synthesis as to why he acted as he did.

Long ago, the British parliamentarian Edmund Burke made a prescient distinction between a statesman and a moralist which has tragic relevance to Wilson's predicament in 1919. Whereas a moralist has a general view of society, said Burke, the statesman has a number of more specific circumstances to take into consideration; a statesman, while not losing sight of his moral principles, must first and foremost be guided by political and diplomatic realities that are forever in a state of flux.[99] A subtly evolving dementia, induced by hypertension and cerebrovascular disease, made this precisely what Wilson could no longer do by late 1919 and 1920. He remained a moralist to the end. The quality that typified him from the beginning was only magnified by his underlying medical condition. Wilson's inability to shift reflectively with changing circumstances was a matter of considerable significance for the treaty's defeat and, ultimately, the emasculation of the League of Nations.

CHAPTER 6

Winston Churchill: Compromised Cold Warrior

That Wilson Churchill suffered all his life from what he called the "black dog" of depression is well known. That this may have contributed to his relatively ineffectual leadership in the postwar years is less appreciated. Moreover, we know that Churchill was in poor health during his second tenure as prime minister, from 1951 to 1955, thanks to the published memoirs of his physician, Lord Moran. Yet the real underlying causes of Churchill's deterioration (hypertension and hardening of the arteries) and their psychophysiologic manifestations (accelerated aging) have yet to be independently analyzed in depth. Like Woodrow Wilson before him, Churchill still perceived himself to be indispensable—though few of his contemporaries felt the same. The perceptions of both, in the end, had as much to do with his tenuous health as with wounded vanity.

To be sure, Moran had already noted some disturbing changes in his patient's behavior and thought processes long before. On December 7, 1947, the doctor observed in his diary: "He is no longer fertile in ideas. Last year his failure as Leader of the Opposition could be put down . . . to a lack of tact and to his indifference to the opinions of others. But now it is more the sterility of his mind that bothers thoughtful people. The once-teeming brain has run dry."[1] Nor had his condition improved four years later. Just prior to Churchill's reelection as prime minister, Moran admitted: "In the fourteen months since my last entry he has lost ground, and has no longer the same grip on things and events. . . . If he wins the election . . . I doubt whether he is up to the job."[2]

In medical terminology, the implication is clear that Churchill was suffering the effects of early dementia, defined as "an irreversible mental state characterized by decreased intellectual function, personality change, and impaired judgment."[3] It was left to a British psychiatrist, Anthony Storr, to reflect on the progression of that process after Churchill left office: "The last five years of his protracted existence were so melancholy that even Lord Moran drew a veil over them."[4] Yet Churchill's daughter allowed fleeting glances behind that veil, with pathetic descriptions of meals eaten in embarrassing silence and the long intervals of depression and apathy that consumed her father's last days. He gave up reading, seldom spoke, and sat for hours in front of the fire in a depressive stupor.[5] These last years for Winston Churchill were sad ones, and the sphinx-like facade of his residual persona gave little indication of talents lost to the ages. There is nothing remarkable in this: he was on the last leg of a lifetime spanning nine decades.

What *is* noteworthy from the historian's perspective, however, is that the process of dementia was well under way during Churchill's last tenure as prime minister. Moran himself had become convinced as early as the last years of World War II that "exhaustion of mind and body" accounted for much that was "otherwise inexplicable" in his patient's behavior.[6] Though few scholars today would take issue with that poignant assessment, it remains to unravel the complexities of this physiologic deterioration as it may have affected his leadership.

To begin with, Churchill's last years in office were characterized by a relative indifference to pressing economic and domestic concerns, subverted all the more by his unrelenting preoccupation with international relations and Britain's waning role in them. This lack of resourcefulness in tackling new problems, while doting on more familiar ones, may be readily attributed to the deleterious impact of incipient dementia on Churchill's behavior, for dementia victims sense the need to establish a means of coping with their increasingly limited mental reserves. By avoiding the complex or unfamiliar, they reduce their failure rate to a level that falls short of being destructive to both social position and self-respect. A physician may regard this as healthy compensation in a patient;[7] the pathographer would hasten to add that such behavior may be distinctly unhealthy for the best interests of a nation being led by one so afflicted.

As if to disguise his deterioration, Churchill's staged performances at the lectern remained relatively effective to the very end. Though the painstaking care he took in editing prepared speeches lent support to his reputation as both speaker and writer, few but the neuropsychologists are aware that some individuals may paradoxically retain their verbal skills in the early stages of dementia. Moreover, remote memory is largely preserved, as a rule.[8] Whereas Churchill could recall many incidents from World War I in vivid detail, events during World War II ran together in his mind, compelling him when writing his memoirs to depend on what had been committed to paper.[9] Yet cognitive decline is a relative matter. In a person of Churchill's formidable aptitudes, a decline of, say, 30 to 40 percent may result in little discernible change to the casual observer. Even so, certain subtleties and nuances in assimilating data are inevitably lost.

A further characteristic of dementia sufferers is their dependence on external sources to maintain self-esteem. That is why Churchill placed such a premium on vigor in his public performances. The well-publicized appearance, a major speech, or the chairing of cabinet meetings all became critical barometers of his vitality, both in his own eyes and in those of his detractors. Deluding himself into believing he had cleared each hurdle successfully, particularly after his major stroke in 1953, strengthened Churchill's resolve to stay on. In the end, this required taking a staggering array of medical stimulants to bolster his confidence and foster the illusion that he was, indeed, indispensable.

Considering, therefore, that Churchill's verbal skills were untarnished, that his cognitive decline was still a somewhat relative matter, and that his public appearances were supported with drugs supplied by his private physician, it is understandable that the insidious influence of progressive dementia was largely lost on contemporaries and historians alike. But two other underlying illnesses aided and abetted the aging process: cerebrovascular insufficiency and depression. The former did not become evident until Churchill's first stroke in 1949; thereafter, it was an increasingly pervasive influence on his leadership. The latter dogged him at every step along the way.

Consider the fact that atherosclerosis can contribute to either the development or the progression of dementia by reducing the supply of oxygen to the brain. Overt strokes are not necessarily required to make the diagnosis; nevertheless, Churchill did suffer at least two permanent strokes and numerous temporary ones during the last six years of his public life. Acknowledging this, the pathographer would do well to ponder the accepted medical axiom that large strokes are but an end stage of vascular dementia, with cognitive changes often occurring long before.[10] That is the basis on which Churchill's medical record can be interpreted to reflect a perceptible degree of mental impairment even before he assumed office for the last time.

It is also true that a disparity is often observed between cognitive impairment and structural changes of the brain in patients afflicted with dementia. This apparent discrepancy can be attributed to several unrecognized factors, among them depression, inactivity, and social deprivation.[11] Certainly Churchill was neither intellectually inactive nor divorced from interpersonal contact, either as leader of the opposition or as prime minister. Yet it is to Anthony Storr's credit that he identified the presence of the significant depression that affected Churchill during his entire public life. This led Storr to conclude that no understanding of his character is possible unless this "central fact" is taken into account.[12]

Certain features of the dementia victim's personality are accentuated as their compromise accelerates. That is what one investigator was driving at when he asserted that hardening of the arteries to the brain "makes it difficult for one to cope with his temperamental difficulties."[13] What one would expect to see in Churchill's case, then, is precisely what occurred: increasingly frequent bouts of depression and periods of soul-searching, enough to compel him to seek pharmacological aids from his physician in order to weather the emotional storm from within and the undertow of criticism from without.

Since premorbid personality traits are often magnified both by the multi-infarct state and by most forms of dementia, perhaps it would be helpful to summarize Churchill's personality profile as succinctly as possible before beginning a chronological evaluation of his progressive illness. Several biographies and character sketches made by closely positioned observers indicate that Churchill's personality was characterized by the following features: egocentricity; a relative indifference to, if not unawareness of, the "common man"; a flair for the romantic and a deeply ingrained belief in the British Empire and its aristocracy; extraordinary skills with both the spoken and written word; hypochondriacal concerns about his health; a propensity to make decisions based on intuition; a crisis orientation; an artistic temperament that allowed for sustained periods of creative activity; a remarkable independence of mind; and last, a recurring depression. This list does not pretend to be exhaustive or all-inclusive (and certainly not all historians would agree with every item), but in the main these features represent the essential qualities of Churchill's premorbid personality. And many were augmented by the effects of his progressive illness.

R. Rhodes James shared the opinion of most historians in asserting that Churchill was not a very effective leader of the opposition in the House of Commons before reassuming the office of prime minister in 1951. For one thing, his stature often seemed greater abroad than in his own country.[14] For another, his egocentricity divorced him from the everyday concerns of common people. Lady Asquith's assessment speaks for itself: "I think that for him human beings fell roughly into three categories: the great figures whom he weighed, measured, and assessed in a historical perspective, . . . the so-called average man and woman who often made no impact on his attention, . . . and lastly his friends."[15]

These observers substantially account for Churchill's obsession during his later years with constructing a lasting peace in face-to-face consultation with world leaders whom he perceived to be of equal historical stature. Yet in relation to the opposition years, they also magnify his principal failing: a lack of genuine communication with commoners. His approach was essentially rhetorical, capsulized now and then in a memorable speech. He had always lived somewhat apart from the bulk of humankind, and his preoccupation only with matters that suited him overshadowed those issues that genuinely concerned the broad majority of the British public. For Churchill during the opposition years there were books to write, paintings to complete, and his health to rejuvenate. He treated his political duties largely as an avocation as he awaited the inevitable time when Labour would be turned out and he could return to center stage. Temporarily barred from the political limelight, his interest in politics lacked the fervor of earlier years. The game was scarcely so important if he could not lead.

Accordingly, Churchill understood two projects in which (at least to his way of thinking) his participation was critical to success: effecting a lasting détente with the Soviet Union, and promoting the movement for European unity. Not that these were the most critical issues of the day for Great Britain; rather, they interested Churchill most, and he perceived them as the only areas in which he might still speak with authority. One observer struck to the heart of the matter: "Ambition is a trait of character which merely reflects a man's desire to find adequate scope for his abilities."[16] The aging process had altered a great many things for Churchill—but obviously not his search for a receptive audience in high circles.

Realistically, two matters of more pressing importance should have captured the attention of a career politician intent upon regaining power: reorganizing his party, and formulating its policy. These were the nuts-and-bolts matters necessary to ensure Churchill's political future. After all, it was the Conservative party, not its leaders, that had failed to impress the electorate in 1945. Yet Churchill left these critical matters of restructuring to others. Discontent within his own party evoked critical comments about his absence from the Commons and his absorption in writing his memoirs. A substantial number of its members called for his retirement, underscoring his ineffectiveness as a party leader during this period. Churchill's response was characterized by a degree of intransigence and suspicion often seen when elderly individuals are opposed or thwarted; he would "react violently, banging the floor with his stick [in anger against] those who were plotting to displace him."[17]

Though many were as concerned about Churchill's health as about his political performance, no obvious red flags of warning unfurled before 1949. Lord Moran painted quite a different picture of his patient behind closed doors, portraying him as increasingly subject to periods of profound depression, possessed of a limited attention span, and preoccupied with reveries of his past triumphs.[18] Others with less accessibility to the aging prime minister saw no obvious changes worthy of note; the *Times* blithely recorded on July 17, 1947 that "he was looking extremely well."[19]

That image was shaken by what is now known to have been Churchill's first stroke on August 24, 1949. At Max Beaverbrook's villa on the French Riviera, he experienced a sudden loss of sensation in his right arm and leg. "He was playing cards," Lord Moran recalled, "when he got up . . . and bent his right leg several times. 'I've got a cramp in my arm and leg,' was all he said."[20] Still another account described the event as a "peculiar sensation of paralysis" that began in Churchill's right hand.[21] The mention of a "sensation" of paresis is important in arriving at a diagnosis, as no genuine paralysis had occurred. Moreover, Churchill had no difficulty in speaking. This allowed him to volunteer that "there is a sensation in my arm that was not there before . . . like a tight feeling across my shoulder blade."[22]

Those descriptions are more than sufficient for the retrospective clinician to diagnose a tiny, hypertension-related stroke involving a deeply seated structure in the left side of the brain known as the thalamus, which is a relay station between the spinal cord and the sensory cerebral cortex. These small infarcts known as "lacunes" usually represent the end stage of hypertension. They are not directly related to large-vessel atherosclerosis; rather, they occur as a result of occlusion of small penetrating arteries deep in the brain.[23] That the outer cerebral cortex supplied by larger blood vessels was not involved in this instance is suggested by the lack of injury to Churchill's speech center, which would have been affected by a large-vessel stroke significant enough to involve both the arm and the leg. In the absence of other clinical findings, his stroke must have occurred where these sensory tracts converge.

For obvious political reasons, Churchill's brush with a serious illness was successfully hidden from the British public. Harold Macmillan confided in his diary entry of August 25, 1949, that "this attack, happily, proved slight, and by *careful control of the news* [emphasis added] was effectively concealed."[24] Beaverbrook had decided that the truth should be hidden and had prepared a bulletin stating only that "Churchill had contracted a chill while bathing and would require a few days [of] rest and quiet."[25] This remained the accepted story until the month after Churchill's death in January 1965.

The entire episode is of significance for several reasons. First, it defines the specific nature of Churchill's cerebrovascular disease, the natural history of which is now well known to physicians. These "minor" strokes occur repeatedly over the years and affect the brain on both sides, frequently giving rise in time to what is known as the "lacunar state." In spite of the victim's apparent recovery from each successive insult, the condition is inexorably progressive. The most devastating consequence is the debilitating syndrome known in medicalese as "multi-infarct dementia."

Second, Churchill's rapid improvement was quite characteristic of a small-vessel stroke, even though it gave his handlers a false sense of security regarding his health and led to some spurious assumptions. "Perhaps it was because he had faced death before and because of his profound will-power that he recovered [so] quickly," one observer surmised.[26] Churchill's recovery had little to do with either; rather, it was compatible with what is usually seen in this disease. Permanent deficits result only with larger lesions, as the aging prime minister would ruefully discover four years later.

Third, and perhaps most significant, the episode led to the duplicity employed by friend (Beaverbrook), colleague (Macmillan), and physician (Moran) alike in disguising its real nature. They withheld access to facts that the British public had a right to know when it came to the next general election, less than two years away. If the cover-up was undertaken at Churchill's behest, as seems to have been the case, then he ignored any consideration of what was in Britain's best interest. Such duplicity, repeated time and again during his remaining years as prime minister, reflects poorly on the professional conduct of the persons responsible for perpetrating the myth of Churchill's vitality and good health.

To return to the chronological narrative, what effects did this brief, albeit portentous, setback have on political events of the day? In relation to Churchill's election two years thereafter, the effects were insignificant, as he seemed by then to have recovered completely and the British public was unaware of the stroke in any event. Nevertheless, it may have adversely affected the speech he gave at Strasbourg in 1949, in which he reversed his position regarding the concept of a united Europe. Churchill had been among the first to call for European unity after the war, and his new position was inexplicable and disappointing to unification enthusiasts both at home and abroad. At about the same time, Lord Moran began to detect in his patient a disconcerting lack of concern about the future. "Winston is aging," he wrote. "The optimism of the war years . . . has oozed out through his wounds, and he has given up planning new worlds. He does not pretend that he is interested in a future he will not live to see."[27] What Moran was alluding to was an accentuation in old age of the depression Churchill had always fought and his recent stroke had rekindled. Yet this observation, made just prior to the Strasbourg speech, may offer some insight into Churchill's inexplicable reversal.

Had European unity become one of those "new worlds" he had

given up planning for in old age? Possibly. Yet whatever else characterized Churchill's later years as prime minister, planning for such
brave new worlds as a "special relationship" with the United States and
détente with Soviet Russia were precisely the two issues that consumed
him. Why, then, had he suddenly abandoned the Continent? Was Europe now extraneous to the other goals? Might Britain lose its way as an
independent mover and shaker in world affairs if it were smothered in a
European embrace? Not only had the timing of Churchill's reversal
raised eyebrows; it also reflected a certain ambiguity in his thinking
regarding Britain's new role in the world.

Whatever the verdict, Churchill's medical record fully two years
before he reassumed office attests to an incipient dementia, documents
his recurring depression, and acknowledges the occurrence of a stroke. If
the last was due to small-vessel disease deep within the brain on the
basis of hypertension, his larger vessels were also beginning to occlude
as early as 1950. Just five months after his first stroke, Churchill mentioned to Moran that "about an hour ago everything went misty. There
was no warning. I could just read with difficulty."[28] In medical terms,
what he was describing was a "transient ischemic attack" related to
decreased blood flow to the posterior portion of the brain where cerebral
impulses for vision are assimilated. This area is supplied by two large
blood vessels of what is known as the "vertebral-basilar system," and
atherosclerosis is nearly always the cause. The fact that Churchill later
complained of "increasing tightness across both shoulders"[29] suggests
an attempt by other vessels at the base of the neck to supply collateral
flow past a partial or total occlusion—much as occurs in patients with
coronary artery insufficiency, who suffer chest pain due to inadequate
blood supply to the heart.

As if to substantiate that diagnosis, Churchill confided to Moran
shortly thereafter that he had a "muzzy feeling" in his brain and
suggested that it came on as a result of "poor circulation to the
head."[30] Giddiness, or lightheadedness, is perhaps the most frequent
complaint of individuals suffering from vertebral-basilar insufficiency.
Even though Churchill implored his physician to give him "something
more substantial" for these attacks, they were both relieved to discover that aspirin seemed to help. That request, in itself, underscored
his hypochondriacal mind set, which included an insatiable appetite
for medications to remedy various maladies both perceived and real.
Just as Lord Moran would be called at a moment's notice to check his
demanding patient's pulse merely to reassure him, by 1953 Churchill
was requesting pharmacologic stimulants on a regular basis when faced
with important public appearances and speeches.[31] Once the usual
defenses fail to alleviate the anxiety that often accompanies aging, drugs

offer the only solution for the host of psychosomatic symptoms that emerge.[32]

Despite his deteriorating health, Churchill did not perceive himself as too old to run again for office once the government called a general election for October 15, 1951. Though the aging warrior must have presented a convincing case with his programmed demonstrations of fitness, he was seventy-seven years old, suffering from cerebrovascular insufficiency, and subject to frequent bouts of depression and apathy when away from the public eye. Only after his death would the public learn that a mere fortnight before the election he had admitted privately to Moran: "I am *not* so sure as I was that I shall be able to see things through."[33]

It is an axiom of politics that reality is often less important than the public's perception of it. Ironically, many of the Labour party's leaders seemed as ill and infirm as only Churchill's physician knew him to be. The charge that could have been directed against him focused instead on the opposition.[34] His carefully orchestrated public appearances, contrasting with Labour's all too obvious compromise and ineptitude, brought the aging giant back for one last curtain call as prime minister. Yet he would return to center stage with an anticlimactic encore that featured a tedious monologue at best, a pathetic soliloquy at worst. Many recognized that the Old Lion could only tarnish the well-deserved fame and prestige of bygone years.[35]

The most pressing issue at the time of Churchill's return was the economy, which was on the verge of collapse. Imagine the concern of his own backbenchers, once they realized that their former hero, now in charge of his first peacetime administration, was facing financial problems for which he had shown only the most rudimentary interest and understanding in the past. An occasionally memorable speech did little to disarm his critics. As historian David Thomson has observed: "The Government was haunted by a curious air of unreality, arising from the disparity between the Churchillian ferocity of its utterances and the tepidity of its deeds."[36] Though Churchill chose his cabinet with care, he offended the younger members of his own party, who correctly perceived that they had no representation in policy-making. Given what is known of the predilections of aging individuals, perhaps there was more in Macmillan's observation than met the eye: "If these faces brought no sense of novelty into our councils, they were his familiars, with many of whom he had worked and striven through the darkest days."[37] Not only did the prime minister's selections fulfill a deeply seated need to retain a sense of familiarity around him; they intimated a reluctance to embark on risky or untested courses of action.

Little wonder, then, that Churchill was unable to please the electorate during his first year in office. The depth of discontent was measured by the gains Labour made in the spring elections of 1952, leading the *Times* to predict "a permanent shift of political power to the Left."[38] These objective results belied Macmillan's subjective assessment that Churchill remained as energetic and industrious as ever.[39] Other observers close to the prime minister would disagree with that characterization—including even some who later came to his defense in the face of Moran's posthumous indictment of their leader-hero.

Though Churchill pursued his usual practice of concentrating on one or two questions at a time, Lord Normanbrook conceded that his instincts in selecting the most important issues were less sure in peacetime than they had been in war.[40] Moreover, the pace of the prime minister's work was decidedly slower. Time allotted for cabinet meetings frequently expired before Churchill arrived at the first item on the agenda. No longer did the ubiquitous label "Action This Day" appear on his messages and transcripts. Such troubling observations were echoed by Sir John Colville, who disclosed that by the spring of 1952 Churchill's periods of "lowness" were increasing and his "zest diminished."[41] He found it increasingly difficult to compose speeches, complaining that "ideas no longer flowed."[42] Added to this litany of disturbing indictments was the response of Churchill's private secretary, Leslie Rowan, when Moran asked whether he had noticed any changes in their old friend: "'Oh yes,' he answered rather sadly, 'he has lost his tenacity; he no longer pushes a thing through. He has lost, too, his power of filling in all of the problems one to another. . . And he forgets figures. In the war he never did.'"[43]

These descriptions by generally supportive associates who probably spent more time with Churchill than anyone but his wife are revealing enough. That aging individuals typically demonstrate a lack of staying power with mental activities or issues they consider mundane or unimportant paradoxically contrasts with a few preoccupations that grab their attention to the exclusion of nearly everything else. The neurologist would identify the latter focus as a dementia-induced "perseveration." Such individuals compensate for an inability to view problems in proper perspective by expending what residual intellectual capacity they have on single issues. Though a single-minded devotion to a solitary discipline or idea has been described as one definition of genius, it becomes a liability for a political leader faced with a wide range of issues.

There are also the frequent references to Churchill's deficient memory to consider, alluded to by Leslie Rowan in relation to numbers and figures. Churchill himself confided to Moran in March 1952 that his memory was failing; he had recently sat between two people he knew very well but whose names he could not remember. On a later occasion Moran proposed that Churchill teach his pet bird, Toby, his telephone number in case the bird got lost—only to discover that Winston no longer knew himself.[44] Nor did the aged prime minister appear to have the capacity to learn new material, yet another liability that became self-evident once unfamiliar economic issues surfaced. These observations had particularly disturbing implications because all of them were made within three months of Churchill's return to Number 10 Downing Street.

Moran's diary entries as early as February 1952 provided intimations of things to come: "There are gaps everywhere in his grip of events. The old appetite for work has gone . . . and how full of qualms he has become! In 1940 when the world was tumbling about his ears—he did not worry over anything. Now that he is Prime Minister and there is peace he seems to worry over everything. Moods come and go. He is not the same two days running."[45] Perseveration with the past, inability to master new material, and apathy are mentioned time and again in these and others' recollections. Moran's observations add two further attributes to this typical portrait of dementia: a propensity to be consumed by unnecessary fear and worry, and an extreme variability in performance from day to day. The former ties in closely with depression and the neurotic tendencies that accompany age-related disorders of the brain; the latter is so characteristic of dementia that even severely afflicted victims occasionally startle their companions with brief displays of lucidity and vitality.

Any suggestion that Churchill might not have suffered from generalized cerebrovascular insufficiency was dispelled by yet another transient ischemic attack on February 21, 1952. As Churchill related to Moran: "I took up the telephone when I woke an hour ago, and I couldn't think of the words I wanted. Wrong words seemed to come into my head, but I was quite clear what was happening and did not say them."[46] This is a classic example of what neurologists term "expressive aphasia." It almost invariably signifies disease referable to the left middle cerebral artery of a right-handed person. This vessel is one of the two major branches of the carotid artery, which (as opposed to the vertebral-basilar artery system described earlier) supplies the more lateral portion of the brain, specifically the temporal and parietal lobes.

Viewed as a continuum of disease, what this last episode underscores is the *diffuse* nature of Churchill's cerebrovascular insufficiency. First, in 1949 a stroke had occurred on account of a small penetrating artery occlusion deep in the left half of the brain. Second, decreased blood flow to both halves of the back of the brain manifested itself as early as 1950. Now, large-vessel disease of the more lateral surface of the left side of the brain was clearly evident. The fourth event, a major stroke in 1953, would occur in still another location, deep in the brain on the right side. The second and third events were attributed to large-vessel disease; the first and fourth were associated with small-vessel changes seen in hypertensive individuals. Churchill's cerebrovascular insufficiency, then, was clearly a pervasive condition, with ominous implications for his evolving dementia and subsequent conduct in office.

The 1952 stroke warning drew attention to what was by then an overriding question: when would Churchill retire? Moran recognized that they had dodged too many bullets already; something more than merely patching up his patient was now required. Accordingly, he sought out some of the prime minister's closest contacts for advice—among them Lord Salisbury (a high-ranking cabinet member), Jock Colville (private secretary to the prime minister), and Alan Lascelles (his parliamentary private secretary). All agreed that Churchill should resign but ruefully acknowledged the difficulty of getting him to do so[47]—and this was but five months into what became a four-year tenure.

Their pessimism was justified. Churchill simply refused to step down until the work he felt only he could do was done. Three issues preoccupied him to the virtual exclusion of all others: reestablishing a meaningful partnership with the United States, as befitted his dream of unity among English-speaking peoples; effecting a meaningful détente with the Soviet Union; and worrying whether either would come to pass before he was goaded into retirement.

Churchill's daughter described the emotional tug of war that haunted her father during his entire second administration. Fits of depression and self-reproach on bad days alternated during better ones with a stubborn resolve to continue in office. The ailing prime minister was once heard to remark that he meant to carry on until "either things become much better, or I become much worse."[48] He made this comment in 1954, but it was representative of his thinking from the moment he took office.

In truth, neither alternative weighed heavily in Churchill's thinking when he ultimately did retire, for neither did things get that much better, nor (at least to his own way of thinking) did he get all that much worse. For four years his pathologically enhanced denial of the implications of his disease had effectively eliminated any consideration of resigning. Not that he was altogether unaware of his restricted abilities; yet one limitation of such afflicted individuals is their inability to gauge the quality of their own performance realistically. What limitations Churchill perceived were (only he believed) both minor and manageable. "I require more prodding to mental effort," he admitted. "I forget names, . . . people whose names I know as well as my own." [49]

Fearing personal retribution in a face-to-face confrontation with his increasingly irascible patient, Moran drafted a letter to Churchill on March 12, 1952, for the express purpose of reminding him of the "instability of his cerebral circulation" that might be increased by what he termed "excessive mental effort." [50] To his chagrin, Churchill continued to deny his illness, while reminding Moran that he was still useful as the world's senior statesman, if not altogether indispensable. That belief became so essential to his sense of self-worth that he demanded both sedatives (barbiturates) and stimulants (amphetamines) to get him over any unavoidable hurdles: "I must have a clear head tomorrow for my speech. . . . I shall want three 'majors' to get me through [it]. I'm short of ideas; they don't come to me as easily as they did." [51] It was left to his worried physician to contain the irrepressible tides of aging as best he could at the same time that he painfully watched the government blunder from one crisis to another. "The weakness in the Prime Minister's administration has taken everybody by surprise," Moran lamented. "Churchill will go on squandering what is left of his capital until he goes bankrupt. . . . The unmistakable signs of old age are apparent . . . and yet he has no intention of giving up." [52]

The pressing nature of that issue abated somewhat in early 1953 with an inexplicable improvement in Churchill's condition, coupled with his renewed zest for exercising leadership. Moran thought that he had uncovered a clue to the temporary improvement: Anthony Eden had gone to the United States for surgery (related to two previous unsuccessful gallbladder operations), obliging Churchill himself to take over at the Foreign Office and giving him a new lease on life. His additional duties as acting foreign secretary were like a breath of fresh air for this septuagenarian, who had been unable to find a forum for his talents in domestic arenas so foreign to him.

Churchill's spirits were further bolstered in early March 1953 when, with the death of Josef Stalin, he perceived that the time might be ripe for a reconciliation with the Soviets through their new leadership. Here was an opportunity that might not recur; indeed, Churchill thought of little else but how to exploit it for both political and personal gain. [53] Besides, it diverted the press from its increasing criticism of his inability to produce any coherent policy in economic matters. This singular preoccupation with leaving a lasting contribution to world peace boded well for preserving Churchill's self-image but poorly for other issues outside his one-dimensional thinking.

In a word, Eden's illness and absence temporarily legitimized the delusion Churchill had held all along—that he was indeed indispensable. Though he had designated Eden as his heir, he still regarded him in a fashion typical of older men for younger subordinates. He had been compelled grudgingly to acknowledge his protégé's opinions in the past; it now buoyed the prime minister's confidence not to be directly exposed to them. Despite his foreign secretary's previously expressed reservations, Churchill leaped at the opportunity to implement his plans for meeting the Soviet Union halfway and drawing the United States into his plan.

So the issue of resignation remained unsolved during the first half of 1953. In June, however, the matter was again brought to the forefront by a fourth—and by far the most serious—breakdown in the blood supply to Churchill's brain. On June 24, 1953, he suffered a second stroke, manifested by weakness of the left side of his face and slurring of his speech. The initial symptoms were so slight that Churchill even managed to get through a scheduled cabinet meeting two hours later. Yet what happened over the next three days was compatible with a condition the neurologist would identify as a "stroke-in-evolution": the weakness progressed to involve his arm and leg.[54] "Look! My hand is clumsy," the prime minister cried out with alarm. Transferring his cigar to his left hand, he made a wavering attempt to put it to his lips, only to find that some loss of power and dexterity had developed since the day before. More worrisome still, he was noted on June 27 to be "dragging his left leg."[55]

This last illness was laden with disturbing implications. First, from the medical perspective, deep seated strokes on both sides of the brain portended the development of the "lacunar state" described above. That syndrome often includes a loss of emotional control, with unprovoked outbursts of laughing or crying.[56] Three weeks after the stroke Moran described what he termed "another disconcerting relic" of his patient's illness: "He is liable to become emotional, so that without warning . . . he [inexplicably] 'blubs like a child.'" Indeed, Moran had to persuade Churchill not to convene any cabinet meetings for fear that if someone made a speech saying how glad they were to have him back, he would break down.[57]

Second, Churchill had suffered at least four separate transient ischemic attacks and strokes over a four-year period, involving not only the large vessels to the left side and both posterior halves of the brain but also the small vessels deep within it. In effect, from the standpoint of vascular supply to the brain, Britain's prime minister was running on only one cylinder by 1953—his right carotid artery.

Third, stroke victims are particularly prone to periods of apathy and depression. Given Churchill's premorbid personality profile, Storr's assertion that cerebral atherosclerosis eventually "broke down his defenses against his lifelong depression" is understandable—not to mention its impact on his leadership.[58] Frequently thereafter, executive function came to a virtual standstill. By way of example, Colville reminded Moran that he had shown the prime minister a number of Foreign Office telegrams "which a month ago would have riveted his attention"; now he hardly glanced at them. He read novels instead or, to use his own words, "merely doodled," taking holidays when he was supposed to be making decisions.[59]

One immediate result of his illness was the need to postpone for at least six months the Bermuda Conference at which Churchill had hoped the Americans would finally agree to later talks with the Russians. He was distraught over the imposed delay, for he mistakenly believed that he was at the peak of his influence with world leaders, particularly the Soviets, just before the stroke occurred. Yet was anything truly lost? Probably not. Churchill's plan was a vainglorious and futile gesture to recapture the past. In the opinion of most observers (including key members of his own government), he clearly overestimated his influence with both Soviet and American leadership at the time.[60]

Moreover, his uncharacteristically pacific stance toward the Russians seemed inexplicable to many at the time, including Beaverbrook: "Like Paul on the road to Damascus, Churchill had suffered a blinding revelation . . . that had overturned some of the convictions by which he had conducted his political life and thoughts for half a century. . . . Churchill had set the heather on fire [in his celebrated Iron Curtain speech at Fulton, Missouri, in 1946]. Now it seemed he was sending for the fire engine."[61] Why?

Contemporary neuropsychologists might offer one plausible explanation: Churchill's vision of a détente between the superpowers, orchestrated by himself, served to bolster his self-image. Having led his nation to victory in the war, he would embellish that feat by obtaining an assurance between East and West that such horrors would not be repeated. This would be the culmination of his political career. Viewed in that perspective, his "revelation" offered him a final opportunity to do what he had at one time done best: meeting with world historical figures to decide the fate of humankind.

The eminent scholar A.J.P. Taylor spoke for many historians in taking a more cynical view of the matter: "In his last senile days as Prime Minister, Churchill once more announced the need for reconciliation with Soviet Russia, and in particular emphasized that he was the man to accomplish it. . . . He lived for crisis . . . and when crisis did not exist, he strove to invent it. . . . It is difficult to discern in him any element of creative leadership. . . . Churchill had no vision for the future, only a tenacious defense of the past. . . . He was no beginning, but an end—a fulfiller, not a prophet."[62]

In assessing Churchill's skill as a strategist, still others emphasized his rigid preoccupation with single issues. "Churchill always had a deep-rooted tendency when concentrating on one problem to forget the other problems which were bound up with its solution," the military historian B. H. Liddell Hart has written. "He lacked the power of relating one part to another, and the parts to the whole."[63] Here is one critical allusion to a quality that explicitly parallels the limitations of the dementia victim's ability to assess things in proportion. In that sense, an aging prime minister's perseveration with Russian détente and American partnership represented as much a form of self-delusion as a failure to employ the abstract attitude in weighing the implications of his actions.[64]

It is perhaps understandable that Churchill, rather than Eisenhower, would feel pressed to assure a culmination of unity between English-speaking nations. Having become the junior partner in this relationship, Great Britain needed the United States (and Churchill needed its president) far more than the reverse. Not that Eisenhower was altogether unaware of Churchill's motivations: "Winston is [merely] trying to relive the days of World War II."[65] As early as January 1952 he had despaired of his old friend's condition after their first meeting since Churchill had reassumed office. "He simply will not think in terms of today," Eisenhower lamented. "He no longer absorbs new ideas." A year later the president confided in his diary the hope that Churchill would withdraw and leave the reins of power to younger men.[66]

What Eisenhower did not know in 1953 was that the prime minister had suffered a stroke that June. Nor was he alone. Professionally sanctioned deception had again become the order of the day. Initially, Moran and his consultants agreed to a vague medical bulletin concerning "a disturbance of the cerebral circulation," while Butler gambled on public assurances that merely lightening his duties would result in a "rapid recovery." Either way, the bulletin of June 17, 1953, made no mention of a stroke as such.[67] Though Macmillan thought this appropriate, his explanation borders on naiveté: "Out of chivalry to Eden . . . [Churchill] must [not resign] unless he feels in conscience unable to serve. . . . To do this it is not necessary to walk or make speeches."[68] Macmillan's apparent inability to see the hollowness of his own assertion is astounding. Certainly there was more to be weighed than a man's abilities to "walk and make speeches" when assessing a prime minister's leadership capability. Nonetheless, Churchill's preoccupation with these minor functions dominated his conduct from that point onward. There was little concern about the quality of his leadership so long as he was able to put up a good front.

Moran remained a party to the deception. "If the Prime Minister is to carry on . . . I now agree with Salisbury that the less we say about the strokes the better," he confided in his diary. Yet his conscience compelled him to view Churchill's illness with foreboding, even if he allowed himself to play a critical role in the cover-up to the very end. "It is strange," he concluded, "that no one around the Prime Minister seems to grasp what is the exact nature of his disability. This is not an acute illness from which he may recover completely. He will never again be the same man as he was before the stroke, because the clot in the artery has cut off some blood which went to his brain and [which] was the ultimate source of all his activities."[69]

If a chosen few knew the facts of Churchill's illness and still failed to grasp its full significance, the overwhelming majority of Britons were left entirely in the dark. A *Daily Mirror* headline on August 17 demanded the truth about Churchill's condition: "Is there any reason why the British people should not be told the facts about the health of their Prime Minister? . . . Let us know whether Sir Winston Churchill is fit enough to lead us!"[70] The next day, as if on cue, Churchill attended his first cabinet meeting since the stroke. Although he appeared to handle himself well, Moran found him in a predictable state of depression the following day.[71] His inability to concentrate and his distaste for work were manifestations of that, for sustained expenditures of effort sap the limited reserves of the dementia victim and depression sufferer alike. His old nemesis would become even more prevalent in the days ahead.

Subsequent cabinet meetings on August 25 and September 8, however, reinforced Churchill's belief that he could still handle his job. Informed medical opinion was less optimistic. Sir John Parkinson, a cardiologist at the London Hospital, was shocked by the degree to which Churchill had aged and felt certain that he could never again act effectively as prime minister. The esteemed neurologist Lord Brain agreed.[72] Yet Churchill simply refused to surrender, believing that he had vital contributions to make to the world situation. If some perceive this attitude as a demonstration of strength of character and will, perhaps one clinical psychologist's assessment of denial reveals its negative side: "The person using the mechanism of denial should not be seen as a courageous person. A courageous person realistically appraises the situation . . . and moves ahead."[73]

From the perspective of the Conservative party's appraisal of his abilities, Churchill's speech at the party conference at Margate in October 1953 was an orchestrated success. As was his custom, he had prepared assiduously. Moreover, one physician was in attendance to spray his throat, and Moran was charged with "inventing" a pill to insure against embarrassment at the rostrum. Moran responded by administering the wonder drug of the decade, Benzedrine, which was then being prescribed for all kinds of ailments.[74] "It completely cleared away the muzzy feeling in my head," Churchill exclaimed to Moran. "I felt just as I did before the stroke. It gave me great confidence."[75]

A sense of enhanced mental powers and self-confidence are two of the most prominent effects of amphetamines like Benzedrine. Yet the perceived cognitive benefits are gained at the expense of a distressing trade-off: psychological dependency that eventually becomes a bona fide addictive state if the practice is continued. The need to make the best possible appearance may have been paramount in Churchill's thinking, but his premorbid personality, which included a neurotic hypochondriasis, was an equally critical factor. He was psychologically "hooked" from the start. From that point forward, the variability of the prime minister's performance reflected both his underlying neurologic condition and the drugs he used to conceal it.

This was how matters stood by the time he had sufficiently "recovered" from his stroke to attend the long-awaited Bermuda Conference in December 1953. To no one's surprise, the results of the meeting were disappointing. Only a Russian proposal for a five-power conference early the following year was accepted—and even that was to be a meeting of foreign ministers, not a summit of heads of state as Churchill had hoped.[76] Since he had failed to sway the Americans and been denied center stage at the next planned meeting, it is little wonder that when Churchill reported to the Commons after his return, he was described by one wag as "Father Christmas without any presents."[77]

Churchill had not been as well at the conference as his physical recovery seemed to imply. On December 5 he complained that he felt "muddled and stupid." The ever present depression tugged at his psyche. He had none of his old tenacity left, being described by his own doctor as "nearly played out." To make matters worse, he suffered yet another transient ischemic attack in the same vascular distribution responsible for the episode of aphasia he had experienced in 1952, manifested on this occasion by numbness of the fingers of his right hand.[78]

The new year brought no improvement in either the prime minister's medical condition or his political standing. In April 1954 he delivered a poor speech in the House of Commons during a debate on the hydrogen bomb and, in the debate that followed, played into the hands of those critics who insisted he was no longer fit.[79] Even the normally supportive *Times* reported that the prime minister's "sensc of occasion had deserted him sadly." This was Churchill's first major stumble in public, and his depression recurred. In May 1954 he said: "I no longer find life attractive. There is no fun in it. People are too base or too stupid to master the new ways of the modern world."[80] Yet mastering the ways of the modern world was precisely what Churchill himself could no longer do.

For one thing, he was reluctant to deal with new and traditionally "unacceptable" powers such as China, referring scornfully to its leaders as "little yellow men." Not only did Churchill's rigid view of what characterized "genuine historical figures" such as himself prevent him from acknowledging other emerging powers in the world; he now evinced a lack of interest, even an inability, to assimilate new facts as they arose. The old imperial prejudices were simply too ingrained in his psyche. In essence, he refused to be educated on issues that did not interest him.

Yet he perseverated on those that did. "It is his belief—and this he holds with fierce, almost religious intensity—that he, and he alone, can save the world from a frightful war," Moran recalled, at the same time his patient refused to confront the issue of his declining political standing at home.[81] Pollsters predicted a Conservative defeat in the next election unless new government and a new prime minister emerged. Given the upturn of economic indicators by 1954, the public's disenchantment with Churchill's conduct must have been a significant issue in itself. The continued uncertainty about his resignation, discussed openly in the press, had in Macmillan's opinion caused the government "to cease to function with full efficiency . . . as no one was coordinating policy." It was only the business of meeting the Soviets and drawing the Americans into his plan that kept him going.[82]

The implication was obvious even to his most supportive associates: Churchill was attempting to shield his weaknesses behind past experience in handling the accouterments of power, without giving much thought to its essence. Even though he deluded himself afterward that his speech at the next party conference was "a huge success," those in attendance did not see it as such; what they had really wanted to hear was when he planned to retire.[83] Following his stroke in 1953, Churchill had used the party's and the public's responses to his speeches and appearances to justify his staying on. Now that those responses were unfavorable, he ignored them and still refused to resign.

That decision was significant for several reasons. First, Churchill's perseveration with remaining in office long enough to meet the world's leaders "without agenda," as he termed it, would allow him maximum exposure with a minimum of effort. Preferring the drama of a face-to-face confrontation (with media coverage, of course), he was unwilling to work through the necessary preparation required, depending instead on his dwindling prestige. That formula was at once naive and delusional. "I believe I can wheedle Eisenhower," he mused. "Then I shall be ready for the Russians." [84] In his view, he needed no further preparation for a summit meeting. Second, Churchill's endogenous depression, always a threat to his well-being even in healthier times, was now activated time and again—both by the continual reminders that he was no longer fit for the job and by those increasingly rare expenditures of energy that invariably left him flat the following day. Finally, and most obvious to political observers of the time, he no longer had the tenacity to pursue issues of foreign policy and defense that would have captured his imagination at any earlier period, much less to consider the less interesting but pressing domestic matters of economics or party reorganization.

In the end, even Churchill's skills as a speaker began to fail him. Just one week before his eightieth birthday, in a speech at Woodford, he inexplicably let the public in on a bit of a secret history. Under the influence of drugs prescribed by his physician, the prime minister rashly volunteered that he had ordered Field Marshal Montgomery to stack the surrendered German arms in May 1945 so that, in his own words, "they could easily be issued again to the German soldiers whom we should have to work with if the Soviet advance continued." [85] The timing of this revelation, coming during a period when he was seeking in vain to bring the West's leaders together with the Soviets to effect a lasting détente, underscored the perverse contradictions in Churchill's conduct. Obviously concerned that posterity should remember him as one of the first to sound the alarm against Soviet aggression, he was attempting in the same breath to achieve reconciliation with that menace—again, partly for the sake of his future place in history. Preoccupied with a favorable historical appraisal, he undermined his only remaining perceived usefulness on the political stage. How were the Soviets to treat Churchill now, after he had admitted to such duplicity and cynicism in 1945? If he were to represent Britain, how could meaningful talks even be conducted?

Only a firm shove from such a close supporter as Harold Macmillan ultimately effected a remedy that the Conservative party should have insisted on long before. Macmillan's new position as defense minister now afforded a despairing vantage point from which to assess Churchill's failing powers. Moran became privy to Macmillan's resolve on January 9, 1955: "You know, Moran," he said, "Winston ought to resign. Since I became Minister of Defense I have found that he can no longer handle the complicated matters properly. He can't do his job as Prime Minister as it ought to be done. Winston has missed so many curtain calls when he could have gone with everyone applauding that it won't be easy now."[86]

In the very week that Churchill would finally announce his retirement, Stalin's successor, Georgi Malenkov, fell from power. To the exasperated prime minister's way of thinking, his last opportunity to meet with the Soviets—his very reason for persevering—was now denied him. Not that such a summit would ever have taken place, given the evidence cited in this review and the Woodford blunder. Still, Malenkov's unanticipated fall seemed to unmask the futility of it all. On April 6, 1955, Winston Churchill therefore resigned—a bit of history long overdue.

Some appraisals of Churchill's last four years in office, perhaps out of deference to an aging hero, have been less than critical.[87] Perhaps, too, the publication of Lord Moran's diaries just one year after Churchill's death evoked supportive attempts to reconstruct a tarnished image. Sir John Colville set the pattern for the reconstructionists: "If he had not achieved all the goals for which he had striven, he could still claim an unusually large score."[88] Yet before tallying the ledger, consider the host of unsettled issues that Colville cited to justify Churchill's staying in office: (1) determining the impact of nuclear arms on strategic considerations; (2) improving Anglo-American relations; (3) unifying Churchill's concept of military commitments with Eden's vis-à-vis the Suez Canal Zone; and (4) ending the Cold War.

With regard to the first, Churchill has been credited with identifying a new set of strategic implications, outlined in the 1954 Chiefs of Staff White Paper on global strategy. If Churchill's influence on its publication is not disputed, the originality of his contribution is less obvious; he had merely elaborated points that must have been obvious to any policymaker in the new age of nuclear armaments. Concerning the second, no discernible improvement in relations with America's leaders was forthcoming. On the third, it was Churchill (and not Eden) who effectively surrendered his position with regard to Suez.[89] Fourth, and most distressing for the prime minister, his efforts to effect a détente with the Soviet Union were essentially ignored.

In but one of the four issues, then, can Churchill's influence even be acknowledged. Moreover, he evinced only passing interest in economic recovery at home and European unity abroad. Although the economic yardsticks *were* favorable at the time of his retirement, Churchill could hardly take credit for that. As for a united Europe, his vacillation had a profoundly negative impact that effectively clouded his earlier vision.[90] To be sure, it would be difficult to find fault with Churchill's view of the future. "Something like a genuine détente has been brought about by those that followed in the trail he blazed," Macmillan later wrote.[91] But it was naive for either man to expect that Churchill alone could assure British leadership in détente with Russia or partnership between the two English-speaking peoples. The war had transformed England into a second-rate power, and it was among the aging prime minister's principal failings that he refused to accept this obvious fact.

That may explain in part Churchill's preoccupation during his final year in office with acquiring the hydrogen bomb. Not only did he believe that its supposed deterrent effect made war less likely; he hoped that possession of such a weapon would improve his country's standing vis-à-vis the United States and assure Britain's position as still a great power. Yet this quest for legitimacy was crucial to more than his patriotic ambitions; it was crucial also to his self-image as a leader.

Churchill's tragic flaw—admitted by even his closest confidants and now argued to have been accentuated by disease—was the overestimation he accorded his own influence. Leaders in the United States and Europe welcomed and revered him much more as Winston Churchill than as the prime minister of Great Britain.[92] Yet he was a very different man by then, as everyone close to him knew. To their chagin, he never perceived either fact. As in the case of Roosevelt at Yalta, one might argue that it was not so much the tactical shortcomings of his conduct that deserve notice; rather, it was the unrealistic nature of the goals he set for himself and his country. And like Roosevelt, Churchill put too much faith in his ability to sway other international leaders in face-to-face encounters.

The parallels between these two very ill men at the end of their respective political careers are striking. Roosevelt was confident that he understood Stalin; if the Soviet leader were simply given all he asked, surely he would help to build a better world after the war. With Churchill's attempts to manipulate Eisenhower and Malenkov in a similar fashion, one senses a disturbing feeling of historical *déjà vu*. To the very end of their respective careers, both leaders embraced similar pretensions, attempting to hammer out delicate and complex international agreements solely through the strength of their personalities.

Having established the illusory character of Churchill's leadership during his last tenure in office, we may now address the ultimate question: how could a person of such previously extraordinary political intuition have misread the signs of his last years so completely? This review has contributed to that answer in the form of a "second opinion": the aged prime minister of Great Britain was suffering from a well-defined medical condition that largely precluded his making an objective assessment of his political and diplomatic alternatives. This is not to suggest that Churchill's intellectual abilities were so compromised that he lacked the intelligence to understand the issues with which he dealt. Rather, early signs of dementia manifested themselves in more subtle ways. Depression became more prevalent, obstinacy and one-dimensional thinking more typical, and denial pervasive. The bulldog had lost his tenacity—and with it, his taste for the fight. As Churchill's secretary quipped on one occasion: "Considering how much a Prime Minister had to do, and how little Winston does, I think we have been quite clever."[93]

Individuals afflicted with dementia may subconsciously postpone the inevitable progression of their affliction by involving themselves in work or other forms of social interaction. Some may even approach near-normal levels of activity that serve to hold in check many elements in their disturbed thought processes.[94] In that sense alone, Churchill's last four years in office were at best therapeutic for his condition. The very requirements of his job assured a degree of personal involvement that may have ameliorated the inexorable physiologic progression of disease. Each orchestrated success served to augment the failing prime minister's denial that anything was seriously wrong with his conduct in office. His oratory, though weakened, was still stirring. Aware that this skill above all others marked his greatness, Churchill used the assiduously prepared spoken word to bolster his flagging self-esteem.

One medical expert tangentially alludes to the problem as Churchill may have subconsciously perceived it: "Two components of self-esteem which are often extremely important to the elderly or demented person are his measure of whether he feels his life has any value to himself and others, and the more subtle . . . measure of his capacity to deal successfully with physical disease."[95] The first, quite simply, explains Churchill's motivation for acting as he did. The second was secured in his own mind through the use of central-nervous-system stimulants and the realization that he continued to make apparent recoveries from each of the strokes and transient ischemic attacks that plagued him. In relation to what we know of his depression, merely remaining in office was one way of maintaining enough self-esteem to ameliorate the effects of this recurring nemesis. Churchill's delusions concerning détente with the Soviet Union and a unification of the English-speaking peoples at least fostered the hope that he would again be useful, sustaining him against the inroads of depression and progressive dementia that ate away at his tenuous reserves.

To be sure, political circumstances came to Churchill's rescue along the way. His foreign policy escaped bankruptcy, thanks to the efforts of a skilled foreign secretary. Had the measure of the government's success been weighed solely on the issues of Russian détente, European unity, and relations with the United States, historians would

have judged these years even more unfavorably than they do. For
Churchill's own reputation, Great Britain's diminished status as a
world power was paradoxically rather fortunate. Her new role one level
below the two superpowers appeared to mirror her prime minister's
increasingly compromised abilities. No historian would argue that he
was responsible for the dissolution of the British Empire or her devolu-
tion as a superpower; the war had done that. Yet this is precisely why his
deterioration as a leader has received so little attention: Great Britain
was suffering from the same circumstance. In that sense alone, Winston
Churchill was quite in step with the role of the nation he governed.

Psychology or physiology: which best accounts for a leader's be
havior once he becomes ill? The intent of the three foregoing chapters is
to suggest that the two are not mutually exclusive. For the short run, it
is obvious that either may impact on thought processes, emotions, and
attention span. Less appreciated are the long-term effects of illness on
personality. No doubt a proper understanding of character must begin
with the psychoanalytical. Indeed, there is little merit in implicating
disease at all unless the pathology in itself can be shown to have affected
those preexisting psychological factors that govern personality. That is
one reason the medical case studies of Stalin, Wilson, and Churchill
have such ironic relevance: all three leaders suffered from the same
illness, one that exacerbated certain attributes of their character and
adversely affected their private and official conduct — with unfortunate
ramifications for twentieth-century history

Hypertension is of course a very prevalent malady continuing to
afflict a sizable portion of the population. Franklin D. Roosevelt fell
victim to the same disease in the end, though that had more to do with
transiently altering his thought process than affecting his personality
per se. More ironic still is the manner in which the respective illnesses
of these four leaders were revealed to the public they served. Whereas
Wilson's, Roosevelt's and Churchill's medical conditions were deliberately withheld in societies that champion openness and an informed
public, Stalin's final illness was depicted by the press in abundant detail,
despite the oppressive restrictions of a totalitarian regime that elevated
secrecy to high art.

The irony grows even larger in relation to the issue of declaring
disability. Whereas Grayson refused to certify an obviously disabled
President Wilson as such, those attending Stalin, as one of their first
official acts, declared that the stricken premier would thereafter be
removed from any decisions affecting affairs of state. Though Stalin was
obviously terminally ill, it bears remembering that in the initial stages
of Wilson's collapse, no one was certain that he was not. As for Church-

ill, the power of his personality alone prevented Moran from acting on what his intuition and medical acumen made all too clear.

These peculiarities aside, the available record now affirms that long-standing hypertension played a major role in prematurely aging all three leaders and accentuating certain features of their personalities. To be sure, Stalin's premorbid paranoia was so pervasive that, with or without an aging brain, he might have behaved as he did. Nor is there much doubt that Churchill's recurring bouts of depression would have continued to plague him, just as Wilson's intrinsic self-righteousness perplexed his opponents and supporters alike. Yet to ignore the adverse influence of malignant hypertension on brain function and behavior would render any retrospective psychological analyses of these men incomplete. Absent that influence, perhaps the worst attributes of their character would not have proved so intractable in the end.

PART III
Drugs and Diplomacy

Substance abuse has reached epidemic proportions during the past decade, transcending class, race, and nationality. Long before the need became apparent to publicize the problem, and unknown to virtually everyone at the time, a few national leaders indulged in drugs while in office. As prime minister of Great Britain, Anthony Eden admitted to consuming large quantities of Benzedrine during the Suez Canal crisis of 1956, and John F. Kennedy received frequent injections of amphetamines throughout his presidency. To date, the pathographer's attention has focused on Eden's intermittent bile duct obstruction and Kennedy's adrenal gland insufficiency. Yet those diseases probably had less impact on their private lives and public conduct than the drugs they took to excess.

For four long years as Winston Churchill's foreign secretary, Anthony Eden chafed under the yoke of his own subservient position to an obstreperous political godfather and his nation's increasingly subordinate role in international affairs. Shortly after Churchill's retirement in 1955, an opportunity arose to redress both grievances when Egypt seized the Suez Canal. Suddenly afforded a convenient excuse to show the flag in the Middle East at the expense of Gamal Abdel Nasser, Eden jumped at the chance, flagrantly rejecting both the personal and official diplomacy that he had used so successfully while serving as Churchill's foreign secretary. That impetuous leap into what proved to be political obscurity was influenced as much by his unstable temperament and poor health as by geopolitical events. Yet one other little-known factor contributed to his inexplicable behavior: at the peak of the crisis, Eden was hooked on amphetamines.

If Suez cost Anthony Eden his political career, many commentators believe that John F. Kennedy's televised debates with Richard Nixon in 1960 won him the presidential election. A British physician, Hugh L'Etang, embellished that pervasive belief with what may seem a simplistic appraisal of his own: "Because of an absence of appropriate make-up, Nixon's 'six o'clock shadow' accentuated on television his sinister and somber characteristics, whilst Kennedy, the victim of chronic pain and glandular deficiency, was carefully stage managed and programmed to radiate charm and vigour."[1] Taking that summation beyond its "face value" raises more questions than it answers. Had previous observers fallen prey to the ease with which Nixon made himself such a ready target, while overlooking the real reasons behind Kennedy's vitality? Just how was Kennedy "stage managed and programmed?" Was there more behind the engaging demeanor of the King of Camelot than his handlers let on—or even knew?

The search for answers leads to a German emigré physician by the name of Max Jacobson, whom Kennedy had met a week before the first debate. The doctor's list of patients reads like a social register. On that day, he added a future president to his stable of affluent socialites. That would have serious implications for Kennedy's health, because the treatment Jacobson administered to his patients was invariably the same: injections of various combinations of stimulants, including amphetamines and steroids. Only a few scholars have made reference to this disturbing indictment.[2] Others have simply concluded that the veil of secrecy surrounding Kennedy's health was so effective that the entire story would never be told.[3] But no pathographer has examined the impact of drugs on Kennedy's conduct in any detail. As in the case of Eden before him, previous accounts may have focused on the wrong disease.

CHAPTER 7

Anthony Eden: Metamorphosis of a Statesman

Winston Churchill's role in Anthony Eden's failure was by no means inconsequential, for theirs had become an increasingly untenable relationship as the younger man agonized over the prize his aging mentor dangled before him. Many of Churchill's associates suspected that the prime minister enjoyed playing upon his protégé's increasingly fragile emotions. Despite Eden's formidable reputation as a diplomat, he had long been regarded by some as a spoiled brat. "You can have a scene with a child of great violence . . . and ten minutes later the whole thing is forgotten," Sir Evelyn Shuckburgh once observed. "This is not possible with grownups, but it's a regular thing with Anthony Eden."[1] To make matters worse, Eden's longing to rid himself of Churchill's oppressive shadow was only magnified by the Old Man's attempts to monopolize any event that lent itself to favorable public exposure. This recurring theme in their relationship suggests that between 1951 and 1955 the political stage had become too small to accommodate them both.

Yet another vexing problem chipped away at Eden's wounded vanity, first as foreign secretary and later as prime minister: Britain's postwar relationship with the United States and recently acquired subservience to its stronger ally. His preeminent biographer, David Carlton, believes that Eden's unwillingness to accept the role of a junior partner was of paramount importance in understanding the last years of his political career.[2] That view is shared by Terence Robertson and others: "Eden . . . was resentful in the presence of [Secretary of State John Foster] Dulles that his country's decline from greatness should deprive him of the right to appear as the decisive presence in world affairs; and that Dulles, representing a new and great power, was given to tactlessly reminding Eden on occasion that despite the authority he had once enjoyed, he now played a lesser role."[3]

Might the effects of Eden's subordination to the likes of a Churchill or a Dulles have carried over into the diplomatic arena? Did the constant exasperation of playing second fiddle, on both a personal and a diplomatic level, push Eden to bolster his flagging self-confidence with amphetamines? Could a combination of perceived inferiority and harmful drugs that magnified his crisis orientation have been enough to foster irrational policies in Eden's relations with Egypt and the United States over the Suez Canal? Unanswerable questions, perhaps, but such a scenario should not be rejected out of hand.

At what date Eden surrendered psychologically to the support of stimulants is not clear, but certainly after 1953 one can trace a critical acceleration in qualities associated with one such drug he is known to have used to excess. Benzedrine, the first member of its class known to induce central-nervous-system stimulation, had found its way into medicine as a stimulant and euphoric in the late 1930s. At one point, it was perceived to be as versatile a remedy as aspirin; a 1946 study listed thirty-nine accepted clinical uses for the drug.[4] Only later did Benzedrine's dependency-producing properties become apparent; subsequently its use was drastically curtailed, and appropriately so. According to one leading pharmacologic authority: "Too freely available, too readily prescribed, and probably more treacherous than any other addicting substance, amphetamines have damaged individuals far more than they have helped."[5] These are disquieting observations indeed when applied to a leader who admitted to being dependent on such drugs in the midst of a grave international crisis.

Like so many others who abused the drug, Eden chose when and how much of it to take.[6] That he self-destructed as a result is more than plausible. For one thing, amphetamine-induced mood changes correlate with the underlying temperament of the individual. Though an average dose may have only negligible effects on a person of calm demeanor, even small amounts impact dramatically on the high-strung, temperamental, anxiety-ridden individual, a personality profile Anthony Eden appears to have exemplified.[7] For another, restlessness, anxiety, insomnia, confusion, and fear to the point of panic are among the drug's adverse short-term psychological effects.[8] There is, then, cause for more than passing interest in the observation of an associate who confided that "the most forbidding aspect of Eden . . . was his growing irascibility and restlessness."[9]

The reasons why people take amphetamines reflect Eden's situation to the letter: the physical need to stay awake; the psychological need to combat anxiety, depression, and feelings of inferiority; and the practical need to think clearly and act forcefully. Laboring through the Suez crisis with less than five hours of sleep a night, perceiving condescension in the American president and his secretary of state, and resolved to send Nasser a forceful message without losing face, the anxiety-ridden prime minister needed a psychological crutch to bolster his self-confidence.

Benzedrine offered a ready solution for one who had already been living on his nerves for some time.

This is of singular importance in understanding Eden's perplexing transformation during the 1950s. The early effects of twenty to thirty milligrams daily (at least two but no more than six tablets) include wakefulness, alertness, and a decreased sense of fatigue. Superficially, amphetamines also increase initiative, embolden self-confidence, and enhance one's ability to concentrate.[10] Exceeding that amount, particularly on an ongoing basis, induces anxiety, irritability, loss of judgment, delusions of persecution, and even a psychological dependency. In fact, an overt amphetamine psychosis may occur in as short a period as five days, even when the drug is taken orally at modest doses.[11] Not that one need postulate a psychosis to understand how adversely Eden's leadership capabilities could have been affected by amphetamines. The motive for taking a central-nervous-system stimulant, the type of personality predisposed to its worst side effects, and the deleterious impact on his behavior are all a part of the historical record.

Before the international crisis that precipitated Eden's character disintegration, Great Britain was still a force to be reckoned with in the Middle East—at least in the minds of archconservative officials in the government who had nurtured imperialistic pretensions for years. As the historian Hugh Thomas emphasized: "The word 'empire' was hardly yet anachronistic. The continuing political weakness of France and of Europe, combined with the unpopular dogmatism of United States diplomacy, gave Britain the illusion of greater power than she actually possessed."[12] This illusion received a substantial jolt when Nasser unilaterally nationalized the Suez Canal during the spring of 1956 as a response to the decision of the United States and Great Britain to withdraw from the Aswan Dam project, which Egypt deemed critical to its economic development.

Britain's distaste for Arab machinations in the Middle East had already been whetted by Jordan's unexpected dismissal of the British commander of the Arab Legion in March, a move that Eden viewed as Nasser-inspired.[13] Piqued by the challenge to Britain's waning prestige Eden had wanted a forceful resolution to that issue, but the United States had refused to follow his lead. Though both nations paid lip service to face-saving diplomatic negotiations, the resulting breach between the two fostered a lingering resentment that contributed to desultory attempts at best on the part of Great Britain's prime minister to resolve the Suez conflict.

While ostensibly playing the diplomatic game, Eden fell under the influence of the French in accepting a conspiratorial plan of military intervention to crush Nasser. The indictment of history rests on the fact that the prime minister promoted the scheme without the knowledge, much less consent, not only of Eisenhower but of his own government. Ignoring any negotiated gains being made on the issue, he cynically and secretly prepared for war. The plan unfolded with the inducement of Israel to invade the Canal Zone, after which the French and British entered the conflict disguised as a "peace-keeping" force. Once hostilities began, however, Eden crumbled under Eisenhower's fierce rebuke and reversed himself completely, after which much of his duplicity in the affair came to light.

Eden's prior track record only magnifies the tragedy of the Suez Canal crisis in relation to compromised British leadership. When he was appointed prime minister in 1956, Eden probably had fewer enemies than any politician of his day. He had been the obvious successor to an aging Churchill for so long that few of his colleagues in the cabinet were prepared to oppose him. Indeed, Eden was said to possess "a silencing authority" in foreign affairs on the basis of his previous diplomatic triumphs.[14] At the beginning of his tenure, the *Daily Telegraph* commented: "Training, knowledge, and courage are the unquestionable assets of our new Prime Minister."[15]

Those assets notwithstanding, there were problems other than Eden's strained relationship with Churchill that would affect his conduct during the Suez crisis. One had already been festering for two years: conflicts between Dulles and Eden had waxed and waned, but by 1956 their mutual distrust was a permanent fixture in the diplomatic order. It had come to a head when Eden reneged on his assurance to participate in an anti-communist alliance with the United States in the Far East.[16] Aside from its unfavorable effect on his relationship with Dulles, such a move led to later charges that Eden was an appeaser of Communism—a harsh and painful indictment against a man who had once resigned from the cabinet of Neville Chamberlain because of his own prime minister's appeasement of Adolf Hitler.

Still another problem arose during Eden's tenure as foreign secretary. Taking a card from Churchill's hand, he had sought to thrust Britain into a unique position linking Western Europe with the United States. That was a vainglorious gesture, considering Britain's depleted economic resources and its status, in American eyes, as just another European state. At this pivotal period in its history, Great Britain seemed to have inherited the worst of both worlds: Europe took Eden seriously as a neo-isolationist; the United States did not take him seriously enough but was too polite to say so.[17] Therein lay the seed of further national and personal humiliation. Even so, few could accuse Eden of significant misjudgments during his tenure in the Foreign office. His performance there stands in stark contrast to his later record as prime minister. Why, then, the change?

The historiography of this period supplies conflicting answers. What might be described as the "official" party line on Suez is outlined in Eden's memoirs and those of his chancellor of the exchequer, Harold Macmillan. Both blamed the United States for failing to support Britain in achieving a rapid solution to the crisis, thereby leaving Eden little alternative but the use of force.[18] Although Nasser claimed that the cancellation of funding for the Aswan Dam was his main reason for nationalizing the canal, Macmillan and Eden saw the seizure in a much more sinister light. To their way of thinking, Nasser was a reincarnation of Hitler and Mussolini rolled into one.[19]

Eden in particular lambasted his critics for failing to draw the appropriate parallel and see its ultimate implications: "From the onset, there had been those who were not prepared to see this dispute for what it was, the denial of an international arrangement recently reaffirmed by the Egyptian government, and the seizure by force of international property. They preferred to look upon it as the expression of a nationalist mood in a country recently emancipated, for which . . . benevolent allowances must be made."[20] He therefore had to institute a secret plan, all the while making public references to the need to settle the dispute by peaceful means. Although Macmillan portrays his prime minister as showing "the greatest moderation and prudence" at this juncture, Eden's real intent was unmasked by the following reflection in his memoirs: "From the start we had to prepare to back our remonstrances with military actions. The Chiefs of Staff were instructed to get ready a plan and a timetable for an operation designed to occupy and secure the Canal, should other methods fail."[21]

It became immediately apparent, however, that the United States would not lend active assistance to such a venture. Dulles favored instead an international Suez Canal Users' Association (SCUA) to manage the canal, and Britain reluctantly backed this proposal as a means of keeping the lines of communication open with the United States. Yet both Macmillan and Eden were soon to indict the United States on three separate occasions for torpedoing efforts to negotiate forcefully with the Egyptians during September 1956, allowing Nasser to believe that he could safely disregard the threat of force. By Eden's own admission, September 13 was the date on which Britain became irrevocably committed to force for lack of a suitable alternative.[22]

Ostensibly, there still remained one last hope for a peaceful settlement: On October 9, direct talks began in New York at the United Nations between Britain's foreign secretary, Selwyn Lloyd, and the Egyptian foreign minister. In truth, these negotiations were nothing but a smoke screen. Eden and the French minister, Christian Pineau, had already met secretly in London on October 2 to firm up their mutual understanding. Terence Robertson's account highlights the importance of that meeting:

> They were alone in the privacy of Eden's study for a meeting which can be recognized in retrospect as the hinge of the crisis. Use of force . . . was reborn and established so firmly as Anglo-French policy that the excited activity and hopes at the United Nations were actually of *no consequence at all.* When the talks at Downing Street ended that evening, there was agreement in principle between Pineau and Eden that their two countries would act jointly in concert with Israel against Egypt; and further, that Eden and Lloyd should go to Paris on October 18, *after the formality* of taking the crisis to the United Nations had been completed, to discuss the next steps in detail. [Emphasis added][23]

Britain and France, unknown to virtually all members of Eden's own government, had already embarked upon their fateful plan.

Following several other clandestine meetings, the military charade commenced on October 29 with Israel's invasion of Egypt. There followed a turbulent week in which the United Nations censured Israeli aggression and the House of Commons was in an uproar over the unauthorized war. Eden retorted that he was not prepared to give any details of what was happening in the Middle East. Only with great reluctance did he finally admit that Great Britain was a cobelligerent.[24]

As opposition to Britain's involvement in the duplicitous scheme arose both at home and abroad, Eden's fortunes slipped as quickly as did his resolve. On November 6 the cabinet precipitately agreed to a ceasefire on the recommendation of its now confused and beleaguered leader. That was a dramatic and inexplicable reversal. No doubt the cornered prime minister was politically compromised by events. Yet his tenuous health may have had more to do with his perplexing behavior than the hostile political and diplomatic climate.

With official papers concerning Britain's involvement in the Suez crisis either nonexistent, unavailable for study, or destroyed,[25] Eden's memoirs have been dismissed by most as a diplomatic apologia. And Macmillan's account is of interest as much for what it omits as for what it says. Hugh Thomas was one of the first historians to assess in an impartial fashion what few data remain. He certainly asked the right questions. Should Dulles be saddled with all the blame? Did Suez represent a military or political failure? If it was a political one, was that the result of a breakdown of cabinet government, or had it been a "collective aberration?" Finally, if it was a personal more than a collective failure, did illness play a decisive role in disturbing the judgment of the prime minister at the time?[26]

To understand Eden's perception of the problem and its political implications, one must know something of the history of British interests in the Middle East. Though realistic enough to sacrifice the Crown's influence in certain regions of the Empire, successive British governments demonstrated extreme reluctance to forfeit control in the Arab world. Not surprisingly, when Nasser seized the Suez Canal in 1956, British reaction bordered on panic. Anthony Nutting, a member of the Foreign Office who later wrote his own critical account of the crisis, explicated the essence of that reaction in captivating metaphor: "If Britain was going to revert to nineteenth-century methods to settle a dispute, it must find a twentieth-century pretext for doing so. If they were going to commit an assault, they must appear to be wearing a policeman's uniform."[27]

Certainly Eden's coconspirators in France had substantial reasons to be involved, the least of which concerned the Suez Canal itself. The French regarded the nationalization of Suez less as a disaster than as an opportunity to crush Nasser. Their consuming objective at this time was to win the war in Algeria—for which they held Egypt ultimately responsible, believing as they did that military support for Algeria was coming directly from Cairo. At least from the standpoint of personalities, Eden and French Premier Guy Mollet saw eye to eye on how to handle the Egyptian upstart. That such a meeting of the minds may have been inappropriate (at least for Eden) was suggested by Lester Pearson: France was already fighting the Arabs and had nothing much to lose, but the British had more to lose and less to gain.[28] The results would ultimately speak for themselves: Britain gained nothing and lost a great deal. Eden, for his part, was to lose his reputation as well.

With Nasser's seizure of the canal, Eden at last had his pretext for a forceful showdown in the Middle East. Even when increasingly effective economic sanctions, combined with growing pressure from the Arab League, induced Nasser three months later to accede to terms that Selwyn Lloyd described as offering "an acceptable compromise," these initiatives became a dead letter because of Eden's refusal to endorse any plan short of military assault.[29]

Anthony Nutting foresaw the dangers of aligning too closely with Israel or France and warned Eden accordingly. The prime minister's reply, as reported by Nutting, revealed his true intent:

> If we did not show strength now, we would eventually lose all our oil to Nasser. The Americans did not really care about the Suez Canal . . . but the Israelis deserved to be allowed to use it. . . . He did not care whether

[opposition leader Hugh] Gaitskell supported or opposed him. As for the U.N., they had proved to be a dead loss. . . . Compromise with Nasser would only serve to whet his appetite. . . . *This man must be destroyed before he destroyed all of us.* [Emphasis added][30]

Against the best advice of his closest advisers, then, Eden uncharacteristically adopted a pro-Israel stance, inaccurately gauged American intentions, ignored the bipartisan support he needed for effective unity at home, abandoned faith in the United Nations, and affirmed a personal vendetta against Nasser.

Other blunders followed in rapid succession. Eden continued to seek American support only on his own terms—"a vainglorious course," his biographer noted, "for a junior partner with much at risk."[31] Nor did he make the most of the opportunities afforded him. For one thing, he could have made any agreement to cancel the dam project contingent upon an alignment of America's Middle Eastern policy with that of Great Britain. In earlier years, such a skilled negotiator would have asked for something in return. At this juncture, however, Eden inexplicably ignored that possibility.

If Eden's goal was really to achieve a peaceful solution, his refusal to support the negotiations at the United Nations was inconsistent. And although he continued to claim that Nasser would never negotiate in good faith, international pressures were already providing strong inducement for the Egyptian leader to do so: by mid-October Nasser had conceded the principle of user participation in the operation of the canal. Yet Eden perceived that his efforts had been abandoned in favor of Dulles's Users' Club arrangement, a fact that wounded his pride and hardened his suspicions.[32] He simply refused to acknowledge that the new proposal gave Britain the essence of what it required to keep the canal open.

Given the paradoxically threatening success of UN negotiations, the French recognized the urgency of bringing Britain into the conspiracy being planned with Israel. Seizing the moment, Mollet's emissaries arranged another clandestine meeting with Eden and Nutting on October 14. For one thing, they needed British bomber bases to protect Israel's cities against retaliatory Eygptian air raids. For another, an unanticipated threat to their tenuous alliance had arisen: Israel had fomented reprisal attacks on Jordan, and Britain, under the Tripartite Declaration of 1950, was obligated to resist any attack across the territorial borders of the Arab-Israeli world. Just prior to the secret meeting, Eden had taken it upon himself to warn Nutting "not to plunge the country into war merely to satisfy the anti-Jewish spleen" of his people in the Foreign Office.[33] Strange words indeed from a man whose intent was to find a pretext for launching a military operation of his own—and who, on the following day, would enter into collusion with France and Israel to drag his country into war after all.

At the meeting on October 14, French emissary Albert Gazier inquired what Britain's response would be if Israel were to attack Egypt. Foreign Secretary Lloyd replied that the Tripartite Declaration effectively bound Britain to a well-defined course of action—to which Grazier countered with the somewhat specious argument that, among other things, Nasser had recently contended that the Tripartite did not apply to Egypt. Eden was ecstatic. "So that lets us off the hook," he exclaimed excitedly. "We have no obligation, it seems, to stop the Israelis attacking the Egyptians."[34] Such thinking, of course, ignored the fact that whatever Egypt said about the declaration, Britain (as a signatory to it) was still bound by its obligations. Yet by then Eden's thinking was anything but clear. Whatever the advice of those few colleagues who knew what he was up to, the prime minister had already made up his mind to go along with the French plan.

The implications were clear at least to Nutting:

> Our traditional friendships with the Arab world were to be discarded; the policy of keeping a balance in arms deliveries between Israel and the Arab States was to be abandoned; indeed, our whole peace-keeping role in the Middle East was to be changed and we were to take part in a cynical action of aggression. . . . And all to gain for ourselves guarantees for the future operation of the Suez Canal which had only a day or so before been substantially gained in Lloyd's negotiations with [the Egyptians] in New York.[35]

In a vacuous defense for posterity, Eden attempted to make the entire cabinet responsible for the affair, claiming that he had discussed the situation with its members in such detail that they "had grown to know each other's minds."[36] Yet cabinet unity, if it existed at all, was more apparent than real. Eden deceived himself into believing that Sir Walter Monckton, his minister of defense, resigned at this time solely on the grounds of ill health. He made no reference whatsoever to the resignation of Anthony Nutting. The testimony of one senior minister highlights the cabinet's predicament in bold relief: "Eden had dictated [to the cabinet] more than Churchill had ever done. In foreign affairs his word was law. Thus, in the unfolding crisis of Suez, each decision taken by the British cabinet *was peculiarly Eden's*" (emphasis added).[37]

No military force of the size required to mount such an offensive had ever before been assembled without the knowledge, much less the support, of the opposition leadership. This was one of Eden's first overt acts of duplicity; another was his failure to inform the United States of his plans. Veiled references to the use of force "as a last resort" hardly covered planned military collusion with France on a specific scale and with an outlined timetable. Just as his treatment of the Foreign Office and the opposition undermined Eden's support at home, so did his conduct toward the United States erode his support abroad.

Eden's precarious position did not pass unnoticed by his allies. Prime Minister Robert Menzies of Australia ruefully recalled asking Dulles whether the British and French had weighed the risks of their venture carefully enough. "I asked Eden the same thing," Dulles replied. "He said they'd rather risk a world war then sink to the level of a third-rate power."[38] Selwyn Lloyd was horrified by the implications of such thinking but powerless to change it, for at this critical juncture Eden had cut himself off from the advice of most of those ambassadors and civil servants who had held him in such esteem.

Over the next few weeks the prime minister entered a surrealistic world. Committing 100,000 men to an undeclared war without bipartisan governmental support was only the tip of the iceberg.[39] Eden refused altogether to seek the advice of his own foreign secretary when the specifics of the plan for Allied-Israeli collaboration were being outlined during his secret meeting with the French in early October. The acceptance of the plan, then, was solely Eden's work, not his cabinet's. To complicate matters, most of his military command remained totally in the dark until the outbreak of hostilities.

Was it out of indecision or deliberate deception that Eden ignored military and governmental input into the final plan? Even his allies-to-be recognized his role as a conspirator to be somewhat out of character for a man considered the world's foremost diplomat. The Israelis had entertained some doubts about Eden's resolve all along. Aware of Great Britain's traditional pro-Arab stance and its prime minister's tendency to vacillate, Israel's Prime Minister David Ben-Gurion was prescient enough to require some form of written agreement. The British foreign secretary's view, on the other hand, suggests an international deception, pure and simple: "Appearances had to be kept. The Anglo-French [forces] should appear at all times to be defending the Canal against both sides. . . . Anything less than a full war could not be said to threaten the Canal and therefore justify the great ruse."[40] Eden and his French allies, then, were not being hesitant, but actually intended to deceive. In the words of one investigator, they "wished to appear virtuous while being Machiavellian." To cover their tracks, the coconspirators took an oath at Sevres on October 24 that "none would in the lifetime of the others reveal what they had witnessed."[41]

Later that same day, Eden gave his own cabinet what was in effect a *casus belli,* and the decision was vaguely made to intervene in some way. At that point Anthony Nutting considered resigning: "I felt no anger; only sadness . . . that Eden, who had always in the past seemed such a model of integrity in public affairs, should now debase our standards of international behavior by this disreputable maneuver."[42] These are not merely the bitter reflections of a colleague out of step with the rest of his team. England had undertaken collusion with Israel in a scheme that ran counter to the spirit of the Tripartite Declaration, as France and Britain attacked the victim rather than the aggressor. The 1954 agreement with Egypt, which allowed the English to intervene militarily only at the request of the Egyptian government, was similarly ignored. Britain was also in violation of the United Nations Charter. The results of all of this were catastrophic. A split with America appeared irrevocable; the Commonwealth itself was divided on the issue; and the Arab world was now firmly aligned against Great Britain.[43]

Yet Eden forged ahead with his scheme like a man consumed. At the next cabinet meeting on October 25, though the "possibility" of conflict between Egypt and Israel was acknowledged for the first time, even then the precise timing of events remained unclear. The cabinet certainly did *not* know that Israel would definitely attack on October 29. And if, as Eden later alleged, detailed discussions did occur a full four days before the outbreak of hostilities, then his later assertion that the British had no time to inform the United States or the Commonwealth nations simply cannot be defended. The truth of the matter is, he knew that Dulles would have torpedoed the project in midstream. Events thereafter assumed an air of black comedy. The British ambassador to Israel took it upon himself to warn Ben-Gurion that, should Israel attack Egypt, Israel must anticipate retaliation on the basis of the Tripartite Declaration. To which Ben-Gurion coolly remarked: "I think you will find your Government knows more about this than you do."[44]

If secrecy was the operation's mother, then dishonor was its stepchild. Once the opposition began asking questions, Eden stood before his critics and announced that "the moment the French government and ourselves had reached conclusions as to what we would do, I authorized the dispatch of a full message to the United States explaining our action before ever coming to the House."[45] Yet the telegram in which Eisenhower was informed of British intentions was not sent until *after* an ultimatum had been delivered and its terms publicly announced. Perhaps taking a card from Adolf Hitler's hand by precipitating an imaginary crisis as an excuse to overrun a neighbor, Eden had belatedly disclosed the ultimatum to the House of Commons as a "response" to alleged inflammatory Egyptian actions along the Arab-Israeli border. When asked why Britain had not acted as required under the Tripartite Declaration, he speciously contended that there was "nothing in it that precluded Britain from acting as she proposed to do." When also asked why the Anglo-French intervention was not delayed pending emergency Security Council deliberations, Eden responded ambiguously that the Council would be prevented by veto from taking the kind of immediate action required to defuse the crisis—the very crisis that Britain and France had engineered with their own ultimatum.[46]

It was at this juncture that the opposition began to smell a rat[47]— and with good reason: Great Britain and France cast vetoes against a United Nations resolution to establish a cease-fire by substituting UN forces for British and French troops. The irony is obvious: for two countries ostensibly bent on limiting hostilities and separating the combatants to use their veto power to defeat a resolution designed to achieve that result testifies to the quagmire into which Eden and Mollet had sunk. Nutting's prediction had proved true: Eden now found himself isolated from the United States, the Soviet Union, the Arab states, and most of the Commonwealth—if not a growing majority of his own parliament.

More than just isolated, the prime minister became the target of accusations from Labourites and Conservatives alike. If at least one-third of Eden's own party felt betrayed, opposition leader Hugh Gaitskell struck to the heart of the matter when he labeled the Suez scheme an "assault upon the three principles which had governed British policy for . . . the last ten years—solidarity with the Commonwealth, the Anglo-American alliance, and adherence to the Charter of the United Nations."[48] Ducking under the crossfire, Eden blandly assured Prime Minister Gerhardsen of Norway that he "knew nothing which might give credence to the charges of collusion being leveled at the British government."[49]

Eden never did fully reveal his intentions to anyone—allies, opposition, cabinet, or the public he served. The United States received confirmation of the Anglo-French collusion only on November 2, and this from the French, not Eden. In response, the cornered prime minister received a thorough dressing-down from Eisenhower. From that point on, the president refused to deal with the broken man. Under duress, Eden rather precipitately announced that if Egypt and Israel would accept a UN peacekeeping force, Britain would not oppose a cease-fire. As an example of the magnitude and transparency of his duplicity, Eden then proposed that the British and French should themselves constitute the UN peace-keeping force![50] The United Nations of course rejected this proposal and immediately demanded a total withdrawal. The desperate statesman had played his last card, and it had been trumped forthwith. Vehement denunciations from the opposition, not to mention Anthony Nutting's resignation on November 4, led Eden to the brink of despair and exhaustion two days later.

Having entered into a war without the knowledge of either his own Parliament or his most formidable ally, Eden compounded his offense by rashly calling for a cease-fire without consulting either his own military advisers or his coconspirators in France. Only belatedly did he telephone his unilateral decision to the latter.[51] In a manner of speaking, one burglar had turned state's evidence against the other when fingerprints of both were found at the scene. Now totally isolated, Eden retreated to Jamaica on his doctor's orders. That more than just his bile duct (damaged by previous gallbladder surgery) was responsible for his deterioration was intimated by his physician, Sir Horace Evans, who warned his beleaguered patient that he no longer could afford to depend on the Benzedrine he had been consuming in large quantities throughout the crisis.[52] It was left for Eisenhower's secretary of state, himself recuperating from cancer surgery, to point out the inconsistencies in all this during Lloyd's visit to his bedside in the hospital. In a question "almost comic in its incongruity," Dulles chided: "Why did you stop?"[53] Lloyd had no answer for Eden's peremptory decision to suspend hostilities. If there is one impression common to nearly every independent account of this tragedy, it is that something unexplained had transformed Eden's political and personal conduct. Anthony Nutting addressed the critical issue years later: "What has not been explained is how and why Anthony Eden came to adopt a policy which [was] morally indefensible and politically suicidal. . . . Little or nothing is known of the pressures, personal and public, physical and political, which explain how and when and why Eden should have come to act so completely out of character."[54]

Nutting initially sought answers in the unsettling domestic and international developments at the inception of Eden's prime ministership. As problems mounted, a perceptible change became apparent in both Eden's personality and the quality of his leadership. Domestic issues, unfamiliar ground for the new prime minister, were among the first to frustrate him. An editorial in the *Daily Telegraph* accusing him of mismanagement in dealing with inflation and an adverse balance of payments cut him to the quick. "I had never seen Eden so stricken," Nutting recalled. "He was positively writhing in the agony of this barbed shaft which . . . struck him at his weakest point."[55] Under duress, the prime minister's health took a turn for the worse.

Although Nutting was referring in this instance to Eden's failure as a tactician, he clearly had in mind a more literal failure of anatomy as well, for he surmised that nervous tension was beginning to eat away at the "patchwork" of the prime minister's previous bile duct surgery.[56]

Hugh Thomas alluded to his increasingly unstable temperament in the same manner: "Eden's health was still problematical, . . . for he was left with a plastic join in the [bile] duct which apparently left him liable to mysterious fevers and the normal consequences of a bad liver: a strong temper and impatience."[57]

These inauspicious qualities had been festering long before Suez; indeed, many associates had wondered whether Eden lived too much on his nerves for the position of power thrust upon him. His own lord chancellor referred to Eden's "chronic restlessness which . . . affected all of his colleagues," and to his "interference in departmental affairs."[58] R.A. Butler registered the same complaint, despairing of "those innumerable telephone calls on every hour of the day." This led some observers to conclude that despite—perhaps because of—Eden's constant interference, government failed to exercise decisive leadership.[59] It was left to Hugh Thomas, however, to drop the most devastating bombshell of all without recognizing its full significance: "Already in July 1956, Eden was taking many pills. When the crisis came he told an advisor that he was *practically living on Benzedrine*" (emphasis added).[60]

Few would dispute that the new prime minister was under intense domestic pressure to assert both his own and his nation's independence of action during the spring and summer of 1956. Yet the deleterious effects of the amphetamines that he was known to have abused have been all but ignored. Without underestimating the impact that Eden's diseased bile duct undoubtedly had on his general health, one can see in retrospect that his increasing anxiety and nervous tension may well have been a manifestation of central-nervous-system-stimulant effect. What is not known for certain is the precise amount of amphetamine he was taking. Medical records are unavailable, and his private physician left no such detailed account as Lord Moran's concerning Winston Churchill. Nevertheless, Evans's parting comment regarding the need for his patient to dispense with his Benzedrine habit warrants further examination.

Certainly Eden's motive for taking amphetamines was clear enough: he needed the courage to make his own way. Yet subsequent pressures resulted in a progressive dependency on these artificial stimulants to steady his increasingly unstable temperament. Nutting was among the first to pinpoint a date when the stress of Eden's new office precipitated a crash. He described the blow to British prestige with Jordan's sacking of the British Commander of the Arab Legion in March, coming on top of domestic unrest over Eden's leadership, as "the last straw."[61] Randolph Churchill felt the same: "The debate [on March 7] marked the beginning of the disintegration of personality and character that the public thought Eden to possess."[62] Backing a high-strung, sensitive individual into a corner where he or she encounters criticism often brings out the worst in that person, who, as pressures mount, is likely to overreact or to seek refuge elsewhere. For those who have access to them, drugs offer an escape.

Sad to relate, the trade-offs that come with taking Benzedrine to excess—volubility, excitement, aggressiveness, paranoia, impulsiveness, and poor judgment—are all mentioned in contemporary descriptions of Eden from that point onward. From the very start the prime minister believed that "if Nasser succeeded, it would be the end of Eden"; accordingly, this Arab prima donna "must be destroyed." That only highlights his aggressive and impulsive behavior. On another occasion, Nutting had counseled Eden to be more charitable toward his critics. "For my pains," Nutting recalled, "I was told that I knew nothing about politics and that I had the mentality of a mere Foreign Office official." That underscores his mentor's volubility and poor judgment. Still later: "Eden's reaction to the Canal seizure was almost as if Number 10 itself had been attacked and a howling mob of Arabs was laying siege to Downing Street." This epitomizes his excitability and paranoia. To complicate matters further, the prime minister's insecurity had become his Achilles' heel: "Eden was not tough," Nutting admitted. "The storm which had struck him so suddenly and so soon after realizing his life's ambition . . . hurt his pride and shook his self-confidence."[63]

The need for Eden to redress these shortcomings was never greater than at that moment. Finally thrust on to center stage where accountability for all decisions now rested with him alone, Eden found himself temperamentally unsuited to bear the burden—not to mention that a swaggering Egyptian dictator was attempting to drive one further nail into the coffin of British imperialism. He needed support—political if possible, pharmachologic if necessary. Under the latter's influence Eden's rationality began to erode, unleashing a stream of intemperate acts and vituperative remarks that deeply disturbed his associates.[64] He no longer was the man they had known, as Nutting acknowledged:

> Eden completely lost his touch. Gone was his old uncanny sense of timing, his deft feel for negotiation. . . . He behaved like an enraged elephant charging senselessly at invisible and imaginary enemies in the international jungle. . . . A feeling [later] came over me that I was talking to a total stranger. No longer did we see things in the same way. . . . What I did not know was how much of this metamorphosis was due to sickness and to the poison from the damaged bile duct which was eating away at his whole system.[65]

The elegant metaphor strikes at the heart of the matter but misses the central mark, for the neurologic and psychiatric manifestations of biliary system disease (known as "hepatic encephalopathy") scarcely match Eden's behavior.[66] Disturbances of awareness and mentation are the harbingers of that condition, yet during his entire illness the prime minister never experienced those symptoms. Then, too, shifting combinations of such neurologic signs as rigidity (rigid body posture), hyperreflexia (increased reflexes), and asterixis (a slow, rhythmic tremor) emerge in conjunction with these mental changes, and are invariably present by the time clouding of consciousness becomes apparent.[67] Again, Eden never demonstrated such physical signs. Bile-duct obstruction as an explanation for his uncharacteristic behavior is not, then, the whole answer. It may account, at best, for only a few of the symptoms described—whereas amphetamine effect fits virtually all of them and would represent a far more sinister illness for a national leader.

Nutting's unflattering portrait reflected the views of others close to the prime minister. Even in his foreign secretary years, "no one in public life lived more on his *nerves* than Eden did," Lord Kilmuir had remarked.[68] Ambassador Winthrop Aldrich registered his own concerns about Eden's mercurial temperament: "I think his physical condition led to his being even more likely than he had been in the past to exaggerate the urgency of any problem with which he was faced. He had a tendency to feel in every case that a crisis had arisen which required immediate action."[69] Such a sense of temporal urgency and impulsiveness, shading into paranoia, are features consistent with amphetamine effect.

Though no one could agree at what point their ever anxious prime minister reached an irreversible turning point, virtually everyone had an opinion. Nutting recalled a conversation with Walter Monckton just prior to the latter's decision to resign over Eden's handling of the Suez crisis: "Before we parted, Monckton and I discussed at some length what had brought about this nightmarish situation, and in particular, what had happened to transform Eden so completely. [Monckton] made no bones about his view that Eden was a very sick man. He had always been excitable and temperamental, but in the last few months he had seemed to be on the verge of a breakdown."[70]

Others maintained that the watershed had been reached at a much earlier date. In defense of the latter view, Eden's legal adviser had decided by early June 1956 that Nasser's seizure of the Canal was justified as long as he did not close it to shipping—to which his prime minister responded by tearing up the report and flinging it in the lawyer's face. Shortly thereafter, Eden received a letter from Eisenhower counseling caution, which the befuddled prime minister somehow interpreted as justifying force at a later date. One biographer, cogently noting that "there were so many qualifiers in the letter that only Eden . . . could have missed the point," concluded that Eden was "out of sync with his old cautious, compromising self. He was obsessed, a driven man, his vast experience and intellect reduced to tunnel vision."[71]

As early as July, Eden's violent moods and peculiar behavior had become the gossip of the corridors of power.[72] As Lord Moran wrote in his diary on July 21: "The political world is full of Eden's moods at No. 10. All this is known to Winston. . . . He sees that things cannot go on like this for long."[73] Yet, if anything, they only got worse. On September 26, Eden enlisted Nutting to explore the possibility of a "present" that he might extend to Mollet as a demonstration of Anglo-French solidarity: "To my astonishment," Nutting recalled, "Eden suggested that the Foreign Office should have another look at Churchill's offer of common citizenship for all British and French nationals, which was made in 1940 in a desperate effort to keep France in the fight against Hitler. I replied that it seemed hardly appropriate to revive such an offer at this stage. . . . In any event, nothing came of this strange notion."[74]

To be sure, John Foster Dulles bore no small responsibility for Britain's isolated position; his stormy relationship with Anthony Eden is well documented. The irony of this situation lies in the dramatic reversal of their positions: during the previous Indochina crisis Eden had cautioned restraint, while Dulles had pushed for immediate action. With Suez, the two leaders exchanged their swords and plowshares. Perhaps one usually well-informed wag was not being entirely facetious, then, when he offered the opinion that Eden was "prostrated by excessive doses of sedatives, pep-pills, and John Foster Dulles."[75]

A transient delirium may also have played a role in Eden's behavioral aberrations as the crisis accelerated. On October 5 he came down with a shivering fever just two days after the critical meeting among the conspirators that one investigator termed "the hinge of the crisis." What is known is that Eden's temperature reached 106 degrees. Its cause was less certain. "His fever was of course connected with his old bile duct trouble," Hugh Thomas concluded,[76] and admittedly, some of the symptoms described might have been due to an acute inflammation of the bile-duct system known as "cholangitis." But Eden's apparent (and temporary) improvement *following* this illness—a state of "acute intoxication," in Nutting's words[77]—suggests instead an untoward confidence and even euphoria that are the primary therapeutic effects of amphetamines in *lower* doses. With Eden confined to bed under a physician's care during his brief illness, his access to amphetamines may well have been restricted sufficiently that for a short period thereafter, at least, he was not subject to the deleterious side effects of the drug taken in larger quantities.

Even though Eden was able to return to his duties within a few days,

he remained "in uncertain health and in *constant need of drugs*" (emphasis added). This led David Carlton to conclude: "The desperate character of the choices facing him at the beginning of October had caused this
relapse [of his cholangitis]."[78] But life-threatening fevers ascribed to
intermittent bile-duct obstruction would scarcely have been induced by
stress or worry. What seems more plausible is that the stress of the
period may have prompted Eden to increase his amphetamine consumption, which precipitated the deterioration and had perhaps contributed
to the high fever he experienced during the acute phase of his illness
before being hospitalized, as unexplained fever is one of the documented
physical signs of amphetamine overdosage.[79]

From the medical perspective, it is noteworthy that the mysterious
fevers began to appear in early October at precisely the time political
pressures were becoming particularly burdensome and the change in
Eden's physical appearance and leadership qualities so apparent. Bear in
mind that David Carlton and Anthony Nutting have both described
Dulles's publicized refusal on October 2 to follow Eden's lead as a
significant turning- or breaking point.[80] In view of what is now known
of the physical effects of increasing amphetamine ingestion, the appearance of "mysterious fevers" three days later may be more than just
coincidental. Acknowledging that Eden was taking large doses of Benzedrine prior to this time and accepting Carlton's observation that after
October 5 he was "in constant need of drugs" makes this belief more
plausible still.

Unfortunately, large gaps in Eden's medical record preclude absolute certainty. That has prompted some retrospective diagnosticians to
continue to defend the "accepted" diagnosis. To cite but one example:
"Doubtless the bile, traditional spring of odd tempers, had had an earlier
effect on Eden's personality."[81] This reference to bile is a throwback to
medieval beliefs about it as one of the "four humors" responsible for
physiologic function and temperament. What Eden's behavior suggests
instead is the presence of a fifth and very evil humor, whose effect goes
far beyond the most fertile imagination of the medieval physician. The
evidence is simply too compelling to ignore: marked deterioration
during a period of intense stress just prior to an exacerbation of Eden's
presumed cholangitis, followed thereafter by a brief interval of apparent
improvement when access to the drug would have been restricted; then,
from mid-October—when a new round of pressures may have induced
Eden to increase his drug intake once again—until the end of the Suez
crisis, a progressive change for the worse in his behavior and decision-
making.

As a measure of the toll the entire affair had taken on the failing
prime minister, one image remains indelibly etched on tabloid copy the

day Eden was forced to pay the piper in explaining his conduct to a woefully uninformed Parliament. Gone was the heady self-confidence of the foreign secretary years, the graceful demeanor, the imposing, almost pristine appearance. "The Prime Minister sprawled on the front bench, head thrown back and mouth agape," a gallery correspondent noted. "His eyes, inflamed with sleeplessness, stared into vacancies beyond the roof, except when they twitched with meaningless intensity to the face of the clock."[82]

It is one thing for some writers to ascribe Eden's physical decline to his incapacity to withstand incessant interrogation and the sleepless nights that ate away at his physical reserves.[83] It is quite another to ignore drug effect. Allusion has already been made to the insomniac properties of amphetamines and their frequent abuse by individuals forced to function without sleep. Both a motive (sleeplessness) and the result (an unkempt physical appearance and perplexing behavior) suggest that during these climactic days Eden's use of the stimulant may have reached a higher plateau than ever. That the casual observer might have overlooked this is understandable; the Benzedrine abuser may not exhibit obvious signs of drug dependence but will show signs of deterioration—such as a rundown physical condition and unkempt appearance—and also tends to become unreliable, irritable, and unstable.[84]

It comes as no surprise, therefore, that indecisiveness characterized the prime minister to the very end. By November 4, for example, Israel had announced that it would accept a cease-fire if Egypt agreed. Yet Eden admonished Lloyd that it would be wrong to call off an operation that had been carried so far, thus ignoring one remaining possible escape route: the United Nations Emergency Force resolution, which might have been used to justify canceling the troop landings in Egypt.[85] In a highly emotional scene, Butler proposed just such an escape in speaking against the pending British airborne assault. That seemed to "nonplus" the prime minister, who could only "respond in silence by going upstairs to consider his position." A more graphic account suggests a far less composed confrontation, with Eden "totally collapsing, weeping unashamedly, and retreating to his bedroom, threatening resignation."[86] After much vacillation, Eden nevertheless authorized the attack. But when on the following day Eisenhower delivered his own ultimatum, Eden capitulated within the hour and accepted a cease-fire.[87] Abandoned by his allies, victimized by a failing biliary tract, and addicted to amphetamines, Eden had finally self-destructed, taking his scheme and his coconspirators with him.

Now he was fighting for his political survival. Whereas Macmillan, Butler, and Salisbury had questioned his thinking enough in the end to challenge his leadership, Eisenhower ignored him completely. Eden no longer had anyone on his side. His isolation allowed the United States to insist on a total British withdrawal before serious negotiations began, a situation that Eden "did not foresee," as he admitted in his memoirs. The same lack of foresight applied to his inability to assess his own position. In an oblique reference to Macmillan and Salisbury, Eden later charged that "there are always weak sisters in any crisis."[88] Had he looked into the mirror, he might have seen the weakest of the lot. From the medical perspective, such self-delusion is readily understood, for one hazard of the self-administration of psychotropic drugs is the inability of the abuser to assess his physical condition, mood, or performance accurately. That goes a long way toward explaining both Eden's bizarre conduct and the equally bizarre conclusion to his nefarious scheme.

Those less medically inclined have concluded that "Eisenhower showed himself to be in no mood to bargain, with the result that Eden . . . saw no rational alternative to unconditional surrender."[89] The complete record now offers a second opinion that may have accounted for Eden's remarkable volte-face: he was in no condition to consider rational alternatives at all. One alternative might have been to acknowledge the whole scheme and play to the chauvinistic side of British popular sentiment by forging ahead against prevailing world opinion. Choosing among options, however, was no longer a part of his intellectual repertoire during those dark hours. In a state of exhaustion and shock, he left to his subordinates the task of announcing a humiliating capitulation and retreated to Jamaica on the advice of his physician.

Unknown to anyone but his own doctor, Eden's final collapse may have been triggered by a belated attempt to dispense with his pharmacologic crutch. Those who try to kick the habit frequently experience a "crash," the symptoms of which include extreme lethargy, fatigue, anxiety, and terrifying nightmares; the victim tends to be extremely irritable and demanding, which drives people away just when their help is most needed.[90] There hardly exists a more apt description of Anthony Eden during the final days of the Suez crisis. In all likelihood, abrupt amphetamine withdrawal indirectly contributed to the isolation he experienced when suddenly confronted with a crisis of overwhelming proportions.

To emphasize the magnitude of one man's poor health on history, the ultimate implications of the Suez debacle speak for themselves. First, the crisis effectively undermined what little clout Britain and France still had in the Middle East, making it necessary for the United States to fill this vacuum lest the Soviets do so.[91] This only enhanced the authority of American presidents to use shows of force in foreign affairs as they deemed necessary. Following Roosevelt's undeclared war in 1940-41 and Truman's dispatch of American troops to Korea without congressional approval, executive fiat in foreign affairs became a self-perpetuating prerogative with the promulgation of the Eisenhower Doctrine in the Middle East—largely through default by weakened European powers.

Second, Suez represented a stroke of good fortune for the Soviets and an intoxicating tonic for Great Britain's detractors. William Hayter, British ambassador to the Soviet Union, bemoaned the fact that "Suez had . . . been a Godsend to Russia" by diverting world attention from Soviet machinations in Hungary to British imperialism in Egypt.[92] Even the Third World bloc in the United Nations used the Suez affair to justify its more aggressive posture toward the superpowers. As Theodore White pointed out: "That fall of 1956 was a moment of transition in international discourse. The massacre of Hungarians by the Russians had not engaged the emotions of the Triple A block—that was white against white. But the strike of the English and French to repossess control of the Suez Canal had thoroughly disturbed them—that was white against colored."[93]

Other losses became obvious with time. In Anthony Nutting's stark appraisal: "We had achieved none of the objectives, whether pretended or real. . . . We had not separated the combatants; they had separated themselves. We had not protected the Canal; it was blocked. We had not safeguarded British lives and property. We had not seized control of the Canal. We had not toppled Nasser. And even the French had turned on Britain for calling a halt."[94] To the bitter end, Eden ignored the increasingly obvious lessons of twentieth-century history that Britain should never venture far in foreign policy matters independent of American support. He had assumed that Eisenhower, as an old friend of the Grand Alliance, could be separated from the influence of Dulles. More than just an unfounded assumption, that was a flagrant exercise in poor judgment.

The biggest mistake the prime minister made, however, was to deceive his own people. Always the epitome of honesty as foreign secretary, now Eden deceived even himself by believing that chauvinistic public opinion required, as he later termed it, "a spot of adventure."[95] If so, he chose the wrong place to accommodate it, despite the warnings of more prescient friends. Nor did he appreciate that by October the public psychology had changed: any agreement reached on the basis of negotiations in good faith would have been far more palatable for the man on the street than the defeat his country was forced to swallow in the aftermath of Suez. Eden's whole career should have prepared him to be the right man at the right time to deal with just such a crisis. He might even have emerged the hero of the negotiation process once again, had he allowed Lloyd's initiatives with Egypt to reach fruition. Instead, "obstinately deciding . . . to scratch out the eyes of his opponent," he did not consider what would happen afterward.[96]

Further, the Suez affair erased much of the popularity Eden had assiduously cultivated in the Middle East during his years as Churchill's foreign secretary. True, there had already been a decline in British power and prestige during the first third of the twentieth century, but it accelerated during the next twenty years, concluding with Suez, when Eden was either close to the helm of or guiding the ship of state. Any historical analysis of this decline, then, will undoubtedly focus upon Eden simply because the extent of Britain's vulnerability was blatantly exposed on his watch. Yet Suez was but one milestone in that process, and for this reason, some historians and biographers would choose to judge his role less harshly. To Carlton's way of thinking, "Suez may seem a relatively unimportant event, more symbolic than seminal, more an effect than a cause of national decline."[97] Few would deny that the debacle was symbolic, yet its importance should not be understated: on the heels of four years of indecisive leadership under Churchill, Eden's Suez adventure confirmed that Britain had lost control of international affairs.

In such a paradoxical fashion might Thomas Carlyle's Great Man theory be vindicated. The lessons inherent in the Suez Canal crisis spotlight the extraordinary influence a single individual can have on events—in this instance, largely a negative influence. Perhaps Lord Mountbatten said it best: "It was astonishing to me to see what one really persistent man could do if he was Prime Minister. [Eden] never let Parliament know what was going on. He really never let the Cabinet know."[98]

Had Eden abandoned his time-honored role as a negotiator under the stress of witnessing Britain's diminishing role in world affairs? Had he chafed for far too long under the thumb of a legendary prime minister, uncertain of his own succession, until he had lost confidence in his ability to make his own way? Or had the effects of chronic amphetamine abuse on a naturally high-strung individual under continuous stresses robbed him of his senses? There is room to debate whether Eden was propelled by extrinsic domestic and diplomatic pressure, as the traditional view suggests, or whether powerful intrinsic pressures, temporarily relieved yet complicated by drugs, were partly responsible.

In defense of the latter point, can it truly be said that the external pressures were greater in the Suez crisis than at any earlier period in Eden's career? For the first time, to be sure, he was as prime minister taking full political responsibility for his decisions, rather than merely implementing another's orders. That may have made the extrinsic pressures harder to handle. Yet this is also to admit that his untoward sensitivity to these pressures could have been predicted on the basis of his personality before the advent of disease. Eden's previous diplomatic record notwithstanding, those political pundits familiar with his mercurial temperament might have done better to consider—long before Suez—the dangers of allowing him to lead.

Historians considering the impact of illness on Anthony Eden's leadership have in part missed the point by emphasizing his bile duct pathology. Peter Calvocoressi spoke for the broad majority of investigators who acknowledged that Eden was ill yet rendered no verdict concerning the implications of his illness. Taking Eden's inexplicable reversal when he called for a cease-fire as an example, Calvocoressi concluded: "There were a number of ingredients to this decision. The principal ones—and I am not trying to put them in any order of importance—were American attitudes, British public opinion, and the Prime Minister's health. We cannot enlarge on this last point because we do not know enough about it." [99] Of course, Hugh Thomas's revelation concerning Eden's injudicious use of amphetamines was made public one year *after* Calvocoressi conducted his investigation. But subsequent investigators, who thereafter possessed the critical link to reconstruct the complete puzzle of Eden's ill health, largely ignored its overriding significance. Bile was not the only evil humor afflicting Anthony Eden. That one-sided thesis may confidently be laid to rest. While increasing his discomfort and compromising his overall health substantially, Eden's damaged bile duct played a lesser role in altering thought processes and behavior (and, consequently, leadership potential) than his abuse of amphetamines.

To ignore the effects of genuine international and domestic pressures as they contributed to Eden's uncharacteristic and irrational decisions during this period is to perpetrate a disservice upon the numerous scholarly words that have emphasized them. Nonetheless, more must be learned of any given leader's day-to-day health, and attempts made to reconcile disease processes with their increasing limitations on performance, if we are to understand why the individual functions as he or she does at any given time. That Anthony Eden, for one, wrestled unsuccessfully with those limitations assured the somber epitaph historians have inscribed on his political tombstone.

CHAPTER 8

John F. Kennedy: Doctoring the Image

Accounts of John F. Kennedy's health both before and during his presidency traditionally fall somewhere between preserving a myth and unraveling a mystery. On the one hand, there is the indomitable JFK of political folklore, wrestling against great odds to overcome chronic back pain and a potentially fatal glandular deficiency. Like another Democratic legend who preceded him in the Oval Office, Kennedy turned his physical handicaps into assets, enough for the mythmakers to conclude that he was more than fit to bear the stress of the office.[1] On the other hand, there are those who see something sinister in the lengths he went to in order to conceal his underlying Addison's disease, leading one to wonder what else may have been hidden once Kennedy reached the sanctuary of the White House.[2] To underscore the point, none of these sources makes more than fleeting reference to his long-standing steroid dependency—much less mentions his abuse of amphetamines while president. A second opinion is therefore in order before accepting out of hand, as his presidential physician once did, that Kennedy's health remained at "optimal efficiency" for the performance of his official duties.[3]

Before exploring the darker side of presidential substance abuse, we would do well to remember that Kennedy had a drug problem of sorts long before being introduced to amphetamines by Dr. Max Jacobson. Not that he had consumed steroids for pleasure or through habit; rather, as a member of Lyndon Johnson's entourage revealed during the Democratic National Convention of 1960, Kennedy had suffered from Addison's disease for years—a condition in which the adrenal glands lack the capacity to produce enough steroid hormones to meet the body's needs. Much has been made of this by subsequent pathographers;[4] only one was prescient enough to ask whether the treatment did not deserve as much attention as the disease.[5]

Taken in excess, steroids elicit a host of undesirable side effects. The most noticeable physical ones are a peculiarly flushed countenance, a full, rounded face ("moon facies"), and excessive fat deposits between the shoulders ("buffalo hump")—the last two induced by fluid retention in the tissues. The behavioral effects are more subtle and sinister, running the gamut from agitation and nightmares to hallucinations and even paranoia. Little wonder that the senator's campaign managers would have preferred to keep the lid on Johnson's disclosure; they appreciated that, drug effect aside, Kennedy's underlying illness had contributed to his lackluster performance as a freshman congressman.[6] With higher stakes now on the table, his spin-doctors opted for second best. By putting the best face on his disease, they managed to transform their presidential candidate into a war hero with a Purple Heart that was worth its weight in political gold.

Their success was hardly a surprise; after all, the Kennedy camp had been well attuned to orchestrating medical cover-ups for some time. Intimations of things to come occurred as early as 1946, during his first campaign for a House seat from Massachusetts. Prone to excessive fatigue, weight loss, chronic infections, and ill-defined stomach problems since his youth, Kennedy had apparently been taking an unknown medication to treat at least some of these symptoms for years. That bit of information we owe to his father, who, upon learning of his son's collapse following one particularly strenuous trek on the campaign trail, had asked a Kennedy aide whether "Jack had his pills."[7] What those pills were, or where they came from, has never been determined. We do know that between 1941 and the conclusion of his successful campaign for the House seat, Kennedy made at least three trips to Rochester, Minnesota. This led some to suspect that he had been receiving treatment at the Mayo Clinic all along. Certainly that had been the case in January 1944, after he sustained a back injury in the now legendary PT-109 accident. Though his father remained optimistic about his son's complete recovery, Kennedy's doctors apparently did not share that opinion.[8] Whether their concern lay with his back problem or his string of mysterious illnesses is uncertain, as no official records of these visits are available. Even so, it should not pass unnoticed that Mayo was then at the forefront of research activities directed at Addison's disease.

Whatever treatment Kennedy might have received there during the early 1940s, steroids were probably not among them.[9] Dr. Elmer C. Bartels of the Lahey Clinic in Boston was the first physician publicly acknowledged to have used an analogue of the drug to treat JFK for an Addisonian crisis in 1947. Kennedy had nearly died of acute adrenal insufficiency while in London and returned to Boston for treatment— but not before having frantially cabled an aide in Washington to have two unknown prescriptions from a "Dr. Sullivan in Baltimore" sent to him.[10] For his part, Bartels asserted that this was the first time Kennedy ever knew he had unequivocal Addison's disease. Only then was he treated with dietary restrictions and subcutaneous implants of desoxy-corticosterone acetate (DOCA).

Who was the mysterious Dr. Sullivan, and what had he been prescribing? Or was "Dr. Sullivan" a code name? If one acknowledges that Kennedy was one of the first Addisonians to receive cortisone in oral form,[11] did that come from the Mayo Clinic or from Bartels? If from both, did the two communicate so as to avoid overmedicating their "shared" patient? In a worst-case scenario, was Kennedy being treated for the same condition by still a third unidentified physician from Baltimore in the late 1940s and early 1950s, with all that implies for the difficulty in regulating the amount of steroid he received?

Speaking under conditions of strict confidentiality, a physician who trained at the Mayo Clinic during the early 1960s asserts that numerous calls were received by the chief of endocrinology from unnamed physicians treating the president, seeking advice on the amount of steroid replacement they were to administer. Despite Dr. Bartels's belief that the mainstay of Kennedy's treatment from 1948 on was his own prescription of 25 milligrams of cortisone and injections of 150-300 milligrams of DOCA every three months, it now seems plausible that his patient may have been receiving more from other unnamed sources.[12] Had the Kennedy penchant for secrecy and the clandestine activities associated with his treatment (including stashes of a ready supply of both cortisone and DOCA in safety deposit boxes around the country)[13] created a potentially dangerous situation in which the right hand of medicine did not know what the left hand was doing?

By 1961 that seems to have been the case. In appearance alone, one of the nation's youngest and ostensibly most vigorous presidents showed unequivocal manifestations of steroid excess. Press photographers were struck by the pudginess of Kennedy's face, which knowledgeable physicians of the day recognized as the telltale "moon facies." More disconcerting still, word circulated in medical circles that he had suffered at least one psychological breakdown as a result of the drug.[14] That happened to have been in the period when Dr. Max Jacobson entered the picture. Though Kennedy's doctors were aware that amphetamines were included in his intramuscular injections to the president, it appears that his concomitant administration of large doses of corticosteroids was overlooked until later analyses revealed their presence in the vials Jacobson had in his possession (see below, p. 173).

The question remains: what was the potential—or real—impact of steroid excess on Kennedy's conduct in office? If appropriately administered and monitored, the fatigue, apathy, and depression associated with Addison's disease can be readily corrected with corticosteroids.

Yet managing that treatment involves a delicate physiologic balance: too little, and the patient lacks adequate reserves to respond to stress, even though the overt signs of Addison's are ameliorated; too much, and peculiar behavior emerges long before any untoward physical manifestations become apparent. Virtually all patients on steroids demonstrate inappropriate euphoria; for those willing to admit it, most at one time or another are also victimized by restlessness, agitation, and insomnia. Higher doses result in manic behavior and even paranoia. Whatever the changes, they closely parallel the dosages administered.[15]

Among the most sinister effects of steroid excess are drug-induced delusional syndromes, defined as the "presence of delusions in a state of wakefulness and alertness," falling just short of overt delirium.[16] And if a slug of steroid is combined with central-nervous-system stimulants such as amphetamines? After all, the documented psychological effects of both are virtually identical: either drug when taken to excess may foster delusions in concert with agitation, anxiety, insomnia, and irritability, not to mention their additive effects when taken in combination.[17]

Hence the alarming significance of Dr. Jacobson's admission (by presidential invitation only) into the medical fraternity engaged in treating the nation's chief executive. Yet the extent to which the doctor was involved became a closely guarded secret of the era. Even though at least one American reporter and one British pathographer drew fleeting attention to the relationship in the 1970s,[18] the most "hidden illness in the White House" remained so obscure that it was not even addressed in a recent and otherwise incisive study under that title, in keeping with previous standard works on Kennedy's health.[19]

It was left to C. David Heymann, in a recent biography of Kennedy's widow, to suggest that the president's abuse of amphetamines was far more pervasive than anyone at the time realized. If Kennedy scholars have taken exception to Heymann's methods, they cannot ignore that he based his charges not only on Jacobson's unpublished autobiography but on court testimony to which he had been given access by the physician's widow, and transcripts of FBI files. To date, no published second opinions by a physician have been advanced regarding the plausibility of Heymann's claims that Kennedy was addicted to amphetamines.[20] Nor have historians assessed the potential impact of that on his presidency.

As with the case of Anthony Eden before him, one must first document beyond a reasonable degree of certainty that Kennedy abused amphetamines, then seek behavioral patterns that match their known side effects, and, finally, assess their impact on events during his tenure that at least raise suspicion. To begin with, Jacobson went on record in the press as having provided indispensable medical services throughout

Kennedy's presidency. In his own words: "I worked with the Kennedys; I traveled with the Kennedys; I treated the Kennedys; they never could have made it without me."[21] To be more specific, Jacobson asserts in his autobiography that his ministrations were instrumental in seeing Kennedy through the Vienna summit meeting, the Cuban missile crisis, a threatened steel strike, and the clash between federal authorities and the state over James Meredith's attempt to enroll in the University of Mississippi.[22] That Jacobson was known to have been treating the president throughout this period only underscores the need to examine these events with the possibility of drug influence in mind.

In the end, however, Jacobson proved to be his own worst enemy. He himself later admitted to being an advocate of what he termed "tissue regeneration," which entailed the injection of "supercharged" particles of animal parts in suspension along with "nerve regenerating chemicals" such as amphetamines, steroids, and vitamins. As Jacobson recorded in a 1968 publication for his Constructive Research Foundation: "Without a general grasp of this [concept of Regenerative Therapy], it is difficult . . . to appreciate the reasons for the departure from the well-trodden paths of conventional medical thinking."[23] This dubious claim notwithstanding, it was by no means difficult for medical authorities to appreciate that the doctor's unfounded practices bordered on quackery. That view, coupled with some unfavorable publicity over the death of one of his patients from an amphetamine overdose,[24] was enough for the New York state attorney general's office to subpoena the records in 1972 from Jacobson's ramshackle and cluttered office, which doubled as an illicit drug laboratory. What they revealed was ample evidence for the state to initiate proceedings to revoke Jacobson's medical license. Much to the chagrin of the Kennedy clan, he was found guilty on forty-eight counts of unprofessional conduct.[25]

Despite assurances to the Kennedy family that Jacobson would not implicate the president during these proceedings (a promise that was apparently kept: in some 4,000 pages of testimony assembled over a two-year period by the New York State Board of Regents' Review Committee on Discipline the White House is mentioned only once, and the subject quickly dismissed),[26] the self-assured doctor glibly spelled out elsewhere his treatment of Kennedy. And there is nothing in the inquiry report to suggest that he would have treated the president any other way than he privately claimed to have done. His injections were all Jacobson knew, a practice he continued to use on himself and all his patients (regardless of the disease he was treating) until the day he lost his license. That said, a universal indictment of the doctor's methods emerges in the labored syntax of one witness: "Treatment for a myriad of diseases all consisted to the extent of almost one hundred percent of administration of injections," which invariably included amphetamines and steroids in combination.[27] For his part, Jacobson downplayed the amount of amphetamine used when he told the press that "the most he ever put in his concoctions [was] a 25 mg dose—usually . . . the dose is less."[28] Forget for the moment that the accepted oral dose is 5 to 10 milligrams in those rare instances when the drug is still used today; an inventory of the vials of medication in his own laboratory revealed that most contained from 30 to 50 mg/cc of amphetamine—"hardly 'trace' amounts," as the inquiry report makes clear.[29]

Boldly manufacturing his concoctions without a license in his rush to dispense them day and night ("Nightly mailings left respondent's office at the rate of twenty to thirty vials to locations throughout the United States and the world"), Jacobson failed to maintain adequate quality control or sterility standards. He was found guilty of malfeasance on both counts; in the words of the inquiry summation: "Adulterated drugs [were found] . . . consisting of filthy, putrid and/or decomposed substances."[30] Jacobson also failed to keep proper records of the stimulants and depressants he prescribed. No doubt he dealt in larger quantities, particularly when it came to the staples of his pharmacopoeia, methamphetamine HCL and dextroamphetamine sulfate. Within a two-year period alone, the doctor was unable to account for 1,474 grams of purchased methamphetamine.[31]

More alarming still was Jacobson's willingness to supply his patients with injectable medication to be self-administered. By the state board's estimate, at least 90 percent of his patients were afforded this dubious luxury.[32] President Kennedy was perhaps among them; the FBI, charged with analyzing these medications in 1961, uncovered five vials that Jacobson had left at the White House, each revealing high concentrations of amphetamines and steroids. Robert Kennedy was so alarmed by Jacobson's increasing access to his brother that he had the Food and Drug Administration analyze fifteen separate vials. Both independent reports coincide with what the state board later disclosed.[33]

Jacobson did not deny that he used amphetamines liberally, on himself as well as his patients. They were not illegal at this early date; nor were their negative attributes and psychological addicting properties common knowledge. That in no way excuses their administration in combination with hefty doses of steroid, garnished with vitamins, ground-up bone marrow, placenta, electric eels, and whatever other solubilized particles Jacobson perceived to be beneficial[34]—particularly when his most esteemed patient was already taking cortisone in large quantities.

The obvious question is how that sordid practice found a willing recipient within the pristine walls of the White House. As most people do, Kennedy obtained his second opinion of sorts concerning Jacobson's skills from trusted friends and other patients. Though Charles Spalding, a close associate and Harvard classmate, recommended the doctor a week before the first presidential debate, it was the Kennedys' photographer and travel companion, Mark Shaw, who spoke so highly of Jacobson that the president finally agreed to see him. That was hardly surprising; Shaw himself was already on the road to addiction, dependent on "Dr. Needles" to supply his habit.[35] Recognizing that this German-trained general practitioner, who billed himself as a "multiple sclerosis researcher," had a dubious reputation at best, Kennedy's other doctors sought in vain to dissociate their patient from him.[36] Yet Janet Travell's warnings regarding the side effects of amphetamines fell on deaf presidential ears, and another Kennedy physician who flatly refused to allow the president to receive further injections from Jacobson was similarly ignored.[37]

Why, then, did Kennedy take so readily to his new doctor? Was Jacobson something of a New Frontier physician, a "can do" innovator who was willing to experiment on the cutting edge of medicine? That seems to have been JFK's perception of the man, or so the brash doctor would have posterity believe: "The treatment of stress had always been one of my specialties," Jacobson confided in his unpublished memoirs. "After his first treatment [the senator] told me his muscle weakness had disappeared. He felt cool, calm, and very alert. . . . First impressions never change."[38] Moreover, Kennedy had been programmed for years in the belief that steroid injections were responsible for keeping him alive, and he had already discovered the dramatic, if transient, benefit of local anesthetics for his back discomfort.[39] Why should another injection be any different? Not that he could turn for answers to Jacobson, who invariably rebuffed those foolish enough to inquire with a brusque "None of your business."[40] As a final measure of Kennedy's guillibility, he later dismissed his brother's horror at what the FDA analysis had uncovered with an equally brusque, Trumanesque reply: "I don't care if it's horse piss. It works."[41]

The president might have thought differently had he known what Jacobson was really concocting behind closed doors in his Constructive Research Foundation. This pharmacologic cottage industry masquerading as a research laboratory rivaled the best bootlegging operation of the Roaring Twenties. To be sure, the times aided and abetted that: purporting to find a cure for multiple sclerosis during the 1950s and 1960s allowed for as much quackery as medicine. Testimony derived from his hearing underscores the point: such quests "encourage the successful exploitation of many forms of quack treatment . . . and orgies of polypharmacy."[42] Jacobson, perhaps unwittingly, took at least part of that lesson to heart. To accommodate (and exploit) those socialites who were naive enough to judge a physician's credentials by his social visibility, there was much to be said for this up-and-comer to erect an impressive facade over his office while cultivating a reputation as "Dr. Feel Good" among those who passed through its doors.

One is reminded of Adolf Hitler's doctor, Theo Morell, who advertised himself as a skin and venereal disease expert while also making a small fortune in the drugs he manufactured, labeled, and sold in his own laboratories. Like Jacobson, amphetamines were the mainstay of Morell's treatment of the Fuehrer, who, like Kennedy, had been introduced to his future physician through social connections. Such well placed contacts played into the hands of two physicians cut from the same cloth, motivated as they were by building a socially prominent clientele that would eventually catapult them to the attention of their respective national leaders.

That Hitler eventually fell captive to his unprincipled physician's administration of a staggering array of central-nervous-system stimulants has been adequately documented.[43] Moreover, Morell's methods were as sloppy as Jacobson's would prove to be. Wandering through the bunker with his bag of drugs in hand and a soiled rag tucked into his belt with which he swabbed off the residue from used hypodermic needles, Morell would pump injections into the Fuehrer's body at a moment's notice. In the White House, aboard Air Force One, at Hyannisport, or within Kennedy's far more fashionable "bunker" at New York's Carlyle Hotel, Jacobson did the same for the president—dumping out drugs and syringes from his ubiquitous bag and rummaging among unlabeled vials, with fingertips blackened by medication, until he found one that had not been used.[44]

If both doctors had a loyal retinue of ardent admirers, those further removed from their needles were more critical. One historian simply dismissed Morell as a "quack and a charlatan"; others drew attention to the fact that by the time he had drawn the Fuehrer into his net of medications, Morell "had probably not practiced serious medicine for twenty years"; and his contemporaries in orthodox medical circles considered him a phony.[45] Max Jacobson's medical status was similar: he belonged to no professional societies; he was granted no staff privileges at any New York hospitals; and the New York State Board's indictment speaks for itself. Some of those who had worked with him couched their criticisms in less measured terms. According to one of his own nurses, "Max was absolutely a quack . . . totally off the wall . . . [and] out of his mind."[46]

Perhaps the shared roots of these two German doctors had something to do with their borderline skills. Both spent their formative years in a country where medical science and training programs were literally transformed by the scourge of National Socialism. In but five short years, one of the most advanced medical systems in the world was bastardized by SS dogma, whose agents chaired the major departments in Germany's medical schools and reduced the nation's best physicians to unwitting converts of the Reich, rewarding those who succumbed. Details of Jacobson's early career in Germany before he fled to France (where he allegedly developed his theories on tissue regeneration and the injections to achieve it) are scant. But one notable irony stands out: in 1934 he claims to have served as medical consultant to the German Davis Cup tennis team.[47] To what did a Jewish doctor owe such good fortune? That unanswerable question aside, it may be said that Germany in the 1930s was hardly a conducive environment in which to hone the skills necessary to treat world figures, whose health and leadership qualities were both at stake.

Before addressing the president's conduct in relation to the drug issue, we need to clarify two prevailing misconceptions. One involves amphetamines themselves; the other, Kennedy's "harmless" sexual exploits. For many amphetamine users, the real danger lies not so much in the ephemeral effects as in the psychophysiologic crash that follows. Truman Capote, himself a devotee of Jacobson's injections, describes a typical amphetamine experience in more graphic terms than medical textbooks afford:

> You feel like Superman. You're flying. Ideas come at the speed of light. You go 72 hours straight without so much as a coffee break. You don't need sleep, you don't need nourishment. If it's sex you're after, you go all night. Then you crash—its like falling down a well, like parachuting without a parachute. You want to hold onto something and there's nothing out there but air. You go running back to [Jacobson's office on] East 72nd Street. You're looking for the German mosquito, the insect with the magic pinprick."[48]

Was there more than meets the eye in the perpetual energy of Camelot? Could drug effect have accounted in part for Kennedy's insatiable sexual appetite? Potentially most damaging of all, did the president ever experience an amphetamine-induced rush (or crash) at a time unpropitious for the national interest?

Yes; probably; and perhaps. Not that the last two considerations were necessarily mutually exclusive in Kennedy's White House, for presidential philandering itself may have left the nation vulnerable on occasion. LeMoyne Billings, Kennedy's former Choate roommate and political confidant, readily perceived what his more cavalier friend let slide: "It never occurred to Jack that some of these women might be considered dangerous."[49] Langdon Marvin, a longtime consultant and aide, recalled one evening when the president had successfully evaded the Secret Service in order to render his own service in secret to a call girl in a townhouse across from the Carlyle Hotel. Looking out the window at an army lieutenant standing on the curb with an attaché case handcuffed to his wrist, Marvin suddenly tumbled to the danger inherent in the tryst he had had a part in arranging: "Jack was off getting laid and the Bagman with the satchel had been left behind. The Russians could have bombed us to hell and back, and there would have been nothing we could have done about it."[50]

If Kennedy's now legendary exploits (adequately detailed elsewhere) might be traced in part to amphetamine effect, the pharmacologist would point out that steroids also enhance one's sexual appetite.[51] Dr. Gerald Erhlich, a specialist in psychosexual conditioning and its related disorders, highlights this side effect in no uncertain terms: "All that cortisone over a prolonged period probably did increase Kennedy's sexual drive. . . . Give a man large doses of cortisone and he often becomes miraculously, wonderfully priapic, or at least rampant." Erhlich saw more in Kennedy's unsatiated libido, however, than a mere physical need, physiologically induced; there were psychological pressures as well that drove him to such behavior, among them "the need to prove himself, the compulsive risk taking, the sense that societal rules didn't apply to him."[52] What the neuropsychologist would hasten to add is that both amphetamines and steroids accentuate those psychological imperatives which Erhlich speaks of and Kennedy personified.[53]

To be fair to both history and JFK, and reaching far beyond his private life, the implications of drug effect on Kennedy's *public* conduct must be addressed and for a very simple reason. Although his association with Jacobson and his use of amphetamines were made known at least as early as 1972, when Boyce Rensberger's bombshell was dropped in the lap of the *New York Times,* it required the 1989 publication of Heymann's biography of Jackie Kennedy to bring the problem into popular focus. Given the public's understandably fallible perception that amphetamine abusers become slaves to the drug's influence, a public figure's job performance would be expected to suffer accordingly. True, the judgment of pathography indicts both Adolf Hitler and Anthony Eden on that count. On the basis of the available record, the same cannot necessarily be said for Kennedy.

To argue the point requires a cursory examination of the president's conduct during the period he was known to have been seeing Jacobson. That in itself is difficult to decipher from the "official" record. Whereas Kennedy's physicians would have us believe that Jacobson had little if any role to play in the president's care, both the doctor and a few of JFK's associates have gone on record to argue otherwise. For one, Charles Spalding later confirmed that Jacobson supplied Kennedy with amphetamines on a frequent basis. For another, one of Jacobson's assistants, Horace Mann, told the *National Enquirer* in 1975 that he had examined the doctor's medical bag after one tryst with Kennedy at the Carlyle Hotel (a short block away from Jaobson's New York office) and found used amphetamine vials and a damp syringe. In retrospect, he recognized that Kennedy's flushed face represented "a sure sign of amphetamine injection." As if on cue the president had exclaimed that he "felt like a new man."[54]

Skeptical historians, of course, would demand better documentation than an unpublished memoir of a physician who had already distinguished himself as a social climber, *National Enquirer* interviews obtained second hand, and a popular biography of the president's widow. Although more "authoritative" sources are scarce, thanks to Kennedy's handlers' ability to camouflage their charge's prolific indiscretions, recent revelations from Secret Service files and the White House gate log substantiate that Jacobson visited Kennedy there no less than thirty-four times through May 1962.[55] Combining that information with data from such primary documents as the record of the New York State Board inquiry, which outlines Jacobson's universal treatment of all his patients in painstaking detail, compels one to accept much of the doctor's claim.

Yet a critical thread of evidence is missing to tie Kennedy's amphetamine abuse to malfeasance in office. Given the drug's relatively short-term effects, it is difficult to attribute cause to effect without a precise account detailing Jacobson's treatment of the president on any given day. Therefore, the evaluation that follows remains circumstantial. Although no one would argue that Kennedy's drug problem was so pervasive as to have become an ongoing day-to-day pharmacologic cross for the president to bear, a few specific instances raise the pathographer's suspicions and demand some comment.

We begin with the intriguing surmise already alluded to: had Kennedy been "staged and programmed" in a more literal sense during the presidential debates than his handlers were aware of? Probably not. For one thing, in Jacobson's own account of his ministrations to the president there is no mention of a role in the debates themselves. For a man who wore his PT-109 tie clasp as a badge of honor commemorating his services to Kennedy,[56] it would have been consistent for Jacobson, had he been even tangentially involved, to take credit for the youthful senator's timely performance. Not only did Jacobson fail to do so, but his next recorded treatment of Kennedy appears long after the debates, while the president-elect was vacationing at Hyannisport.[57] Moreover, the debates occurred very early in their evolving relationship, and Kennedy was probably circumspect enough not to entrust his performance to the vagaries of a drug he had taken only once before.

Shortly after assuming office, Kennedy became embroiled in perhaps the biggest eyesore of his presidency, the Bay of Pigs debacle. On the surface, this disastrous debut into covert operations was so similar to Anthony Eden's involvement in the Suez Canal crisis as to suggest historical *déjà vu*. Both operations were undertaken by free-world Cold Warriors reacting to headstrong dictators who were careening dangerously toward the Communist bloc and despotism. Nasser's unlawful seizure of the Suez Canal and denunciation of Western interests there was mirrored by Castro's suspension of due process of law and renunciation of a military pact with the United States. And just as a swaggering Egyptian upstart invited a forceful confrontation with Great Britain, a cigar-chomping Cuban dared the *yanquis* to invade Cuba.

The casts of characters even bear a family resemblance: John Foster Dulles was calling the shots for Eisenhower during the prelude to the Suez crisis; his brother Allen, as director of the CIA, was responsible for overseeing the day-to-day preparations for both Ike and JFK during the Cuban buildup. Then too, the motivation of the respective national leaders was the same: to teach small-fry dictators that snubbing the major Western powers would not be taken lightly. Finally, both ventures met with disaster—and both Eden and Kennedy took amphetamines to excess during their respective tenures. Since that certainly affected Eden's conduct in the one crisis, it would seem only natural to look for similar effects in Kennedy.

Yet much the same problem that applies to the presidential debates arises when one considers the possible contribution of amphetamines to a president's poor judgment in sanctioning an invasion of Cuba. Again, Jacobson makes no reference to having seen, much less treated, Kennedy during the time when the fiasco occurred. To be sure, the impact of steroid excess cannot be discounted so readily; that alone might still have predisposed the president to some inexplicable and impulsive behavior. Yet Kennedy was, if anything, both more cautious and more dubious about the merits of this holdover project from the Eisenhower administration than were his advisers, who had virtually all assured him that there was an excellent chance of its succeeding.[58]

The problem, it seems, lay with the CIA's slipshod preparations and faulty intelligence. Indeed, it would be difficult to construct a more ill-starred venture or one more susceptible to Murphy's Law. Suez had been a political more than a military failure; the Bay of Pigs debacle proved just the opposite—but not for want of a rational president in charge. If in retrospect one sees cloudy thinking on Kennedy's part, he was at least willing to acknowledge that himself: "How could I have been so far off base?" he mused. "All my life I've known better than to depend on the experts."[59] That is something Anthony Eden would never have admitted in the aftermath of Suez; moreover, intuitive reflection and self-reproach are hardly qualities that doctors associate with an amphetamine abuser. Though Kennedy's advisers apparently confused image with reality, as one commentator has suggested,[60] that had little to do with a befuddled president—much less amphetamines.

Rather, the new president had been in office only briefly when the CIA informed him that the time was ripe for an invasion of Cuba. Advisers like Allen Dulles, steeped in Cold War rhetoric, played on Kennedy's fears by reminding him that there would be a heavy political price to pay in the 1964 election were he to betray the trust of those Cuban emigrés whose opportunity to restore a free government in their homeland only U.S. support could assure.[61] Yet the president bided his time, seeking any opinion from an informed source that might confirm his skepticism. None appeared, at least from the senior ranks. Arthur Schlesinger, Jr., later admitted that had just one senior adviser spoken against the plan, it would have been cancelled.[62]

And well it should have been, for what Kennedy was told and what in fact was true were two entirely different things. An elite band of 1,400 CIA-trained guerrillas was to establish a beachhead on a remote, abandoned stretch of shoreline with a full seventy-two-hour window of opportunity before Castro could even respond. There they were to be joined by thousands of their countrymen and a second wave of U.S. troops if necessary. Failing that, the invaders would "melt into the hills" to continue insurgent warfare until the tide swung in their favor under cover of American air support.

So much for the image. In reality (and unknown to Kennedy), all military training had been suspended a full five months before, at which time La Brigada's effective force numbered fewer than three hundred men. As for Castro, he was aware of the invasion at least twenty-four hours beforehand; moreover, the "abandoned" strip of beach the CIA had chosen three years earlier had become a public park glittering with lights (one commentator likened the charade to a handful of Russian commandos making a hostile landing on Coney Island).[63] And what of the mountains that would serve as a refuge should the initial invasion falter? Not only were they some eighty miles away, but this contingency had never been spelled out to the insurgents in advance. Nor was any second wave made up of U.S. support troops even considered, as Kennedy himself made clear, despite CIA assurances to the contrary. The president's horror in the aftermath of the failure speaks from the heart as much as for itself: "My God, the bunch of advisers we inherited. . . . Can you imagine being President and leaving . . . all those people there?"[64] In the final analysis, Kennedy's willingness to depend on subordinates had more to do with inexperience than with drug-induced impulsiveness.

Though Max Jacobson's footprints emerged for the first time after Kennedy's election in the sands of Hyannisport, the doctor's trail to the White House itself remains cold until we discover that he treated the president there shortly before Kennedy's first state visit to Canada in May 1961. The effects must have been beneficial, because four days after Kennedy's return he asked Jacobson to fly to Palm Beach to "treat" his wife for migraine. From that moment on, the stings of the "German mosquito" became a family affair. The real importance to Kennedy's drug habit of the trip to Canada was that he continued to receive one injection after another for the painful back spasms he suffered after planting a tree there. According to Jacobson, that convinced the president that his new doctor was irreplaceable.[65]

It was not until Kennedy's next diplomatic journey that the doctor's trail to the president began to heat up considerably. Still reeling from his disastrous debut in Cuba, Kennedy accepted Nikita Khrushchev's invitation to meet at Vienna. This would be his first summit, preceded by a stopover in Paris and followed by a layover in London to meet with Charles de Gaulle and Harold Macmillan, respectively. As events proved, Kennedy needed a doctor who could treat his back and bolster his confidence during these encounters with older and more experienced statesmen. To secure both, the president spared no expense. That included chartering a separate transatlantic airliner for Dr. Jacobson and his wife alone, at no small cost to the American taxpayer.

Although Dr. Travell was taken along as a more visible part of Kennedy's entourage aboard Air Force One, Jacobson provided the essential treatment—the first of which took place with the president's plane still perched on the tarmac at Idlewild Airport. Alleged to have become "mildly addicted" to amphetamines by this time, Kennedy requested an injection before taking off.[66] The morning after their arrival in France, Jacobson gave him a second slug of amphetamine prior to a round of talks with De Gaulle. Those discussions appear to have been "substantive," though Jacobson thought the old general seemed more intent upon catching Jackie's eye than lending an ear to her husband.[67]

His wife's charm would hold the visiting couple in good stead (at least socially), but Kennedy was not about to rely on that alone when it came to meeting Khrushchev in Vienna. "No sooner had we arrived," Jacobson recalled, "when I was hurried up to . . . the President's room.

'Khrushchev is supposedly on his way,' Kennedy said. 'You'd better give me something for my back.'"[68] With his dependency on drugs now clearly accelerating, the question remains whether that was reflected in the president's performance at Vienna. Perhaps we will never know for certain: the two men met alone in the presence of a single interpreter, and as of this writing the Kennedy Library has not yet released the official transcripts of the Vienna summit. What we do know is that Kennedy failed to anticipate the ultimatum that Khrushchev cast before him, threatening to sign a separate accord with East Germany unless the United States yielded on the Berlin issue. If some have questioned the president's judgment in attending the summit at all, so soon after the Bay of Pigs debacle,[69] the question arises whether inexperience and a lack of preparation account for his poor showing—or whether amphetamines were now playing a greater role than Jacobson's gullible patient was willing to acknowledge.

To complicate matters, the administration's press policy proved woefully inadequate in either explaining what really happened or diffusing its impact. Leaving such spin-doctors as Charles E. Bohlen to whitewash the meetings through the press with banalities about their "amiable nature," Kennedy took it upon himself to grant an incriminating interview to James Reston. Bear in mind that few really knew things had gone so badly for the president in Vienna, much less that an ultimatum had been placed on the table. That information had to be gleaned by the press corps secondhand, a fact that disturbed them and damaged the president's credibility.[70]

Reston's revelations didn't help matters: Kennedy seemed to be "in a state of semi-shock" when he met the reporter in a dimly lit room in the American Embassy. "Pretty rough?" he asked the president. "Roughest thing in my life," Kennedy replied, describing Khrushchev as "rude" and "savage." The president's confidence had been severely shaken; he even intimated that the Soviet premier's suspicions of his shortcomings had probably been confirmed. By demanding that the "bone" of Berlin be "removed from the Soviet throat," Khrushchev was serving notice that Kennedy could be intimidated and blackmailed.[71] And for the moment, he clearly was. Little wonder that Khrushchev would later reflect that he had been "genuinely pleased" with the meeting in Vienna.[72]

As for Max Jacobson, left alone in a darkened foyer outside the Vienna meeting to ponder how his medicated patient was faring, the truth of the matter seemed to have escaped him. Greeting the president as he emerged, Jacobson asked how he was feeling. Kennedy replied with a touch of sarcasm: "May I be permitted to take a leak before I respond?" Returning, he sent Jacobson packing to the hotel, as his services were no longer required.[73] Was Kennedy implying that the doctor's ministrations had failed him?

Jacobson's pharmacologic props notwithstanding, the inexperienced president had clearly been intimidated by Khrushchev. Arriving in London the following day in a state of thinly disguised depression, Kennedy sought out Jacobson for yet another "treatment."[74] Whether his back pain (as was alleged) or his wounded psyche required the doctor's services is not entirely clear. Suffice it to say, the aura of despair did not lift, even after the presidential party had returned to Washington. Despite the Reston interview and a nationally televised address, the public was in the dark as to what Kennedy's next move would be.

So, it seems, was he. Rather than "mobilizing the nation," as more than one commentator publicly urged him to do, Kennedy failed to respond. Allegedly "ill with his back ailment" for several days after returning from Vienna,[75] the president held no press conferences for an entire month. Though some believed that merely reflected his indecision over what to say about Berlin, one wonders whether Kennedy might have been rendered unable "to sort out his thoughts"[76] at least in part by amphetamine withdrawal. After all, other Jacobson patients (one of whom had also received a series of injections for back pain) later testified that they had become psychologically and physically addicted to amphetamines in as short a time as six months, only to suffer from severe depression once the drug was withdrawn.[77] Was it a coincidence that Kennedy's return from Vienna marked a six-month milestone in his relationship with Jacobson, following which the president became mysteriously less visible in his official duties? Jackie was away from Washington during the time in which Jacobson makes no allusion to further drug treatments, and that roughly correlates with the period of Kennedy's "illness." Indeed, it was only after Mrs. Kennedy's return, Jacobson wrote, that he began to be called into service on a regular basis, "at least once a week and occasionally as often as three and four times weekly."[78]

Had two successive setbacks so early in Kennedy's presidency set the stage for Jacobson's increasing role in energizing the king of Camelot and his court? Whether in recharging the president's voice with an emergency injection before his scheduled speech to the United Nations General Assembly on September 25, or steadying his hand during the Cuban missile crisis, the threatened steel strike, or the Meredith confrontation (as Jacobson alleged he was charged to do),[79] how pervasive was the influence of amphetamines on the Kennedy presidency?

The Vienna setback and its immediate aftermath perhaps excepted, probably not as much as Jacobson would have us believe. As history recalls, the president's patience and sense of timing during the Cuban missile crisis are the stuff of which the Kennedy legend is made. On October 16, 1962, McGeorge Bundy informed the president of unassailable photographic evidence that the Russians had offensive missiles in Cuba. Kennedy called an emergency session of the executive committee of the National Security Council to assess his alternatives, only to find that the majority was initially in favor of immediate air strikes against the missile sites. Had Kennedy been under the influence of amphetamines or overdosed with steroids, such an impetuous course might have been consistent with the behavior those drugs are known to induce.

On the contrary, the president carefully weighed the options still open to him in a series of round-table discussions with his advisers. He was also prescient enough to discount the Air Force chief of staff's claim that no Russian response would be forthcoming should the alternative of military force be followed.[80] Taking his cue from cooler heads (which included Robert McNamara, his brother Robert, and legal advisers from the State Department), he settled upon a blockade instead. Once informed by Nicholas Katzenbach that a "quarantine" could be legally justified under the circumstances (and only after learning that the majority of the executive committee was now in favor of it), Kennedy seized the initiative and delivered a nationally televised revelation in conjunction with a carefully worded letter to Khrushchev.[81]

As still another measure of Kennedy's ability to keep things in perspective, he joined others in condemning Adlai Stevenson's suggestion that the United States should agree to withdraw its missiles from Turkey in exchange for Russian withdrawals from Cuba.[82] That had been, after all, one of Khrushchev's secondary aims in fomenting the Berlin crisis at Vienna, and Kennedy was not about to fall prey to that ploy now. Moreover, he exercised enough reflection to acknowledge, when congressional reaction to the quarantine plan proved more militant than he would have liked, that this mirrored his own thinking upon first learning of the missiles' presence in Cuba just six days before.[83]

What the record of this thirteen-day period depicts, then, is a calm, detached president coolly weighing his alternatives as changing circumstances dictated. Had he been hyped up on amphetamines, at the very least he would have failed to cover all his bases. Yet his diplomatic orchestration of events proved flawless. Gaining the support of the United Nations Security Council and the Organization of American States was precisely the kind of skilled nuts-and-bolts diplomacy that Anthony Eden had neglected in a similar crisis. Nor did Kennedy miss any cues when it came to safeguarding American interests at home. In response to a Pentagon report that the Cubans had lined up their planes wingtip to wingtip as the Americans had done at Pearl Harbor, inviting destruction, the president was wise enough to ask whether U.S. air bases in Florida had done the same thing. They had—and Kennedy ordered the aircraft to be immediately dispersed.[84]

With Khrushchev now on the ropes but not yet down for the count, Kennedy shelved his advisers' suggestion to order an air strike two days later if the Russians had still not capitulated. He instructed his brother instead to answer Khrushchev's separate and contradictory responses with a draft that agreed only to those items that met with American conditions already agreed upon. The rest, as they say, is history. Kennedy managed to compel Khrushchev to agree to a proposal that the Soviet premier, in effect, had never really made.[85] The blockade held, and the Russians capitulated.

Yet even in victory, Kennedy was empathetic enough to appreciate the price Khrushchev had paid for backing down. There would be no gloating over an American victory. Unlike Eden, he sought some modicum of gain in what he and Khrushchev had just endured by using the crisis as a catalyst to suggest the need for a nuclear test ban treaty. Kennedy's cool judgment under fire made the best of a very frightening situation. That is hardly what one would anticipate of someone truly addicted to amphetamines or overmedicated with steroids.

If anything, John F. Kennedy seemed to grow in office with each passing crisis. So what, one might ask, is the problem? "The problem," we are told, "is not what actually happened, but what potentially could have happened."[86] The intent of this chapter has been to deflect attention from what proved to be a manageable glandular ailment to a more sinister affliction that has yet to be critically addressed. Not that the impact of steroids can be ignored, as their psychological effects are much the same as those induced by amphetamines.

Given the huge dosages of amphetamines and steroids to which Kennedy was subjected, it is a wonder that his performance as president was as exemplary as history recalls. Even if the management of Kennedy's Addison's disease had something to do with "the remarkable success of modern medicine,"[87] we are left with the question whether the treatment was potentially or actually as bad as the disease. Moreover, who was really orchestrating and monitoring this "remarkable success" story? Those ostensibly in charge by the time Kennedy became president failed to appreciate that there was a loose cannon on deck, freely firing off steroids and amphetamines in combination during some very critical happenings in our history.

That Kennedy was taking amphetamines frequently, if not regularly, is now a matter of record. Whether he was truly "addicted" to them is difficult to tell, as there is little in the way of irrational behavior in his professional conduct to suggest that. Despite some notable early stumbles in the arenas of covert operations and diplomacy, the drug factor seems to have had no appreciable impact on what came to pass— at least as far as we have yet been allowed to know.[88] That caveat in itself remains a source of grave concern. Are there still other snakes— and perhaps other Jacobsons—in the woodpile? Have previous patho-graphical accounts emphasized the wrong issues of health?

One wonders, too—assuming that Jacobson's involvement was as prevalent as the record suggests—what might have happened as a result of Kennedy's drug indulgence had he survived to live out his term. In the final judgment, perhaps we dodged that bullet only because the real thing on November 22, 1963, made such considerations painfully moot.

Of one thing, however, we can be certain: the largely successful cover-up of Kennedy's medical history represented the rule and not the exception with respect to presidential health. That subject deserves further consideration.

PART IV

The Crippled Presidency

December 1799: The Father of His Country is dying. Scarcely able to speak as a result of severe tonsillitis, George Washington's life hangs in the balance between choking spasms of breathlessness. The first physician to make his way through the snows enveloping Mount Vernon that morning, Dr. James Craik, hastily bleeds the former president in a vain attempt to assuage his suffering. Defying the prescribed medical practice of his time, Washington fails to respond.

Within the day two other physicians arrive, and a heated discussion ensues over the alternatives of treatment available to them. The youngest of the three, Elisha Cullen Dick, is a thirty-seven-year-old doctor from Alexandria, Virginia. He argues in favor of an aggressive surgical approach: cutting a hole in the windpipe below the area of swelling to bypass the blockage. With a penchant for innovative thinking perhaps rare for his day, Dick surmises that if they can temporarily reconstruct Washington's breathing passage, the life-threatening swelling may yet run its course as the inflammation subsides.

Fearing to take responsibility for possibly contributing to the death of the country's first president, Dr. Gustavius Brown convinces Craik that such a novel and risky treatment might meet with disaster. Dick counters with a willingness to absolve them both of any blame for Washington's death should that occur through his surgery. Common sense tells him that the hallowed practice of bleeding an elderly patient might well prove fatal in itself. As the young doctor summarizes the situation for his more conservative colleagues: "Our patient needs all of his strength—bleeding will only diminish it."[1]

Here is a physician willing to take a stab at the problem (in a very literal sense) by eschewing tincture of time in favor of reason. Yet the views of his older and more respected colleagues, tempered by caution and circumstance, win the day. Washington is bled for a fourth time. Later that evening, with his ebbing vitality spent in dried blood stains on crumpled bedsheets, the president dies. Established medical principles, not to mention the views of the medical establishment itself, have prevailed—and with that, some dubious precedents for the future have been set.

Dr. Craik later confessed to his associate that "our good friend might have been alive today" had he and Dr. Brown listened to their younger colleague.[2] Although Washington was no longer in office, their predicament presaged what future presidential physicians would all too often ignore: when it comes to treating sick presidents, establishing diagnoses and rehashing therapeutic alternatives demand the very best, which only a second professional opinion (or even a third) can assure.

This assumes that the president's doctors know their patient is ill and are willing to divulge such information to the public they also serve. Neither proposition is as straightforward as one might imagine. Recognizing subtle disability in the chief executive can be a vexing task. It also happens to be a chastening one for those charged with protecting the president's political health. That is why the American public will probably require a second opinion for itself at some future date to fill a constitutional vacuum that remains today. Despite the 1967 ratification of the Twenty-fifth Amendment, dealing with presidential disability, this sensitive issue bears reexamination—if only to highlight the amendment's loopholes and to suggest how those might best be closed.

CHAPTER 9

Precedents and Pitfalls

Though some precedents had arguably been established through the shared failure of George Washington's doctors, Dr. James Craik's admission of error was not among them; humility would hardly become a trademark of later presidential physicians. Nor, in a few cases, was withholding desperate operations of the sort that might have saved the life of our nation's first president. To be sure, some were as futile as many scholars have suggested a tracheostomy would have been for Washington. Abraham Lincoln, well beyond the benefits of the surgery that a bullet fired into his brain at point-blank range had already made moot, was still subjected to a frantic bedside operation in a vain effort to debride the bullet's track. The futility of that exercise remains enshrined today on a surgical probe covered with presidential brain and blood, buried in the cluttered archives of a military medicine museum in Washington, D.C.[1]

Some sixteen years later, the searching fingers of a handful of intrepid physicians were added to the list of probes used to violate presidential anatomy. On this occasion, the attempted assassination of James Garfield in 1881, the depth to which they penetrated was measured with the full knowledge, if not macabre fascination, of a captivated public. The object of their search was the bullet that had been fired into the president's back. The newspapers of the day not only chronicled Garfield's progress but openly discussed the methods available for retrieving the bullet. This approach to keeping the public informed perhaps justified in the eyes of some the later practice of reserving such weighty matters to the physicians in charge.

In a word, Garfield had become something of a medical curiosity. Every quack had access to the ears of the White House, suggesting the use of large magnets, suction machines, and other imaginative devices to locate the bullet and extract it. One inventor described a jet stream device for flushing out the wound's passages. Another at least brought some name recognition to the task at hand: Alexander Graham Bell constructed an electro-magnetic apparatus, which he claimed operated on the principle of "induction balance," to reveal the projectile's location (Bell would have done well to seek a second opinion from bedmakers of his day, for he failed to take into account the metal bedsprings, which altered the magnetic fields).[2]

Primitive principles of the scientific method were also used to tackle the problem. One Faneuil Weisse, described as a "publicity-seeking anatomist" at New York Medical College, sought to reconstruct the projectile's trajectory through an experiment in which bullets of the same caliber as that used in Garfield's attack were fired at similar angles into a series of cadavers. His charts depicting the bullet's path and supposed location were paraded before the public but served no useful function other than to sell more newspapers. Dr. D. W. Bliss, a Washington surgeon who had taken charge of Garfield's case at the wounded president's request, dismissed that charade in favor of his own theory. Yet after Garfield died and an autopsy revealed the precise location of the bullet, neither the surgeon nor the anatomist proved to have been anywhere near correct in their estimations. That prompted one solicitous medical editorial to conclude: "Where ignorance is Bliss, 'tis folly to be Weisse."[3]

The peculiar manner in which Garfield's medical care was handled had serious implications for dealing with presidential disability. Of singular importance, this was America's first long-term challenge with a seriously incapacitated president in office. Garfield hovered at death's door for fully eighty days before passing through it. Still another ex post facto precedent was all but ignored by future generations: though certainly of no impact on Garfield's disability, presidential medical care ultimately had the benefit of retrospective review in the autopsy that was performed. For all the questions that have been raised with regard to the deaths of other presidents while in office, their physicians (and the public they serve) have rarely been afforded the chance to confirm the "accepted" diagnosis.[4]

Although Bliss's tireless ministration to President Garfield became the stuff of which doctors' reputations are made (one writer referring to it as "the longest house-call on record"),[5] his approach was flawed in one critical respect: he preempted all important decisions in the case for himself and spurned the help of others, including the president's own primary-care physician. How that situation was handled reflected poorly on the man and set a dubious precedent for other presidential physicians to follow. A reported encounter between Bliss and Garfield's personal doctor, John H. Baxter, illustrates the point:

> *Baxter:*   I have come to ask you to take me in to see the President. . . . I have, for many years, been his physician.
> *Bliss:*   Yes, I know your game. You wish to sneak up here and take his case out of my hands. . . . I know you are sneaking

> around to prescribe for those who have influence and will
> lobby for you.[6]

This would hardly be the last time that professional jealousy and court intrigue would impact on the care of a disabled president in office.

On the positive side of the ledger, Garfield's case proved to be the first instance of presidential disability of which the American public was fully informed. The assertion that the intensive search for the bullet "took people's minds away from public matters and gave them little opportunity to become panicky"[7] may seem hollow today, but at least they were not hoodwinked, for all the specious merit of the revelations made. In some subsequent cases of presidential disability the public would be victimized by failed or misrepresented disclosures of the facts.

History took precious little time to reveal how prevalent that practice would become. Not only did history refuse to wait; it repeated itself, as it is prone to do. Twenty years later, in Buffalo, New York, yet another assassin's bullet struck down President William McKinley. Both McKinley's travails and the national crisis that threatened were mercifully short-lived. He died nine days after the assassination attempt, but not before other precedents of very dubious distinction were established in ministering to seriously ill presidents. As fate would have it, the physician in charge had been openly critical of the impasse that had resulted during Garfield's medical management. Suddenly entrusted with the sobering responsibility of caring for a seriously wounded president whom he had just met the day before, Dr. Matthew D. Mann vowed that any appearance of uncertainty would not be repeated. For that error in judgment, he has been pilloried ever since.

Mann chose to operate immediately and without first transferring his esteemed patient to the nearby University of Buffalo, where one of the first x-ray machines available might well have aided him in locating the bullet he was unable to find. That he failed to locate and extract it is no surprise. Not only was he an obstetrician and gynecologist who had never operated on a male victim of a gunshot wound, but he operated with poor illumination and without a trained surgical assistant. Resigned to his failure, Mann could only repair the injured stomach lining and close the gaping wound he had made. Worse, he failed to allow for postoperative drainage, recognized even at that early date as an important adjunct of surgical treatment to prevent subsequent infection.[8]

That was but a part of the tragedy and subsequent irony to be visited on a critically ill president of the United States. Tragic, because McKinley would die as a result, the victim of an overwhelming infection buried deeply in his abdomen. Ironic, because shortly thereafter an expert in the treatment of gunshot wounds belatedly offered himself as a consultant in the case.[9] But the damage had already been done. McKinley had fallen victim to one of the horrors of medicine: being operated upon by a surgeon unfamiliar with the disease process, in compromised circumstances, and without benefit of second opinions and consultations.

Sad to relate, some of those who consulted after the fact only complicated matters. The most counterproductive on record were the services of Dr. Charles McBurney of New York City. Like later presidential physicians he took it upon himself to be the obligate spokesman for the group and, in so doing, became one of the first in a long line of doctors to release only news that was not politically damaging to the president. Unrestrained (and unfounded) optimism pervaded his every press release. As if to underscore the political aspect, one critic charged, not entirely tongue-in-cheek, that the garrulous doctor had been sent by none other than J.P. Morgan to prevent a precipitate drop in the stock market.[10]

Grandiloquently describing Mann's operation as marking "the epoch of the century in surgery," McBurney assured his anxious audience that "the door had been bolted against the green monster of death by the skilled hand of modern medicine."[11] Better he had bolted shut his mouth; for one of those listening was Vice-President Theodore Roosevelt, who was so assured by what McBurney told him that he packed up and went hunting in the Adirondacks while his president hung in the clutches of death and his nation in limbo. Everyone (Roosevelt included) was aghast when, on the ninth day after the assassination attempt, McKinley suddenly died of fulminant peritonitis.

Not all subsequent presidential operations were emergencies triggered by the twitching fingers of crazed assassins. A few were not even reported at the time. Some twelve years after James Garfield's assassination, President Grover Cleveland underwent clandestine surgery aboard a yacht to remove a cancerous growth from the roof of his mouth. During the procedure he was anesthetized and strapped unconscious to a deck chair propped against the ship's mast while nervous, if close-lipped, surgeons explored the presidential mouth.

As befitted their perceived role (based as much on past experience with a sensationalist press as presidential edict), the doctors involved either refused to confirm or denied altogether the rumors that arose as a result of the president's abrupt and unexplained disappearance from the capital. In fact, the conspirators disguised their work so well that almost a quarter of a century would elapse before one of the physicians told the story. Even those indirectly involved in the scheme at the time were unaware that the health at issue was that of the president. After the lesion was biopsied by Dr. Joseph D. Bryant, an esteemed head and neck surgeon from New York, it was sent unlabeled to the Army Medical Hospital for microscopic analysis. Cancer was confirmed in a specimen identified only as "the most important ever submitted for examination" because the nation's security was said to be at risk.

Cleveland himself set the tone for his conspirators: "If a rumor gets around that I'm dying, then the country is dead too."[12] Far more than just the president's health was at stake during that sultry summer of 1893—or so at least he perceived it. America was in the grip of a rapidly burgeoning depression, and Cleveland, a staunch gold-standard adherent, balked at the prospect of relinquishing the office to his vice-president, Adlai Stevenson of Illinois, who was a free-silver man. Believing that the surgery had to be as secret as it was necessary, the president and his family physician, Dr. Robert O'Reilly, took it upon themselves to initiate a string of clandestine activities that would rival the best efforts of our later CIA. Through secret meetings with trusted envoys, Cleveland persuaded his friend Commodore Elias C. Benedict to allow his yacht to become a floating operating room in the less-than-antiseptic environs of Long Island Sound. It was then left to Dr. Bryant to enlist the services of an anesthesiologist and a dentist to assist him, while underscoring the seriousness of the scheme with a warning to Benedict: "Should anything happen to the President, run us on the rocks and sink us all!"[13]

In late June the president was furtively whisked out of the White House and transported by rail and dinghy to the *Oneida*, where he steeled himself for the ordeal. The doctors' task was not made any easier by what was found during surgery on July 1: the cancer extended so deeply that a portion of Cleveland's jaw had to be removed, necessitating a second and equally secret operation to insert a prosthesis in the gaping hole so that the president's speech would not be affected.

As luck would have it, the surgeons' skills matched their stealth. Cleveland survived both operations and returned to his duties within the month. The public remained unaware of the inordinate risks that had been taken on their behalf at the behest of presidential whim. To be sure, at least one investigative reporter had caught wind of the story by late August.[14] But the participating physicians hid behind the ethics of patient confidentiality. The crossfire of charges and countercharges eventually passed, and the earlier explanation stood: "No operation [had] been performed, except that a bad tooth was extracted." Not until 1917 did the famed surgeon Dr. William W. Keen, who had assisted in the operation, disclose the entire story in the *Saturday Evening Post*.[15]

No doubt presidential physicians and political subordinates alike were only beginning to warm to the task of withholding potentially damaging information concerning the president's health. That practice came to a boil on at least two notable occasions in the twentieth century. Nearly 150 years after Elisha Dick's futile encounter with presidential medical care by fiat, another youthful doctor found himself at loggerheads with older physicians more closely linked to a president than he. In March 1944 Lieutenant Commander Howard Bruenn was commissioned by Franklin D. Roosevelt's personal physician, Vice Admiral Ross McIntire, to examine the obviously failing president. The results of the young cardiologist's examination were so disturbing that Bruenn hastily convened a conference of medical experts to wrestle with the despairing facts: Roosevelt's blood pressure was running out of control at the same time that his heart was playing out. Bruenn forcefully argued for administering digitalis to prime the failing pump, but he was opposed by the committee on this and other recommendations. Only by threatening to resign did Bruenn eventually get his way and the president of the United States get appropriate treatment for the alarming symptoms he had been experiencing all along.[16]

Much to Bruenn's chagrin, McIntire reserved for himself the final say not only in what treatment would be administered but in what the public would be allowed to know on the eve of another reelection campaign; after all, he was the lieutenant's superior officer. Denying Roosevelt's infirmities to the end, McIntire evinced self-serving surprise and dismay when Roosevelt suddenly died of a hypertension-related brain hemorrhage at Warm Springs, Georgia, a year later.[17] Bruenn, recognizing that most of his communications to his military superior had been altered to put a better face on their "public" patient, was equally dismayed to find that the medical records had mysteriously disappeared from the hospital safe the day that Roosevelt died.[18]

Ross McIntire was an ear, nose, and throat doctor who had learned both his card-playing and his press relations well from another navy doctor who oversaw the last tragic year of Woodrow Wilson's administration. Taking a card from the hand of his older associate, Dr. Cary T. Grayson, McIntire believed that the political health of the president should weigh as heavily as his physical well-being.[19] Any damaging revelations had to be held close to the vest or placed face down on the table of public review, just as his predecessor had done when Wilson was felled by a severe stroke in 1919. In clear disregard of Article 2 of the Constitution, Grayson had never considered certifying the invalid president disabled.[20] Our national interest, not to mention the stability of international relations, suffered as a result (see Chapter 5.)

The pent-up steam of public frustration with such practices temporarily blew off the lid of complacency after successive insults to the heart, bowel, and brain of Dwight D. Eisenhower. Concerned lawmakers, immersed in this public pressure-cooker, gave the problem a detailed look in the 1960s. The Twenty-fifth Amendment, dealing with presidential disability, resulted. With its ratification in 1967, Congress placed a constitutional seal on the issue, having assured itself that all contingencies were finally covered. Yet even now the amendment seems little more than a purge-valve to some skeptics, constructed largely for the purpose of diffusing political fallout. What its authors neglected to seek was a second opinion from organized medicine, which by its very nature would be concerned with knowing something more of disability's essence than merely its unsavory political aroma.

Events in Washington during Ronald Reagan's tenure (see Chapter 10) suggest that it is time to reexamine the distasteful ingredients of presidential disability. To do so requires a review of the history leading to the adoption of the amendment. For nearly two centuries before its formulation the public welfare had been bound by imprecise wording below a constitutional sword of Damocles that threatened to sever the legal discovery from the occurrence of inability in our chief executive. On at least four occasions during the last one hundred years alone, executive function has been paralyzed by medically defined presidential inability, while two perplexing questions restricted a satisfactory resolution to the problem. First, in such a circumstance, does the office of the presidency devolve to the vice-president, or does the latter merely serve as an acting president? Second, who shall determine when the president becomes disabled and at what point that disability has ended?

In the first instance, the amendment's sponsors deemed it appropriate for the vice-president to assume the powers and duties (but not the office itself) if the president became disabled. As for the second, they proposed that the vice-president and the cabinet should be jointly responsible for determining the duration of inability when, for medical or other reasons, the president himself is unable to do so. These noteworthy advances notwithstanding, the Twenty-fifth Amendment still suffers from some glaring inadequacies. Today, as in the past, we remain dependent on the presidential physician, whose opinions may not afford an unbiased and unrestricted revelation of the medical facts should the question of disability arise. Certainly our past experience with the duplicity of presidential physicians is cause for grave concern, yet their conduct was but one symptom of a long-standing and unresolved constitutional problem.

By all accounts the framers of the Constitution produced a remarkable document that has endured since those stifling summer months of 1787 in Philadelphia. They spent little time, however, discussing the issue of presidential succession and said virtually nothing about what would happen should a president become disabled while in office. These shortcomings did not pass unnoticed by at least one participant there, though John Dickinson's warnings were all but ignored as the sessions drew rapidly to a close. Not surprisingly, scholars and politicians alike spent the next two centuries grappling with what one senator later termed "this blind spot" in our Constitution.[21]

Intimations of problems to come arose for the first time in the new republic when President James Madison fell victim to a three-week siege of "bilious fever" in 1813. The press played on the fears of some of its readers with perhaps unsubstantiated hyperbole when the *Federal Republican* reported that "not a few who have recently visited [the President] have left his chamber under a full conviction of the derangement of his mind."[22] True, these fears eventually receded with Madison's full recovery; yet the disquieting specter of a disabled president in office had at least been raised.

Nearly three decades later the first death of a president in office occurred, compelling Vice-President John Tyler to succeed the deceased William Henry Harrison. In subsequent Senate debates a vexing question arose: what would happen if a *temporarily* disabled president recovered, only to find a vice-president occupying his office? As later scholars pointed out, in this instance the vesting clause of the Constitution was at variance with its succession clause.[23] Clearly the former provided for a single, and not plural, chief executive. Yet the framers failed to recognize that the latter precluded the use of an "acting" president when the legitimate bearer of that office was disabled. Accordingly, more than one political observer began to realize that in practice the succession clause would have to be reinterpreted to allow the temporary discharge of executive power by someone else when the president was unable to perform the duties of office.[24]

James Garfield's protracted disability in 1881 underscored, however, that there was really no chief executive at all when a president was incapacitated. Caught between an ill-defined legal position and charges of being a usurper, Vice-President Chester Arthur fell victim to the limitations of the succession provision. Both his actions (or lack of them) and those of the cabinet defined the problem in practical terms. Public business was suspended, ultimately compelling the cabinet to consider asking Arthur to act.

Yet Arthur never moved to end the crisis. The vice-president had his own reasons, both political and constitutional, for refusing to assume the office. To begin with, Garfield and Arthur were from opposite wings of the party. This led to a second consideration: the cabinet feared Garfield's ouster for the remainder of his term lest he improve—and his doctors were predicting full restitution of powers, despite compelling evidence accumulating to the contrary.

From the constitutional perspective, moreover, there was no agreement on the meaning of disability, its determination, or its permanency in Garfield's case. Although his mind was sound during the first weeks following the assassination attempt, Garfield was clearly unable to discharge the duties of his office. During the entire eighty days of his disability the president completed only one official act, the signing of a minor State Department paper. Meanwhile, foreign relations deteriorated, and fraud in the Post Office reached scandalous proportions. Though the cabinet continued to conduct affairs of government, the fact remained that important questions of public policy could be resolved only by an active president.

Despite earlier optimistic press releases, Garfield's mental state eventually deteriorated. Two months into his disability, the previously supportive *Boston Evening Transcript* was forced to admit that Garfield's mind had become "weak" and that he suffered "hallucinations."[25] With his decline, many persons agreed that the vice-president should now be free to declare the president disabled, but no one knew how to compel him to do so. Others, cabinet members among them, agreed neither to such a declaration nor to the contingent assumption of the office itself by the vice-president. Proposals abounded, including a plan for delegating but not devolving executive powers to Arthur. The country continued to flounder about in its first real succession crisis until Garfield expired. Yet political scars remained, and fears for the future grew.

Those fears had already arisen some fifteen years earlier after Abraham Lincoln's assassination. From the standpoint of disability in office, the deadly aim of an assassin had rendered that consideration moot with Lincoln's death the same day. Few persons were aware, however, of less dramatic forms of disability lurking behind the doors of the White House long before "John Wilkes Booth" became a household name. Unknown to the public at the time, Lincoln not only had to wrestle with very personal forms of covert and overt disability but also had to minister to the perplexing illness of his anxiety-ridden wife. Moreover, the president himself was unaware of a physical ailment that at least one investigator claims would have taken his life within the year had Booth not been afforded the leap (in a literal sense to the stage below) into the blackest pages of our history. For Lincoln is said to have been a victim of Marfan's syndrome. If so, his heart and aorta were rapidly playing out long before his visit to Ford's Theater.[26]

Whereas such festering disability had no effect on Lincoln's conduct in office, one equally subtle condition arguably did: an inbred depression that had plagued him since its activation by the failed loves of his early manhood.[27] Whether as a result of migraine or depression, he was often prostrated for days on end by excruciating headaches. In the absence of other symptoms related to the nervous system, it is doubtful that these headaches were the result of a blood clot sustained in his youth with consequent brain damage, as has been alleged.[28] More to the point, physicians of the present day are aware of the deleterious effect depression alone may have on the decision-making process, with or without headaches.

Obviously, the Founding Fathers and those who have later wrestled with the disability issue had no intention of removing a president from office on the basis of depression. Yet Lincoln's experience attests to the fact that not all burdens borne in the office are the product of politics, diplomacy, or physical infirmity. If Mary Todd's detractors are to be believed, "social diseases" should be added to the list—though firm evidence is lacking to link hers to the sort now associated with the term. Still, some social diseases *did* impact on a few of America's presidents that could result in disabling others in the future. By far the most prevalent of these is alcoholism, which had victimized both Franklin Pierce and Ulysses S. Grant. Yet the two men differed in one respect: whereas Pierce continued to embrace the bottle when a crisis emerged during his presidency, Grant was disciplined enough to eschew its allure, for the most part, during his eight-year tenure.

In recent decades medical knowledge and public education have advanced to the point of accepting alcoholism as a disease—and like all diseases discussed in these pages (Lincoln's alleged Marfan's syndrome excepted), it shares the indictment of affecting the way one thinks. For all of alcohol's superficial virtues of loosening the tongue and inhibitions (enough, perhaps, to make one a proficient and prolific speaker), the drug has few other redeeming virtues—particularly when it is used as a crutch in times of crisis, a lubricant in social interaction, or a mask to hide unhappiness.

A more devastating form of presidential disability visited itself upon the office when Woodrow Wilson fell victim to a serious stroke in 1919 during a very critical time in our history. The complete story and its implications have already been detailed (see Chapter 5), including the conclusion that Wilson may have been disabled, in the medical definition of the term, by poorly controlled high blood pressure long before his debilitating stroke.[29] For the purpose of this review, the impact of the president's less controversial stroke-induced disability bears repeating. A recurring scenario unfolded—and with it, recurring questions begging for answers. No one was willing to address the question of who should judge the president's impairment or what in fact signified constitutionally defined disability—including a befuddled vice-president, Thomas R. Marshall. Consequently, whatever veneer of executive function remained was vested in Wilson's wife and his personal secretary for the next four months. During the debate over America's entry into the League of Nations, Mrs. Wilson's pithy response to senators begging to deal directly with their president epitomized the plight of an isolated and broken man: "Gentlemen, I am not interested in the President of the United States. I am interested in my husband and his health." [30] In the long run, ratification of the Treaty of Versailles was dealt a fatal blow, a victim as much of presidential illness as of partisan politics.

Much else was lost in the interim following Wilson's stroke besides American participation in the League of Nations. Venerable principles of executive accountability and checks-and-balances headed the list. Fully twenty-eight acts of Congress became law without presidential review. One scholar has surmised that public policy was formulated by those "whose stand was not necessarily Wilson's, by persons whose capabilities were not always commensurate with their loyalty to Wilson, and by people who had no legal mandate." [31] Secretary of State Robert Lansing convened a score of cabinet meetings in an attempt to transact neglected executive business, thereby indirectly forestalling any congressional moves to establish a case for presidential disability. His reward was a demand for his resignation from the stricken and paranoid president. This was but one intimation that by the time Wilson began to resume a more active role in affairs of state, he was captive to the dictates of an organic brain syndrome that marked him as a changed man. [32]

No one outside the inner circle was aware of Wilson's true condition, as Dr. Grayson had stipulated that potentially damaging information regarding the president's health be withheld from the vice-president and cabinet, not to mention the American public. [33] If Marshall never considered assuming Wilson's office for fear, in part, of being assassinated, others hesitated on less personal grounds to voice their concerns. Though several justices of the Supreme Court suspected that Wilson was seriously ill, any certification of presidential inability was argued to be outside their purview on the basis of separation of powers. Since neither Congress, the vice-president, nor the court could or would make a move, it was left to the cabinet or the White House itself to take the next step. But the cabinet was led to believe by Grayson's palace guard that the president was well on his way to a complete recovery; accordingly, no action was deemed necessary. As his trusted aide Joseph P. Tumulty admitted, the sole motive was loyalty to the president. [34]

Twenty-five years later virtually every question that remained unanswered during the period of Wilson's disability reappeared when Franklin D. Roosevelt became seriously ill during his last year in office.

Victimized by malignant hypertension, heart failure, and progressive pulmonary insufficiency, Roosevelt began to experience transient periods of clouded consciousness that arguably affected his conduct in several intrawar conferences. The parallels are striking. Both Roosevelt and Wilson fell prostrate with exhaustion while attempting to act as world peacemakers; one presidential physician's failure to disclose unpleasant facts presaged another's denial of his patient's failing health. Such thinking ultimately allowed Roosevelt to run for an unprecedented fourth term despite the fact that he was dying.[35]

Certainly Roosevelt's manifestations of disability were far more subtle; he neither suffered a major stroke nor disappeared from view altogether as president until the day he died. This brings to mind a question that haunts the succession process to this day: how compromised must a president be to warrant a certification of disability under the letter and intent of the Constitution? No doubt a strictly medical determination would have been enough to certify both Wilson and Roosevelt as impaired (see Chapter 10). But medicine is not the law—and law, most assuredly, is not politics. The restrictions to legal discovery of potential disability in our chief executives remain as formidable now as they were in the past, largely for political reasons. Beyond a doubt, had the Twenty-fifth Amendment then been in effect, neither Wilson nor Roosevelt would have willfully exercised his duty under Section 3 and declared his disability. Thus (under Section 4) we would have been solely dependent on the opinions of the presidential physician, who, in both instances, would have similarly refused to support findings of disability that the cabinet and the vice-president might otherwise have jointly declared.

Taking this argument one step further, a division of opinion between the vice-president and the cabinet—had the facts been known—might well have arisen in either case. Without Robert Lansing's forced resignation, he might ultimately have succeeded in bringing the issue of Wilson's health to a vote in the cabinet, even though Vice-President Marshall steadfastly refused to become involved in any declaration of presidential disability. As for Harry Truman, he had been so far removed from any working relationship with Roosevelt that he would have been unlikely, whatever his suspicions, to certify his superior as being disabled under Section 4's provisions. Nevertheless, more than one member of the cabinet was bothered enough by what he had seen of the president's appearance at his fourth inauguration in 1945 to register doubts about his ability to speak for the United States at Yalta.[36]

Any determination of disability, then, had the Twenty-fifth Amendment applied, would have devolved to "such other body as Congress by law shall provide." In practice, McIntire in all likelihood would have had the final word, as he alone reserved the right to be Roosevelt's exclusive medical spokesman; and as we now know, potentially damaging facts about the president's health, uncovered by McIntire's subordinate, were either hidden or destroyed.[37] Nothing, it seems, had been learned from past experience. Public awareness in the Roosevelt era was as restricted as it had been in Wilson's time, dependent upon both the fallibility and duplicity of a presidential physician.

Perhaps that is why the country's next experience with presidential inability was both precedent-setting and cause for optimism in future cases, or so it was believed at the time. With Dwight D. Eisenhower's succession of illnesses, a consensus evolved regarding several unresolved issues, among them the right of a president to certify the onset of his own disability and its termination. Yet other vexing problems remained: the lack of accessibility to medical facts concealed by physicians bound by a unique relationship; the hesitancy of a vice-president to act for fear of being labeled a usurper; the forced resignation of cabinet members aware of a president's compromised ability and willing to testify to it; and the potential for turning the whole issue to the political advantage of the opposing party.

On September 24, 1955, Eisenhower suffered his first heart attack. Recalling the Wilson debacle, he decreed that the facts of his illness and their implications be revealed to the public as well as to Richard Nixon. Unlike Wilson, Eisenhower approved of his vice-president's assumption of the powers and duties of the presidential office. Within a week Eisenhower had recovered enough to declare his disability ended, thereby setting a precedent for what would become the essence of Section 3 of the Twenty-fifth Amendment. A similar scenario unfolded during and immediately after Eisenhower's later emergency operation for a bowel obstruction. As it turned out, no crises occurred during either of the two illnesses.

A year and a half later, red flags of warning unfurled again when Eisenhower suffered a small stroke that affected his speech, only to be lowered just as quickly with his rapid improvement within twenty-four hours. Ominously enough, this disability affected brain function; equally significant, the president denied that such was the case.[38] We will never know whether his intransigence would have endured had the effects of his stroke been permanent. Yet Wilson and Roosevelt's respective encounters with similar neurologic disability underscore the serious implications involved when a national leader's brain dysfunctions. Disorders of the presidential heart and bowel are sources of legitimate concern; when the thought processes and decision-making of the chief executive are at risk, concern becomes alarm. A transient speech disturbance in and of itself may not disaffect the political process, but it may presage future problems. Will the next stroke carry a stricken president into the twilight of inactivity, if not into clouds of incomprehension altogether? Might the disappearance of overt disability camouflage subtle underlying injury to the powers of abstraction and problem solving?

At the time, politicians were faced with more concrete considerations. As Richard Nixon pointed out, Eisenhower's stroke had come at the worst possible moment, just before a NATO summit and amid burgeoning insecurity vis-à-vis the Russians. Yet in the wake of this brief flirtation with disaster, the Justice Department reached no conclusion as to what procedure would be legal should the president be unable (or, as in this case, refuse) to certify his own disability. Not all hesitation was grounded in constitutional considerations; political factors also weighed heavily in the failure to reach a consensus. For example, the distasteful option of handing over the keys of the White House to Nixon arguably discouraged a skeptical Congress from taking Eisenhower's admittedly brief inability more seriously.[39]

The Eisenhower experience had at least broken ground in the field of presidential succession; for one thing, Section 3 became a logical extension of what had already occurred in practice. Yet much remained to be clarified. Just how disabled can a president be and still remain a salvageable political entity in the eyes of his colleagues? Does presidential disability cover only mental compromise? Should it be declared only when the public interest suffers? Most troubling of all, did political scientist Clinton Rossiter have the final word in suggesting that the presidential inability problem was in practice "insoluble?"[40]

Answers to these and other questions began to crystallize by consensus during public debates and Senate hearings in the early 1960s, preceding the passage of the Twenty-fifth Amendment—but not before the American public unwittingly dodged yet another bullet that may have disabled its president, at least on occasion, long before he fell victim to the real thing. Aware enough that John F. Kennedy had suffered a wartime back injury that necessitated a major (and what proved to be a life-threatening) operation, we all but ignored the more troubling revelation in 1960 that he had been suffering all along from a glandular deficiency for which he required drug replacement.[41] For those with access to medical journals of the day, that startling revelation would have come as no surprise. A 1955 issue of the *Archives of Surgery* discussed an unnamed thirty-seven-year-old patient with Addison's disease who had undergone a back operation on October 21, 1954, and nearly died from the stress of surgery. When Kennedy's name later surfaced as a legitimate presidential contender, it required no mental gymnastics to put two and two together: in 1954, Kennedy had been thirty-seven years old and had undergone a lumbar fusion on October 21 of that year at the same institution.[42]

What the public never knew during Kennedy's lifetime about substance abuse in high office was potentially even more harmful. The intent of the preceding chapter was to point out that Kennedy's prolific use of drugs is now a matter of record, even if their impact on his conduct in office is less apparent. That Kennedy required chronic steroid replacement before and after his brush with death in 1954 would hardly be a cause for concern, could we assume that it had been properly administered and monitored. But the specific drugs used (cortisone orally, and its intramuscularly injected analogue desoxycorticosterone acetate, or DOCA) and the doses administered were at time both poorly controlled and excessive, as has already been detailed. Moreover, we now know that DOCA is so slowly metabolized by the body when given intramuscularly that an excess of steroid often results—even without such additional injections as those the president received at the hand of Max Jacobson. On balance, that practice seems to have been less a factor than those familiar with both steroid and amphetamine effects might have expected. That it was allowed to occur at all, however, remains a source of grave concern.

The record, as in all things medical pertaining to Kennedy, remains clouded by the restrictions placed on today's scholars by his family. Yet thanks to the Freedom of Information Act and the diligence of a handful of relentless investigators, the fog is beginning to lift, presenting future pathographers with much still to ponder and recalling the questions with which formulators of the Twenty-fifth Amendment wrestled during the same decade.

Acknowledging that a few among them perceived the problem of presidential disability to be insoluble, less fatalistic participants at Senate hearings on the issue sensed that the public welfare demanded more than "patience, prayers and improvision" in what one skeptic aptly described as "a messy situation."[43] To their credit, they eventually agreed that disability was recognizable, certifiable, and applicable to an incumbent president who was unable to exercise his powers as public business required. Moreover, they agreed that a president should have the right to declare both the beginning and end of his or her disability.

Yet what to do with a president who could not, or would not, declare disability remained the burning question. Experts who had already studied the problem could not agree. Opinions ran gamut from a verdict of "insoluble" proposals of various instruments for making a determination: a panel of distinguished citizens, the Supreme Court, an ill-defined "disability commission." In the absence of informed medical second opinions, each proposal foundered on its own weaknesses both perceived and real.

No group had more impact on the deliberations than did a powerful committee of twelve lawyers from the American Bar Association. Not only were physicians excluded from that panel; a review of the lengthy transcripts of Senate hearings during 1963-64 fails to uncover any meaningful testimony from either organized medicine or individual physicians skilled in the determination of disability. Hence, perhaps, the bias that crept into the ABA committee's recommendations against any proposed disability commission: "A commission of purely medical personnel would be undesirable, because a determination of whether inability exists is more than a medical question."[44] Such a determination is undoubtedly more than a matter of health; yet the ABA committee and the senators and representatives who listened failed to perceive that what little allowance they did make for medical input into the question had already proved inadequate in the past. In effect, those ultimately empowered to decide the issue were merely "expected" to consult with the president's physician and "others."[45]

History was ignored and the issue eventually resolved through general consensus: if the president did not declare his disability, that determination should fall to members of the executive branch, as would be compatible with the doctrine of separation of powers. Since the Constitution reserves the power to act through the contingent grant-of-power principle to his successor when the president is disabled, the vice-president (with the help of the cabinet) was perceived to be the rightful judge of the facts.[46] Congress, however, reserved the right to involve itself in the process through "such other body" as it might provide, should the provisions for keeping the matter within the executive branch prove inadequate. That was at least in keeping with the original (albeit ambiguous) intent of Article 2, Section 1, Clause 6 of the United States Constitution, which stipulates, in part, that "the Congress may by Law provide for the Case of Removal, Death, Resignation or *Inability* [emphasis added], both of the President and Vice-President."

These guidelines, then, were embodied in the Twenty-fifth Amendment as eventually passed by Congress in 1965 and ratified by the states two years later. For the moment, at least, the vexing issue of presidential disability was laid to rest.

CHAPTER 10

Resuscitating the Twenty-fifth Amendment

The Twenty-fifth Amendment has been hailed as a providential safe-guard against virtually every contingency likely to be faced in future cases of presidential inability. Yet precisely where the vice-president and cabinet are to obtain the pertinent medical facts to pass judgment, should a stricken president fail to certify his or her own disability, was all but ignored by the amendment's sponsors. They chose instead to honor the dubious precedent of depending on presidential physicians. If these doctors have occasionally misled us, it is now naively assumed that the media at least will not. We expect to be immediately and fully informed of a change for the worse in the president's health. As Clinton Rossiter put it: "If we cannot have confidence in our ability to make such a judgment [based on these revelations] . . . then what in heaven's name can we have confidence in at all?"[1]

The one thing we can be confident of in this age of the public presidency is that any determination of presidential disability will be argued in a political forum, for that determination is strictly a political decision—or so it has been erroneously argued. History would suggest instead that much more than politics is at stake—including the nation's best interests and on occasion even its security. That is why *both* the state of the President and the state of the Union must be taken into account in any judgment of disability.[2]

Few would take exception to that view. Yet the modest proposal of this chapter entails a corollary: let professionals skilled in disability determination but not directly responsible for the chief executive's care be the initial judges of the presidential state in a medical sense; *then* let the politicians judge the state of the Union, as the president might effect it, through the procedural guidelines of the Twenty-fifth Amendment. To assure this proper division of responsibility, certain clarifications are required in that amendment as currently worded. We simply must maximize the public's assurance that the data which the vice-president and the cabinet use to determine the duration of inability, when the president cannot, are valid.

A Presidential Disability Commission, staffed at least in part by physicians skilled in disability determination, could be chosen or appointed *before* the inception of the next administration. Potential nominees could be asked to testify beforehand in House and Senate hearings as to their professional qualifications for (and personal views on) disability determination in general, in order to assure selection of the best and most unbiased candidates. Equally divided by political persuasion, such a commision would be charged with monitoring the president's health on a yearly basis and reporting its findings to the vice-president. It would have no power to intitiate proceedings against the president, much less to depose him; its duties would be restricted to gathering medical facts to assist the vice-president in making an informed decision should the question of inability arise. As the amendment expressly states, only the vice-president or cabinet can initiate any deliberations relevant to a determination of presidential inability.

Nor would the implementation of such a commission require further amendment, since Section 4 already acknowledges the right of Congress to provide "such other body."[3] A simple concurrent resolution of both houses of Congress might satisfy this most compelling need, and would be compatible with both the spirit and the letter of the law as currently worded. Moreover, such a resolution would hardly represent a usurpation of power. Because a concurrent resolution is but an expression of congressional opinion (and therefore has moral but not necessarily legal force),[4] the commission's findings would serve only as a guide—but a useful and necessary one—for the vice-president should disagreement arise between him and the cabinet.

One mechanism to expedite the process already exists: specific guidelines for evaluating disability and permanent impairment, which have been in force since the American Medical Association published its first *Guides to the Evaluation of Permanent Impairment* in 1971. As earlier discussed, the *Guides* go to great lengths to differentiate between *impairment* (which is "directly related to the health status of the individual") and *disability* (which "can be determined only within the context of the . . . occupational demands or statutory or regulatory requirements that the individual is unable to meet as a result of the impairment").[5] The determination of impairment can be done only by physicians, whereas determination of disability is recognized as having "social, administrative, economic and legal consequences beyond the domain of medicine."[6] An impairment rating, then, merely serves as a useful starting point for subsequently weighing the *consequences* of that impairment.

To make the procedure as uniform as possible, today's physician breaks down the process into four steps. Any proposed Disability Commission would act accordingly. First, a thorough medical history and physical examination are undertaken, supported by appropriate diagnostic tests. Second, these findings are analyzed to determine the nature and extent of the patient's impaired bodily functions. The third step entails a comparison of the results of that analysis with the criteria specified in the *Guides*. That need not be performed by the same physician (or physicians) responsible for the initial examination. The final step in rating medical impairment takes into account all relevant considerations in order to reach a "whole person" impairment rating on a percentage basis.[7]

Examples from recent history may illustrate what a "percentage of impairment of the whole person" means. To begin with, several criteria are included in the evaluation of brain impairment, among them disturbances in language, complex and integrated cerebral functions, and emotions, as well as the presence of temporary or permanent neurologic deficits.[8] Applying these 1984 *Guides* criteria to Franklin D. Roosevelt during his last term in office allows the pathographer not only to substantiate but to *quantitate* his impairment retrospectively.

Though medical evidence suggests that Roosevelt's impairment was less pervasive than, say, Woodrow Wilson's (see Chapter 5), the last criterion of "episodic neurologic disturbances" may be readily applied to FDR, who was frequently stricken with transient periods of impaired awareness on the basis of poorly controlled hypertension. This is termed an "encephalopathy."[9] Categorizing that impairment at its first and lowest level as an "an episodic neurologic disorder of slight severity . . . such that most of the activities of daily living can still be performed," Roosevelt would have been rated as 15 percent impaired as early as March 1944. Later, particularly after the 1945 inauguration, it can be argued that his compromise extended to a higher level; that is, it was "of such severity as to interfere moderately with the activities of daily living," thereby extending his percentage of impairment to 20-45 percent.[10] In addition, he suffered from life-threatening disturbances of heart, lung, and blood-pressure function, each category with its own particular percentage of impairment. What should concern us most, of course, is *neurologic* impairment as it impacts on cognition and decision-making—and both Wilson and Roosevelt were quantitatively impaired in that respect by strictly defined criteria. Would the American public choose to be led by presidents with certifiable impairment, from the standpoint of brain dysfunction alone, at more than 50 percent?

The *Guides* acknowledge that the concept of "permanency" may vary considerably, but the guidelines for permanency are more than adequate to declare disability constitutionally as applied to the presidency per se: "The concept of permanency . . . relates to a provision in a contract, policy, or regulation in which the time limit for permanency of disability is defined."[11] The election of a president is, barring malfeasance in office or inability, a four-year contract. Therefore this definition could be used by the vice-president and cabinet in those circumstances where they are charged by Section 4 of the Twenty-fifth Amendment to determine the duration and termination of the inability of the chief executive. Should a proposed Disability Commission anticipate the president's impairment to extend beyond a four-year period—and, therefore, be defined as "permanent" as far as the office's "contract, policy, or regulation" is concerned—the vice-president and cabinet would be on more solid ground in denying the president's resumption of powers and duties, absent improvement.

Such a decision presupposes that they have certified in kind that the "urgency of public business" requires an active president to act. This judgment would extend beyond the domain of any Disability Commission, as the *Guides* applied in a more general sense make clear: "Each administrative or legal system . . . should *define its own process* for translating the [permanent impairment] rating into an estimate that the individual's capacity to meet occupational demands . . . *is limited by the impairment*" (emphasis added).[12]

This is all to reemphasize, as the *Guides* have done, that physicians must refrain from speculating about nonmedical consequences of any impairment they have certified. They should consider only whether or not the specific medical condition *can* cause the type of observed failure. That is a medical decision; it is left to others to decide whether in a particular case it *did* cause failure. And that, most assuredly, is beyond the profession's mandate. While a physician may properly make an inference about the risk of allowing an impaired individual to continue in his or her present employment, it is not the medical examiner's duty to determine the *acceptability* of that risk. That decision is more properly made by nonphysicians on the basis of nonmedical considerations.[13]

If those entrusted with Wilson's and Roosevelt's care were guilty of allowing their own opinions on nonmedical issues to influence what should have been strictly medical determinations, how has the present system of impairment determination fared today when applied to executives of major corporations and the like? Independent clinical studies substantiate that when the *Guides* are used properly, permanent impairment can be rated with reasonable accuracy, uniformity, and dispatch.[14] In essence, the machinery for such determinations has been in place since 1971 and has worked well. It would seem, then, no great leap of principle to extend the practice to the workings of the Twenty-fifth Amendment.

One can hardly imagine a more politically charged event threatening to blow the succession mechanism apart than disagreement between the vice-president and the cabinet as to whether the president is disabled. This potential bombshell must be defused. The findings of a Disability Commission with no political axe to grind would be of immeasurable benefit to a vice-president, who might otherwise be accused of being a usurper. Such distasteful suggestions, coupled with the formidable restrictions placed on the public's right to remain informed about the health of its most powerful and trusted servant, blocked the transfer of power on more than one occasion in our past. Nor does the potential for subterfuge end here. Other less obvious but equally formidable problems remain.

Section 3 of the Twenty-fifth Amendment deals with situations in which the chief executive is aware of his or her disability and is able to communicate to the vice-president the date of both its onset and its termination. Fewer problems might have arisen in such cases in our history in which Section 3 would have been invoked had the amendment then been in force. Take, for example, the issue of general anesthesia for surgical procedures: Grover Cleveland could have notified the vice-president of his impending surgery and effected a temporary transfer of power until his recovery. For political reasons, he refused to do so. Two later presidents, Dwight Eisenhower and Lyndon Johnson, did choose to relinquish their powers temporarily to their vice-presidents, in keeping with at least the spirit of Section 3 as later written: Eisenhower's experience has already been detailed, and similar provisions were made by Lyndon Johnson prior to two separate operations for the removal of his gallbladder and of colon polyps.

Yet providing for temporary inability under the Twenty-fifth Amendment has had its share of problems. Ronald Reagan twice underwent general anesthesia for surgery: the first as an emergency following the attempt on his life in 1981; the second on an elective basis for removal of a colon cancer. Though no disasters resulted, both events were fraught with disturbing implications. One became immediately obvious to many Americans who saw Secretary of State Alexander Haig announce to a skeptical television audience after the assassination attempt that he was "fully in charge" of matters at the White House. Though the president had been awake just prior to undergoing emergency surgery, a formulation of policy prescribed by Section 3 for temporarily devolving his powers to the vice-president was not put into effect.

The second implication remains obscure to all but physicians familiar with the effects of general anesthesia on the thought processes of the elderly in the immediate postoperative period. That manifested itself with serious consequences following Reagan's elective colon surgery in 1985. The question was, when did the period of Reagan's inability (that is, the effects of general anesthesia on mentation) really end? The president had signed a document temporarily delegating the powers of the presidency to the "acting" president, George Bush. Then, following his surgery, he signed another document declaring that his inability had ended. But medical purists would point out that Reagan was arguably incapacitated for far longer on the basis of anesthetic effect, during which period of time some key decisions were made regarding proposed arms sales to Iran. A similar argument could have been applied to the lingering effect of general anesthesia on Dwight Eisenhower following his bowel operation in 1956. Within two days of his surgery, the president had actively resumed the powers and duties of his office. Fortunately, nothing of consequence was occurring in political or diplomatic affairs at that time, in contradistinction to Reagan's experience some thirty years later.

The Reagan experience aside, past performances suggest that the provisions of Section 3 are well defined and not subject to much improvement. The murky issue of determining when a period of disability has *ended*, however, is less well defined under Section 4. In essence, application of that provision has yet to undergo trial by fire. Critics of the amendment would argue that we simply may have been lucky or, at least in Reagan's case, merely improvident. Here is why.

Though constitutional scholar Ruth Silva has argued that the determination of presidential inability is a policy matter based on political circumstances,[15] one discerning senator during the 1960s, Roman Hruska, disagreed—perceiving correctly that such a determination is, at least in its initial stages, first and foremost a medical matter divorced from politics.[16] History spoke to at least this one critic of the Twenty-fifth Amendment quite clearly. After all, many suspect that it was the partisan fears of facing Richard Nixon in the White House that kept Congress from acting with dispatch during the period of Eisenhower's disability. And as noted, the risk of appearing as usurpers accounted in part for the inaction of Chester Arthur and Thomas Marshall during their respective superiors' protracted illnesses. Whether or not any of the three vice-presidents would have performed more capably than their disabled superiors is not (at least from the standpoint of impairment determination) the salient issue. What *is* important is the need for a timely, apolitically motivated gathering of the facts to initiate such a determination in the first place. Depending solely on elected or appointed officials to pass judgment on a president's impairment without legislatively mandated medical expertise runs the risk of putting the political cart in front of a questionably disabled horse.

It goes without saying that such officials should seek out the best advice available before acting. Yet under the provisions of Section 4, soliciting medical opinions per se is merely *suggested*—and then only during the eleventh hour when disagreement has already arisen between the vice-president and cabinet. Recall, for the moment, the sticky dilemma facing Garfield's cabinet during his prolonged disability: in the absence of a realistic medical appraisal of the president's prognosis, political and personal considerations only contributed to the gridlock.[17] If dispatch is the key to preserving the integrity of ongoing and effective executive function, potential pitfalls in such a scenario today can well be imagined—not to mention that the selection of medical experts *after* the fact by a politically conscious Congress or presidential physician might well depend on the doctors' party affiliations as much as (or more than) on their medical skills.

A second potential problem exists with the current wording of Section 4 in that the language employed is hardly specific enough to satisfy the degree of authority and urgency required. Disagreement arose at the start over how specifically to spell out the procedure for handling a case of disability. Everett Dirksen successfully argued for keeping the wording simple ("such method as Congress may by law provide"), consonant with the tenor of the remainder of the Constitution. Senators Birch Bayh and Samuel Erwin opposed Dirksen, believing that such generalities would give too much power to Congress. As they pointed out, provisions for impeachment, a situation argued to be in some ways analogous to disability proceedings, were quite specific.[18] Because their opinions were eventually overriden, critics continue to voice concern that Section 4 fails to specify how "such other body" is to determine disability. Having provided the legal framework for both initiating and concluding the process, Section 4 is vague on how "such other body" arrives, if you will, at point B from point A. The solution seems clear: medical expertise of the highest order should be either mandated by law or cloaked with the moral authority implicit in a joint resolution of Congress.

Section 4 also fails to address a third and very real potential problem: a cornered president might lash out defensively, before the issue reaches crisis proportions, and force the resignation of any cabinet members perceived as threatening. Wilson did precisely that during his period of disability. That is why the Disability Commission should be linked not to the cabinet but to the vice-president, who cannot be forced by the president to resign. In like manner, it would be naive to argue that Congress could act by statute (as Section 4 leaves it open to do) should disgreement arise between the vice-president and the cabinet. After all, the president has a constitutional right to veto any legislation passed by the legislature and might be inclined to exercise that power should such an emergency statute be perceived as a threat to his political survival.

Therein lies the rationale for a concurrent resolution of Congress to define the procedural issues *prospectively*. This would carry with it such moral force that any president would appear less than circumspect in overriding its intent—an intent well defined and already outlined prior to the onset of any future crisis. Hastily handpicking a group of medical experts after the fact, and only after disagreement has arisen between the vice-president and the cabinet, would foreseeably divide the selection process of the commission along partisan lines and bog down the proceedings at precisely the time the data required to make a decision should be arrived at with dispatch.

As currently provided for, there simply is not much time allowed for wrangling over such issues. Sponsors of the Twenty-fifth Amendment, acknowledging that the powers and duties of the chief executive must never lie dormant, recognized the need for prompt action once a previously disabled president declared the intention to resume office. As matters now stand, the cabinet and the vice-president are given but four days to review the data and make a determination. If disagreement exists, then the vice-president retains the powers and duties of the office while Congress considers the matter. A decision in the legislature must then follow within twenty-one days.[19]

In order to expedite that determination during the first four days before risking the pitfalls of a longer process, a prospectively selected committee already in force is essential. As presently mandated, such a committee or any other "body as Congress may by law provide" cannot even be formed, much less solicited, before disagreement arises. The fourth potential problem with the current wording of the amendment, then, is this matter of expediting the procedure without surrendering exactitude. Bringing a medically staffed commission into the process at an earlier stage than presently provided for would go far toward assuring both.

Yet if the findings of the commission are not bound to the vice-president, the validity of that determination might well be called into question long enough to frustrate the entire process. The examples of both Arthur and Marshall during the disabilities of their superiors showed that though the cabinet may be willing to declare a president still disabled, a squeamish vice-president (for either personal or political reasons) may choose to abstain, thus leaving the determination to the whims of Congress. A vice-president to whom the findings of a Disability Commission were made known before the four-day deadline would be more inclined to act. Without the force of an authoritative body that has prospectively evaluated the relevant medical data, it is doubtful that any consensus could be arrived at in such a short time.

During the debate over the Twenty-fifth Amendment, Senator Bayh posited a view that risks confusing the responsibilities of the participants involved: "The cabinet, as well as the Vice-President and Congress, are going to have to judge the severity of the disability and the problems that face our country."[20] Lumping the two responsibilities into one, without making specific provision for which instrument is responsible for either, introduces a fifth potential problem for any future case. Few would dispute that judging the severity of the problems facing the country should remain within the purview of government officials. That they might also be called upon to judge the severity of the president's medically defined impairment, however, would represent an unskilled exercise of power. The burden of that particular responsibility should rest with medical experts.

A sixth potential problem arises as an extension of the fourth and fifth just discussed. As a constitutional scholar points out: "In deciding the issue [of inability in a president] Congress can proceed as it thinks best. . . . Thus, it *may* request that the President undergo medical tests and examinations or submit to questions at hearings" (emphasis added).[21] In short, under current provision, medical examinations are not necessarily required, though surely such a requirement is the very least the public deserves. Yet even if they are performed at congressional request, precedent virtually assures us that the president's personal physician will have the last word. That has been shown to have its share of limitations; few of these doctors in the past possessed the necessary training in neurologic and psychiatric disease to play such a dominant part in any impairment determination related to brain dysfunction. Nor should we assume that they would take seriously opinions elicited from experts in that field. Not only do presidential physicians guard their preeminent positions jealously; they may be inclined to dismiss or even hide revelations that would be politically harmful.

Tests and examinations alone, then, are not enough. *Who* conducts them, and *how* the findings are revealed are equally crucial matters. Is it too much to ask that those experts who gather the data do so without consideration for personal gain or political proximity to the president? Should the rendering of opinions on those data be bandied about by laypersons in a public forum? Our proclivity today to entrust sensitive or classified information to the televised charades we now know as open House and Senate committee hearings, complete with prime-time political exposure for the participants, disregards the solemn warning of more prescient individuals to divorce the initial process from any consideration of political advantage, personal prejudice, or other extraneous factors. Yet in this age of mass media exposure the cynic cannot conceive of the twenty-one-day period of debate currently mandated under Section 4 *not* being televised in open hearings. Public demand in the post-Watergate and post-Iranscam era has so whetted the collective appetite for information that televised hearings have become the citizen's inalienable "right" of passage into the political process. The current arrangement, then, begs for media exploitation. It is one thing to spill our political guts out on the table for public consumption in open hearings on covert government activities; it is quite another to lay open sensitive matters of presidential health in a public forum, complete with hand-picked medical experts waxing philosophical under the kleig lights.

This assumes, of course, that any information as serious as medical impairment would be divulged by those entrusted with the president's health. Such has not always been the case, either for political reasons or as a result of restrictions inherent in the physician-patient relationship. It assumes, too, that all domestic and diplomatic concerns at the time the impairment occurs would be known to those entrusted with determining the seriousness of the problems facing the country. Yet in this era of covert operations such activities might remain unknown not only to those responsible for such a determination but even to the president.[22]

The implications are clear: past executive styles of leadership and methods of monitoring the president's health have often precluded an effective determination of his ability to lead and the problems facing the nation at the time that ability has been called into question. Nothing exemplified this more than our experience with Ronald Reagan's recurring medical impairment and, arguably, his lingering disability. With all due respect to President Reagan, revelations regarding the Iran-Contra debacle and other matters appear to affirm at least one underlying suspicion: a perceptible transition occurred in the effective exercise of the president's powers and duties during the last half of his tenure. Did Reagan's advanced years constitute another form of subtle disability? That was a question I myself raised in 1988.[23] Whether any proposed Presidential Disability Commission, had one existed, would have agreed at the time is admittedly a tough call. The indisputable lesson to be learned from the Reagan experience, however, is that the provisions of the Twenty-fifth Amendment were never invoked to protect the presidency and the nation, though at three different times their consideration was clearly warranted.

The first, during Reagan's emergency surgery after the assassination attempt in 1981, has been eloquently detailed elsewhere.[24] For the purpose of this review, two conclusions bear reemphasizing: on the basis of the trauma itself, the general anesthetic he underwent, and his prolonged convalescence, Reagan was impaired in the medical sense and perhaps disabled constitutionally for far longer than we knew; moreover, the mechanism specifically provided for determining the onset of his disability and its termination was ignored, compelling reasons for invoking it to the contrary. Ironically, similar errors of omission were repeated in 1985 before and after Reagan's elective colon surgery, which would have singular implications for the Iran-Contra scandal. Finally, as late as 1987, at least one Reagan associate was bothered enough by what he had seen and heard of the president's performance to ask whether Section 4 of the Twenty-fifth Amendment should be invoked. Yet the issue went no further, nipped in the bud by one individual on the basis of a single presidential interview.

What still defies explanation is that in all three instances no specific medical inquiry into those aspects of impairment necessary to raise the issue of presidential disability was even considered, much less undertaken. More ironic still (and emblematic of the limitations of relying on presidential physicians), two of the doctors closest to Reagan were neurological surgeons, professionally trained to recognize and treat disorders of the brain that affect the way one thinks and behaves.[25] The available record now affirms that a Presidential Disability Commission might well have judged his degree of impairment obvious enough to warrant an inquiry, or for Vice-President George Bush and the cabinet to at least consider the matter—which is precisely what architects of the Twenty-fifth Amendment had in mind.

If the assassination attempt provided the first opportunity to test the provisions of the Twenty-fifth Amendment, Reagan's handlers clearly failed to seize the moment. Neither Section 3 nor Section 4 was invoked, despite the president's obvious disability. No doubt such factors as ignorance concerning those provisions on the part of the cabinet and vice-president, the latter's willingness to defer to the wishes of the White House staff, political concerns for the message that might be conveyed to the American public, and the guile of one staffer in particular played major roles in that impasse.[26] Yet the real deterrent to prompt action, as has forever been the case in such matters, was the lack of authorized medical opinion necessary to certify the president's obvious impairment in the first place. Even the White House physician involved, Dr. Daniel Ruge, intimated as much when he later reflected on the failure to consider the Twenty-fifth Amendment. "I think that it should have been invoked," he recalled. "Maybe I am responsible, because I really hadn't thought about it too much." In Ruge's defense, no one specifically *asked* him about the president's cognitive capacities.[27] That would have been a task tailor-made for a Disability Commission already established prospectively.

Years later, virtually every doctor involved agreed that the Twenty-fifth Amendment should have been invoked, not only during and immediately after Reagan's surgery but for a considerable period of time thereafter.[28] Though the president himself later professed little doubt about his ability to handle his office effectively, that speaks volumes to the often misguided perceptions of those suffering from the lingering effects of general anesthesia in particular and subtle brain dysfunction in general. If a president will not or cannot acknowledge the residua of disease-induced disability, Section 4 offers a remedy—one inexplicably ignored by all concerned.

True, Reagan's aides would have us believe that something akin to a review process did in fact take place. While the president was in surgery, Howard Baker and Edwin Meese briefly consulted with the head of the trauma service at George Washington University Hospital concerning his potential inability to function in the immediate postoperative period. To Dr. Joseph Giordano's credit, he acknowledged the effects of a general anesthetic and "heavy-duty" pain medication as reasons why Reagan should not be asked to make major decisions. Despite that, the White House staff decided not to invoke the amendment. Not only was this the sole instance in which Reagan's aides consulted a physician (and only one at that) regarding the president's *anticipated* medical impairment, but the subsequent judgment of both impairment and disability was made by them—and not by the cabinet and vice-president, as envisioned by the amendment's authors. As White House Communications Director David Gergen admitted, everyone was hesitant to act for fear of expressing "less than full confidence" in their chief executive rather than the "serene view" they wished to convey to the American public.[29]

That inaction would present its share of problems when it came to assuaging the concerns of those who had already questioned Reagan's ability to govern on the basis of his age alone. In one press conference after another following his formal return to an office he had never really relinquished, Reagan fumbled questions from the press and was unable to remember even the most general details of important events. Witness the embarrassment of everyone in the room (including the president himself) during one such briefing when he lost his thought in midsentence concerning a compromise on the MX missile project and left its explanation to a startled John Tower standing in the wings.[30] Whether he knew anything of the details to begin with or lost them under the heat of the kleig lights is immaterial. Perhaps we were seeing the lingering effects of his trauma and general anesthetic—if not the vintage Reagan of years to come.

To be sure, those in the administration had already passed some troubling signposts along the way. Within weeks of his return to the White House, the president began to doze off during meetings. That practice gave rise to one tongue-in-cheek description of the cabinet room: "seats thirteen, sleeps one." Though his staff was more alarmed than amused, Reagan seemed to find it funny. "When I leave here," he quipped, "they'll probably put a plaque on the back of my chair inscribed 'the President slept here.'"[31] Other problems could not be laughed away so easily. During the first presidential debate of 1984, Reagan appeared irresolute and failed to field questions with his usual aplomb. Few will forget the period of suspense between the two debates as we awaited the verdict on whether Reagan had grown too old to be entrusted with the duties of his office. Within the year that verdict would be called into question by yet another disabling illness.

What makes the following indictment all the more disturbing is that the White House staff and its doctors had ample opportunity to make preparations, once the president announced his plans to go under the knife for his colon cancer in 1985. Pleading ignorance in the heat of battle as the staff had done in 1981 would not suffice this time. Yet they seemed to have learned little. That would eventually embroil an impaired president in the gravest threat to his political health—which brings us to a brief discussion of Reagan's mental health vis-à-vis the Iran-Contra scandal.

If the failure to invoke the Twenty-fifth Amendment in 1981 was related in large measure to ignorance of its provisions on the part of those involved, the amendment's inherent ambiguity as to who was responsible for determining the presence of any medical impairment in the first place had a great deal to do with the similar failure in 1985. True, Reagan's handlers had at least learned enough from their earlier experience to urge the invocation of Section 3, whereby the president was allowed to declare his own disability before undergoing a general anesthetic. Yet Reagan's sadly uninformed stand set the tone for his staff: he issued a strong disclaimer that the temporary transfer of power to George Bush had anything to do with the Twenty-fifth Amendment—for fear of establishing "a poor precedent"! He even went so far as to stipulate that anesthesia and surgery were conditions for which the amendment's provisions were not intended.[32] (Its architects, of course, saw things differently; Senator Birch Bayh, for one, flatly asserted that Reagan had botched the chance to set an *important* precedent.)[33] That would color every subsequent aspect of what transpired in 1985, including the critical need to determine the end of the president's disability, defined all too broadly by Section 4.

Any knowledgeable physician would view with unveiled skepticism the method the White House staff ultimately chose as an appropriate test of the president's mental capacities during the immediate postoperative period: they simply asked him to read a few lines of a letter. Sad to relate, chief of staff Donald Regan and others were operating in a medical capacity totally outside their expertise. It was left for Dr. Herbert Abrams to elucidate later what should have been obvious to the palace guard: "To read is not necessarily to understand." [34]

So what might this have to do with the Iran-Contra scandal? Just *two* days after emerging from his surgery, during a meeting in the hospital with Regan and Robert McFarlane, Reagan agreed in principle to open up the Iranian initiative for the sale of arms.[35] Having assumed the president was thinking clearly, his associates gave little consideration to the effects of a general anesthetic and narcotics on Reagan's thought processes. Nor was any medical opinion on the matter even solicited. That oversight would return to haunt them all once the scandal broke and the president was left to fend for himself—only to compromise his credibility further with seven distinct contradictions during a press conference in which he bungled his attempt to lay the whole affair open.[36]

Within a subsequent three-week period Reagan first stated that he had not approved the arms sales; then, that he had; and finally, that "he could not remember—period."[37] Strangely, the last admission seems the most plausible, for medical studies uniformly affirm that elderly individuals in particular suffer a distressing degree of memory loss during the first *week* after anesthesia and are routinely advised to make no major decisions during that time. Some studies extend this period of compromise to six weeks.[38] That the president specifically approved the plan a second time some six weeks after the first meeting, then, is no assurance that the lingering effects of his general anesthetic had cleared, as some would argue.[39] I, for one, believe that the president truly forgot—and that frightens me more than the acts of duplicity that have apparently become routine among government officials. The key question is no longer, what did Reagan know and when did he know it? It is, rather, what did he know and when did he forget it? A deficient memory is a poor servant for any public figure. For an aging president, it threatened thereafter to become a mainstay in his intellectual repertoire— as might be anticipated in most individuals seventy-seven years of age, the effects of two general anesthetics within a four-year period notwithstanding.

How else to explain the Tower Commission's frank portrayal of a man wholly out of touch and of "ineptitude verging on incompetence, from the President on down"? Having earlier adopted comprehensive procedures for monitoring covert activities, Reagan subsequently ignored them. He did not recall signing one Covert Action draft concerning the CIA, and he later signed (*but did not read*) a second draft making the United States a direct supplier of arms to Iran. To make matters worse, Reagan so perseverated on the release of victims of an airline hijacking as to overlook the obvious fact that bargaining with terrorists for their hostages' release merely justifies their methods. Such behavior brings to mind the most sinister effect of cognitive compromise on any executive: conduct that impacts negatively on occupational duties. As the *Tower Commission Report* concluded, the president "did not seem to be *aware* of the full consequences of his actions" (emphasis added).[40] That indictment alone should raise red flags even among those without medical training.

Arthur Schlesinger, Jr., once aptly portrayed Ronald Reagan as "the Master Illusionist." But illusions go only so far in dealing with terrorists and arms merchants—or in being dealt with by a cynical media. The fragile yolk of credibility becomes scrambled once the protective Teflon ages and erodes. Enter a befuddled Reagan, no longer sunny side up, as a skeptical Congress leaves a bag of burning questions concerning his involvement at the presidential door. Hastily stomping on the bag to snuff out the flames licking at his credibility, Reagan discovers to his dismay that it contains incriminating excrement that explodes underfoot. Like many an old codger victimized by the pranks of neighborhood jackals, the president was described by an unnamed adviser at the time as "still not understanding what's happening; but every time those guys come down from the Hill and beat up on him, he just gets his back up more."[41] Kids on the block understand this obstreperous quality in their elderly neighbors; as for aging leaders, so do opposing politicians.

To accuse Ronald Reagan of subconscious duplicity or overt dishonesty squares with neither the image nor the essence of the man. On balance, it appears that the president really may not have known the details of what was being done in his name. Yet what little he was allowed to know, he seemed to have forgotten—including his approval for opening up the Iranian initiative in the first place. Like The Speech he continually revised to reinterpret history while picking up a few votes along the way, Reagan's explanations for half-baked schemes were typically long on narrative and short on substance. By 1986 they were often wrong as well, for the Great Communicator was no longer mastering his briefs. His pledge that "as long as Iran advocates the use of terrorism, the U.S. arms embargo will continue" belied the revelation that shipments to Iran had already begun some fifteen months before.[42]

That was enough for Schlesinger to describe the Iran-Contra scandal as a watershed in the Reagan presidency: "The fact that he does not command or even comprehend details of policy need not be of major political consequence—until Iran."[43] The question remains whether medical circumstances at the time likewise signified a watershed in Reagan's health.

Subsequent evidence affirms just how prevalent such concerns were to become among many White House associates. By February 1987 disorder in the Oval Office seemed to have reached epidemic proportions, and Howard Baker replaced Donald Regan as White House chief of staff. Baker asked James Cannon to interview a number of aides to ascertain the cause. What Cannon learned of the president himself disturbed him so much that he wrote Baker a memorandum reading in part: "Consider the possibility that section four of the 25th Amendment might be applied." Though Cannon doubted that Reagan had slipped that far, and even suggested later that loyalty to the deposed chief of staff may have motivated the charges, almost everyone else said in one way or another that "the president was inattentive," that he had "lost interest in his job."[44] Not unexpectedly, both Regan and Baker later came to Reagan's defense. "I didn't take Cannon's memo lightly," Baker recalled, "but from the first time I saw [the President], he was fully in control and I never had any question about his mental competence."[45] Though doubts had been raised, neither Baker nor Regan solicited informed medical opinion at the time to support their own favorable assessment.

Personalities, like stores of knowledge, become to some degree more rigidly defined with age. While meticulous preparation may aid in obscuring that, all the coaching in the world cannot immunize an aging actor against foot-in-mouth disease during a press conference when the mind fails to turn the page of its notebook of prepared answers. Sam Donaldson described the confusion that often resulted: despite his dress rehearsals, the president was still "perfectly capable of getting things mixed up . . . forever calling up figures that [were] wrong, asserting facts that [weren't], and re-writing history."[46] Little wonder that the press conference became an endangered political species during Reagan's second tenure.

Perhaps that would have been all for the better. Take one press conference in particular in June 1986, in which Reagan clearly outdid himself in making mistakes. When asked about the Supreme Court ruling on abortion, he launched into a discussion of a completely unrelated court decision. Queried about a Warsaw Pact proposal to reduce standing armies in Europe, he responded with a dissertation on missile deployment. The president then revealed that new plans for the space shuttle were in the works, when in fact no such plans were yet being considered. Finally, he denied that cruise missiles were being installed in the B-52, though he had authorized that decision himself two weeks before.[47]

Elder statesman may not only have trouble recalling what they think they know; they may also have difficulty learning new information. As one measure of both, a year after leaving office, Reagan fell back on the same accounting of the Iran-Contra affair that he had embraced from the beginning. No matter what revelations had subsequently surfaced, it was as if the myth had been rehearsed so many times in the past that he could scarcely divorce it from his mind. Yet the realities of the matter Reagan left hanging in clouds of memory lapses to which he readily confessed. Though even the most skeptical reporters believed he was telling the truth, his truth was almost eerily at odds with the facts. And that was precisely what made his performance during the 1990 trial of John Poindexter so unnerving. If this represented what *Newsweek* called "fresh evidence of the workings of Reagan's mind," [48] it may also have reflected a progressive change for the worse in what knowledge-able observers had recognized long before.

Not that subtle deterioration in cognitive function necessarily follows a steadily progressive course. Good days alternate with bad, camouflaged in part by the universal observation that aging individuals perform best in structured situations. This is why the teleprompter may be of immeasurable benefit for an actor-president turned revered senior citizen, as Reagan's convincing performance at the 1992 Republican National Convention in Houston attests. Yet ghosts of extemporaneous performances past would remain to haunt him. Describing Reagan's testimony at the Poindexter trial as "sad and embarrassing," [49] an increasing number of observers are now willing to attest to his tenuous grasp on the office we once felt he had firmly in hand.

For all of the indictments implicit in this review, let me be the first to admit that I have never met Ronald Reagan, much less ministered to his medical needs. Moreover, I genuinely *like* the man, as I suspect most Americans on either side of the political fence do. The Poindexter affair aside, I would also admit that it is difficult to discern a clear progression of cognitive and behavioral deficits some six years after the president stumbled through the Iran-Contra fiasco.[50] Nor can one ignore that Reagan succeeded in elevating the art of politics to a new level. Two questions, then, come to mind: (1) Are we reading too much into anesthetics and aging as they affected Reagan's presidency? (2) If not, then how did he manage to survive it virtually unscathed?

To be sure, other journalists who observed Reagan on a day-to-day basis at close range were less than sanguine about this sensitive issue.

At a recent Washington conference, "Medical Care of the VIP," four panelists from the news media were as one in admitting that they did a poor job of reporting the effects of mental compromise on Reagan's occupational duties during his last two years in office. Jack Nelson, Washington bureau chief for the *Los Angeles Times*, spoke for them all when he asserted: "It was all too obvious to us that the President was not processing information very well." In their defense, former White House spokesman Ron Nessen pointed out that following the unseemly coverage of the president's bowel movements after his colon operation, Mrs. Reagan had taken it upon herself to limit the medical news coming out of the White House. Nevertheless, Reagan's performance led these commentators to admit that "our handling of this issue of mental compromise remains remarkably unsophisticated to the present day."[51]

In retrospect, the implications are sobering. Reagan may well have remained to the end the premier spokesman for law, order, and virtue, but he arguably debased public ethics at home and made the United States a law unto itself abroad.[52] Ignoring the rules of international diplomacy, the president created a few of his own. He violated the UN Charter by occupying Grenada; he defied the World Court in refusing to face its ban on mining the harbors of Nicaragua; and some would argue that he was devoid of good sense in attempting to assassinate terrorist Libyan leader Muammar Qaddafi. Time and again, Reagan imposed his own brand of frontier justice on world affairs. Military aid to the freedom fighters of Nicaragua in clear violation of congressional mandate was but an extension of a myopic world view grown old and more dangerous with time.

If some of those actions found a receptive audience at home, thoughtful economists had problems with his persistent harangue about the federal deficit, even as it was allowed to balloon to its highest level in history. Once Reagan began to believe in something—even something as fantastic as increased defense spending, reduced taxes, and a decreased deficit rolled into one—he adhered to it with the tenacity of a pit bull. Yet pit bulls, like old men, may become so impassioned that they shred the object of their attention—or rip out their own teeth trying. Though the presidential dentist has yet to be heard from, the American public is still paying the bill.

The suspicion remains, then, that the flexibility of Ronald Reagan's mind weathered neither the storms of a crisis that nearly toppled his presidency nor the inroads of aging that in the end came to define it. If his subsequent behavior happened to square with public sentiment, such inflexibility paradoxically became a source of political strength. Perhaps this, as much as anything, explains his enduring popularity through a decade that seemed to worship materialism and abhorred making waves on domestic shores. Like Eisenhower's before him, Reagan's style fit the times—times that demanded less innovation and more avarice. Riding the crest of conservatism, Reagan's ship reached the presidency. Fortunately for the sake of his reputation, he happened to have been on the right boat.

When measured against a youthful if naive predecessor, Reagan's record seems deceptively impressive. In Jimmy Carter's case we reaped the harvest of what we sowed: substituting a seasoned infighter with an inexperienced outsider in the Washington game. Our satisfaction with having survived that oversight should not blind us to the fact that we failed to recognize what effect aging and anesthetics may have had on Carter's successor. In that sense, future historians may be less kind to Ronald Reagan than his popular acclaim in the twilight of his presidency implied.

As regards the three instances of presidential inability during Reagan's tenure, it bears reemphasizing that *one* individual was largely responsible in each case for withholding the application of the Twenty-fifth Amendment: Richard Darman (acting through James Baker) in 1981; the president himself in 1985; and Howard Baker in 1987. What that dubious legacy suggests is the need to seek a second opinion from someone other than "official sources" should we again be faced with a disabled person in office. Establishing a source for that second opinion is a formidable task, and the attempt is likely to be opposed by presidential physicians and politicians alike. For both have something to lose—the one, a seat next to the throne; the other, control over a process that has immense political implications. In the passage of the Twenty-fifth Amendment, the views of the politicians and a handful of lawyers carried the day; pathographers, with a critical eye on the past and a worried look to the future, have yet to have their say. For all the amendment's good intentions, a second opinion in the form of a proposed Presidential Disability Commission is long overdue. Can objections to that proposal be overcome? To that question we now turn.

The concept of a Presidential Disability Commission staffed at least in part by physicians is hardly new. Harry Truman first proposed the idea in 1957 in a letter to the *New York Times*. He called for a "select group of medical authorities from the top medical schools in the country" to monitor the health of the president and "so inform Congress" should questions of presidential inability arise.[53] Dwight D. Eisenhower initially favored physician representation in the process as well, and numerous academicians—among them such heavyweights as James MacGregor Burns and Paul Freund—argued the same in Senate hearings during those critical months of 1964 antedating formulation of the Twenty-fifth Amendment.[54]

Three major objections to the concept were raised as early as 1957 by Eisenhower's attorney general, Herbert Brownell: first, presidential inability is argued to be a political, and not exclusively a medical, issue; second, entrusting the question to non-elected officials such as physicians would grant them too much power; and third, the doctrine of separation of powers, in and of itself, precludes individuals outside the executive, legislative, or judicial spheres from participating.[55]

On the basis of the first objection, Clinton Rossiter stridently opposed the creation of such a commission: "Let us not go beyond the President and Vice-President in search of machinery to decide doubtful cases of disability, lest we construct a monstrosity." He concluded that "physicians should not have a say" in the matter and, presumably, should speak "only when spoken to." Rossiter added as an aside that certain members of the Supreme Court would agree.[56] Perhaps. Yet most members of the medical profession even remotely familiar with the problem would certainly differ. That may come as a surprise to those who participated in the 1964 Senate subcommittee hearings, as the opinion of organized medicine was not solicited, much less considered, during those proceedings (though Birch Bayh later conceded that they "might have been in error" in excluding medical testimony).[57]

Another opponent of the commission proposal, Dr. Ruth Silva, has pithily observed that "Congressmen, editors, lawyers and professors of political science had had a field day trying to imagine the identity or composition" of such a commission.[58] Doctors, it appears, have yet to have their say. Yet since these medical Moseses in the political wilderness are routinely charged with determining disability in corporate executives, it would seem shortsighted to deny those most skilled in this combination of art and science a part in Silva's call for "an organ so legitimate in its own right" that the nation "would be disposed to accept its judgment without hesitation."[59] Indeed, one suspects that the American public is justifiably cynical enough to resist leaving the *medical* aspects of such weighty determinations to the vagaries of the political process alone.

At least one participant in the proceedings leading to the Twenty-fifth Amendment was wise enough to define presidential inability in its proper medical context as "some very grave disability visited upon [the President], nervous, mental, or physical."[60] What Senator Roman Hruska understood better than most was that any subsequent decision must first rest on relevant and reliable facts regarding the president's mental and physical faculties. Leaving such a delicate determination solely to the discretion of elected or appointed public officials has served our nation poorly in the past, and one doubts that their diagnostic acumen has improved with the passage of time.

It would seem implicit in Senator Bayh's clarification of the word "inability" appended to the body of the amendment ("an impairment of the President's faculties") that the second objection raised against involving physicians in the determination must be reconsidered. Empowering such expert opinion as can only be found in the medical profession for judging presidential inability would hardly represent a usurpation of constitutional power. After all, the amendment gives Congress the expressed right to substitute another body for the cabinet. Moreover, that body would still be required to act *with* the vice-president, as the revised wording and punctuation of Section 4 ultimately agreed to make clear: "the Vice-President *and* a majority of either the principal officers of the executive departments *or* of such other body as Congress may by law provide" (emphasis added).[61] Binding the Presidential Disability Commission to the vice-president by concurrent resolution or statute would eliminate the fear of a physician-induced witch-hunt. The commission could neither raise the question of inability for discussion unless asked to do so by the vice-president nor act alone on the matter.

There is one additional benefit of binding the proposed commission's members to the vice-president rather than to the cabinet: neither could appear the usurper, whether a vice-president allegedly acting for personal gain or physicians assuming constitutional powers not accorded them. Though the potential successor has been granted the right to be part of the determination process, he or she should be relieved of the embarrassing duty of taking the initiative—at least without firm medical grounds for doing so. Senator Hruska might also have appreciated the strength of an arrangement which, in his own words, would provide the "advantages of a disinterested group . . . without extraneous motivations."[62]

One not so disinterested motivation, to be sure, is hardly extraneous. In a very real sense, the role of presidential physicians is an unenviable one. They are required to weigh a doctor's obligate respect for the patient's privacy against the implications for society of any compromise found in its leader. Given the restrictions inherent in this "central ethical dilemma," according to two scholars, "it seems simplistic to argue that the President's physician should always be candid with the public. . . . [After all], if the President cannot confide in his or her physician, he or she might let symptoms stay untreated. Moreover, a worrisome medical report at certain junctions could readily lead to overreaction or the weakening of the United States in a crisis. Secrecy [therefore] plays a legitimate role in effective government."[63]

Because no one would dispute that, one of the merits of a Presidential Disability Commission is that it would relieve the presidential physician of *sole* responsibility for judging the patient impaired. Naturally, the White House doctor's opinion would be solicited; in all likelihood he or she would act as the president's advocate by adding personal insight and necessary balance to any incriminating data the commission might gather. Failing that, one might even choose to hide behind the Hippocratic oath of confidentiality. A president who understands that his or her physician has that right would feel more inclined to be candid with the doctor without fear of public disclosure.

This is all to say that to warrant consideration of the removal of a president from office, inability should be so obvious to a majority of physicians on the commission that breaches of confidentiality in the doctor-patient relationship would hardly be necessary. Moreover, if secrecy is an obligate part of the game in Washington, the deliberations of such a commission should be accorded the same protection: the public would not need to know that a current review of the president's health was underway. Should circumstances require it, the president's physician could still speak optimistically from a whitewashed bully pulpit. Only if the commission's findings pointed to a health problem that the vice-president and cabinet found relevant to current political circumstances and decision-making would revelation become necessary.

The third objection to the concept of a Presidential Disability Commission assumes that introducing participants outside appointed or elected government positions would violate the constitutional principle of the separation of powers. Most who have studied the problem agree that the executive branch should be responsible for ironing its own laundry; hence the decision to conduct "in house" any investigation of a prospective case of presidential inability, the ultimate decision to be made in concert with the potential successor.

It is hardly surprising that those who see a determination of presidential inability as a political matter rather than what it really is to begin with—a medically based determination of physical or mental impairment enough to effect executive function—would deem any organ composed of non-executive-branch officials as a breach of the doctrine of separation of powers. But Congress has already refused to surrender all possible jurisdiction to its executive counterpart by retaining the right to appoint some "other body," should a future case not be adequately provided for by the arrangement outlined in the amendment. Vesting a preestablished Presidential Disability Commission with the power to investigate cases when they arise and to report its findings to the vice-president would assure that such deliberations remain tied to and function within the executive branch. Moreover, should the collective wisdom of any cabinet—wisdom that accrues from being close to the president, in a position to know the facts, and not likely to rule against the chief executive without good reason—come in conflict with the individual wisdom of the vice-president, both parties would benefit from the conclusions of medically trained experts having both the trust of the general public and the professional skill to evaluate the president's state of health.

The take-home lesson is this: under the current wording of the Twenty-fifth Amendment, Congress has been granted a constitutional right to resolve by statute or concurrent resolution this last remaining blind spot in our presidential succession policies. If a Presidential Disability Commission were mandated as an advisory panel answerable to the vice-president, there could be no objection to the concept on the grounds of separation of powers. As has already been made abundantly clear: "The Vice-President [remains] the key to the effectiveness of the procedures prescribed in the Amendment."[64] Rather than being shackled by the restraints of a hasty congressional move to assemble "such other body" in the eleventh hour, when agreement cannot be reached with the cabinet, the vice-president would be immeasurably strengthened by the contributions of a committee skilled in determining individual cases of impairment from the onset of any such potential crisis.

These last two chapters have outlined the pervasiveness of presidential inability in our past history and the limitations of the original constitutional provisions for dealing with the problem; traced the genesis of the Twenty-fifth Amendment from the important precedents set during Eisenhower's administration through its ultimate formulation; and shown that not all contingencies have yet been adequately provided for.

Certainly our experience with Ronald Reagan exemplifies the difficulties inherent in determining disability. What may have appeared as adequate (even normal) behavior and function from the perspective of those empowered with that determination was viewed with alarm by many physicians outside of government who deal on a daily basis with the effects of aging and general anesthetics. For some within the administration who shared that disquiet, further investigation was precluded by the charge that they were only being more loyal to their deposed chief of staff than to the president. By such political sleight-of-hand can legitimate concerns be swept under the rug.

That perplexing case will hardly be the last we shall see of this grave threat. The emergence of a youthful Bill Clinton notwithstanding, national leadership is often awarded those experienced enough to master its intricacies yet, paradoxically, aged enough to be subject to diseases that impact adversely on the way they think and behave. Many believe that the blinders to the problem we wore for so long were removed by passage of the Twenty-fifth Amendment. This study offers a second opinion to the contrary. Are we forever willing to entrust the health of our chief executives—and the decisions about how much to reveal—to medical friends of the president's family or military physicians? Will the political establishment accept the perhaps distasteful but urgent and necessary proposal to allow medical experts divorced from this unique physician-patient relationship a role in preventing recurrences of our physiologic flirtations with disaster? Can we afford to ignore the proposals of previous presidents and distinguished academicians who have suggested variations on this theme?

Legislative means are still at our disposal to strengthen the provisions of an amendment that has only begun to focus on the problem of presidential disability.

Postscript—
or Apologia?

Two eminent writers from distinctly different generations and cultures have made cogent observations about the discipline of history that have particular relevance to this study. The better known, the early twentieth-century Italian philosopher-historian Benedetto Croce, once remarked, in effect, that the only real history is modern history. Taken to its lowest common denominator of understanding, "If it ain't recent, it can't be relevant." The other, Arno Karlen, is an American editor and writer who has used the best elements of eclecticism to elevate the relatively modern disciplines of biohistory and pathography to high art. Karlen's work reflects his own understated ability to perceive the study of history as "a changing state of mind."

Both views have influenced the tenor and methodology of this book. What began as a rather lighthearted survey of select kings, emperors, and mystics of the past was transformed in midstream into a more pedantic examination of figures prominent in our own time. One suspects that Croce would have understood: the closer history is to us, the more relevant it becomes to our own lives. From the studies of Stalin, Churchill, and Eden through the examination of America's presidents, even the most casual reader should have tumbled to the realization that we are suffering today from the consequences of what has recently ailed others. What should interest us most about these pathographical dilemmas is the hope of avoiding them in the future. It is one thing to be entertained; deciphering the implicit message and learning from it is quite another, as Croce would surely have argued.

Karlen, too, would perhaps recognize my transition in style and content for what it is intended to represent. As he so succinctly described historical scholarship, "Each generation repaints the portraits of its past, keeps seeking a new present, and revises its expectations of the future." This book, viewed as a continuum, began by refurbishing a few musty pathographic portraits of the distant past, only to shift its focus toward rethinking those cases that have had more direct impact on our present circumstances. The last chapter detailed at least one proposal for a way of revising the future to the benefit of the American public as a governed people.

Certainly the conclusions drawn from the first few chapters are subjective and inferential, a direct reflection of the distance between the medical records of my subjects and the current methods that modern science can defensibly apply to them. In medical practice today, diagnoses are usually missed not on account of faulty reasoning but because our initial observations are wrong in the first place. The passage of years, not to mention the murkiness of the data at a modern physician's disposal, arguably reduce our judgments in these remote cases to speculative exercises in mental gymnastics.

The same should not apply to the twentieth century, for which most of the data have been painstakingly recorded somewhere, if the pathographer only knows where to look. Not that it's always available. Close-lipped physicians to the rich and famous continue to keep medical records to themselves. This is precisely why the observations and testimonies of friends, associates, and family members become so important. As every good clinician knows, probably 80 percent of diagnoses come from the medical history the patient or family gives the physician. The pathographer, like the prudent diagnostician, must be an eclectic of the Karlen mold to track down whatever data remain outside those withheld by the historical subject's physician.

There is no such excuse when the primary data *are* available but not sought—a lesson I once had to relearn: without the benefit of as yet unpublished primary sources, I had assumed that Wilson's viral illness in early April 1919 had more impact on the proceedings of the Paris Peace Conference than probably was the case (see Chapter 5). Without diligence and circumspection, we all too easily brand our historical patients with unwarranted diagnoses, at least insofar as they are alleged to have influenced history at a given point in time. In fact, I still feel somewhat uncomfortable with two of the diagnoses rendered in this study. For one, I am not at all certain that Adolf Hitler really suffered from temporal lobe epilepsy. Not that a lack of data is to blame; the problem in Hitler's case is the breadth of data to master. Above all, it is difficult to sort out the psychopathic god of the psychoanalyst's studies from the host of central-nervous-system stimulants Hitler took to excess. Or perhaps allowances simply have to be made for a few madmen in our past after all.

Another questionably relevant diagnosis applies to Ronald Reagan. How much was his conduct a mere reflection of the man, and how much was it exacerbated by the signs of aging that the record cannot ignore? Would anything really have happened differently during his administration had he been in his fifties rather than his seventies? What troubles me most about my observations and assessments, I suppose, is that for all the foibles and obvious missteps during his second term, it is difficult to discern the clear progression in the aging process that often typifies such cases. Either Reagan's public conduct was so controlled and orchestrated that further inroads of aging were not allowed the light of day, or the process itself was relatively static. Knowing something of our past experience with presidential health is justification enough for the cynicism that has emerged in my treatment of the man; even so, my instincts as a physician may have misled me.

That said, it is still the case that those who choose to ignore the impact of Reagan's age on his behavior risk being charged with sticking their heads in partisan sands. Nor would it be consistent with what the media have done to the private lives of public figures for the physician to continue to ignore their medical records on the basis of "ethical" restraints. Surely how a president thinks in the Oval Office is more important for the national interest than how he performs in the bedroom—or bedrooms. Yet insofar as the impact of Reagan's age on history is concerned, there is definite room for argument. For I suspect that the presidential synthesis view of history—that the president himself has the power to mold events as he sees fit despite whatever historical and political processes come to bear—has its weaknesses when applied to the office as we know it today. Indeed, the Reagan experience may be the best example one can conjure up of the institution of the presidency running itself even if no one is home. Quite apart from the person who holds the office, the modern presidency appears to be a self-perpetuating force on the world stage.

If that is true, then what is the point of the whole chapter on American presidents? Perhaps the answer lies in the fact that, at least on occasion, the bearer of that office—and of its counterparts elsewhere—does indeed supersede the historical process. With a potential nuclear holocaust not yet altogether out of the question, we should not remain oblivious to what effects disease might have on the thought processes of unstable terrorists in the Middle East and elsewhere.

On the more mundane level of scholarship, this whole area is something the American public is only now beginning to warm to, given the increasing number of publications dealing with leadership health. Yet to be a part of this new genre compels the need to be as circumspect and impartial as one can be. Pathography is a delicate area, full of pitfalls for the unwary and untrained. There will continually be the need, as Arno Karlen has so amply demonstrated, to rethink our history with new methodologies as they become available. To do so will serve to make modern history as real as possible. And that, one suspects, Benedetto Croce might well have appreciated.

Notes

Introduction

1. Frederick F. Cartwright, *Disease and History* (New York: Crowell, 1972), p. 83.
2. Elizabeth W. Marvick, review of *The Impact of Illness on World Leaders* by Bert E. Park, *Los Angeles Times*, July 12, 1987.
3. Sidney Walker, "Should Leaders Be Tested for Brain Integrity?" *Leaders*, January 1989.
4. Arno Karlen, *Napoleon's Glands and Other Ventures in Biohistory* (New York: Warner Books, 1984), p. 45.
5. I. MacAlpine, R. Hunter, and C. Rimington, "Porphyria in the Royal Houses of Stuart, Hanover, and Prussia," *British Medical Journal* 1 (1968): 7-18.
6. Sten Forshufvud et al., "Arsenic Content of Napoleon I's Hair Probably Taken Immediately after His Death," *Nature* 92 (1961): 103-5.
7. J.C. Howden, "The Religious Sentiments in Epileptics," *Journal of Mental Sciences* 18 (1872-73): 491-97.

Part I. Sick Heads and Tall Tales

Chapter 1. Napoleon Bonaparte

1. Cartwright, *Disease and History*, p. 110.
2. Ibid., pp. 108-9.
3. William Ober, "Seats of the Mighty," cited in Karlen, *Napoleon's Glands*, p. 8.
4. Karlen, *Napoleon's Glands*, p. 9. Most historical events have a precedent, if one only knows where to look. Some are buried in obscure libraries; Karlen has made us aware that a few are found in the gutter. A century earlier another pile of piles had done more than soil the regal underwear of French leadership. Though venerated by his contemporaries as the Sun King, Louis XIV was sorely vexed by a painful condition located, ironically enough, where the sun never shines: it seems that he suffered from swollen hemorrhoids and an anal fistula for fifteen years, during which period outbursts of rage and intemperate decisions marked his reign. One of the earliest surgical cures of this malady on record came at a propitious time. For the next thirty years Louis enjoyed good health and a stable temperament, and France embarked on the *grand siècle* of its history. Lest one think the prurient researcher is making too much of this, the esteemed historian Jules Michelet understood, as protocologists of a later time discovered, that the mind alone does not govern behavior; according to Karlen (p. 10), Michelet considered Louis's recovery from chronic rectal pain the turning point of his reign.

5. Victor Hugo, *Les Miserables*, bk. 4, chap. 7; cited in Wardner D. Ayer, "Napoleon Bonaparte and Schistosomiasis or Bilharziasis," *New York State Journal of Medicine* 66 (1966): 2298.

6. Cartwright, *Disease and History*, pp. 85-88.

7. Quoted in William Manchester, *The Glory and the Dream* (Boston: Little, Brown 1974), p. 405.

8. Archibald Arnott, *An Account of the Last Illness, Decease, and Post-Mortem Appearances of Napoleon Bonaparte* (London: J. Murray, 1822); cited in Ayer, "Schistosomiasis," p. 2300.

9. James Kemble, *Napoleon Immortal* (London: John Murray, 1959); Wilhelm Stekel, *Impotence in the Male* (New York: Liveright, 1927).

10. Augustin Cabanes, *Curious Bypaths of History* (Paris: A. Michel, 1898).

11. Leonard Guthrie, "Did Napoleon Bounaparte Suffer from Hypopituitarism?" *Lancet* 2 (1913): 823.

12. Kemble, *Napoleon Immortal*, p. 147.

13. Cabanes, *Curious Bypaths*; see also Karlen, *Napoleon's Glands*, p. 22.

14. Guthrie, "Hypopituitarism?" p. 823; Kemble, *Napoleon Immortal*, p. 147.

15. Walter Henry, *Events of a Military Life* (London, 1843), p. 148; Arnold Chaplan, *The Illness and Death of Napoleon Bonaparte* (London: Hirschfeld, 1913).

16. Henry, *Events*, p. 148.

17. Karlen, *Napoleon's Glands*, p. 23.

18. Frank Richardson, *Napoleon: Bisexual Emperor* (New York: G.P. Putnam's, 1972); cited in Karlen, *Napoleon's Glands*, p. 25.

19. Lewis Way, *Adler's Place in Psychology* (London: Allen and Unwin, 1950); Sigmund Freud, "Letter to Arnold Zweig," both cited in Karlen, *Napoleon's Glands*, p. 26.

20. Boris Sokoloff, *Napoleon: A Doctor's Biography* (New York: Prentice-Hall, 1937), p. 168 (first attributed to Cesare Lombroso).

21. Ibid.; Chester Dale, *Medical Biographies of Thirty-Three Famous Persons* (Norman: Univ. of Oklahoma, 1958), p. 157.

22. Cartwright, *Disease and History*, p. 105; Sokoloff, *Napoleon*, p. 168.

23. Quoted in Sokoloff, *Napoleon*, p. 155.

24. Dale, *Medical Biographies*, p. 157.

25. Sokoloff, *Napoleon*, p. 154; Dale, *Medical Biographies*, p. 157.

26. D. Bear, R. Freeman and M. Greenberg, "Changes in Personality Associated with Neurologic Disease," in *Psychiatric Aspects of Neurologic Disease*, ed. D.F. Benson and D. Blumer (New York: Grune & Stratton, 1975), 28:1-13.

27. Dale, *Medical Biographies*, p. 157.

28. Sokoloff, *Napoleon*, p. 167.

29. Attributed to the Spanish psychiatrist Dr. C. Juarros; cited in Sokoloff, *Napoleon*, p. 166.

30. Sokoloff, *Napoleon*, p. 159.

31. Cartwright, *Disease and History*, p. 106.

32. Ayer, "Schistosomiasis," p. 2295.

33. Karlen, *Napoleon's Glands*, p. 19.

34. Ayer, "Schistosomiasis," p. 2296. It stretches neither the bounds of literary license nor the open mind of the biohistorian to assert that whereas an indifferent Roman emperor once fiddled as his city burned, a French emperor-to-be was guilty of lounging more literally in troubled waters, unaware of his empire's mortgaged future. Taking historical analogies one step further, Troy's defenses were once penetrated by a fabled horse whose belly was filled with the armed seeds of her

destruction. As for Napoleon, an equally pernicious parasite may well have penetrated the imperial protective covering, discharging eggs that threatened to destroy its unwary host. Yet to suggest that the fate of Napoleon's *levée en masse* was ultimately linked to the larva of a parasite makes the skeptic uneasy. A kingdom for a horse is one familiar refrain; a levee for a larva is quite another—and admittedly runs the risk of falling on deaf, if incredulous, ears.

35. Paul B. Beeson and Walsh McDermott, *Cecil-Loeb Textbook of Medicine,* 12th ed. (Philadelphia: Saunders, 1967), pp. 389, 391.

36. Ibid., p. 392.

37. Emil Ludwig, *Napoleon* (New York: Boni & Liveright, 1926), p. 140; Vincent Cronin, *Napoleon Bonaparte: An Intimate Biography* (New York: Morrow, 1972), p. 149.

38. Ayer, "Schistosomiasis," p. 2297; Karlen, *Napoleon's Glands,* p. 19.

39. Arnott, *Last Illness;* Francesco Antommarchi, *The Last Days of Napoleon* (London, 1825); cited in Ayer, "Schistosomiasis," pp. 2300-2301.

40. W.A.D. Anderson, *Pathology,* 6th ed. (St. Louis: C.V. Mosby, 1971), p. 1404.

41. Forshufvud et al., "Arsenic Content," pp. 103-5.

42. Peter K. Lewin, Ronald Hancock, and Paul Voynovich, "Napoleon Bonaparte—No Evidence of Chronic Arsenic Poisoning," *Nature* 299 (1982): 627-28.

43. A.S. Lyons and R.J. Petrucelli, *Medicine: An Illustrated History* (New York: Abrams, 1978), p. 524; Beeson and McDermott, *Textbook of Medicine,* p. 392.

44. Ayer, "Schistosomiasis," p. 2296.

45. Contemporaries of Napoleon subscribed to this belief, as did a number of subsequent investigators, including (among those cited here) Cartwright, Wallace, Dale, and Kemble.

46. Antommarchi, *Last Days.* He later changed his mind and implicated hepatitis. See David Wallace, "How Did Napoleon Die?" *Medical Journal of Australia,* March 28, 1964, pp. 494-95.

47. Dale, *Medical Biographies,* p. 169.

48. Antommarchi, *Last Days;* cited in Wallace, "How Did Napoleon Die?" pp. 494-95.

49. Wallace, "How Did Napoleon Die?" p. 494.

50. Ibid.; Gilbert Martineau, *Napoleon's St. Helena* (Chicago: Rand McNally, 1969), p. 211.

51. Charles-Tristan Montholon, *History of the Captivity of Napoleon at St. Helena* (London: H. Colburn, 1846).

52. Forshufvud et al., "Arsenic Content," p. 105.

53. Ben Weider and David Hapgood, *The Murder of Napoleon* (New York: Congdon & Lattes, 1982), pp. 8, 255; Sten Forshufvud, "Napoleon's Illness 1816-1821 in the Light of Activation Analysis of Hairs from Various Dates," *Archiv fur Toxikologie* 20 (1964): 210-19.

54. "Death of Napoleon Bonaparte" (correspondence), *Lancet* 1 (1962): 101, 272, 428, 749, 914, 1128.

55. Lewin, Hancock, and Voynovich, "No Evidence," p. 627; Karlen, *Napoleon's Glands,* p. 18; Ayer, "Schistosomiasis," p. 2296.

56. Weider and Hapgood, *Murder of Napoleon,* p. 202.

57. Sir Russell Brock, "Death of Napoleon," *Nature* 195 (1962): 841; Lewin, Hancock, and Voynovich, "No Evidence," p. 627; Wallace, "How Did Napoleon Die?" p. 494.

58. Weider and Hapgood, *Murder of Napoleon,* p. 202. If the precise scientific explanation of chronic arsenic intoxication remained an enigma to Napoleon's

contemporaries, their predecessors in the Court of Louis XIV understood enough of its effects to use it as a poison in eliminating undesirables; see Frantz Funck-Brentano, *Le Drame des Poisons* (Paris: Hachette, 1920).

59. Forshufvud et al., "Arsenic Content," pp. 103-4; National Academy of Science, *Medical and Biologic Effects of Environmental Pollutants* (Washington, D.C., 1977), p. 175.

60. Arnott, *Last Illness*; Antommarchi, *Last Days.*

61. National Academy of Science, *Medical and Biologic Effects*, p. 176.

62. Forshufvud et al., "Arsenic Content," p. 104; Wallace, "How Did Napoleon Die?" p. 495; Ayer, "Schistosomiasis," p. 2297.

63. Martineau, *Napoleon's St. Helena*, p. 224.

64. Wallace, "How Did Napoleon Die?" pp. 494-95; Lewin, Hancock, and Voynovich, "No Evidence," p. 628.

65. Forshufvud, "Napoleon's Illness," p. 212.

66. Martineau, *Napoleon's St. Helena*, p. 224.

67. Weider and Hapgood, *Murder of Napoleon*, p. 206; Forshufvud, "Napoleon's Illness," p. 211.

68. Lewin, Hancock, and Voynovich, "No Evidence," p. 627; Martineau, *Napoleon's St. Helena*, p. 223; Forshufvud, "Napoleon's Illness," p. 211; Weider and Hapgood, *Murder of Napoleon*, p. 20.

69. Lewin, Hancock, and Voynovich, "No Evidence," p. 628; Martineau, *Napoleon's St. Helena*, p. 223.

70. Forshufvud, "Napoleon's Illness"; Weider and Hapgood, *Murder of Napoleon.*

71. Lyons and Petrucelli, *Medicine*, p. 524.

72. Weider and Hapgood, *Murder of Napoleon*, p. 19; Wallace, "How Did Napoleon Die?" p. 495.

73. Sokoloff, *Napoleon*, p. 216; Forshufvud et al., "Arsenic Content," p. 103.

74. Wallace, "How Did Napoleon Die?" p. 495.

75. National Academy of Science, *Medical and Biologic Effects*, pp. 176-77.

76. Lyons and Petrucelli, *Medicine*, p. 524; Ayer, "Schistosomiasis," p. 2296.

77. Whether Napoleon's dermatitis was psychosomatic in origin (i.e., neuroder-matitis) or related to the scabies so prevalent among his own troops is still in dispute. Nevertheless, he did take medication for it on a regular basis, eventually obtaining a cure with a mixture of cevadilla powder, olive oil, and alcohol (Dale, *Medical Biographies*, p. 156). Arsenic may have been among other medicines used, though this cannot be documented.

78. John Rose, *The Life of Napoleon* (London: G. Bell and Sons, 1934), p. 50; Sokoloff, *Napoleon*, p. 145; Wallace, "How Did Napoleon Die?" p. 495.

79. Karlen, *Napoleon's Glands*, p. 18.

80. National Academy of Science, *Medical and Biologic Effects*, pp. 175, 217.

81. Ibid., p. 174.

82. Ibid., p. 179.

83. Louis Marchand, *Memoirs de Marchand* (Paris, 1955); cited in Weider and Hapgood, *Murder of Napoleon*, p. 21, and Forshufvud, "Napoleon's Illness," p. 210.

84. Weider and Hapgood, *Murder of Napoleon*, p. 255.

85. Quoted in ibid., p. 21.

86. Forshufvud, "Napoleon's Illness," p. 212. Forshufvud covers his tracks by surmising that still other unnamed opponents had been poisoning Napoleon long before. That would be stretching the point. See Brock, "Death of Napoleon," p. 842.

87. National Academy of Science, *Medical and Biologic Effects*, p. 179.

88. Martineau, *Napoleon's St. Helena*, p. 226.

Chapter 2. Henry VIII

1. Cartwright, *Disease and History*, pp. 54, 63.

2. Andrew S. Currie, "Notes on the Obstetric Histories of Catherine of Aragon and Anne Boleyn," *Edinburgh Medical Journal* 34 (1888): 294-98.

3. Charles McLaurin, *Mere Mortals* (New York: George H. Doran, 1925), pp. 54-55, 73.

4. Ibid., p. 57; Ove Brinch, "The Medical Problems of Henry VIII," in *Tenements of Clay*, ed. Arnold Sorsby (London: Julian Friedman, 1974), pp. 47-49; James Kemble, *Idols and Invalids* (London: Methuen, 1933), p. 167.

5. Brinch, "Medical Problems," pp. 47-49; Kemble, *Idols and Invalids*, p. 167; James Kemble, "Henry the Eighth: A Psychological Survey and Surgical Explanation," *Annals of Medical History* 3 (1931): 619-25.

6. McLaurin, *Mere Mortals*, p. 56.

7. I.C. Flugel, "On the Character and Married Life of Henry VIII," *International Journal of Psycho-Analysis* 1 (1920): 30-31.

8. McLaurin, *Mere Mortals*, p. 56.

9. Brinch, "Medical Problems," p. 30.

10. J.F.D. Shrewsbury, "Henry VIII: A Medical Study," *Journal of Medical History*, 1952, p. 153.

11. Brinch, "Medical Problems," pp. 31, 44; Dale, *Medical Biographies*, p. 25.

12. Brinch, "Medical Problems," p. 44.

13. M.A.S. Hume, *Chronicle of King Henry VIII of England* (London, 1889); cited in Shrewsbury, "Henry VIII," p. 160.

14. McLaurin, *Mere Mortals*, p. 59.

15. Shrewsbury, "Henry VIII," p. 160; attributed to Dr. J.W. Orr.

16. William Osler, *Modern Medicine* (Philadelphia: Lea Brothers, 1907), 2:489.

17. McLaurin, *Mere Mortals*, p. 60; originally proposed by Dean Inge.

18. Lyon Appleby, "The Medical Life of Henry Eighth," Bulletin/*Vancouver Medical Association* II (1934): 94.

19. In defense of the syphilis thesis, one might argue that Henry may have become less infectious with time, so that the spirochete was not passed along to either Anne or Jane (Dale, *Medical Biographies*, p. 29). Yet one investigator exceeded the bounds of prudence by staking his reputation as a retrospective diagnostician on the assertion that, had the Wasserman blood test for syphilis been available in the sixteenth century, all of Henry's wives (except the Flemish mare Anne of Cleves) would have tested positive (Kemble, "Henry the Eighth," p. 624). More authoritative opinion from at least three obstetric/gynecologic experts has argued to the contrary: after reviewing the data, none found evidence to support syphilis as a cause for this tragic string of obstretrical histories (cited in Frederick Chamberlin, *The Private Character of Henry VIII* [London: J. Lane, 1932]; acknowledged by Brinch, "Medical Problems," pp. 41-42).

20. Currie, "Notes," pp. 299-300; Kemble, "Henry the Eighth," p. 623.

21. McLaurin, *Mere Mortals*, p. 86.

22. Osler, *Medicine*, 2:453, 493; *Harrison's Principles of Internal Medicine*, 11th ed., ed. Eugene Brauwald et al. (New York: McGraw-Hill, 1987), p. 644.

23. McLaurin, *Mere Mortals*, p. 92.

24. Shrewsbury, "Henry VIII," p. 162. To respond to one syphilophile's open-

ended invitation: any doctor looking at the portrait would probably say, "That woman must have been a hereditary syphilitic" (McLaurin, *Mere Mortals*, p. 92). But what I, for one, saw was nothing more than a rather homely woman framed at best in guilt-edged inference.

25. See Chamberlin, *Private Character*; cited in Shrewsbury, "Henry VIII," pp. 162-63.

26. Kemble, "Henry the Eighth," p. 623.

27. Shrewsbury, "Henry VIII," p. 162. "Overstudy," astoundingly enough, was also said to have accounted for Mary's menstrual irregularities.

28. Osler, *Medicine*, 2:493.

29. Shrewsbury, "Henry VIII," p. 146.

30. R.S. Ellery, "Must Syphilis Still Serve?" *Medical Journal of Australia* (1947): 393.

31. *Harrison's Principles*, p. 840.

32. Dale, *Medical Biographies*, p. 29; *Harrison's Principles*, p. 644.

33. J.J. Abraham, "The Early History of Syphilis," *British Journal of Surgery* 32 (1944): 235.

34. Cartwright, *Disease and History*, p. 77.

35. Barrett, "King Henry," pp. 224-25; Ellery, "Syphilis," p. 392; Shrewsbury, "Henry VIII," p. 175.

36. Abraham, "Early History," p. 230. The medical records of Henry's doctors are silent on this and all other matters pertaining to the king's health. It has been suggested that caution compelled them to avoid recording damaging information (Barrett, "King Henry," p. 221). For whatever reason, this same sort of silence has been practiced time and again in similar physician-patient relationships during the twentieth century; see Chapters 9 and 10.

37. Houston Merritt, *Textbook of Neurology*, 6th ed. (Philadelphia: Lea & Febiger, 1979), p. 136.

38. John Gary, "The Tudor Age," in *The Oxford Illustrated History of Britain*, ed. K.O. Morgan (Oxford: Oxford University Press, 1984), p. 237; J.J. Scarisbrick, *Henry VIII* (London: Eyre & Spottiswoode, 1968), p. 458; L.B. Smith, *Henry VIII: The Mask of Royalty* (Boston: Houghton Mifflin, 1971), pp. 229, 232.

39. Gary, "Tudor Age," p. 237.

40. Flugel, "Character and Married Life," p. 27.

41. A.F. Pollard, *Henry VIII* (Edinburgh: Gospen, 1902), p. 69.

42. Gary, "Tudor Age," p. 238.

43. *Henry VIII*, act 2, sc. 2; A.S. McNalty, *Henry VIII: A Difficult Patient* (London: Christopher Johnson, 1952), p. 72.

44. Pollard, *Henry VIII*, pp. 427-28; Smith, *Henry VIII*, p. 236.

45. Gary, "Tudor Age," p. 238.

46. Brinch, "Medical Problems"; Currie, "Notes"; McLaurin, *Mere Mortals*.

47. Shrewsbury, "Henry VIII," pp. 182-83.

48. Barrett, "King Henry," p. 230.

49. Cartwright, *Disease and History*, pp. 72-73.

50. *Harrison's Principles*, p. 652.

51. Appleby, "Medical Life," p. 96; Dale, *Medical Biographies*, p. 30.

52. Ibid., p. 31; Smith, *Henry VIII*, p. 230; McNalty, *Henry VIII*, p. 109.

53. Brinch, "Medical Problems," p. 44.

54. Ibid., p. 45; Kemble, *Idols and Invalids*, p. 168.

55. Dale, *Medical Biographies*, p. 27; McNalty, *Henry VIII*, p. 74.

56. McNalty, *Henry VIII*, p. 159.

57. Scarisbrick, *Henry VIII*, p. 485. Sir D'Arcy Power deserves credit for first suggesting this diagnosis; see Chamberlin, *Private Character*.

58. Shrewsbury, "Henry VIII," p. 178; Appleby, "Medical Life," p. 98.

59. *Harrison's Principles*, p. 1044.

60. Barrett, "King Henry," p. 231.

61. Brinch, "Medical Problems," p. 45; original description attributed to the French ambassador de Castillion.

62. Cartwright, *Disease and History*, p. 75.

63. Shrewsbury, "Henry VIII," pp. 144, 182-85.

64. Ibid., p. 183.

65. *Harrison's Principles*, pp. 1624-25.

66. Shrewsbury, "Henry VIII," p. 144; description originally attributed to Chamberlin.

67. Brinch, "Medical Problems," p. 49.

68. McLaurin, *Mere Mortals*, p. 86.

69. Kemble, "Henry the Eighth," p. 624.

70. Shrewsbury, *Henry VIII*, pp. 142-43; McLaurin, *Mere Mortals*, p. 54; Brinch, "Medical Problems," p. 53; Appleby, "Medical Life," pp. 99, 101.

71. Smith, *Henry VIII*, p. 232.

72. John Bowle, *Henry VIII: A Biography* (Boston: Little, Brown, 1965), p. 15.

73. Ibid.; McNalty, *Henry VIII*, p. 173; Smith, *Henry VIII*, p. 23; Gary, "Tudor Age," pp. 246-48.

74. Scarisbrick, *Henry VIII*, p. 458.

75. McNalty, *Henry VIII*, p. 170.

76. These were parliamentary statutes proclaiming convictions for treason that were punishable by death. Henry VII had elevated this practice to a high art, arguably overextending himself in the latter part of his reign as he sought to wipe out hostile landed magnates and to augment the power and income of the Crown. See Gary, "Tudor Age," p. 236.

77. Bowle, *Henry VIII*, p. 15.

78. Smith, *Henry VIII*, p. 17.

79. Ibid., p. 18; Gary, "Tudor Age," p. 252.

80. Francis Hackett, *The Personal History of Henry the Eighth* (New York: Modern Library, 1945), p. 368.

81. Cartwright, *Disease and History*, p. 77.

82. Gary, "Tudor Age," p. 246.

83. Cartwright, *Disease and History*, p. 77.

84. Osler, *Medicine*, 2:711.

85. Ibid., 2:716.

86. Ibid., 2:712.

87. Merritt, *Textbook of Neurology*, p. 144.

88. Kemble, *Idols and Invalids*, p. 171.

89. Brinch, "Medical Problems," p. 45.

90. Ibid.

91. Cartwright, *Disease and History*, pp. 72-73.

92. Osler, *Medicine*, 2:693.

93. Quoted in Cartwright, *Disease and History*, p. 50.

94. Quoted in ibid.

95. McNalty was the first to bring attention to this heretofore neglected aspect of Henry's medical history; see his *Henry VIII*, pp. 84-97.

96. Ibid., pp. 85-94; Barrett, "King Henry," p. 225.

97. McNalty, *Henry VIII*, pp. 95-96.

98. Julian Youmans, ed., *Neurological Surgery* (Philadelphia: Saunders, 1985), p. 970.

99. Ibid.

100. Smith, *Henry VIII*, p. 228.

101. Quoted in ibid.

Chapter 3. Fanatics and Saints

1. Bear, Freeman, and Greenberg, "Changes in Personality," 28:1-13.

2. Bert E. Park, *The Impact of Illness on World Leaders* (Philadelphia: University of Pennsylvania Press, 1986), pp. 160-76.

3. David Bear, "Behavioral Alterations in Patients with Temporal Lobe Epilepsy," in *Psychiatric Aspects of Epilepsy*, ed. Dietrich Blumer (Washington: American Psychiatric Press, 1984), p. 197.

4. See D. Landsborough, "St. Paul and Temporal Lobe Epilepsy," *Journal of Neurology, Neurosurgery, and Psychiatry* 50 (1987): 659-64; Cesare Lombroso, *L'Homo de Genie*, trans. as *The Man of Genius* (London: Scott, 1891), p. 189; Kenneth Dewhurst and A.W. Beard, "Sudden Religious Conversions in Temporal Lobe Epilepsy," *British Journal of Psychiatry* 117 (1970): 502.

5. Dewhurst and Beard, "Religious Conversions," pp. 502-4.

6. Steven G. Waxman, and Norman Geschwind, "The Interictal Behavior Syndrome of Temporal Lobe Epilepsy," *Archives of General Psychiatry* 32 (1975): 1580; Bear, "Behavioral Alterations," p. 159.

7. John Guerrant, W. Anderson, A. Fisher, et al., *Personality in Epilepsy* (Springfield, Ill.: Charles C. Thomas, 1962); Waxman and Geschwind, "Interictal Behavior Syndrome," p. 1585.

8. Norman Geschwind, Richard I. Shader, et al., "Case 2: Behavioral Changes with Temporal Lobe Epilepsy: Assessment and Treatment," *Journal of Clinical Psychiatry* 4 (1980): 89-95.

9. David Bear and Paul Fedio, "Quantitative Analysis of Interictal Behavior in Temporal Lobe Epilepsy," *Archives of Neurology* 34 (1977): 454-67; Geschwind, et al., "Behavioral Changes," pp. 89-95.

10. Eliot Slater, and A.W. Beard, "The Schizophrenia-like Psychosis of Epilepsy: Psychiatric Aspects," *British Journal of Psychiatry* 109 (1963): 95, 110.

11. Ibid.

12. Bear, Freeman, and Greenberg, "Changes in Personality," p. 8.

13. Bear and Fedio, "Quantitative Analysis," p. 465.

14. Ibid.; Dewhurst and Beard, "Religious Conversions," p. 497.

15. Bear and Fedio, "Quantitative Analysis," p. 465.

16. Ibid., p. 464; Geschwind, et al., "Behavioral Changes," p. 91.

17. John Gilroy and John S. Meyer, *Medical Neurology*, 2d ed. (London: Macmillan, 1969), p. 309.

18. Francis Forster and Harold Booker, "The Epilepsies and Convulsive Disorders," in *Clinical Neurology*, ed. A.B. Baker and L.H. Baker (Hagerstown, Md.: Harper & Row, 1976), 2, ch. 24, pp. 20-21.

19. Donald MacRae, "Isolated Fear: A Temporal Lobe Aura," *Neurology*, 4 (1954): 497.

20. Gilroy and Meyer, *Medical Neurology*, p. 310.

21. D. Frank Benson and Norman Geschwind, "Psychiatric Conditions Asso-

ciated with Focal Lesions of the Central Nervous System," in *American Handbook of Psychiatry*, 2d ed., ed. Sylvano Arieti (New York: Basic Books, 1975), 4:231.

22. Attributed to H.L. Mencken.

23. Park. *Impact of Illness*, pp. 177-85.

24. David Bear and George Arana, "Nonfunctional Disorders of Emotion," in *Neurology and Neurosurgery*, ed. Peritz Scheinberg (Princeton: Biomedia, 1978), 1, ch. 2, p. 7.

25. Robert G.L. Waite, *The Psychopathic God: Adolf Hitler* (New York: Basic Books, 1977).

26. Howden, "Religious Sentiments," pp. 491-97.

27. G. Sedman, "Being an Epileptic: A Phenomenological Study of Epileptic Experiences," *Psychiatria et Neurologia* 152 (1966): 1-16.

28. S. Karagulla and E.E. Robertson, "Physical Phenomena in Temporal Lobe Epilepsy and Psychoses," *British Medical Journal* 1 (1955): 748-52.

29. Dewhurst and Beard, "Religious Conversions," pp. 497-505.

30. Landsborough, "St. Paul," pp. 659-64.

31. 2 Corinthians 12:1-4.

32. Dewhurst and Beard, "Religious Conversions," p. 497.

33. Ibid.; Waxman and Geschwind, "Interictal Behavior Syndrome," p. 1580.

34. 1 Corinthians 15:6-8.

35. Galatians 4:13-15.

36. P.T. Manchester, "The Blindness of St. Paul," *Archives of Ophthalmology* 88 (1972): 316.

37. 2 Corinthians 11:6.

38. Quoted in Dewhurst and Beard, "Religious Conversions," p. 502.

39. Ibid., p. 503.

40. J.H. Neuba, *The Psychology of Religious Mystics* (London: Kegan Paul, 1925).

41. Dewhurst and Beard, "Religious Conversions," p. 503.

42. Quoted in F.M. Davenport, *Primitive Traits in Religious Revivals* (London: Macmillan, 1905).

43. Quoted in Willard Trask, *Joan of Arc: Self-Portrait* (New York: Collier Books, 1961), pp. 15, 96.

44. Quoted in Wilfred T. Jewkes, *Joan of Arc: Fact, Legend, and Literature* (New York: Harcourt, Brace & World, 1964), p. 53; Trask, *Joan of Arc*, pp. 98, 44, 49.

45. Trask, *Joan of Arc*, p. 107; Francis C. Lowell, *Joan of Arc* (Boston: Houghton Mifflin, 1896), p. 31.

46. Lowell, *Joan of Arc*, pp. 20-26.

47. Ibid., pp. 28, 29; Jewkes, *Joan of Arc*, p. 50; Trask, *Joan of Arc*, p. 106.

48. Charles E. Welles, "Organic Mental Disorders," in *Comprehensive Textbook of Psychiatry*, 4th ed., ed. H.I. Kaplan and Benjamin Sadock (Baltimore, Md.: Williams & Wilkins, 1985), 18:881.

49. Dewhurst and Beard, "Religious Conversions," p. 505.

50. Bear, "Behavioral Alterations," p. 165.

51. Jewkes, *Joan of Arc*, p. 50.

52. Dewhurst and Beard, "Religious Conversions," p. 497.

53. Quoted in Trask, *Joan of Arc*, p. 19.

54. Dewhurst and Beard, "Religious Conversions," pp. 499, 501.

55. Jewkes, *Joan of Arc*, p. 55.

56. Dewhurst and Beard, "Religious Conversions," p. 500.

57. Waxman and Geschwind, "Interictal Behavior Syndrome," p. 1584.

58. Trask, *Joan of Arc*, p. 71; Jewkes, *Joan of Arc*, p. 52.

59. Slater and Beard, "Schizophrenia-like Psychosis," p. 10.

60. Stephen B. Oates, *To Purge This Land with Blood* (New York: Harper & Row, 1970), p. 61.

61. Louis Ruchames, ed., *A John Brown Reader* (New York: Abelard-Schuman, 1959), pp. 63, 64.

62. Bear and Fideo, "Quantitative Analysis," pp. 459, 464-65.

63. See, e.g., the reproduction in David Donald, *Liberty and Union* (Lexington, Mass.: Heath, 1978), p. 74.

64. Bear and Fideo, "Quantitative Analysis," p. 465.

65. Barrie Stavis, *John Brown: The Sword and the Word* (South Brunswick, N.J.: Barnes, 1970), p. 14.

66. Ruchames, *John Brown Reader*, p. 168; Stavis, *John Brown*, p. 19.

67. Oates, *Purge This Land*, pp. 42-43.

68. Quoted in Jules Abels, *John Brown and the Cause of Liberty* (New York: Macmillan, 1971), p. 187.

69. Ibid., pp. 2, 38, xv.

70. In Ruchames, *John Brown Reader*, p. 169.

71. Abels, *Man on Fire*, p. 92.

72. Oates, *Purge This Land*, p. 353-54.

73. Abels, *Man on Fire*, p. 92.

74. Oates, *Purge This Land*, p. 330; Abels, *Man on Fire*, pp. 251, 85.

75. Abels, *Man on Fire*, p. 250; see also Oates's excellent discussion (*Purge This Land*, pp. 410-11); and Allan Nevins, *The Emergence of Lincoln* (New York: Scribner, 1950), 2:5-27, 70-97.

76. Abels, *Man on Fire*, p. 251.

77. S.E. Morison, *The Oxford History of the American People*, (New York: Oxford University Press, 1965), p. 601; quoted in Abels, *Man on Fire*, p. 250.

78. Stavis, *John Brown*, p. 32.

79. Abels, *Man on Fire*, p. 397.

80. Oates, *Purge This Land*, p. 59.

81. In Ruchames, *John Brown Reader*, pp. 65-66.

82. Quoted in Oates, *Purge This Land*, p. 73.

83. Stavis, *John Brown*, pp. 29, 84.

84. Ibid., p. 84; Ruchames, *John Brown Reader*, pp. 97, 125.

85. Welles, "Organic Mental Disorders," 18:879.

86. Bear, "Behavioral Alterations," p. 211.

87. Quoted in Abels, *Man on Fire*, pp. 10, 302.

88. Bear, "Behavioral Alterations," p. 162.

89. Oates, *Purge This Land*, pp. 251, 256; Stavis, *John Brown*, pp. 112, 133.

90. Quoted in Abels, *Man on Fire*, pp. 161-62.

91. In Ruchames, *John Brown Reader*, p. 129.

92. Abels, *Man on Fire*, pp. 161-62, 252.

93. Ibid., p. 251.

94. Quoted in Oates, *Purge This Land*, p. 231.

95. Abels, *Man on Fire*, pp. 170, 173.

96. Oates, *Purge This Land*, pp. 288-89.

97. Stavis, *John Brown*, p. 97.

98. Quoted in Abels, *Man on Fire*, pp. 294, 250.

99. Ruchames, *John Brown Reader*, p. 121.

100. Quoted in Abels, *Man on Fire*, pp. 294.

101. In Ruchames, *John Brown Reader*, p. 159.

102. Dewhurst and Beard, "Religious Conversions," p. 506.

Part II. Brain Failure at the Top

Chapter 4. Josef Stalin

1. Arthur M. Schlesinger, *The Age of Jackson* (Boston: Little, Brown, 1945); Edward Pessen, *Jacksonian America: Society, Personality, and Politics* (Homewood, Ill.: Dorsey Press, 1978).

2. Julius W. Pratt, *America's Colonial Experiment* (New York: Prentice-Hall, 1950); William A. Williams, *The Tragedy of American Diplomacy* (New York: Dell, 1959).

3. Walter Lippmann, *The Cold War: A Study in U.S. Foreign Policy* (New York: Harper, 1947); Denna F. Fleming, *The Cold War and Its Origins, 1917-1960* (Garden City, N.J.: Doubleday, 1961). For the more traditional view, see George F. Kennan, "The Sources of Soviet Conduct," *Foreign Affairs* 25 (July 1947); and Herbert Feis, *Roosevelt, Churchill, and Stalin* (Princeton, N.J.: Princeton University Press, 1957).

4. Fleming. *Cold War*; Lippmann, *Cold War*.

5. Thomas G. Paterson, *Soviet-American Confrontation: Post-War Reconstruction and the Origins of the Cold War* (Baltimore, Md.: Johns Hopkins University Press, 1973), pp. 260-67.

6. Thomas G. Paterson, "American Expansionism and Power," in *Major Problems in American Foreign Policy*, ed. Thomas G. Paterson (Lexington, Mass.: D.C. Heath, 1978), 2:314.

7. Arthur M. Schlesinger, "Soviet Ideology and Stalinist Paranoia," in *Major Problems in American Foreign Policy*, 2:308.

8. Kennan, "Sources of Soviet Conduct."

9. George F. Kennan, "Long Telegram," February 22, 1946, in *Major Problems in American Foreign Policy*, 2:276.

10. Schlesinger, "Soviet Ideology and Stalinist Paranoia," 2:308.

11. Harry Hopkins and Joseph Stalin, Memorandum, May 27, 1945, in *Major Problems in American Foreign Policy*, 2:275; Schlesinger, "Soviet Ideology and Stalinist Paranoia," 2:296.

12. Betty M. Unterberger, "Did the United States Try to Overthrow the Soviet Government, 1918-1920?" University Lecture Series, Texas A & M, November 18, 1986.

13. A.W. DePorte, *Europe between the Super-Powers* (New Haven, Conn.: Yale University Press, 1979), p. 135.

14. Kennan, "Long Telegram," p. 277.

15. Schlesinger, "Soviet Ideology and Stalinist Paranoia," p. 307.

16. Kennan, "Long Telegram," p. 279; Gustav Bychowski, "Joseph V. Stalin: Paranoia and the Dictatorship of the Proletariat," in *The Psychoanalytical Interpretation of History*, ed. B.B. Wolman (New York: Basic Books, 1971), p. 140.

17. Sigmund Freud, "Dostoevsky and Parricide" (1928), in *Collected Papers* (London: Hogarth, 1950), 5:222.

18. Bychowski, "Stalin," p. 138.

19. Ibid., p. 130.

20. Klara Zetkin, *Reminiscences of Lenin* (London: Modern Books, 1929), p. 7.

21. Zbigniew Brzezinski, *The Grand Failure* (New York: Scribner, 1989), p. 7.

22. Bychowski, "Stalin," pp. 125-26.

23. Leon Trotsky, *Terrorismus und Kommunismus* (Petrograd: Kommunistische Internationale, 1921).

24. V.I. Lenin, *The State and Revolution* (New York: International Publishers, 1932); Bychowski, "Stalin," p. 122.

25. Brzezinski, *Grand Failure*, p. 21.

26. Lenin quoted in Louis Fischer, *The Life of Lenin* (New York: Harper and Row, 1964), pp. 648-49; Bychowski, "Stalin," p. 122.

27. P. Pomper, "Necaev, Lenin, and Stalin: The Psychology of Leadership," *Jahrbucher fur Geschichte Osteuropas* (Weisbaden: Plesse Verlag, 1978), p. 129.

28. Bychowski, "Stalin," p. 123.

29. Alexis Scherbatov, introduction to N. Romano-Petrova, *Stalin's Doctor: Stalin's Nurse: A Memoir* (Princeton, N.J.: Kingston Press, 1984), p. viii.

30. Brzezinski, *Grand Failure*, p. 23.

31. Fischer, *Life of Lenin*, pp. 647-48.

32. Jerrold M. Post, and Robert S. Robins, *When Illness Strikes the Leader* (New Haven: Yale University Press, 1993), p. 51.

33. Quoted in Bengt Ljunggren, *Great Men with Sick Brains and Other Essays* (Park Ridge, Md.: American Association of Neurological Surgeons, 1990), p. 57.

34. Post and Robins, *When Illness Strikes*, p. 54.

35. Lidiya Shatunovskaya, *A Life in the Kremlin* (New York: Harper and Row, 1982), p. 241.

36. Romano-Petrova, *Stalin's Doctor*, p. xv.

37. Ibid., pp. xxv, 27-28.

38. Ibid., p. xxx.

39. Diana Spearman, *Modern Dictatorship* (New York: Columbia University Press, 1939); cited in Bychowski, "Stalin," p. 124.

40. See Robert C. Tucker, "The Dictator and Totalitarianism," in *The Soviet Political Mind: Stalinism and Post-Stalin Change* (New York: Norton, 1971), pp. 20-46.

41. George F. Kennan, *Russia and the West under Lenin and Stalin* (Boston: Little, Brown, 1960), p. 169.

42. Quoted in Paterson, "American Expansionism," p. 314.

43. Stimson and Kennan quoted in Schlesinger, "Soviet Ideology and Stalinist Paranoia," pp. 294-95.

44. Quoted in ibid., p. 295.

45. Ibid., p. 305.

46. Paterson, "American Expansionism," p. 313.

47. Quoted in Schlesinger, "Soviet Ideology and Stalinist Paranoia," p. 298.

48. Pomper, "Necaev, Lenin, and Stalin," p. 26.

49. Charles L. Mee, *Meeting at Potsdam* (New York: M. Evans, 1975), p. 50.; H. Montgomery Hyde, *Stalin: The History of a Dictator* (New York, 1978), p. 559.

50. Georges Bartoli, *The Death of Stalin* (New York, 1975), p. 201.

51. Ibid., p. 209.

52. Romano-Petrova, *Stalin's Doctor*, p. 57. That should also suffice to explain his sudden death, if only to dispel the ever popular rumor that he was murdered by a member of his entourage. See, e.g., Robert Payne, *The Rise and Fall of Stalin* (New York: Simon and Schuster, 1965), pp. 767-70, which argues the point unconvincingly. Not only do the autopsy findings correlate perfectly with his clinical presentation as a massive stroke, but nine separate physicians in attendance at the time of

Stalin's death attested to the autopsy report's authenticity (cited in Bartoli, *Death of Stalin*, p. 209).

53. Hyde, *Stalin*, p. 559.

54. Nikita Khrushchev, *Khrushchev Remembers* (Boston: Little, Brown, 1970), pp. 307-11.

55. O. Moroz, "The Last Diagnosis: A Most Probable Version Which Deserves Further Research," *Ziteraturnaya Gazeta* 28 (1988): 12.

56. Jelena Rzhevskaya, "Vtotden Pofdnejosenyur," *The Flag*, 1986, p. 12; cited in Ljunggren, *Sick Brains*, p. 66.

57. Post and Robins, *When Illness Strikes*.

58. Romano-Petrova, *Stalin's Doctor*, p. 29.

59. G.E. Vaillant and J.D. Perry, "Personality Disorders," in Kaplan and Sadock, *Comprehensive Textbook of Psychiatry*, 22:1574.

60. Bartoli, *Death of Stalin*, pp. 16-17; Romano-Petrova, *Stalin's Doctor*, p. 7.

61. Lawrence Kolb, "Multi-infarct Dementia and Delirium States," in *Modern Clinical Psychiatry*, 9th ed. (London: Saunders, 1977), p. 142.

62. Ronald Hingley, *Joseph Stalin: Man and Legend* (New York: McGraw-Hill, 1974), pp. 416-17; Bartoli, *Death of Stalin*, p. 15.

63. Svetlana Alliluyeva, *20 Letters tó a Friend* (New York: Harper & Row, 1967), p. 20.

64. Hingley, *Stalin*, p. 417.

65. Quoted in Hyde, *Stalin*, p. 563.

66. Charles E. Welles, "Organic Syndromes: Dementia," in Kaplan and Sadock, *Comprehensive Textbook of Psychiatry*, 4th ed., 1:859.

67. J.I. Walker and H.K. Brodie, "Paranoid Disorders," in H.I. Kaplan, Alfred M. Freedman, and Benjamin J. Sadock, eds., *Comprehensive Textbook of Psychiatry*, 3d ed. (Baltimore, Md.: Williams & Wilkins, 1980), 16:1288.

68. American Psychiatric Association, *Diagnostic and Statistical Manual of Mental Disorders*, 3d ed. (Washington, D.C.: APA, 1980); Walker and Brodie, "Paranoid Disorders," p. 1296.

69. Vaillant and Perry, "Personality Disorders," p. 1574.

70. Walker and Brodie, "Paranoid Disorders," p. 1290.

71. Ibid., pp. 1289, 1291.

72. N.A. Cameron, *Personality Development and Psychopathology* (Boston: Houghton Mifflin, 1963), p. 151.

73. Ibid.; Walker and Brodie, "Paranoid Disorders," p. 1291.

74. Walker and Brodie, "Paranoid Disorders," p. 1291.

75. Ibid.

76. Vaillant and Perry, "Personality Disorders," p. 1574.

77. Bychowski, "Stalin," p. 145.

78. Romano-Petrova, *Stalin's Doctor*, p. viii.

79. Bychowski, "Stalin," p. 141.

80. Romano-Petrova, *Stalin's Doctor*; Alliluyeva, *20 Letters*.

81. Khrushchev, *Khrushchev Remembers*; quoted in Schlesinger, "Soviet Ideology and Stalinist Paranoia," p. 308.

82. Bychowski, "Stalin," p. 146.

83. Blaine Taylor, "Josef Stalin: A Medical Case History," *Maryland State Medical Journal* 24 (November 1975): 35-46.

84. See Park, *Impact of Illness*, pp. 3-79; and Chapter 5.

85. Schlesinger, "Soviet Ideology and Stalinist Paranoia," p. 308.

86. Paterson, "American Expansionism," p. 315.

87. Ibid., p. 316.

88. Ibid., p. 318.

89. Schlesinger, "Soviet Ideology and Stalinist Paranoia," p. 308.

90. Nikita Khrushchev conceded that it may have been Stalin's "right to be suspicious," but it was *not* right to kill people just because he was. And that, Krushchev concluded, "was what made him crazy" (*Khrushchev Remembers*, p. 310).

Chapter 5. Woodrow Wilson

1. To be sure, that thesis has already been established, defended, and revised: see Edwin A. Weinstein, *Woodrow Wilson: A Medical and Psychological Biography* (Princeton, N.J.: Princeton University Press, 1981); and Park, *Impact of Illness*, chap. 1 and appendix. Neither account, however, had the benefit of primary sources that have since come to light. Hence the need to reexamine the effect of neurologic illness on Wilson's behavior with these new data in hand—particularly when an otherwise meticulous scholar concluded as recently as 1992 that the details of Wilson's medical history will never be known because pertinent records disappeared or were destroyed long ago: see Robert Ferrell, *Ill-Advised: Presidential Health and Trust* (Columbia: University of Missouri Press, 1992), p. 167. Such is simply not the case, as this chapter makes clear.

2. Alexander George and Juliette George, *Woodrow Wilson and Colonel House*, rev. ed. (1956; New York: Dover, 1984).

3. Ibid., p. 323. Would that other scholars were so prescient and candid. A recent publication that fails to address the entire record is Ferrell, *Ill-Advised:* "A few years ago [emphasis added] Arthur S. Link . . . explained President Wilson's illness in 1919-1921 and made available . . . special materials on the subject, including the diary of Dr. Cary Grayson [Wilson's physician]" (p. xi). But Ferrell ignores that subsequent analyses have shed new light on Wilson as a medical case study—enough for Link and the editorial staff of *The Papers of Woodrow Wilson* (Princeton, N.J.: Princeton University Press, 1966-1993) to accept some critical revisions of the original thesis so eloquently detailed by Weinstein in *Woodrow Wilson*. Not only have many of the remembrances in Dr. Grayson's diary proved transparent in the extreme; recent revelations among the "special materials" in Link's possession now validate the thesis as it was revised in 1986. As a review of the latest volumes of the Wilson *Papers* acknowledges: "The events documented [in vols. 62-64] are so complex that it is doubtful that a biographical study or a monograph could convey to the reader the same depth of understanding" (Raymond A. Esthus, *Journal of Southern History* 58 [August 1992]). As one of the contributors to that project, I would echo such sentiment. Nevertheless this chapter attempts to convey just such understanding.

4. See Weinstein, *Woodrow Wilson*, and *Journal of American History* 70 (1984): 845-53, 945-55, for the origins of this academic dispute.

5. Ferrell, *Ill-Advised*, p. 12.

6. George and George, *Wilson and House*, p. 278.

7. Ibid., p. 271.

8. See, e.g., Weinstein, *Woodrow Wilson*, pp. 339-44; Park, *Impact of Illness*, pp. 40-41; J.M. Keynes, *The Economic Consequences of the Peace* (New York, 1920), pp. 52-53.

9. Zbigniew Lipowski, "Organic Mental Disorders," in Kaplan, Freedman, and Sadock, *Comprehensive Textbook of Psychiatry*, 3d ed., 2:1375.

10. Park, *Impact of Illness*, pp. 335-36. Lacunar infarcts are small strokes, often clinically unappreciated, that occur deep in the brain on both sides. They are caused by hypertension and may eventually predispose the patient to the development of an organic brain syndrome.

11. Weinstein, *Woodrow Wilson*, pp. 323-24.

12. George and George, *Wilson and House*, p. 285.

13. Bert E. Park, "Wilson's Neurologic Illness at Paris," in Appendix, *WWP*, 58:613-14.

14. Ibid., pp. 624-25.

15. Ibid., p. 625.

16. Kolb, "Multi-infarct Dementia," p. 141.

17. Gilbert Close to his wife, April 7, 1919, in the Gilbert Close Collection, Firestone Library, Princeton University; Irwin Hood Hoover, *Forty-Two Years in the White House* (Boston: Houghton Mifflin, 1934), p. 98.

18. Kolb, "Multi-infarct Dementia," pp. 142-43.

19. Hoover, *Forty-Two Years*, pp. 98-99.

20. Edwin A. Weinstein, "Woodrow Wilson's Neurologic Illness," *Journal of American History* 57 (1970): 324-51.

21. Quoted in Editor's Commentary to Park, "Wilson's Neurologic Illness at Paris," *WWP*, 58:639; from Walter C. Alvarez, *Little Strokes* (Philadelphia: Lippincott, 1966), p. 34.

22. Appendix, *WWP*, 58:607.

23. Editorial comment, *WWP*, 58:278.

24. Grayson to J.P. Tumulty, April 30, 1919, *WWP*, 58:248.

25. Grayson Diary, *WWP*, 58:367.

26. *WWP*, 58:598-600.

27. Edwin A. Weinstein, "Woodrow Wilson's Neuropsychological Impairment and the Paris Peace Conference," Appendix, *WWP*, 58:632-33.

28. Charles Seymour Papers, May 14, 1919, and House Diary, May 10, 1919, *WWP*, 59:159, 34.

29. Henry Cabot Lodge, *The Senate and the League of Nations* (New York: Scribner's, 1925), pp. 226, 212-13, 218-19; cited in George and George, *Wilson and House*, p. 277.

30. *Washington Post*, July 22, 1919; *WWP*, 61:578-79.

31. Lodge to Wilson, July 22, 1919, and Wilson to Lodge, July 25, 1919, *WWP*, 61:582, 623.

32. Tumulty to Wilson with enc., August 4, 1919, *WWP*, 62:150-51.

33. Wilson to Lodge, August 8, 1919, *WWP*, 62:219.

34. Wilson to Lansing, August 8, 1919; and Lansing memorandum, August 11, 1919, *WWP*, 62:235, 258-59.

35. Lansing to Polk, "Strictly Confidential," August 12, 1919, *WWP*, 62:265; news report August 15, 1919, *WWP*, 62:35.

36. U.S. Senate, *Treaty of Peace with Germany: Report of the Conference between Members of the Senate Committee on Foreign Relations and the President of the United States*, 66th Cong. 1st sess. 1919, S.Doc. 76, *WWP*, 62:335-411.

37. Wilson memorandum to G.M. Hitchcock, September 3, 1919, ibid.

38. Woodrow Wilson, *Constitutional Government in the United States* (New York: Harper and Bros., 1908), pp. 139-41; see also editor's comment, *WWP*, 62:632-33.

39. "Leaders of Men," *WWP*, 62:633.

40. Lansing's Desk Diary, August 25, 1919, and editor's comment, *WWP*, 62:507.

41. Lansing memoranda, August 25 and September 1, 1919, *WWP*, 62:507, 613.

42. American Medical Association (hereafter AMA), *Guides to the Evaluation of Permanent Impairment*, 2d ed. (Chicago: AMA, 1984); cited in Appendix to *WWP*, 62:633-34.

43. *AMA, Guides*, p. x.

44. Kurt Goldstein, "Functional Disorders in Brain Damage," in Arieti, *American Handbook of Psychiatry*, 4:43-66.

45. Baker Diary, July 4, 1919, *WWP*, 61:383.

46. George and George, *Wilson and House*, p. 291.

47. Ibid., p. 114.

48. Quoted in Edith G. Reid, *Woodrow Wilson: The Caricature, the Myth, and the Man* (London: Oxford University Press, 1934), pp. 48-49.

49. Grayson Diary, September 25, 1919, *WWP*, 63:489.

50. Ibid.

51. Quoted in Baker Diary, November 5, 1919, *WWP*, 63:620.

52. News report, October 17, 1919, cited in *WWP*, 63:579.

53. See Park, *Impact of Illness*, p. 17.

54. Grayson Diary, September 26, 1919, *WWP*, 63:518-19; Weinstein, *Woodrow Wilson*, p. 355.

55. Grayson Diary, September 26, 1919, *WWP*, 63:518.

56. *New York Times*, October 13, 1919; *Washington Post*, October 3, 1919; news report of October 17, 1919, cited in *WWP*, 63:579.

57. Memoir of Irwin H. Hoover, "The Facts about President's Wilson's Illness," cited in *WWP*, 63:634.

58. See, e.g., *A Text Book of Medicine*, ed. R.L. Cecil (Philadelphia: Saunders, 1927), pp. 1308-9, 1419-24. This edition would represent the current thinking on strokes and neurasthenia as of 1919.

59. Ibid., p. 1309.

60. Ibid., pp. 1419-26.

61. *Washington Post*, October 4, 1919.

62. See Dercum's memorandum, cited in *WWP*, 64:500-507; and Grayson memorandum and subsequent statement of October 29, 1919, *WWP*, 64:507-13, as well as Cary T. Grayson, *Woodrow Wilson: An Intimate Memoir* (New York: Holt, Rinehart and Winston, 1960), pp. 97-114.

63. Appendix to *WWP*, 63:645.

64. Weinstein, *Woodrow Wilson*, p. 192.

65. Percentages are not strictly additive; see AMA, *Guides*, p. 240.

66. See Appendix to *WWP*, 64:526.

67. See *WWP*, 64:23, 53, 159, 204, including Tumulty to Edith Wilson, December 18, 1919.

68. Hitchcock to Edith Wilson, with enc., November 18, 1919, *WWP*, 64:58.

69. *Washington Post*, November 30, 1919.

70. Lansing memorandum, December 16, 1919, *WWP*, 64:192-94; Baker Diary, November 18, 1919, *WWP* 64:61.

71. *New York Times*, December 3, 1919.

72. House Diary, December 11, 1919, *WWP*, 64:183.

73. Lansing memorandum, December 10, 1919, *WWP*, 64:179.

74. Draft of a public letter, December 17, 1919, *WWP*, 64:199-202; Jackson Day message, January 8, 1920, *WWP*, 64:257.

75. See editorial comment appended to Hitchcock to Wilson, March 20, 1920, *WWP*, 65:109.

76. Lansing memorandum, January 10, 1920, *WWP*, 64:267; Lipowski, "Organic Mental Disorders," p. 1389.

77. House Diary, January 11, 1920, *WWP*, 64:270-71.

78. Ibid., January 3, 1920, *WWP*, 64:243.

79. Editorial, *New York World*, January 10, 1920, *WWP*, 64:271.

80. *New York Times*, February 11, 1920; *Baltimore Sun* interview with Dr. Hugh H. Young, February 10, 1920. Dr. Grayson declined comment on the report.

81. *Literary Digest*, 64 (February 28, 1920): 13-15.

82. Ibid. (attributed to Dr. Young in *Sun* interview).

83. Ibid.

84. Editorial, *Philadelphia Evening Public Ledger*, February 11, 1920, *WWP*, 65:5.

85. Mark Sullivan, *New York Evening Post*, February 11, 1920, *WWP*, 65:6.

86. Lansing memorandum, February 23, 1920; House Diary, February 18, 1920, *WWP*, 64:454, 444. That was not the first time Wilson had indulged in selective amnesia; at one point he claimed that he had no knowledge of the Treaty of London before 1919, again at variance with the record.

87. Lansing memorandum, February 13, 1920, *WWP*, 64:415; Lipowski, "Organic Mental Disorders," p. 1389.

88. Baker Diary, February 15, 1920, *WWP*, 64:434.

89. Wilson to Lansing, February 3, 1920, *WWP*, 65:352.

90. Baker Diary, February 3, 1920, *WWP*, 64:359-60.

91. Cummings Diary, February 14, 1920, *WWP*, 64:427-28.

92. Weinstein, *Woodrow Wilson*, p. 369.

93. Baker Diary, February 15, 1920; Lansing memorandum, February 22, 1990, *WWP* 64:434, 451-58.

94. House Diary, February 18, 1920; *WWP*, 64:444.

95. Wilson to Hitchcock, March 5, 1920, *WWP*, 65:49-55.

96. *Literary Digest*, February 28, 1920.

97. *New York World*, March 20, 1920. Wilson's letter was published on March 9 in the *New York Times*.

98. Loring Chapman and Harold Wolff, "Diseases of the Neopallium," *Medical Clinics of North America* 42 (1958):677-89.

99. Cited in Arthur M. Schlesinger, *The Cycles of American History* (Boston: Houghton Mifflin, 1986), p. 82.

Chapter 6. Winston Churchill

1. *Churchill: Taken from the Diaries of Lord Moran* (Boston: Houghton Mifflin, 1966), p. 350 (hereafter Moran, *Diaries*).

2. Ibid., p. 361.

3. H.A. Skinner, *The Origin of Medical Terms*, 2d. ed. (New York: Hafner, 1970), in *Aging and Dementia*, ed. W. Lynn Smith and Marcel Kinsbourne (New York: Spectrum, 1977), p. 8.

4. Anthony Storr, "The Man," in *Churchill Revised: A Critical Assessment*, ed. A.J.P. Taylor (New York: Dial Press, 1969), pp. 231, 273.

5. Mary Soames, *Clementine Churchill* (Boston: Houghton Mifflin, 1979), p. 631; Storr, "The Man," p. 273.

6. Moran, preface to *Diaries*, p. ix.

7. Marcel Kinsbourne, "Cognitive Decline with Advancing Age," in Smith and Kinsbourne, *Aging and Dementia*, p. 229.

8. Jack Botwinick, *Cognitive Processes in Maturity and Old Age* (New York: Springfield, 1967), p. 89.

9. Moran, *Diaries*, pp. 71, 72.

10. Michael O'Brien, "Vascular Disease and Dementia in the Elderly," in Smith and Kinsbourne, *Aging and Dementia*, p. 88.

11. H.S. Wang, "Dementia of Old Age," in Smith and Kinsbourne, *Aging and Dementia*, p. 16. Interested readers may consult L.G. Kilik, "Pseudo-dementia," *Acta Psychiatrica Scandinavica* 37 (1961):336-51; and L.S. Libow, "Pseudo-senility: Acute and Reversible Organic Brain Syndromes," *Journal of the American Geriatric Society* 21(1973):112-20.

12. Storr, "The Man," p. 231. Lord Moran likewise had developed this theme of depression in his book *The Anatomy of Courage* (Boston: Houghton Mifflin, 1967) published prior to the *Diaries*, which caused such a furor.

13. Wang, "Dementia of Old Age," p. 17.

14. R. Rhodes James, "The Politician," in *Churchill Revised*, p. 124.

15. Violet Bonham Carter, *Winston Churchill: An Intimate Portrait* (New York: Harcourt, Brace & World, 1965), p. 116.

16. Storr, "The Man," p. 272.

17. Henry Pelling, *Winston Churchill* (New York: Dutton, 1974), p. 573. See also James Stuart, *Within the Fringe* (London: Macmillian, 1967).

18. Pelling, *Winston Churchill*, p. 574.

19. *The Times* (London), July 17, 1947.

20. Moran, *Diaries*, p. 355.

21. Kenneth Young, *Churchill and Beaverbrook* (London: Eyre & Spottiswoode, 1966), p. 285.

22. Quoted in Moran, *Diaries*, pp. 355-56.

23. Merritt, *Textbook of Neurology*, p. 196. The original article describing this syndrome (C. Miller Fisher, "Pure Sensory Stroke Involving Face, Arm, and Leg," *Neurology* 15 [1965]:76-80) makes several points in distinguishing this entity from large-vessel, middle cerebral artery branch thrombosis or embolism. The power of the limbs is preserved, and there is no speech deficit, visual field deficit, or acute memory loss: "When only the ipsilateral extremities are affected [as in Churchill's case] we are inclined to suspect pure hemosensory syndrome [of lacunar infarction] rather than a superficial middle cerebral territory lesion."

24. Harold Macmillan, *Tides of Fortune, 1945-1955* (New York: Harper & Row, 1969), p. 179.

25. Young, *Churchill and Beaverbrook*, pp. 284-85. This account of events is corroborated in Moran, *Diaries*, p. 356.

26. Young, *Churchill and Beaverbrook*, p. 286.

27. Moran, *Diaries*, p. 351.

28. Quoted in ibid., p. 358.

29. Ibid., p. 359.

30. Quoted in ibid., p. 368.

31. Ibid. Ironically, modern medicine now recognizes aspirin to be a safe and effective antidote for reducing sludging and augmenting flow in vessels narrowed by atherosclerosis. If Churchill was suffering from vertebral-basilar ischemic episodes, then he was receiving the very medication prescribed today for that condition.

32. Kolb, *Modern Clinical Psychiatry*, p. 253.

33. Moran, *Diaries*, p. 368.

34. Young, *Churchill and Beaverbrook*, p. 287.

35. Lord Normanbrook, *Action This Day: Working With Churchill*, ed. John Wheeler Bennett (New York: St. Martins Press, 1969), p. 38.

36. David Thomson, *England in the Twentieth Century* (New York: Penquin Books, 1983), p. 244. That there was more than political rhetoric in this assertion is suggested by Basil Liddell Hart, who believed that Lord Esher's verdict in 1971 on the subject was as true in the end as it was in the beginning: Churchill "handles great subjects in rhythmical language, and becomes quickly enslaved by his phrases. He deceives himself into the belief that he takes broad views, when his mind is fixed upon one comparatively small aspect of the question" (quoted by Liddell Hart in "The Military Strategist," in *Churchill Revised*, p. 221).

37. Macmillan, *Tides of Fortune*, pp. 484-85.

38. *The Times* (London), April 5, 1952.

39. Macmillan, *Tides of Fortune*, p. 491.

40. Lord Normanbrook, *Action This Day*, p. 40.

41. Sir John Colville, *Action This Day*, p. 123.

42. Moran, *Diaries*, pp. 377-78.

43. Ibid., p. 408.

44. Ibid., p. 663.

45. Ibid., pp. 395-96.

46. Quoted in ibid., p. 398.

47. Ibid., pp. 401-4. This was not the first such meeting held by Churchill's associates regarding the need for him to resign. See Anthony Seldon, *Churchill's Indian Summer: The Conservative Government 1951-1955* (London: Hodder & Stoughton, 1981), p. 38.

48. Quoted in Soames, *Clementine Churchill*, pp. 591, 590.

49. Quoted in Moran, *Diaries*, p. 406.

50. Ibid., p. 407. Unfortunately, Moran's letter gave Churchill breathing room by allowing him to believe that lightening the load would rectify the problem. Yet no medical evidence supports the notion that excessive mental effort increases the instability of the cerebral circulation—or its corollary, that decreasing such effort would improve the natural history of the disease, which progresses inexorably.

51. Quoted in ibid., pp. 546, 564.

52. Ibid., pp. 412, 420, 421.

53. Ibid., p. 429.

54. Macmillan, *Tides of Fortune*, pp. 516-17.

55. Moran, *Diaries*, pp. 434-38.

56. Merritt, *Textbook of Neurology*, p. 190.

57. Moran, *Diaries*, pp. 460, 473.

58. Storr, "The Man," p. 273.

59. Moran, *Diaries*, pp. 461, 466.

60. Ostensibly, this three-power summit conference involving Britain, France, and the United States had been planned to discuss the upkeep of military forces in Western Europe, but Churchill had hoped to use the meeting as a springboard to catapult himself into the position of indispensable mediator between the Americans and the Soviets.

61. Young, *Churchill and Beaverbrook*, pp. 293-94.

62. A.J.P. Taylor "The Statesman," *Churchill Revised*, pp. 58-60.

63. Liddell Hart, "Military Strategist," ibid., p. 222.

64. This is what Goldstein ("Functional Disorders," pp. 43-66) has identified as "impairment of the abstract attitude" in individuals stricken with dementia: "Tasks which demand choice or shifting particularly reveal the defect."

65. Quoted in David Carlton, *Anthony Eden* (Boston: Houghton Mifflin, 1981), p. 333.

66. *Eisenhower Papers*, Dwight D. Eisenhower Library, Abilene, Kansas, 12:51, 53.

67. Pelling, *Winston Churchill*, p. 604. Anthony Seldon (*Indian Summer*, p. 69) indicted the conspirators in the cover-up with the caustic assessment that they had been "often far from frank in the information they passed on."

68. Macmillan, *Tides of Fortune*, p. 517.

69. Moran, *Diaries*, pp. 439, 444.

70. *Daily Mirror*, August 17, 1953.

71. Moran, *Diaries*, p. 486.

72. Cited in ibid., pp. 488, 489, 492.

73. Ewald Busse, "Aging and Psychiatric Diseases of Late Life," in Sylvano Arieti, ed., *American Handbook of Psychiatry*, 2d ed. (New York: Basic Books, 1975), 4:77.

74. Moran, *Diaries*, p. 507.

75. Quoted in ibid., p. 509.

76. Macmillan, *Tides of Fortune*, p. 527.

77. *Hansard*, December 17, 1953.

78. Moran, *Diaries*, p. 491. "Older subjects become depressed when they cannot find ways of gratifying their needs. They are likely to have a loss of self-esteem; hence, they feel depressed" (Busse, "Aging and Psychiatric Diseases," p. 74).

79. Moran, *Diaries*, pp. 570-73.

80. Quoted in ibid., pp. 579-80.

81. Ibid., pp. 595, 596, 598.

82. Macmillan, *Tides of Fortune*, pp. 543-41; Moran, *Diaries*, p. 623. For most of his second tenure, Churchill's approval by the public he served remained at or below 50 percent. See Seldon, *Indian Summer*, pp. 42, 46, 428; Thomson, *England in the Twentieth Century*, p. 245.

83. Moran, *Diaries*, p. 642. Churchill's egocentricity was highlighted by his response to a threatened newspaper strike at the time: he was concerned lest the public not be able to read about his speech the following day (Macmillan, *Tides of Fortune*, p. 547).

84. Quoted in Moran, *Diaries*, p. 635.

85. Quoted in Pelling, *Winston Churchill*, p. 612.

86. Quoted in Moran, *Diaries*, p. 666. This was not the first time Macmillan had attempted to get Churchill to resign. In July 1954, when there was much unrest in the cabinet over the issue, Macmillan confronted Clementine with the news that many in the government thought Churchill should resign (Soames, *Clementine Churchill*, p. 591).

87. See, e.g., Seldon, *Indian Summer*, p. 37.

88. Colville, *Action This Day*, p. 138.

89. An agreement signed July 27, 1954, specified that all British troops were to be evacuated from the Canal Zone. That this solution was not in accord with Churchill's wishes is a matter of record.

90. Allan Sked and Chris Cook, *Post-War Britain* (Harmondsworth: Penguin Books, 1984), pp. 104-5.

91. Macmillan, *Tides of Fortune*, p. 550.

92. Colville, *Action This Day*, p. 130.

93. Quoted in Moran, *Diaries*, p. 518.

94. Kolb, *Modern Clinical Psychiatry*, p. 253.

95. Busse, "Aging and Psychiatric Diseases," p. 75.

Part III. Drugs and Diplomacy

1. Hugh L'Etang, *Fit to Lead?* (London: William Heinemann, 1980), p. 26.
2. Ibid., pp. 94-97; James F. Giglio, *The Presidency of John F. Kennedy* (Lawrence: University Press of Kansas, 1992), p. 263.
3. Ferrell, *Ill-Advised*, p. 157.

Chapter 7. Anthony Eden

1. Carlton, *Anthony Eden*, p. 298.
2. Ibid., p. 299.
3. Terence Robertson, *Crisis: The Inside Story of the Suez Conspiracy* (New York: Atheneum, 1984), p. 106.
4. W.R. Bett, "Benzedrine Sulphate in Clinical Medicine," *Postgraduate Medical Journal* 22 (1946): 202-9; Kaplan, Freedman, and Sadock, *Comprehensive Textbook of Psychiatry*, 3d ed., 2:1619.
5. Eric Martin, *The Hazards of Medication* (Philadelphia: Lippincott, 1971), pp. 334-35.
6. Hugh Thomas, *Suez* (New York: Harper & Row, 1967), p. 35.
7. John von Felsinger, Louis K. Lasagna, and Henry Beecher, "Drug-Induced Mood Changes in Man," *Journal of the American Medical Association* 157 (1955): 1113; A. Goodman, Louis S. Goodman, and Alfred Gilman, *The Pharmacologic Basis of Therapeutics*, 6th ed. (New York: Macmillan, 1980), p. 158.
8. Kaplan, Freedman, and Sadock, *Comprehensive Textbook of Psychiatry*, 3d ed., 2:1619; Martin, *Hazards of Medication*, p. 335.
9. Quoted in Carlton, *Anthony Eden*, p. 298.
10. Goodman, Goodman, and Gilman, *Pharmacologic Basis of Therapeutics*, p. 158.
11. Kaplan, Freedman, and Sadock, *Comprehensive Textbook of Psychiatry*, 3d ed., 2:1620; see also J.H. Biel and B.A. Bopp, "Amphetamines: Structure-Activity Relationships," in *Handbook of Psychopharmacology*, ed. Lawrence Iverson et al. (Philadelphia: Lippincott, 1982), p. 30.
12. Thomas, *Suez*, p. 11.
13. Anthony Nutting, *No End of a Lesson* (New York: Potter, 1967), p. 6.
14. Lord Kilmuir, *Political Adventure* (London: Cassell, 1964), p. 193.
15. Quoted in Sked and Cook, *Post-War Britain*, p. 146.
16. Ibid., pp. 116, 118; Carlton, *Anthony Eden*, p. 338.
17. Carlton, *Anthony Eden*, p. 311.
18. Anthony Eden, *Full Circle: The Memoirs of Anthony Eden* (Boston: Houghton Mifflin, 1960); Harold Macmillan, *Riding the Storm* (New York: Harper & Row, 1971).
19. Eden, *Full Circle*, p. 481; Macmillan, *Riding the Storm*, pp. 99-100.
20. Eden, *Full Circle*, p. 560.
21. Ibid., pp. 475-76.
22. Ibid., pp. 539-40.
23. Robertson, *Crisis*, pp. 139-40.
24. Ibid., p. 172.
25. Thomas, *Suez*, p. 2.
26. Ibid., p. 1.
27. Nutting, *No End of a Lesson*, p. 8.
28. Cited in Robertson, *Crisis*, p. 85.

29. Nutting, *No End of a Lesson*, pp. 50-51.

30. Ibid., p. 58.

31. Carlton, *Anthony Eden*, p. 405.

32. Nutting, *No End of a Lesson*, p. 78.

33. Ibid., p. 89.

34. Ibid., p. 92.

35. Ibid., p. 94.

36. Eden, *Full Circle*, pp. 580-81.

37. Quoted in Thomas, *Suez*, p. 34.

38. Quoted in Robertson, *Crisis*, p. 81.

39. Thomas, *Suez*, p. 92.

40. Ibid., p. 112.

41. Ibid., p. 113.

42. Nutting, *No End of a Lesson*, pp. 99, 106.

43. Ibid., p. 107.

44. Thomas, *Suez*, pp. 116, 117, 119.

45. Ibid., p. 124.

46. Nutting, *No End of a Lesson*, pp. 112, 117.

47. Ibid., p. 119; Thomson, *England in the Twentieth Century*, p. 254.

48. *Hansard*, November 3, 1956.

49. Quoted in Thomas, *Suez*, p. 126.

50. Robertson, *Crisis*, p. 178.

51. Thomas, *Suez*, pp. 134, 138.

52. Robertson, *Crisis*, pp. 264, 266.

53. Quoted in Thomas, *Suez*, p. 149.

54. Nutting, *No End of a Lesson*, p. 14.

55. Ibid., p. 25.

56. Ibid., p. 26. No medical evidence supports the claim that nervous pressure threatens the anatomy of the bile duct.

57. Thomas, *Suez*, p. 35.

58. Quoted in ibid., p. 35; Kilmuir, *Political Adventure*, p. 308.

59. Sked and Cook, *Post-War Britain*, p. 126.

60. Thomas, *Suez*, p. 35.

61. Nutting, *No End of a Lesson*, p. 27.

62. Quoted in Donald Neff, *Warriors at Suez* (New York: Simon and Schuster, 1981), p. 181.

63. Nutting, *No End of a Lesson*, pp. 27, 26.

64. Neff, *Warriors at Suez*, p. 183.

65. Nutting, *No End of a Lesson*, pp. 32-33.

66. Alterations in mentation (encephalopathy) on the basis of liver disease usually occur in the face of both intrinsic (liver) and extrinsic (bile duct) pathology, the former of which Eden did not have. It is true that in some cases of bile duct obstruction transient behavioral changes occur, but this is the exception. The disease was certainly contributory but not as overriding as some investigators have argued in Eden's case. Dr. Hugh L'Etang's opinion is illustrative: "Such episodes [of obstructive cholangitis] may be accompanied by high fevers . . . together with pain and jaundice. Some patients become introspective, querulous, and suspicious" (*The Pathology of Leadership*) [New York: Hawthorne Books, 1970], p. 163). The significance of fever and the absence of jaundice in Eden's case may have important implications, which are discussed below.

67. Frederich Plum and Jerome Posner, *The Diagnosis of Stupor and Coma* (Philadelphia: Davis, 1966), p. 246.

68. Quoted in Nutting, *No End of a Lesson*, pp. 34-35.

69. Quoted in Carlton, *Anthony Eden*, pp. 376, 391.

70. Nutting, *No End of a Lesson*, p. 107.

71. Neff, *Warriors at Suez*, p. 278.

72. Ibid.

73. Moran, *Diaries*, p. 747.

74. Nutting, *No End of a Lesson*, pp. 67-68.

75. Malcolm Muggeridge quoted in L'Etang, *Pathology*, p. 167.

76. Thomas, *Suez*, p. 99.

77. Nutting, *No End of a Lesson*, p. 26; Carlton, *Anthony Eden*, p. 428. Donald Neff (*Warriors at Suez*) deserves credit for indicting amphetamines as a possible explanation for Eden's "mysterious fevers," which others have ascribed to an inflammatory condition of the bile duct. See Thomas, *Suez*, pp. 99, 100.

78. Carlton, *Anthony Eden*, p. 428.

79. AMA Council, "Aspects of Amphetamine Abuse," *Journal of the American Medical Association* 240 (November 17, 1978): 2318.

80. Carlton cites Ramsay MacDonald as his source (*Anthony Eden*, p. 427); see also Nutting, *No End of a Lesson*, p. 70.

81. Thomas, *Suez*, p. 162.

82. Quoted in Robertson, *Crisis*, p. 259.

83. Carlton, *Anthony Eden*, p. 446; Robertson, *Crisis*. p. 259.

84. AMA Council, "Aspects of Amphetamine Abuse," p. 2318.

85. Carlton, *Anthony Eden*, p. 450. On November 3-4, the General Assembly passed a resolution authorizing the establishment of a United Nations Emergency Force for deployment along the Suez.

86. Butler quoted in ibid., pp. 450-51; James Morgach, *The Abuse of Power* (London: Cassell, 1978), p. 113.

87. Carlton, *Anthony Eden*, p. 452. Eisenhower informed Eden that "the resort to force, condemned in our enemies, should not be permitted by our friends" (quoted in Robertson, *Crisis*, p. 253).

88. Quoted in Carlton, *Anthony Eden*, p. 453.

89. Ibid., p. 454.

90. Kaplan, Freedman, and Sadock, *Comprehensive Textbook of Psychiatry*, 3d ed., 2:1625. Periods of drug abstinence also result in painful gastrointestinal cramps. That leads one to wonder whether the abdominal discomfort Eden suffered during this time was solely attributable to his bile duct pathology. No account mentions the appearance of jaundice in concert, which would be expected to occur if the bile duct is obstructed or inflamed.

91. Neff, *Warriors at Suez*, p. 25.

92. William Hayter, *The Kremlin and the Embassy* (New York: Macmillan, 1972), p. 154.

93. Theodore H. White, *America in Search of Itself* (New York: Warner Books, 1982), p. 92.

94. Nutting, *No End of a Lesson*, p. 145.

95. Quoted in Thomas, *Suez*, p. 161.

96. Nutting, *No End of a Lesson*, p. 160.

97. Carlton, *Anthony Eden*, p. 479.

98. Quoted in Neff, *Warriors at Suez*, p. 439.

99. Peter Calvocoressi, *Suez: Ten Years After* (New York: Pantheon Books, 1967), pp. 19-20.

Chapter 8. John F. Kennedy

1. John B. Moses and Wilbur Cross, *Presidential Courage* (New York: Norton, 1980), pp. 214-30.

2. Joan Blair and Clay Blair, *The Search for JFK* (New York: Berkley Books, 1976); Nigel Hamilton, *J.F.K.: Reckless Youth* (New York: Random House, 1992), specifically "Notes on Sources," p. 809.

3. Janet Travell, *Office Hours, Day and Night: The Autobiography of Janet Travell, M.D.* (New York: World Publications, 1968), cited in Edward B. MacMahon and Leonard Curry, *Medical Cover-ups in the White House* (Boston: Farragut, 1987), pp. 128-29.

4. Blair and Blair, *Search for JFK*; Moses and Cross, *Presidential Courage*; Kenneth R. Crispell and Carlos F. Gomez, *Hidden Illness in the White House* (Durham, N.C.: Duke University Press, 1988); Herbert S. Parmet, *Jack: The Struggle of John F. Kennedy* (New York: Dial Press, 1980).

5. L'Etang, *Fit to Lead?* pp. 93-131.

6. Crispell and Gomez, *Hidden Illness*, p. 188.

7. Blair and Blair, *Search for JFK*, p. 476. One author, perhaps unwittingly, makes a convincing case that Kennedy suffered from a relative degree of adrenal insufficiency as a teenager, or so a physician would surmise from the data presented. See Hamilton, *Reckless Youth*, pp. 110-11, 141, 144, 147-49, with particular reference to Kennedy's recurring abdominal pain, weight loss, fainting spells, and "yellowish-brown tan, almost as if he'd been sunbathing."

8. Crispell and Gomez, *Hidden Illness*, pp. 172, 177, 180, 182. Indeed, Kennedy had been a frequent patient at the Mayo Clinic as early as the mid-1930s (Hamilton, *Reckless Youth*, pp. 110, 141).

9. Recently opened medical files pertaining to Kennedy's medical treatment elsewhere (specifically, the Lahey Clinic in Boston) during the late 1930s and 1940s confirm that he had Addison's disease. A letter to his urologist, Dr. William P. Herbst, revealed that "Senator Kennedy has been a patient of the Lahey Clinic at intervals since 1936, and has had quite a variety of conditions. The most serious of these has been Addison's disease which was first discovered and treatment instituted in October of 1947" (by Dr. Elmer Bartels). William P. Herbst, "Clinical Notes", 1950-1963, Medical File, M5-83-38, John F. Kennedy Library.

10. Herbst, "Clinical Notes"; Blair and Blair, *Search for JFK*, p. 560.

11. Crispell and Gomez, *Hidden Illness*, pp. 187-89.

12. Blair and Blair, *Search for JFK*, pp. 578-79. The trail leading to and from the Mayo Clinic remains cold. As patients' records are the "property" of the clinic, Mayo has steadfastly refused to confirm or deny the story. Nor has it allowed any of the physicians involved to comment for the record.

13. Crispell and Gomez, *Hidden Illness*, p. 189.

14. L'Etang, *Fit to Lead?* p. 93. To be sure, L'Etang cites no specific reference to support the claim.

15. Gerald C. Peterson, "Organic Mental Disorders Induced by Drugs or Poisons," in Kaplan, Freedman, and Sadock, *Comprehensive Textbook of Psychiatry*, 3d ed., 2:1446.

16. Lipowski, "Organic Mental Disorders," p. 1385.

17. Ibid., p. 1439.

18. Boyce Rensberger, "Amphetamines Used by a Physician to Lift Moods of Famous Patients," *New York Times*, December 4, 1972; L'Etang, *Fit to Lead?* pp. 93-95.

19. Crispell and Gomez, *Hidden Illness*; Blair and Blair, *Search for JFK*; Moses and Cross, *Presidential Courage.*

20. C. David Heymann, *A Woman Named Jackie* (New York: Carol Communications, 1989), p. 308.

21. Quoted in Rensberger, "Amphetamines."

22. Max Jacobson, memoir, with chapter entitled "JFK," pp. 14, 26. A copy of Jacobson's unpublished memoir (the original is in the possession of his wife) has been supplied to the author.

23. Annual Report of the Constructive Research Foundation; cited in New York State Board of Regents, "Reports of the Regents' Review Committee on Discipline," University of the State of New York, March 22, 1973, to February 25, 1975, p. 2.

24. Rensberger, "Amphetamines." The patient's name was Mark Shaw, a photographer to and frequent traveler with the Kennedys. There is more to this connection than meets the eye, as the reader will soon discover.

25. "Review Committee on Discipline," pp. 1-2.

26. Heymann, *Jackie*, p. 543.

27. "Review Committee on Discipline," p. 22.

28. Rensberger, "Amphetamines."

29. "Review Committee on Discipline," pp. 3-4. Indeed, the majority of vials contained 50 mg/cc of amphetamine, as Jacobson's own corporate reports from 1958 and 1961 attest.

30. Ibid., pp. 22, 5.

31. Ibid., pp. 2, 8.

32. Ibid., pp. 17, 22.

33. U.S. Government Memorandum, August 18, 1972, FBI file 62-84930; "Review Committee on Discipline," pp. 2-4. Jacobson himself admitted to supplying the vials to Robert Kennedy for analysis ("JFK," Jacobson memoir, pp. 27-8).

34. "Review Committee on Discipline," pp. 11, 12.

35. Ibid., p. 26.

36. Jacobson was no genuine researcher. Not only did he fail to keep adequate records or evaluate the effect of his treatments in a systematic prospective or retrospective scientific fashion; he himself admitted that finding a cure for M.S. was not his real intent. Rather, he reasoned, why should his patients not feel better if he could help them do so? One of his defenders explicated the essence of the man in captivating, if somewhat paradoxical, terms when he described Jacobson in the same breath as both a "futurist" and a "medical anarchist" (Heymann, *Jackie*, p. 310).

37. Rensberger, "Amphetamines." Ironically, Travell was roundly criticized for the numerous procaine injections she gave the president, and by late 1961 was alleged to have been dismissed for doing so (T.H. Baker, interview with White House physician George G. Burkley, December 3, 1968, LBJ Library). Oddly enough, Burkley never acknowledged Jacobson in the same interview. Jacobson himself implied that Travell became expendable because of her professional distrust (or jealousy) of his access to the president ("JFK," Jacobson memoir, pp. 13, 21).

38. Quoted in "JFK," Jacobson memoir, p. 2. Charles Spalding later corroborated this account in a telephone interview on February 20, 1990, with James N. Giglio, author of *The Kennedy Presidency* (personal correspondence).

39. L'Etang, *Fit to Lead?* p. 93; Burkley interview, December 3, 1968, LBJ Library.

40. Myrna Green, *The Eddie Fisher Story* (Middlebury, Vt.: Paul S. Erickson, 1978), p. 18.

41. Quoted in "JFK," Jacobson memoir, p. 28.

42. "Review Committee on Discipline," p. 8.

43. Park, *Impact of Illness*, pp. 177-89; interview with Ernst-Gunther Schenck, *American Medical News*, October 11, 1985.

44. "JFK," Jacobson memoir, pp. 8-10, 23, 28, 35; Heymann, *Jackie*, p. 311.

45. Hugh, Trevor-Roper, *Last Days of Hitler*, 3d ed. (New York: Collier Books, 1962), pp. 122-23; L. Leonard Heston and Renate Heston, *The Medical Casebook of Adolf Hitler: His Illness, Doctors, and Drugs* (New York: Stein & Day, 1979), p. 35; Joseph Goebbels, *The Goebbels Diaries, 1942-1943* (Garden City, N.Y.: Doubleday, 1948), p. 314.

46. U.S. Government Memorandum, August 18, 1972, FBI file 62-84930; "Review Committee on Discipline," p. 41.

47. "JFK," Jacobson memoir, p. 14.

48. Quoted in Heymann, *Jackie*, p. 301.

49. Quoted in ibid., p. 371.

50. Quoted in ibid., p. 391. The president's philandering may have exposed him to more than political hazards. Recently released medical files document that he suffered from relapsing venereal disease long before, and throughout, his presidency. For at least a ten-year period, Dr. William Herbst repeatedly treated Kennedy for postgonoccocal urethitis, first with sulfonamides and later with penicillin. Though Herbst proudly proclaimed that his antibiotics were responsible for the president's "profound psychochemical influence for the better in a spectular way" (Herbst, "Clinical Notes"), one wonders whether the amphetamines and steroids (about which the doctor knew nothing) accounted for his observation.

51. See L'Etang, *Fit to Lead?* p. 132.

52. Quoted in Heymann, *Jackie*, p. 175.

53. Kennedy's sexual indiscretions and substance abuse have been linked to another presidential paramour named Mary Pinchot Meyer. James Truitt, a friend and confidant of Meyer, was quoted as saying that just two weeks after Kennedy had presided over a White House conference on narcotic abuse, she and the president smoked marijuana in bed together (see Bernie Ward and Granville Toogood, "JFK's 2-Year White House Romance," *National Enquirer*, March 27, 1978; and Herbert S. Parmet, *JFK: The Presidency of John F. Kennedy* [New York: Dial Press, 1983], p. 306). Secret Service White House Police Gate Logs, containing specific identification of those who visited Kennedy on any given day via a guarded elevator to his private quarters, confirm that Meyer frequently visited Kennedy during 1963 (Gate Logs, boxes 15-18, John F. Kennedy Library). So far as is known, he did not use marijuana again, but if Timothy Leary (*Flashback: An Autobiography* [New York, 1983]) is to be believed, Kennedy's penchant for experimenting did not exclude LSD.

54. Spalding interview with Giglio, February 20, 1990; Harvey Mann, *National Enquirer*, May 25, 1975, quoted in L'Etang, *Fit to Lead?* p. 94. This article appeared roughly a month after Jacobson's license was revoked.

55. Records of the United States Secret Service (Record Group 87); White House Police Gate Logs, boxes 2-11, JFKL.

56. Rensberger, "Amphetamines."

57. "JFK," Jacobson memoir, pp. 27-28.

58. Arthur M. Schlesinger, Jr., *A Thousand Days: John F. Kennedy in the White House* (Boston: Houghton Mifflin, 1965), pp. 246-69.

59. Quoted in David Halbertstam, *The Best and the Brightest* (New York: Random House, 1972), pp. 66, 69; Schlesinger, *Thousand Days*, p. 292.

60. Manchester, *Glory and the Dream*, p. 895.

61. *New York Times*, April 21, 1961.

62. Schlesinger, *Thousand Days*, p. 259.

63. Manchester, *Glory and the Dream*, p. 900.

64. Quoted in Schlesinger, *Thousand Days*, p. 295.

65. "JFK," Jacobson memoir, pp. 8, 9.

66. Heymann, *Jackie*, p. 308; "JFK," Jacobson memoir, p. 10.

67. "JFK," Jacobson memoir, p. 12.

68. Ibid., p. 14.

69. Patricia Levering, Montague Kenn, and Ralph Levering, *The Kennedy Crisis: The Press, The Presidency, and Foreign Policy* (Chapel Hill: University of North Carolina Press, 1983), p. 63.

70. Ibid., pp. 63-64.

71. James Reston, "Kennedy and Khrushchev Find Limited Laos Accord but Split on Berlin and Key Arms Issues," *New York Times*, June 5, 1961, and November 15, 1964.

72. Khrushchev, *Khrushchev Remembers*, p. 458.

73. "JFK," Jacobson memoir, p. 18.

74. Ibid.; Jacobson alludes to five separate "treatments" of the president during Kennedy's European tour ("JFK," Jacobson memoir, pp. 10, 13, 14, 17, 20).

75. Robert Chalmers, *Washington Post*, June 10, 1961.

76. Ibid.

77. "Review Committee on Discipline," pp. 20-21.

78. Heymann, *Jackie*, p. 308.

79. "JFK," Jacobson memoir, p. 26.

80. Schlesinger, *Thousand Days*, pp. 806-7.

81. *New York Times*, October 20, 1962.

82. Manchester, *Glory and the Dream*, p. 964.

83. Robert Kennedy, *Thirteen Days: A Memoir of the Cuban Missile Crisis* (New York: Signet, 1969), p. 55.

84. Elie Abel, *The Missile Crisis* (New York: Bantam Books, 1969), pp. 95-109.

85. Kennedy, *Thirteen Days*, pp. 96-97.

86. Crispell and Gomez, *Hidden Illness*, p. 201.

87. Ibid.

88. The record, both medical and diplomatic, is far from complete, as James N. Giglio's recent analysis of available sources makes clear. "My impression was that the Kennedy Library [is] more overly protective . . . than were other presidential libraries that I have utilized. . . . [Moreover,] material on the Cuban missile crisis, the Bay of Pigs, Vietnam, and other foreign policy matters remains under security restrictions or unprocessed because of insufficient staffing" ("Past Frustrations and New Opportunities Researching the Kennedy Presidency at the Kennedy Library," *Presidential Studies Quarterly*, Fall 1992, pp. 371, 376-77).

Part IV. The Crippled Presidency

1. Quoted in James T. Flexner, *Washington: The Indispensable Man* (New York: New American Library, 1974), pp. 403-04.

2. Quoted in Rudolph Marx, *The Health of the Presidents* (New York: Putnam, 1960), pp. 25-28.

Chapter 9. Precedents and Pitfalls

1. John K. Lattimer, "The Wound That Killed Lincoln," *Journal of The American Medical Association* 187 (1964): 118-127.

2. *Harper's Weekly,* August 13, 1881; cited in Nancy Roth, "Tracking by Telephone: Locating the Bullet in President Garfield," *Medical Instrumentation* 15 (1981): 190.

3. Quoted in Moses and Cross, *Presidential Courage,* p. 120.

4. Abraham Lincoln was one notable exception; see Lattimer, "Wound That Killed," p. 483. The peculiarly handled case of Zachary Taylor threatened to become another, until a recent analysis of samples of his hair and fingernails for alleged arsenic poisoning failed to reveal any trace of the heavy metal in his exhumed body (*Wall Street Journal,* June 15, 1991).

5. A.J. Bollet, "Wounded Presidents: 1981 Almost Repeats the Events of 1881," *Medical Times* 10 (1981): 19-23.

6. Quoted in E.P. Raines, "The Best That Medical Science Has to Offer," *Nebraska Medical Journal* 70 (1985): 22-25.

7. Moses and Cross, *Presidential Courage,* pp. 115-16.

8. Selig Adler, "The Operation on President McKinley," in *An American Historian: Essays to Honor Selig Adler,* ed. Milton Plesur (Buffalo: State University of New York Press, 1980), pp. 37-49.

9. Ibid., pp. 41, 43. The consultant, Dr. Roswell Park, was later openly critical of Mann's handling of the case.

10. Moses and Cross, *Presidential Courage,* p. 47.

11. Quoted in ibid., p. 45.

12. Quoted in Allan Nevins, *Grover Cleveland: A Study in Courage* (New York: Dodd, Mead, 1932), p. 178.

13. Quoted in J.J. Brooks, "The Final Diagnosis of President Cleveland's Lesion," *Transactions and Studies of the College of Physicians of Philadelphia* 2 (1980): 1-26. Bryant had good reason to be concerned, having performed but two such operations previously. See E.B. MacMahon and Leonard Curry, *Medical Cover-ups in the White House* (Washington: Farragut, 1987), p. 44.

14. Moses and Cross, *Presidential Courage,* p. 19.

15. *New York Times,* July 7, 8, 1893; WilliamW. Keen, "The Surgical Operations on President Cleveland in 1893," *Saturday Evening Post* 190 (September 22, 1917): 24-25, 53, 55. An excellent discussion of the implications can be found in Robert S. Robins and Harold Rothschild, "Ethical Dilemmas of the President's Physician," *Politics and the Life Sciences* 1 (1988): 9.

16. See Park, *Impact of Illness,* p. 229.

17. Ross T. McIntire, *White House Physician* (New York: Putnam, 1946), p. 239.

18. Jim Bishop, *FDR's Last Year* (New York: Morrow, 1974), p. 202. Robert Ferrell has conducted an extensive investigation into the fate of those records, leading to the inescapable conclusion that McIntire destroyed them (*Ill-Advised,* pp. 172-73).

19. Park, *Impact of Illness,* p. 220.

20. Joseph Tumulty, *Woodrow Wilson as I Know Him* (Garden City, N.Y.: Doubleday, 1921), pp. 443-44.

21. Birch Bayh, *One Heartbeat Away* (Indianapolis, Ind.: Bobbs-Merrill, 1968), p. 4.

22. Quoted in Iva Brant, *James Madison: Commander in Chief, 1812-1836* (Indianapolis, Ind.: Bobbs-Merrill, 1961), p. 210.

23. Ruth D. Silva, *Presidential Succession* (New York: Greenwood Press, 1968), pp. 31, 75-82, 86; Clinton Rossiter, *The American Presidency* (New York: New American Library, 1960), p. 201.

24. Silva, *Presidential Succession*, p. 81.

25. Ibid., p. 53.

26. Harold Schwartz, "Abraham Lincoln and Aortic Insufficiency: The Declining Health of the President," *California Medicine* 116 (1972): 82-84.

27. Benjamin Thomas, *Abraham Lincoln*. (New York: Knopf, 1952), pp. 86-88.

28. Moses and Cross, *Presidential Courage*, p. 79.

29. See also Park, *Impact of Illness*, pp. 3-63.

30. Quoted in Tumulty, *Woodrow Wilson*, p. 438.

31. Silva, *Presidential Succession*, p. 58.

32. See Bert E. Park, Appendices to *WWP*, vols. 58, 60, 62, 63.

33. For the press, historically presumed to be the gatekeeper of public awareness, Victorian-style prudence seemingly overrode any consideration in this instance of the public's right to know. As a belated admission by the then editor of the *Washington Post* attests, newspaper editors were aware that Wilson was not performing his duties but agreed to refrain from publishing articles on the subject (cited in W.A. White, *Woodrow Wilson* [Boston: Houghton Mifflin, 1924], p. 448). We can only marvel at the remarkable volte-face today's media have undergone concerning the exposure of public officials. Ironically enough, the *Washington Post* has recently led the way, as every Watergate aficionado is aware. As comforting as this transition may seem, events beyond Wilson's era suggest that such safeguards still have their limitations.

34. Tumulty, *Woodrow Wilson*, p. 443.

35. Park, *Impact of Illness*, pp. 221-28.

36. See Bishop, *FDR's Last Year*, p. 270; E.R. Stettinius, *Roosevelt and the Russians: The Yalta Conference* (Garden City, N.Y.: Doubleday, 1949), p. 12.

37. Bishop, *FDR's Last Year*, p. 202.

38. Sherman Adams, *Firsthand Report: The Story of the Eisenhower Administration* (New York: Harper & Row, 1961), p. 193. True, there is reason to question whether Eisenhower really denied suffering a stroke. See his own account in Dwight D. Eisenhower, *The White House Years* (Garden City, N.Y.: Doubleday, 1963-64), 2:227; and the November 25, 1957, journal entry of Howard McC. Snyder the day the stroke occurred, in his "Diary and Papers," American Heritage Center, University of Wyoming, Laramie. What the stricken president wished to convey was that he would not become another Woodrow Wilson. See Ferrell, *Ill-Advised*, p. 131.

39. J.D. Feerick, *The Twenty-fifth Amendment: Its Complete History and Earliest Applications* (New York: Fordham University Press, 1976), p. 22. The most detailed analysis of Eisenhower's illnesses in office is found in Ferrell's *Ill-Advised*, pp. 53-133.

40. Rossiter, *American Presidency*, p. 213.

41. Dr. Janet Travell indulged in what seems a classic case of "doublespeak" in the same year when she assured Kennedy's brother-in-law that "Jack hasn't taken cortisone in years. Of course, he does take some relatives of cortisone, but the way he uses them, in physiological doses, they're not drugs" (quoted in Moses and Cross, *Presidential Courage*, p. 227).

42. John Nichols, "President Kennedy's Adrenals," *Journal of the American Medical Association* 201 (1967): 129-30; James Nicholas, et al., "Management of Adrenocortical Insufficiency," *Archives of Surgery* 71 (1955): 737-42.

43. Rossiter, *American Presidency*, p. 213. The same applies to some scholars who should know better. One otherwise incisive book about medical cover-ups in the White House largely dismissed the cases of both Kennedy and Ronald Reagan "partly because . . . their situations *seem obvious, hardly subtle* [emphasis added]" (Ferrell, *Ill-Advised*, p. x). Any physician familiar with their medical histories would differ. See Chapter 8 on Kennedy and the discussion of Reagan in Chapter 10.

44. Quoted in Silva, *Presidential Succession*, p. 101.

45. Feerick, *Twenty-fifth Amendment*, p. 63.

46. J.D. Feerick, *From Failing Hands: The Story of Presidential Succession* (New York: Fordham University Press, 1965), p. 250.

Chapter 10. Resuscitating the Twenty-fifth Amendment

1. Rossiter, *American Presidency*, p. 215.

2. Ibid., p. 206.

3. Feerick, *Twenty-fifth Amendment*, p. 76.

4. Silva, *Presidential Succession*, p. 92.

5. AMA, *Guides* (1984), p. x.

6. Ibid., p. vii.

7. Ibid., p. viii.

8. Ibid., p. 63.

9. Park, *Impact of Illness*, p. 227.

10. AMA, *Guides*, p. 63.

11. Ibid., p. ix.

12. Ibid.

13. Ibid.

14. D.S. Glass and M.G. Wordle, "Reliability and Validity of American Medical Association's Guides to Ratings of Permanent Impairment," *Journal of the American Medical Association* 248 (1982): 2292-96.

15. Silva, *Presidential Succession*, p. 92.

16. See Feerick, *Twenty-fifth Amendment*, p. 86.

17. Ibid., p. 90.

18. Ibid., p. 104. Bayh was also prescient enough to insist upon clarifying the respective terms "inability" and "unable" for the record. "Inability," he proposed, should refer to "an impairment of the President's faculties," whereas the term "unable" implies the inability to "either make or communicate his decision as to his own competency to execute the powers and duties of his office." The latter equates with "disability" as it is understood today.

19. Ibid., p. 201.

20. Quoted in ibid., p. 206.

21. Silva, *Presidential Succession*, p. 93.

22. The impact of illness on such covert activities as those in the Iran-Contra scandal at least forced Congress to awaken to the problem—above and beyond the health of the president. Certain unnamed Senate subcommittees monitored the deteriorating mental state of the CIA director, William Casey, as it may have related to the revelations concerning Iranscam (*U.S. News and World Report*, July 24, 1987).

23. Bert E. Park, "Presidential Disability: Past Experiences and Future Implications," *Politics and the Life Sciences* 7 (1988): 50-66.

24. Herbert L. Abrams, *"The President Has Been Shot"*: Confusion, Disability, and the 25th Amendment in the Aftermath of the Attempted Assassination of Ronald Reagan (New York: Norton, 1992).

25. Through the years, friends and intimates of the family have typically had the last word in presidential physician selection. Reagan's physician, Dr. Daniel Ruge, was selected because of his former association with Dr. Loyal Davis, also a neurosurgeon and—more important—Nancy Reagan's stepfather.

26. Abrams, *President Has Been Shot*, pp. 253-54. Richard Darman, assistant to Chief of Staff James Baker, was authorized by the latter to confiscate the pertinent letters of invocation relating to Sections 3 and 4 and lock them away in his office safe to preclude their consideration. Laurence I. Barrett, *Gambling with History* (Garden City, N.Y.: Doubleday, 1983), pp. 115-16.

27. Ruge interview, cited in Abrams, *President Has Been Shot*, pp. 192-93.

28. Abrams, *President Has Been Shot*, p. 196.

29. Ibid., pp. 181-82.

30. Sam Donaldson, *Hold On, Mr. President!* (New York: Fawcett Crest, 1987), p. 116.

31. Ibid., p. 118.

32. "Reagan Transfers Power to Bush for 8-Hour Period of 'Incapacity.'" *New York Times*, July 14, 1985.

33. Testimony of Birch Bayh in White Burkett Miller Center of Public Affairs at the University of Virginia, *Report of the Miller Center Commission on Presidential Disability and the Twenty-fifth Amendment*, Kenneth W. Thompson, ed. (Lanham, MD.: University Press of America, 1988), p. 33.

34. Abrams, *President Has Been Shot*, p. 212.

35. Congressional Quarterly, *The Iran-Contra Puzzle* (Washington, D.C.: Government Printing Office, 1987), p. 44; U.S. Senate, Select Committee on Intelligence, *Preliminary Inquiry into the Sale of Arms to Iran and Possible Diversion of Funds to the Nicaraguan Resistance*, 100th Cong., 1st sess., 1987, p. 5.

36. *New York Times*, November 20, 1986.

37. John Tower, Edmund Muskie, and Brent Scowcroft, *The Tower Commission Report* (New York: Bantam Books and Time Books, 1987), pp. xiv, 139. See also "Reagan May Have Acted While Ill," *San Jose Mercury News*, December 12, 1986.

38. J. Riis, B. Lomholt, et al., "Immediate and Long-term Mental Recovery from General vs Epidural Anesthesia in Elderly Patients," *Acta anaesthesiologica Scandnavica* 27 (1983): 44-49; J.R. Flatt et al., "Effects of Anesthesia on Some Aspects of Mental Functioning of Surgical Patients," *Anesthesia & Intensive Care* 12 (1984): 315-24.

39. Jane Mayer and Doyle McManus, *Landslide: The Unmaking of the President* (Boston: Houghton Mifflin, 1988), p. 113; Abrams. *President Has Been Shot*, p. 210.

40. Tower, Muskie, and Skowcroft, *Tower Commission*, pp. xvi, 67-76, 79.

41. Schlesinger, *Cycles*, p. 292; *Newsweek*, December 15, 1987.

42. *Newsweek*, December 15, 1987.

43. Schlesinger, *Cycles*, p. 293.

44. Dale Nelson, *Washington Post*, September 16, 1988; Mayer and McManus, *Landslide*, p. ix; Michael K. Deaver and Marvin Hershkovitz, *Behind The Scenes* (New York: Morrow, 1987), p. 261.

45. Jack Nelson, "Removal of Reagan from Office Suggested to Baker," *Los Angeles Times*, September 15, 1988.

46. Donaldson, *Hold On*, p. 141.

47. Ibid., p. 142.

48. *Newsweek*, March 5, 1990.

49. Ibid.

50. Other scholars have at least suggested that a continuum of disease existed, citing Reagan's behavior at the Reykjavik Conference in 1987, where "signs sometimes indicative of early dementia were reportedly intensified" (Robins and Rothschild, "Ethical Dilemmas," p. 3). Donald Regan believed that Reagan's abrupt termination of the conference reflected not so much cloudy thinking as fatigue and impatience—perhaps ignoring the fact that both qualities typify the aging individual when frustrated; see his *For the Record* (New York: Harcourt Brace Jovanovich, 1988), pp. 349-51.

51. "Medical Care of the VIP," conference at George Washington University Medical Center, Washington, D.C., 1990.

52. Schlesinger, *Cycles*, p. 295.

53. *New York Times*, July 24, 1957.

54. Feerick, *Failing Hands*, p. 254.

55. U.S. Congress, *Hearings before the House Special Subcommittee on Study of Presidential Disability*, 85th Cong., 1st sess., 1957, pp. 26-27. Brownell's arguments were recapitulated in "Presidential Disability: The Need for a Constitutional Amendment," *Yale Law Journal* 68 (December 1958): 198-201.

56. Rossiter, *American Presidency*, p. 210.

57. Quoted in Miller Center, *Report on Presidential Disability and the Twenty-fifth Amendment*, p. 29.

58. Silva, *Presidential Succession*, p. 206.

59. Ibid.

60. Quoted in Feerick, *Twenty-fifth Amendment*, p. 64.

61. Ibid., p. 87.

62. Quoted in ibid., p. 98.

63. Robins and Rothschild, "Ethical Dilemmas," p. 9.

64. Silva, *Presidential Succession*, p. 149.

Index